Rose of the World

DANIEL LEONIDOVICH ANDREEV
October 20, 1906 – March 30, 1959

ALLA ALEKSANDROVNA ANDREEVA (BRUZHES)
February 12, 1915 – April 29, 2005

Photo taken February 24, 1959, about a month before the death
of Andreev at the age of 52 years.

DANIEL LEONIDOVICH ANDREEV

Rose of the World

A New Translation from the Russian of Selections
for the American Reader, with Introduction,
by:

DANIEL H. SHUBIN

DANIEL ANDREEV

ISBN 978-0-9662757-9-7
Copyright 2015
Daniel H. Shubin

Email: peacechurch at jps dot net

TABLE OF CONTENTS

1. Introduction   7

2. Brief Biography of Daniel Leonidovich Andreev   11

3. Brief Chronology of Events   15

4. Glossary of Major Terms, Names and Places   21

5. The Strata or Worlds of the Universe   33

SELECTIONS FROM *ROSE OF THE WORLD*

6. Book I: *Rose of the World* and its Place in History   53

7. Book II: About the Meta-Historical and Trans-Physical
               Method of Comprehension   121

8. Book III: Structure of *Shadanakar*: The Worlds of the
               Ascending Series   183

9. Book IV: Structure of Shadanakar: The Infra-Physical 221

10. Book V: Structure of Shadanakar: The *Stikhials*   261

11. Book VI: The Higher Worlds of *Shadanakar*   287

12. Book VII: Regarding a Meta-History of Ancient Russ   331

13. Book VIII: Regarding the Meta-History of the Muscovite Realm
                                                            345

14. Book IX: Regarding the Meta-History of the Petersburg
               Empire   351

15. Book X: Regarding a Meta-History of Russian Culture 359

16. Book XI: Regarding a Meta-History of the Previous Century
                                                            373

17. Book XII: Possibilities   391

18. Appendix: Brief Eschatology of ROSE OF THE WORLD   441

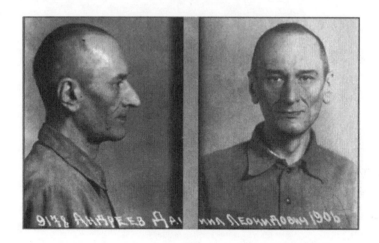

Official Photograph of Daniel Leonidovich Andreev,
taken shortly after his arrest on April 21, 1947.

INTRODUCTION

As used in this book, in italics, *Rose of the World* is the title of
the book composed by Daniel Andreev. In capital type, ROSE OF
THE WORLD is Andreev's ideology, his concepts of religion, polity,
culture, and history.

Daniel Andreev explained ROSE OF THE WORLD in the following
manner:

> ROSE OF THE WORLD can be compared to an inverted
> flower whose root is in heaven, while the pedal bowl is
> here, among humanity, on earth. It's stem is the
> revelation through which the spiritual sap flows,
> sustaining and strengthening its pedals – the fragrant
> choral of religion. But other than the pedals, it also has a
> pith; this is its individual teaching. This teaching is not
> just a mechanical combination of the more or less high
> theses of various theosophies of the past. Other than the
> new attitude toward religious legacy, ROSE OF THE
> WORLD materializes the new attitude toward nature,
> toward history, toward the destinies of humanity's
> cultures, toward their tasks, toward creativity, toward
> love, toward the routes of cosmic ascension, toward the
> subsequent illumination of *Shadanakar.*

In Russian, *Роза Мира* literally means A Rose for the World, or The World's Rose, although the popular translation prevalent in literature is *Rose of the World*.

Andreev has many meanings assigned to the appellation Rose of the World.

It first refers to the future epoch of which Andreev foretold as the golden age of humanity, whose essence will developed fully as history progresses in the close connection between God and people. Second, there is a society of ROSE OF THE WORLD that consists of a world-wide ecclesiastical fraternity. Third, there is an inter-religion or summation of religion of ROSE OF THE WORLD. Fourth, ROSE OF THE WORLD is an inter-culture, a meta-culture to encompass all of humanity. Finally, ROSE OF THE WORLD is also a supra-governmental organization or institution, that will possess ethical and moral control over the activities of government.

Another facet of ROSE OF THE WORLD is Andreev's description of the structure of the universe and the human's part of it, its purgatories and heavens. His concepts of divinity, salvation, redemption, sin, and restoration of humanity are included.

Fluent in comparative religion, Andreev proceeds to provide his approach to the impact of the various major religions on history, and the benefits and detriments of all the major religions on society and polity, morality and ethic. Andreev also delves into the specific character of the major figures of these religions and their impact on history. He also has his personal interpretation of the concept of the Divine Triune Deity in 3 Hypostases, and its extension into the inclusion of a female facet. The volume includes his journeys through the heavenly regions and nether regions.

The teaching of Daniel Andreev has no analogy in global esoteric thought, and it has been subject to tremendous popular interpretation. In his revelations, Andreev envisioned the reign of ROSE OF THE WORLD on earth in the 23rd century, the future epoch being a golden age of humanity, whose essence will developed fully as history progresses into a close connection between God and people. It includes a society that consists of a world-wide ecclesiastical fraternity. It is an inter-religion or summation of religion, as well as a culture to encompass all of humanity. At this time, a worldwide Federation of governments will be installed, an organization or institution that will possess ethical and moral control over the activities of government, all in the interests of the spiritual development of a person.

ROSE OF THE WORLD will install a genuine golden age on our planet. It will abolish the exploitation of one person by another and all violence against the individual. It will motivate the personal strengths of human nature and direct them to the comprehension of nature and continual creativity. With the powers of science it will raise the evolution of animals to possess communication and increase their level of intellect. People will forget words like: tyranny, war, revolution, famine, poverty, and illness, since none of this will ever exist again. Genuinely spirit-filled leaders of all humanity, called pontiffs, will govern the land.

NOTE ON THE TRANSLATION

This volume is an original translation into English directly from the original Russian source. I have done my best in this area, although sometimes the text may be difficult to read or interpret due to the subject matter and how Andreev conveys his visions and concepts. To explain matters of mysticism, sometimes even 2 or 3 words are necessary to convey the proper meaning into English. No text has been inserted into the translated passages, except if located in [brackets].

Because Andreev has many words that either he invented or which were revealed to him in visions and revelations, these are all in *italics*.

STRUCTURE OF THE VOLUME

Essentially, this translation includes almost 70% of Andreev's complete text of *Rose of the World*, as well as a glossary of the major terms used, and the list of all the worlds or strata of the universe, and their purpose, if defined in *Rose of the World*.

The selections that I selected for this translation are those that would interest the American reader and would be understandable and applicable. Those portions that deal specifically with details of Russian ancient history, or details of historical events and persons and geography and its relative impact on Russia of that era, have not been included. Also much of the text of his meta-history of various other countries, those apart from Russia and America, was also not included.

Where the text jumps due to a skipped section, but the topic continues, I have inserted a gap between paragraphs. If the topic changes in the center of a chapter, then I have inserted asterisks to indicate this:

*   *   *

Because Andreev's eschatology is very complex and lengthy, I have provided a short summary of it, instead of translating the entire verbose text dealing with this topic.

DANIEL H. SHUBIN

April 14, 2018
Second Edition

Brief Biography of

Daniel Leonidovich Andreev

Daniel Andreev was a complex genius encompassing many spheres of comprehension and ideology. He was simultaneously a mystic entity having a connection to and communication with the realms beyond the terrestrial and mundane corporeal one of our own, and he traversed the heavenly regions and the nether regions, and recorded them. Andreev's life beginning at age 14 was infused with a series of encounters with the spirit realm, where he was saturated with the fullness of spirit-deity. This allowed him to transcend the mundane and secular progress of contemporary existence, experience it and record it.

Over the years after leaving the Literary Institute in 1925, and up to his conscription into the military during World War 2, in 1942, Andreev spent innumerable hours at Moscow libraries delving into world history, religion, philosophy, culture and political science. His personal library at his apartment consisted of over 2,000 books. He had an unfathomable memory in the social sciences and an excellent ability to synthesize information. In addition to his mystic experiences and education Andreev's character was also molded over his lifetime with his arrest and incarceration. With his perseverance and endurance he survived his 10 years of extreme prosecution interrogations and sufferings in Soviet high security prisons. Along with this was overcoming his spinal handicap causing spondyloarthrosis, and the accompanying pain, with the necessity of wearing an iron corset.

All of this molded Andreev into the person necessary to create such a treatise as *Rose of the World* and all of his other compositions, and perseverance under the Soviet penal system.

During Andreev's 8-1/2 year incarceration at Vladimir high security prison, for a thousand nights on his prison cell cot, beginning in September 1949, and until the final revelation in November 1953, Andreev departed on trans-physical journeys in his nightly visions, as he called this transcendent state.

Andreev also had his theological speculations of the Bible with his own original concepts of deity, the Logos-incarnate Jesus, angels, sin and redemption and judgment. In *Rose of the World* he expounds his views of the apostles and saints and ecclesiastical history. Andreev was also fluent in Islam, Buddhism, and Hinduism, and discusses these religions and their positive and negative contributions to world society. At the same time, Andreev proposes his own meta-religion, one that transcends all religions and yet permits their existence as subservient to his supreme ideal, which materializes as the Temple of the Sun.

Even with Andreev having beliefs and convictions that more agreed with Hinduism than Christianity, he still considered himself a devout Russian Orthodox all his life. He attended services regularly, and he took communion, confession and last rites from a family priest on his deathbed and was buried according to Russian Orthodox rites. In one respect, true religion as far as Andreev was concerned had to be pragmatic and purposeful, yet he still details the precise movements of priests and parishioners in his description of temple services during the future era of ROSE OF THE WORLD and the exact construction of the temples dedicated for worship.

If there was a single experience or event in Andreev's life that could be isolated as being the most definitive in molding his ideology, the author would select the year or so that he was assigned to the funeral corps while in the military during World War 2. Because of his spinal handicap, Andreev was unfit for combat duty and so was first assigned to the supply train behind the troops heading toward Leningrad to break the blockade.

After the Germans withdrew from the city, Andreev was assigned to the funeral corps. His duty was to record the remains, if identifiable, of the dead and then bury them in the field, in unmarked graves. The work was difficult and horrifying. Many of the dead had been lying in the snow frozen for several months and now with the spring they were thawing, and with the weather warming the bodies were putrifying. Andreev had to gather the bodies and parts and pile them on carts, cover with canvas and haul them to some open pit just dug for burial.

Andreev stared at the horror of war before his very eyes and all of this left its indelible impression on his psyche. The scene of massive death and the job of disposing bodies as objects, bodies and pieces that were once living humans just like himself, molded his attitude toward war and military service, making it repulsive and objectionable.

All of the above, and while under the circumstances of his incarceration and physical handicaps, developed the person necessary to compose all the compositions that Andreev did, traverse the heavenly regions and nether regions, develop his ideology, and create the volume of *Rose of the World*.

Alla Andreeva describes Andreev in her memoirs:

Daniel was handsome in an original fashion, something different than the typical sense of Moscow beauty. He was talk, agile, thin, and dark complexioned. His face was narrow and thin, he had a high forehead, thin nose, small lips, and dark eyes. His hair was straight and dark, with a few strands always longer than the rest, and longer than the era, when most men had their hair short. He did not wear a tie, but when he had to, he wore a black bowtie, a small one, almost non-pretentious.

His hands did not match the balance of his stature. Daniel's palms were masculine and large, but his fingers were thick and short. It would seem he was embarrassed of his hands and he would regularly hide them under the table.

13

Daniel was a genius. As applying to him, there was no pride, no conceit. This was a very difficult burden, a heavy cross, which the Lord only gives to a few. Such people are recognizable and are distinct due to the awesome qualities and some non-conformity with the balance of men. They seem to know, hear, see what is impossible for another to hear or see. They are like buildings arranged in some locality that are inaccessible to us.

Such special children of God possess a dreadful frailty and infantile vulnerability. I noticed these traits with Daniel, and sometimes attempted to work them out of him, but sometimes I was surprised they were to his benefit, but then finally I just accepted this as his inherent character and no longer tried to change him. At the same time, Daniel was painfully dissatisfied with his external self. He wanted to be a precious and loving figure of a radiant and bright and bold and joyful person. As a result of this attitude toward his external self, he ended up in unexpected situations.[1]

I should also add that Daniel was very attentive to others and very polite with women. He always wanted the best for others, although not every person understood this.

When Daniel Andreev died at the age of 52, he no doubt thought his memory would terminate likewise, as well as all his writings. But 30 years after his death, Andreev resurrected to life through the publication of his poetry and *Rose of the World*, including a present movement in Russia to implement its concepts into a functioning organization in order to better Russia.

After his death, Daniel Andreev ascended to the *sakuala* of the Heavenly Russia as a result of his merits.

---

[1] Referring to his spinal deformity and the necessity of wearing an iron corset to alleviate the pain and allow him to function.

Brief Chronology

of Daniel Andreev's Life

Pre-historic Era to the 17th Century:

> Daniel Andreev lives several previous lives or incarnations in the following regions: Atlantis, Java, Urartu, twice in India, England and Italy.

1898
> Daniel's parents, Leonid Nikolaievich Andreev and Aleksandra Mikhailovna Veligorski, marry in Moscow.

October 20, 1906
> Daniel Leonidovich Andreev is born in Germany. His mother Aleksandra dies 7 days later, and Daniel is taken to Moscow with his maternal grandmother. Daniel's Uncle Dr Philipp Dobrov and Aunt Elizabeth become his foster parents and raise him. Daniel's older brother Vadim remains with the father.

1907
> Father Leonid Andreev remarries and has 3 more children.

1919
> Father Leonid Andreev dies in Finland. The balance of the family moves to Paris to escape the Russian revolution and civil war.

1921
> Daniel receives his first revelation at the age of 14. So begin his journeys and mystic experiences that continue on a regular basis until 1953.

1926   Daniel marries Aleksandra Gublyor, he is 20 and
               she is 19. He falls ill with scarlet fever that
               evening and the marriage is never consummated
               and it ends just as quickly.

1926-1942   Daniel's life is consumed with writing prose and
               poetry, and studying at Moscow's libraries for
               long periods. He supports himself with odd jobs
               and regularly attends Orthodox Church. His
               studies are in history, philosophy, religion and
               polity. Especially important is his attachment to
               India and the study of Hinduism and Buddhism.
               He likewise devours books on theosophy,
               transcendentalism, and other mystic authors.

1931   Daniel begins his first of several visits and mystic
               experiences in the various wildernesses of central
               and southern Russia. He would visit these areas
               many times over the next decade, until the start
               of World War 2.

               Alla Bruzhes marries Sergei Ivashev-Musatov.
               Their married does not last long. She meets
               Daniel and the 2 of them commit to a long term
               relationship.

1942   Daniel is conscripted into the Red Army against
               Germany in World War 2. He is first assigned to a
               supply train behind the army ranks as they break
               the blockade of Leningrad..

1943   After the liberation of Leningrad, Daniel is
               assigned to the funeral corps (as described above
               in the Introduction). Later, Daniel contracts
               malaria and is assigned to the army camp
               hospital. After his recovery, he remains in the
               hospital corps as an attendant and follows the
               Red Army into Europe.

1944   During Daniel's short leave from the military and
                visit to Moscow, Alla abandons Sergei and moves
                into Daniel's apartment, but he then returns to
                the front. Alla files for divorce from Sergei.

1945   Daniel is discharged from the military and
                returns home. He and Alla legally register as a
                couple.

1945-1947   Daniel and Alla take odd jobs to survive: she is a
                graphics artist and he is a writer. They are
                assisted by her parents: Aleksandr Petrovich and
                Yulia Gavrilovna Bruzhes. Daniel works at night
                on his novel *Night Wanderers*, regarding events
                surrounding a family of 1937 Moscow. Some parts
                are critical of Soviet Russia of the era.

                At the same time, Daniel is unable to work much
                due to his disabilities from military service in
                World War 2 and he is placed on pension as a
                disabled veteran. He also suffers with his spinal
                deformation that is very painful and he needs to
                regularly wear a metal corset.

April 21, 1947

                Daniel is arrested by the secret police for the
                contents of his novel *Night Wanderers*. For the
                next 19 months he is held, first in Lubyanka
                Prison, and then Lefortovo Prison, with regular
                interrogations and beatings. Another 20 or so
                members of the family and associates are also
                arrested.

April 23, 1947

                Alla is arrested by the secret police. She likewise
                spends the next 19 months at the same prisons
                and same types of interrogations.

October 30, 1948

> Daniel and Alla are both sentenced to 25 years: Daniel at a high security prison, and Alla at a labor camp. The other alleged conspirators receive sentences from 10 years to 25 years.

1949-1953

> Daniel is incarcerated at Vladimir high security prison. There he continues to receive visions and revelations, and has trans-physical journeys to heavenly worlds and nether worlds. This occurs over the course of one thousand nights from September 1949 to November 1953.
>
> He also develops his concept of a new meta-religion called ROSE OF THE WORLD, beginning its composition on December 24, 1950. Daniel's concepts of meta-history and meta-philosophy along with his other revelations are recorded over these years and will form the content of his book of the same title. At the same time Daniel also composes much poetry.

1949-1956

> Alla is confined to several labor camps in Mordovia province. In October 1956, Alla's term is reduced to time served and she is released from labor camp. She returns to her parents in Moscow.

1957

> Daniel's term is reduced to 10 years, and he is released from prison on April 23, 1957. He returns to Moscow to live with Alla at her parent's home.

June 4, 1958

> Daniel and Alla formally marry in a Russian Orthodox Church.

1957-1958

> Daniel and Alla attempt to build a new life for themselves in Moscow. They bounce around from one friend to another, while attempting to find a permanent residence in Moscow. Daniel is unable

to work very much due to his disabilities and spends considerably time in hospitals and physical therapy treatments centers. Alla works as an artist to bring in some finances. Much of their support comes from friends and her parents. They spend some time together in southern Russia, to help Daniel due to his loss of health. He now suffers regularly from heart attacks. Eventually they acquire a new apartment in Moscow.

Alla has cancer and goes to radiation treatments and eventually recovers.

All of Daniel's excess time is dedicating to completing *Rose of the World*, which he considers his divinely assigned task and which needs to be completed before his death.

October 12, 1958 Daniel completes *Rose of the World.*

January-March 1959

Daniel and Alla return to Moscow from southern Russia. Daniel spends the initial months in a physical therapy treatment center and then moves into their apartment in March.

April 30, 1957

Daniel Leonidovich Andreev dies of a heart attack, and literally in his wife's arms. He was 52 years of age.

1962   Alla Andreeva remarries to an old family friend who is also widowed, Sergei Beloyusov. He dies in 1977.

Decade of 1970s and 1980s

After Daniel's death, Alla hides the text of *Rose of the World*, but then soon after allows a few copies to be made for safe-keeping. However, more copies are clandestinely reproduced by mimeograph and duplicating machines and distributed without her consent or knowledge. As a result interest grows in the book.

1989-1991   The initial selections of *Rose of the World* are formally published in local magazines in 1989. The first complete publication is in 1991, with an edition of 10,000 copies.

2005   Alla leads a quiet life in Moscow until her death the night of April 29-30, 2005. She dies from smoke inhalation due to a fire in her apartment.

Glossary of Names, Terms and Places,

Often used in the Text of

Rose of the World [2]

Agga: All forms of materiality of our *bramfatura* created by demonic principles. Structurally they are distinct from physical materiality and in general from *siaira* because the quantity of initially arranged *aggas* are extremely limited and not one of its elemental parts possesses any free will or soul-enlivenment.

Anti-cosmos: A conditional denotation for the collection of all worlds created by demonic principals as a presumptive substitution for the divine cosmos. The following strata belong to the anti-cosmos of our *bramfatura: Shog, Digm, Gashsharva, Sufetkh* and *Dno.*

Arimoiya: The *zatomis* of the meta-culture of humanity in general, presently being created.

Arungvilta-Prana:

The impersonal, imperceptible substance of an alien materiality spilled into *Enrof,* overflowing from body to body and securing the possibility of individual organic existence. The feeling of the

---

[2] Most of these were defined by Daniel Andreev personally as a epilogue to his book, and which accounts for the difficulty in rendering them into English in an understandable manner.

presence of *Arungvilta-Prana* was the axis of the intrinsic life of pre-non-mystical humanity and appeared, as it seems, as the most ancient of revelations.

Astrafayr: The center of the universe.

Astral: Used here as the 2nd of the alien-materialities with which the monads are clothed. The *shelt* is created by the monad itself. The great *stikhial* Mother-Earth participates in the creation of the astral, and it also participates in the creation of individual astrals of all entities of Shadanakar: people, angels, *daimons*, animals, *stikhials* and demons, and even the Great Hierarchies when they descend into strata where such a body is indispensable. The astral is the highest utensil of the *shelt*. The capability of spiritual vision, audio, smell, profound memory, ability to fly, ability of communication with entities of other strata, ability of contemplation of cosmic panoramas and perspectives – is concentrated here.

Bramfatura: Almost every heavenly body possesses a series of diverse-materiality strata, forming a mutually connected and mutually dependent system. Such a system is called a *bramfatura*, and their strata are united due to a common process flowing through them. In the majority of the *bramfaturas* of our galaxies, the basic process that unites the strata of each of them is the progression of struggle between the Providential and the demonic powers. There are other *bramfaturas*, however, that have entirely succumbed to demonic authority, and such have entirely severed themselves from Providential powers.

Daimons: The higher humanity of *Shadanakar*, the residents of the *sakuala* of the worlds with four-dimensional spatial coordinates and a various number of time coordinates. *Daimons* traverse a route of installation, similar to ours, but their beginning is earlier and is consummated more successfully. With our humanity, they are connected with different types of threads.

Demiurge: as used here: The demiurges are all who create for the glory of God, from their love of the world and its primordial Creator. The demiurge is absolutely good and is omnipotent.

Digm: The residence of the *Gagtungr*, one of the worlds of five-dimensional space and a large number of time dimensions.

Druekkarg: The *shrastra* of the Russian meta-culture.

Duegguer: One of the strata of the demonic *stikhials*, having a special significance for humanity. The entities traversing their incarnations in *Duegguer* supplement the losses of their life's strengths with *eifos* – the emanations of the passions of humanity.

Egregore: Used here as the other-materiality forms appearing out of certain intrinsic influences of humanity over large collectives: tribes, governments, certain political parties and religious organizations. They are deprived of a monad, but temporarily possess a conceptual volition along with an equivalent consciousness.

Eytzekhore: Used here as representing the demonic portion of each entity whose material incarnation evolved with the participation of the *Leeleet*, and not only people, but also titans, *igvies*, and *yuitzraors*.

Enrof: The name of our corporeal stratum, understood as equivalent to the contemporary astronomical universe. It is characterized due to its possession of a three-dimensional space and one-dimensional time.

Ethereal Body:

The 3rd of the alien-materiality clothing or crust of the monad. It is impossible to have any organic life in the worlds of three- and four-dimensions without it.

Gagtungr: The name of the planetary demon of our *bramfatura*. He possesses 3 faces, just as do certain others of the mature hierarchs.

The first hypostasis of *Gagtungr* is the great torturer, *Gisturg*; the 2nd is the great prostitute, *Fokerma*; the 3rd is the great implementer of the demonic plan, *Yurparp*. He will be redeemed at the conclusion of the 2nd Eon with the entrance of the 3rd Eon.

Gavvakh: The alien-materiality emanations as a result of human suffering, exerted by our essence during our life as well as in the post-mortem nether-world. The *gavvakh* supplements the many losses of life's strength we incur as a result of demonic influences and the *Gagtungr* himself.

Gashsharva: One of the basic strata of the demonic anti-cosmos in *Shadanakar*; the world of two-dimensional space; the nest of various types of potent demonic powers.

Great Sisters: The national conciliar Souls of the meta-cultures.

Heavenly Russia (Holy Russ):
> The *zatomis* of Russian Meta-culture, the residence of its *Sinklit*.

Hierarchy: This word is utilized in the present book with 2 meanings:
1. The hierarchy that is the staircase of ranks, the lower subject to the higher, whether ecclesiastical, military or administrative.
2. The hierarchies that are the various categories of other-worldly, other-materiality or spirit entities, for example, the hierarchy of angels, demons, the hierarchies of *stikhials*, *daimons* and many others.

I: The individual human living soul as an inherent self-conscious entity.

Igva (plural: *igvies*):
> The head or first of the race of anti-humanity. The highly developed intellectual demonic entities, residents of the world-fugitives – the *shrastras*.

Iroln: One of the worlds of the five-dimensional spatial coordinates, the residence of the monads of humanity.

Karossa: Local manifestations of the sole great *stikhial* of humanity, *Leeleet*, connected with distinct nations or supra-nations, The *Karossas* are deprived of monad, but exist due to having an equivalent conscious and will. They are directly involved with human reproduction in the absence of *Leeleet*.

Karrokh: A corporeal organic body analogous to a physical, possessing some attributes of demonic entities, for example, the *igvies* and *raruggas*, created not from *seiayra*, but from *agga*.

Leeleet: The great *stikhial* of humanity, at one time the spouse of the First-Angel, and then the female sculptor of the corporeal body of the human race and some other entities. She was inseminated by the *Gagtungr* a long time before the appearance of humanity in *Enrof,* as it exists at present. She is also queen of the eternal garden and mistress of the plant kingdoms. The *Dingra* is her local manifestation.

Meta-culture: The inner *sakuala* of *Shadanakar* presents itself through a segmented series of some of its lower strata. Meta-culture consists of various numbers of strata, however each of them possesses definitely 3:
1. The corporeal: a place of residence in *Enrof,* of its relative supra-nation, that has created its own culture;
2. The *zatomis:* the heavenly country of the enlightened souls of this nation;
3. The *shrastra:* the demonic nether-region that is contradistinctive to the *zatomis*.

Other than this, all the meta-cultures include one or another number of strata of Enlightenment and strata of Retribution.

Meta-history:
1. The conglomeration of processes that presently are located outside the field of vision of science and outside its methology, flowing into those strata of alien-materiality existence that, existing in other forms of space and in

other dimensions of time, penetrate through the process, and which we accept as history:

2. The religious teaching of these processes.

Monad:
As used here: the primordial, indivisible, deathless, spirit-entity, either born of God or created by God. The universe is the accumulation of the innumerable quantities of monads and the various and diverse forms of materiality of which they are composed.

Monsalvat:
The *zatomis* of European meta-culture.

Muedgabr:
The *shrastra* of European meta-culture.

Navna:
A monad born of God, one of the Great Sisters, the ideal conciliar Soul of the Russian meta-culture.

Nertis:
One of the worlds of Enlightenment, the country of radiant rest and blissful tranquility.

Olirna:
The first of the worlds of the ascending series, the country of the dead, common for all of humanity, although the *Olirna* of each meta-culture possesses it own character.

Planetary Logos:
The great monad born of God; the intrinsic expression of God the Son; the divine intellect of our *bramfatura*; the most ancient and very first of all of its monads, expressing itself in humanity as Jesus Christ, and installed as the head of the preparation of our world for the change of the eon. The planetary Logos is the Leader of all powers of Light in *Shadanakar*.

Rarugga: The second of the race of anti-humanity, presenting itself as those entities that traversed innumerable incarnations in the strata of demonic materiality.

Rif: Frail demonic entity that acquired an incarnation and eventually in time was turned into the monsters of our days. Residents of *Gashsharva.*

ROSE OF THE WORLD:

The meta-religion of the final ages, unifying within itself the churches of the past, and connecting it all based on the concept of open cooperation with all religions of the bright direction. Its fundamental task is the salvation of the greater number of the souls of humanity to the extent possible and the removal of dangers of religious enslavement of the coming anti-God. The evidence of the installation of ROSE OF THE WORLD in humanity will be the ethereal birth of *Zventa-Sventana* in one of the *zatomises.*

Sakuala: Used here as the system of 2 or several diverse-materiality strata, tightly connected together structurally and meta-historically.

Salvaterra: The conditional appellation of the summit and heart of *Shadanakar,* the highest of its *sakualas,* composed of 3 worlds: the residence of the planetary Logos, the residence of the Virgin-Mother, and the residence of *Zventa-Sventana.*

Seiayra: All the forms of materiality, created or in the process of creation by Providential powers.

Shadanakar: personal name of the *bramfatura* of our planet. It is composed of an immense number, above 240, of diverse-materiality strata, with varying space and time dimensions.

Shavva: The alien-materiality radiance of certain compositions of the human mentality or psyche. *Shavva* complements the loss of the living strengths of the *yuitzraors, igvies* and *raruggas.*

Shelt: The first of the material clothing or crust of the monad. The *shelt* is created by the monad itself from materiality of five-dimensional spatial worlds. It is the receptacle of monads together with their divine qualities and their near appurtenances.

Shrastra: The other-spatial material strata, connected with certain zones in the corporeal body of the planet Earth. It is the residence of demonic anti-humanity, consisting of 2 simultaneously living races: the *igvies* and *raruggas.* The *shrastras* possess their unique immense cities and a very high demonic technology.

Sinklit: Masses of enlightened human souls that are residents of the *zatomises* of the meta-cultures.

Skrivnous: The highest of the purgatories of Christian meta-culture, having its analogy also in other meta-cultures of humanity. This is an inescapable post-mortem stage of all souls, other than those that, after physical death, enter unimpeded and directly into *Olirna* and further along the stages of the worlds of Enlightenment.

Stikhial: The category of monads created of God that have traversed their route of installation in *Shadanakar* through the kingdom of nature for the most part, but the majority of them do not have a corporeal incarnation.

Supra‑nation: A group of nations or nationalities having a common union and simultaneously creating a common culture.

Voglea: A demon of female gender, responsible for catastrophes that have affected the humanity of the lunar *bramfatura* in the past. For a long while she was held in partial isolation, warring against Providential powers and, in part, against *Gagtungr.* At present the *voglea* has harnessed its efforts together with the efforts of the planetary demon.

Yarosvet: A monad born of God; one of the great demiurges of humanity; the national leader of the Russian meta‑culture.

Yuitzraor: The potent, intellectual and extremely ruthless entities residing in strata intermixed with *shrastras.* From the point of view of a person, this is the demon of massive and despotic government, but there are very few of them. The *yuitzroar* play an immense contradictory and dual role in meta‑history.

Yuppum: One of the strata of Retribution, the Rain of Eternal Regret, the hell of the *yuitzraors.*

Zatomis: The *zatomises* are the higher strata of all the meta‑cultures of humanity, their heavenly countries, support of the powers that lead the nations, the residents of the *Sinklits*. Along with the *Arimoiya* presently being created, which is the *zatomis* of ROSE OF THE WORLD, their quantity will reach as high as 34.

Zhrugrit: Genderless demon of the Russian state, materialized in the past as Stepan Rezan, Pugachov, Joseph Stalin, and other rebels. It is the offspring of the *Zhrugr* and *karossa*.

Zventa-Sventana:

The great monad born of God expressing eternal Womanhood, the Bride of the planetary Logos, which descended from the spirit-cosmic heights to the high strata of *Shadanakar* about 1-1/2 centuries ago, and has the responsibility to accept an enlightened incarnation in one of the *zatomis* of humanity. This meta-historical event will be reflected in the earthly *Enrof* as the evident appearance of ROSE OF THE WORLD.

List of the Strata or Worlds of the Universe with Available Explanations

1. *Enrof* – the physical universe

THE INFRA-PHYSICAL WORLDS (54 WORLDS)

    The *Sakualas* of the *Shrastras* (15 worlds)

        Active Shrastras

2. *Fu-Chezhu* – China

3. *Yunukamn* – Roman-Catholicism under Gregory VII. Loyola, and the majority of popes

4. *Mudgabr* – Europe after Karl V, Napoleon, and others

5. *Druekkarg* – Russia after Tsar Ivan IV

        Dissolving *Shrastras*

6. *Tugibd* - India

7. *Aru* – Indo-Malaysia

8. *Alfokk* – Islamic

Agonizing *Shrastras*

9.   *Dabb* – Atlantis

10.   *Bubgisch* – Gondwana

11.   *Setkh* – Ancient Egypt

12.   *Nergal* – Babylon-Assyria

13.   *Devan* – Iranian

14.   *Tartar* – Greek-Roman

15.   *Zing* – Hebrew

16.   *Babilon* – Byzantine

THE *SAKUALAS* OF THE *YUITZRAORS* (16 WORLDS)

The Residences of the *Yuitzraors* (14 worlds)

Active Dynasties

17.   *Nissush* and *Lai-chzhoi* – Mongolia, Manchuria and Japan

18.   *Istarra* - Spain

19.   *Baggag* – western Europe

20.   *Zhrugr* – Russia

21.   *Shostr* – new Arabia, after the Ottoman Empire

22.   *Avardal* – new India, after its independence

23.   *Yustr* – England

24.   *Bartrad* – France

25.   *Charmich* – Yugoslavia

26.   *Stebing* – United States of America

27.   *Yukurmia* – New Germany, after the Third Reich

Perished Dynasties

28. *Yunigr* – ancient Babylon, Assyria and Carthage

29. *Kharada* – ancient India

30. *Ariman* – ancient Iran

31. *Forsuf* – ancient Macedonia and Rome

32. *Foshtz* – ancient Hebrew

33. (no name provided)   ancient Byzantium

34. (no name provided)   Middle Ages of South-East Asia

35. *Efror* – the caliphates of ancient Turkey

Special 2 Worlds of the *Sakualas* of the *Yuitzraors*

36. *Kragr* – the stratum of the battle of *yuitzraors*

37. *Yuppum* – the hell of the *yuitzraors*, the Rain of Eternal Sorrow

The Worlds of Torment (19 worlds)

This consists of 18 words of Retribution and the Cemetery of *Shadanakar*. These strata are common to all supra-nations, but have for worlds (except the Kernel) their own coloration and their own distinction. In some meta-cultures, the zones of the individual worlds of retribution appear empty, but this is not always the case.

Sakualas of the Purgatories:

The Higher Strata of the Purgatories:

38. *Skrivnous* – for those whose conscious is defiled for crimes committed

39. *Ladref* – short-term residence; mostly empty; for those primarily who had little belief.

40. *Morod* – for criminals and those who imposed tragic destinies on others

The Middle Strata of the Purgatories:

41. *Agra* – for those deprived of sympathy toward close associates

42. *Buistvich* – for those who have earned and accomplished nothing in their life

43. *Rafag* – for those devoted to tyranny, treachery and greed

The Lower Strata of the Purgatories:

44. *Shim-Bieg* – for those who caused many deaths

45. *Dromn* – for those who initiated unbelief and promoted atheism

46. *Fukabirn* – for those who condemned the innocent

Sakualas of the Trans-Physical Magma:

47. *Okruis* – for immense cruelty; persecution of defenseless children and ideological enemies

48. *Gvegr* – burning red-hot

49. *Yukarvayr* – for corrupting high ideals, for those who practice sadism and enjoy imposing pain on others.

50. *Propuilk* – for executioners, and blood-thirsty soldiers

51. *Erl* – for those returning again to the Magma

Sakualas of the Kernel:

52.   *Biask* – for those who corrupt the spirit

53.   *Amiutz* – for those involved in immense crimes and sadism

54.   *Etrech* – planetary night lasting to the 2nd zone

55.   *Zhursch* – residence of Judas Iscariot

56.   *Sufetkh* or *Sufel* – cemetery of *Shadanakar*

The Anti-Cosmos – The Worlds of *Osnova*

57.   *Gashsharva* – the anti-cosmos of *Gagtungr*

58.   *Shog* (also part of the anti-cosmos galaxy) – the storage of the great demons of the macro-*bramfatura*.

59.   *Digm* – residence of *Gagtungr, Gisturg, Fokerma* and *Yupatr*, united with the demonized *shelts* of the monads of people, the great *igvies*, and Torquemada.

60.   Bottom of *Shadanakar* · indescribable suffering; the purgatory of the demonic *shelts*; the invocation of the satellite of *Antares* (the heart of the scorpion); the anti-cosmos of the galaxy.

61.   Bottom of the Galaxy: A hole in time; the purgatory of the great demons; the realm of dark eternity. (Not one of the worlds of *Osnova*, but independent.)

The Worlds of the *Stikhials* (37 worlds)

The *Sakualas* of the Animals (5 worlds)

62.   *Nigoida* – the world of collective souls of the insects and simple life forms.

63.   *Zhimeira* – the world of the better part of the underground animals

64. *Eesong* – the world of the souls of the present animals

65. *Ermastig* – the world of the higher animals

66. *Khangvilla* – the *zatomis* of the animal kingdom

The *Stikhial* of Demonic Nature (5 worlds)

67. *Shartamakhum* – the *stikhial* of the volcanoes, earthquakes

68. *Nugurt* – the *stikhial* of the ocean depths

69. *Ganniks* – the *stikhial* of bogs, swamps, tropical growths

70. *Sviks* – the *stikhial* of the deserts, sandy regions

71. *Duegguer* – the demons of the great cities of *Enrof*

The *Stikhial* of the Intermediate Groups (5 worlds)

72. *Kattaram* – the *stikhial* of the mineral kingdom

73. *Ron* – the region of the mountain stikhial

74. The stratum of the *nibrusks*, the genus of places

75. *Maniki* – the stratum of the household spirits

76. *Shalem* – the *Olirna* for the *stikhial* of the 4 preceding strata.

The Single World

77. *Orliontana* – the world of spirits of mountain summits; queen of the snow-capped heights.

THE BRIGHT *STIKHIALS:*

The *Sakuala* of the Small *Stikhials* (14 worlds)

78. *Darainna* – the region of spirits penetrating roots and seeds

79. *Faltora* – the *stikhial* of meadows and fields

80. *Murokhamma* – the *stikhial* of forest land

81. *Arashamf* – the *stikhial* of trees

82. Country of the Elfs

83. *Liyurna* – the *stikhial* of rivers

84. *Vlanmim* – the *stikhial* of the surface of seas

85. *Vayieta* – the *stikhial* of soft breezes

86. *Eerudrana* – the *stikhial* of storms and hurricanes

87. *Zoongoof* – the *stikhial* of dew, clouds, rain, moisture and fog

88. *Nivenna* – the *stikhial* of frost and falling snow

89. *Akhash* – the Arctic and Antarctic *stikhials*

90. *Diramn* – the *stikhials* of the stratosphere (lower temperatures)

91. *Sianna* – the *stikhials* of the higher levels of the atmosphere (high temperatures)

The *Sakualas* of the Highest *Stikhials* (7 worlds)

92. *Povurn* – King of the Flaming Body, the potentate of subterranean magmas

93. *Zaranda* – King of all animal kingdoms

94. *Ea* or *Vlarol* – King of Fresh Waters[3]

---

[3] Or, life-providing waters (as opposed to salt water)

95.   *Vauimn* – King of the Blessing Wings, the spirit of the atmospheric ocean

96.   *Estira* – Queen of the Eternal Garden, the mistress of plant kingdoms

97.   *Leeleet* – the international Aphrodite and progenitress of all humanity

98.   *Mati* – Mother of *Shadanakar* (Mother-Earth); the personification of love toward all.

BEGINNING OF THE ASCENDING SERIES (38 WORLDS)

Sakualas of Enlightenment (4 worlds)

99.   *Olirna* – Stratum of all meta-cultures; residence of the angelic pre-humanity.

100. *Fayir* – World of the joy over an entering soul.

101. *Nertis* – Radiant calm.

102. *Gotimna* – Garden of Supreme Destinies

Sakualas of the Built and being Built *Zatomises* (19 worlds)

103. *Mayif* – Atlantic meta-culture, 12,000 to 9,000 years BC.

104. *Leenat* – Gondwana meta-culture, consisting of Java, Sumatra and south-east Asia and local regions.

105. *Eealu* or *Atkheam* – Ancient Egyptian meta-culture.

106. *Eyanna* – Babylonian-Assyrian-Canaanite meta-culture

107. *Shan-Ti* – Chinese and Japanese meta-culture

108. *Sumera* or *Meru* – Indian meta-culture

109. *Zervan* – ancient Persian meta-culture

110. *Olymp* – ancient Greek and Roman meta-cultures

111. *Nikhord* – Hebrew meta-culture

112. *Rai* (Paradise) – Byzantine meta-culture

113. *Zhunfleiya* – Ethiopian meta-culture

114. Eden – Roman Catholic meta-culture

115. *Monsalvat* – meta-culture of the European north-west, North America, Australia, and parts of Africa.

116. *Aireng-Dalyahu* – Indo-Malayan, Indo-Chinese, and Ceylon meta-culture

117. *Dzhannet* – Islamic meta-culture

118. *Sukkhavati* – Tibetan and Mongolian meta-culture

119. Heavenly Russia – the meta-culture of Russia, Ukraine, early Bulgaria, Georgia and Armenia; the demiurge of *Yarosvet* and the conciliar soul of *Navna*. This *sakuala* was founded by Apostle Andrew.

    It is the residence of Vladimir Solovyov, Tsar Ivan IV, Taras Shevchenko, Pavel Florenski, Gavrila Derzhavin, Aleksandr Pushkin, Mikhail Lermontov, Nikolai Gogol, Leo Tolstoy, Aleksei K. Tolstoy, Feodor Dostoyevski, Ivan Aksakov, Aleksandr Vitberg, Mikhail Kutuzov, Glinka,[4] Evgrof Chemezov, Vasili Surikov, Modest Musorski, Matvei Kazakov, Vasili Bazhenov, Nikolai Leskov, Nikolai Rimski-Korzakov, Vasili Kluchevski, Nikolai Gumilyov, Maximillian Voloshin, Sergei Rachmaninov, Anna Pavlova, Sergei Bulgakov, John of Kronshtadt, Patriarch Tikhon, Tsarevich Aleksei Nikolaevich, Afanasi Fet, Leonid Andreev, Aleksandr Blok, Feodor Shalyapin, Tsar Aleksandr II, Konstantine Romanov, and scientist Ivan Pavlov.

120. (no name provided) *Zatomis* of the African and Negro meta-culture; residence of Harriet Beecher-Stow.

121. *Arimoiya* – future *zatomis* of the general meta-culture. Founded by Zoroaster.

---

[4] This could be either of the brothers Sergey or Feodor.

> *Sakualas* of the *zatomises* not yet built in the *Enrof* meta-culture (15 worlds)

122. *Nambata* – Ancient Sudan
123. *Tzen-Tin* – Pra-Mongolian meta-culture
124. *Pred* – Dravidian meta-culture
125. *Asgard* or *Valgalla* – Ancient Germany
126. *Tokka* – Ancient Peru
127. *Bon* – Ancient Tibet
128. *Gaouripur* – the Himalayas
129. *Yunkif* – Mongolia
130. *Ieroo* – Ancient Australia
131. *Taltnom* – Toltec-Aztec meta-culture
132. *Kertu* – Yucatan, Mayan
133. *Intil* – Inca
134. *Daffam* –American Indian
135. *Lea* – Polynesia
136. *Nikisaka* – Japan, the Shinto religion.

The Middle Strata (76 worlds)

Sakualas of the Egregores (7 worlds)

137. *Zativ* – egregores of the initial tribes
138. *Zhag* – egregores of the governments
139. *Foraoun* – egregores of the churches
140. Yudgrogr – egregores of the anti-churches
141. (name not provided) egregores of the population of the *shrastras*

142. (name not provided) egregores of the world of the *daimons*

143. *Tsebruemr* – egregore of the coming anti-church anti-christ

Sakualas of the *Daimons* (3 worlds)

144. *Zheram* – world of the *daimons* corresponding to the *Enrof,* where the planetary Logos incarnated 10,000 years ago.

145. *Yurm* – the purgatory of the *daimons*

146. *Kartiala* – the *zatomis* of the *daimons*

The Single World

147. *Fongaranda* – the stratum of the residence of the *shelts* of great architectural creations: the architects of Orthodox monasteries, Egyptian pyramids, ziggurats, Catholic abbeys, German fortresses, Cathedral of St Peter in Rome, the Cathedral of Vasili the Blessed, the Chinese Temple of Heaven, Versailles, Peter the Great's Summer Palace, London parliament, Petersburg Admiralty.

Sakualas of the Angels (8 worlds)
Angels of the Lower Circle

148. Cherubim

149. Seraphim

150. Thrones

Angels of the Higher Circle

151. *Astrals* or Authorities

152. Powers

153. Dominions

154. Principalities

155. Archangels

SAKUALAS OF THE HIGHER OBLIGATION (12 WORLDS)

156. *Yusnorm* – the general temple

157. *Gridruttva* – great creative plan of humanity

158. *Alikanda* – first residence of human monads, united with their assigned souls

159. *Tovia* – second residence of the same

160. *Ro* – third residence of the same

161. *Mageeree* – the residence of the monads of meta-prefigures, united with all their *shelts* and with their transfigured Astral clothing or crust.

The meta-prefigures residing here are: Ivan Karamasov and Pavel Smerdyakov of Dostoyevski;, Sobakevich and Chichinov of Gogol; and Peter Bezukhov, Andrei Bolkonsky, Princess Maria, and Natasha Rostova of Tolstoy's *War and Peace.*

162. *Kaermis* – residence of the monads of animals, united with their assigned souls

163. *Deytrast* – residence of the monads of *daimons*, united with their assigned souls

164. *Sibrana* – residence of the monads of angels, united with their assigned souls

165. *Flyauros* – residence of the monads of *stikhials*, united with their assigned souls

166. *Niatos* – residence of the monads of demons, united with their assigned souls

167. *Iroln* – residence of the monads of people, united with their assigned souls

Sakualas of the Invocation of Orion (10 worlds)

168. *Yumaroyya*

169. *Odgiana*

170. *Ramn*

171. *Vualra*

172. *Leegeya*

173. *Fianna*

174. *Eramo*

175. *Veyatnor*

176. *Zaolita*

177. *Natolis*

Sakualas of the Invocation of the Planets (5 worlds)

178. Jupiter

179. Jupiter's moons

180. Saturn

181. Uranus

182. Neptune

Sakualas of the Invocation of the Planet *Daiya* (3 worlds)

This planet rotated in the past between Mars and Jupiter. The efforts of the demiurges on it banished the demonic powers there. *Daiya* then entered the 3rd eon, meaning it was physically transfigured and so disappeared from the global *Enrof.*

183.　　*Eeora*

184.　　*Akhos*

185.　　*Gebn*

Sakualas of the Sun's Invocation (9 worlds)

186.　　*Raos*

187.　　*Flermos*

188.　　*Tramnos*

189.　　*Gimnos*

190.　　*Aryer*

191.　　*Nigbeya*

192.　　*Trimoyya*

193.　　*Derayn*

194.　　*Eeordis*

Sakualas of the Invocation of *Astrafayr*, the Center of the Galaxy

195.　　*Grezuar*

196.　　*Maleyn*

197.　　*Virueana*

198.　　*Luevarn*

The *Bramfatura* of the Moon (5 worlds)

199. World of *Boglea* – the lunar female demon

200. The lunar hell of the demonic *Boglea*, the sacrifices of *Duegguer* descend here.

201. *Soldbiis* – the lunar *zatomis*

202. *Laal* – the lunar Elite

203. *Tanit* – the residence of the lunar goddess

The Worlds of the Trans-Myths of Supreme Religions (9 worlds)

204. *Azur* – Zoroasterism, The white pyramid

205. *Aye* – Judaism, the gold pyramid

206. *Niruddkhi* – Hinduism, the first layer of the lilac pyramid, the *Sinklit* of India

207. *Eroyya* – second layer of the lilac pyramid, only guests reside here.

208. (name not provided, it transcends mention)

209. *Shatrittva* · final layer of the lilac pyramid, the Hindu pantheon

210. Nirvana – the first layer of the green pyramid, Buddhist meta-culture

211. Stratum of Dhyani-Bodhisattvas – second layer of the green pyramid

212. Heavenly Jerusalem – the blue pyramid, the Christian teaching.

THE HIGHEST WORLDS OF *SHADANAKAR*

Sakualas of the *Sinklit* of Humanity; the *Sinklits* of the World (7 worlds)

Residents are the elect of the elect, and its number does not increase any more than about a thousand. They are no longer humans, but figures consisting of a higher, enlightened image. Those residing here are: Ramakriskna, Mohammed, Ezekiel, Daniel, Basil the Great, Vladimir the Great of Kiev, Yaroslav the Wise, Antonius and Fedosius of Pecher Monastery, Nestor the Chronicler, Aleksandr Nevski, Sergei Radonezhski, Andrei Rublyov, Nil Sorski, Mikhail Lomonosov, Ambrosi Optinski, Seraphim Sarovski, the meta-prefigures Venus de Milo, Don Quixote, and Faust.

213.   *Arvantakernis*

214.   *Diyegarnis*

215.   *Ranmatirnis*

216.   *Serbaraynis*

217.   *Magraleynic*

218.   *Ivaroynis*

219.   *Nammaraynos*

The *Sakualas* of the Great Hierarchies (11 worlds)

220.   *Aolinor*

221.   *Ramnagor*

222.   *Pleyragor*

223.   *Foraygor*

224.   *Stranganor*

225.   *Tzeliror*

226. *Likhanga*

227. *Devenga*

228. *Siringa*

229. *Khranga*

230. *Ganga*

Sakualas of the Demiurges (3 worlds)

231. *Rangaraydr* – the meta-ethereal birthplace and residence of the monads of the Demiurges and Great Sisters

232. *Astr* – the birthplace and residence of the monads of the spirit-leaders of the nations and Lesser Sisters

233. *Oamma* – (nothing is communicated)

Waves of Global Womanhood (6 worlds)

234. *Limuarna* – the female *Sinklit* of humanity

235. *Bayushmi* – the residence of the Great Female Monad at the preset time

236. *Faolemmis*

237. *Saora*

238. *Naolitis*

239. (name not provided) the 6th world remaining a secret

Sakualas of the Worlds of Communication of *Shadanakar* with the Hierarchies of the Macro-*Bramfaturas* and Universe (3 worlds)

240.   (name not provided)

241.   *Raoris* – residence of the Great Female Monad at the beginning of its emanation in *Shadanakar*

242.   (name not provided)

The Elite of *Shadanakar* (3 worlds)

Thése worlds include the residence of Zoroaster, Moses, Hosea, Lao-tze, Gautama Buddha, Akhenaten, Mahavira, Ashoka, Chandragupta Maurya, Patanjali, Nagarjuna, Kanishka, Aristotel, Plato, all the apostles except Paul, Tertullian, Mary Magdalene, John Chrysostom, Dante, Augustine, Joan d'Arc, Leonardo de Vinci, and Francis of Assisi.

243.   (name not provided)

244.   (name not provided)

245.   (name not provided)

The Global *Salvaterra*

246.   Region of the Ever-Virgin Mary

247.   Region of the Great Female Monad – *Zventa-Sventana*

248.   Region of the Planetary Logos, incarnated in *Enrof* as the human Jesus Christ.

Rose of the World

(selections)

TRANSLATED FROM THE RUSSIAN

BOOK ONE

Rose of the World and its Place in History

CHAPTER 1

Rose of the World and its Immediate Tasks

This book began when the danger of unprecedented calamity was already hanging over humanity; when the generation that barely began to depart from the upheavals of the Second World War was shockingly convinced that over the horizon there was already condensing, thickening, a strange deep darkness, the warning sign of a catastrophe that is even more terrible, a war that is even more devastating. I began this book in the extremely mute years[5] of tyranny that prevailed over 200 million people. I began it in a prison that had the designation of political isolation. I wrote it clandestinely. The manuscripts I hide, and good efforts of people – and even those who were not human – hid it for me during times of search. And every day I expected that the manuscript would be confiscated and destroyed, just as

---

[5] Meaning that news of what was occurring in the Soviet Union was not being spread.

my preceding work was destroyed, which deprived me of 10 years of my life and brought me to political isolation.

The book *Rose of the World* concludes a few years after, not when the danger of the 3rd world war is only rising like storm clouds from beyond the horizon, but is already hovering over our heads, having covered the zenith and quickly descending from it, spreading to every side of the sky.

But perhaps it will circumvent us? Such a hope remains warm in the soul of each person and without a similar hope it would be impossible to even live. Some attempt to reinforce it with logical reasons and effective actions. Some manage to convince themselves that as though the danger is exaggerated. A third strive not to think about it at all, delving into the concerns of their puny world and once and for all having decided about themselves: what occurs is what will occur. There are also others whose hope smolders in their soul like a spark ready to extinguish, and they live, move, work only as a result of previous inertia.

I finished the manuscript of *Rose of the World* in freedom, in a gold-colored autumn garden.[6] The person, under whose yoke the country weakened, already for a long while is reaping in other worlds the fruits of what was sown in this world.[7] And nonetheless the final pages of the manuscript I hide in the same manner as I hid the first pages, and I am unable to dedicate its contents to even one living soul. And as in the past, and so now, I have no assurance that this book will not be destroyed, or that the religious experience that saturates it will actually be transmitted to at least someone.

But perhaps all of this will circumvent us and the tyranny will never return? Perhaps, humanity will preserve forever the memory of the horrible historical experience of Russia? Such hope smolders in the soul of each person, and without such hope life would be nauseous.

---

[6] This was at Gorachi Kluich, southern Russia, October 12, 1958.
[7] Referring to Joseph Stalin burning in purgatory.

But I am a member of those who were fatally wounded by 2 great calamities: world wars and autocratic tyranny. Such people do not believe that the roots of war and tyranny are long obsolete in humanity or will become obsolete in some short while. Maybe the danger of such tyranny, such war, can be postponed, but after a certain interval passes the threat of the following will surface. Both these calamities were for us their own type of apocalypses – revelations of the potency of world-wide evil and its eternally perennial struggle against the powers of light. People of other epochs, assuredly, would not understand us. Our alarm would seem exaggerated to them, that our attitude towards the world is hypochondria. But such a conceptualization of the consistent pattern of history is not exaggerated, and which has flared in myself as a human being after half-a-century's contemplation and participation in events and progress of unprecedented scope. And that result can only be painful, that which has materialized in a human soul as the fruit of the activities of its supposedly brightest and deepest facets.

I am immensely ill, the years of my life are numbered. If this manuscript will be destroyed or confiscated, I will not have the time to recreate it. But if it will reach at some time even a handful of persons, whose religious thirst will compel them to read it to the end, overcoming all of its difficulties in comprehension – the ideas inherent in it – it cannot but become seeds that will sprout in strange hearts.

And whether this will yet occur before a third world war or after it, or even if the third war will not be unleashed in the near future at all, this book will not die anyway if just some friendly eyes will gaze over it, chapter by chapter, over its pages. Because the questions to which it is attempting to provide answers will agitate people still into the distant future.

These questions do not settle the problematic of war and state organization. But nothing agitates me in the conviction that the most terrifying dangers that threaten humanity and presently do and will threaten yet and more than just one century, this will be a great suicidal war and an absolute worldwide tyranny. It just may be that humanity is capable of overcoming a third world war to occur during our epoch, or at least be able to survive it in the same manner as it survived the first and the second world wars. It just may be that it will be able to outlast one way or another a tyranny that is even more extensive and ruthless than the one that we outlasted. What might also occur is that after a hundred or 2 hundred years new dangers for the nations will surface, not any less disastrous than the tyranny and the Great War,[8] but something else. This is possible. This is probable. But no type of strengths of reason, no type of reflection or intuition is capable of depicting the future dangers that would be tied in one way or another with one of 2 basic criteria: the danger of physical annihilation of humanity as the result of war and the danger of its religious annihilation as the result of absolute worldwide tyranny.

This book is directed, first of all, against these 2 evils, these 2 radical and fundamental evils. It is directed against them, not as a pamphlet, not as an exposing satire, not as a sermon. The most consuming satire and the most fiery sermon are fruitless if they only slap evil, and prove that what is good is good, and what is bad is bad. They are fruitless unless they are based on knowledge of the basics of this world ideology, this universal teaching, and an effective program – one that is expanding from mind to mind and from will to will. Only this would be capable of turning humanity from these 2 radical dangers.

To share my experience with others, to disclose the picture of historical and meta-historical perspectives, the branching chain of dilemmas rising in front of us, which must of necessity surface, and the panorama of worlds created of diverse materials mutually tied tightly with us in good and bad – this is the task of my life. I strove and strive to fulfill this in the form of a piece of literature, in fictional prose and in poetry, but especially this art did not permit me to disclose the entire concept with the sufficient completeness, to expound it exhaustively, precisely and in a manner accessible to everyone. To unfold this concept particularly in a manner that it could be understood, how it

---

[8] Russians refer to WW2 as the Great Patriotic War.

handles explaining the other-world nature, and at the same time how the key to the flowing progression of history and the fate of each of us is concealed from us – this is the task of the present book. The book – and if the Lord should preserve it from destruction – is just one brick among many to be installed into the foundation of the ROSE OF THE WORLD, the basis of the Fraternity of all humanity.

Institutions have existed over many ages that have claimed to be the sole, stable unification of people, repelling them from the dangers of wars of all against all and the danger of falling into chaos. Such an institution is the state. From the time of the end of the dynastic successions in all the historical stages, the state surfaced as an essential indispensable institution. Even the hierocracy, which was attempting to change it using religious authority, was transformed also into another version of the same state. The state cemented society on the principle of force, while the level of moral development, indispensable in order to cement society on some type of other principle, was not attained. Of course, this has not been attained even to this day. The state to this time remains the sole tested means to restrain social chaos. But its presence in humanity's ethical principles must be understood in a more higher sense, one capable of not only supporting, but also to consummate social harmony. And what is even more important, paths must be designated for a speedy development of these principles.

In the political history of the most recent era, 2 universal orientations are easily differentiated, although at opposite ends of the pole from one another.

One of them aspires to the redevelopment of the government principle in order to strengthen on every side the dependence of the individual on the state, more precisely, on that institution in whose hands the state bureaucracy is located: party, army, leader. Governments can be of the fascist or socialist-nationalist type,[9] which are the most flagrant examples of the phenomena of this type.

---

[9] Nazi

The other current that surfaced back in the 18th century, if not earlier, is the current of humanist orientation. Its sources and its most primary stages are the English parliament, French declaration of the Rights of Man, the German social-democracy, and finally, the wars of independence against colonialism. The distant goal of this current is to weaken the violence that cements the life of nations, and to transform the state from an overwhelming police bureaucracy that defends the national or class dominion, into a bureaucracy of general economic balance and with the preservation of individual rights.

Historical reality possesses other original forms that can be displayed as though hybrids. Essentially abandoning the phenomena of the first type, they change the shape of their personal appearance to the extent necessary into something more expedient to attained its designated goal. But this is just some tactic or masquerade; nothing more.

Anyway, disregarding the polarity of these currents of events, one trait unites them, characteristic of the 20th century: the aspiration to be worldwide. The external pathos of the various movements of our age resides in their constructive programs of building nations. But the inner pathos of the most recent history resides in the elemental aspiration to be worldwide.

The most potent movement of the first half of our century was distinctive due to its international doctrine and its planet-wide scope. The Achilles heal of this movement, the opposite effect of its intentions, surfaced as racism, National-Socialism.[10] This was their narrow nationalism, more precisely, the borders of their blessed zones were based on their narrow view of race and nationalism, by which they deceived and fascinated people in a chimerical manner. They aspired toward a world domination and even then with colossal energy. Now cosmopolitan Americanism is worried on how to escape the mistake of its predecessors.

---

[10] Nazi effort toward the annihilation of the Jews and other minorities.

So to what does this sign of the time direct us? Is it not because becoming world-wide is not just an abstract idea, but now has become a general necessity? Is it not because the world has become indivisible and integral, as never in the past? Is it not, finally, because the resolution of all essential problems can become fundamental and stable only under the condition of implementing this resolution on a worldwide scale?

Education under despotism systematically causes the principle of extreme violence to materialize or else it veils it partially through some subtle union of methods. The tempo increases speed. Such state armadas appear that earlier would have taken centuries to arm. Each one acts in a predatory manner according to its nature, each one strives to bind humanity particularly under its authority. Their military and technical potential causes a person's head to spin. How many times already have they thrown the world into the abyss of war and tyranny. Where is the guarantee that they will not throw it in again and again. And finally the most powerful will gain the victory on a worldwide scale, although this will be at the cost of transforming one-third of our planet into a moonscape environment and then the cycle will end and in order to yield its place to a considerably greater of evils: a sole dictator over the surviving two-thirds of the world. First, perhaps, an oligarchic system, and then, as this usually occurs as the second stage of dictatorship, one individual as despot. This is the threat, the most terrible of all that is hanging over humanity: the threat of tyranny over all humanity.

Consciously or unconsciously having a premonition of this danger, humanitarian-oriented movements are attempting to consolidate their strengths. They babble about cultural cooperation, disseminate slogans of pacifism and democratic freedoms, seek a transparent salvation in neutrality, or else they are scared by the aggression of the enemy, and so they enter themselves on the same path. Influencing some goal that is inarguable and trusting by all, that is, the idea that ethical control over the activity of the state is essentially indispensable, yet not one of them is instituted. Certain societies, traumatized by the terrors of the world wars, attempt to unite with them, in order for political union to encompass the entire world in the future. But to what will all this now lead? The danger of war, truly, would be estranged, or at least temporarily. But where is the guarantee that this supra-state, depending on ethically-obsolete, expansive layers (and there are so many of these in the world, more than we would even want) and rousing unfulfilled instincts in humanity of megalomania and torture, will not again grow into a dictatorship and eventually into a tyranny, and one that will make all previous ones seem like a child's amusement?

It is significant that particularly religious denominations were the first of all to announce international ideals of fraternity, but now seem to have become the rear guard of the general aspiration for its worldwide proliferation. It is possible that here the characteristic concentration of their attention on the inner person is explained, while disdaining all the external. At the same time the problems of the social development of humanity is directed at the external person. But if we were to delve deeper, if we were to publicly announce what is usually spoken just in narrow circles of people living an intensively religious life, then something will be revealed, but not taken into consideration by everyone. This mystical horror surfaced earlier in the face of the impending unification of the world during the era of the ancient Roman empire, this unstoppable alarm on behalf of humanity, because this sole state that encompassed all of humanity sensed a trap ahead of time, and the sole exit was an absolute autocracy, toward the kingdom of *the Prince of this world*, to the final cataclysm of history and to its catastrophic rupture.

Yes and indeed, where is the guarantee that a great ambitious man will not appear at the head of the supra-state, and science to benefit him as belief and virtue, as weapons for the transformation of this supra-state particularly into a monstrous machine of torture and psychological crippling, of which I speak? Can anybody doubt that even at the present preconditions are being created to acquire complete control over people's conduct and over their manner of thinking? Where are the limits of such dreadful perspectives that surface right in our imaginations as a result of the crossing of 2 factors: terrorist autocracy and the techniques of the 21st century? The tyranny will be even more absolute, so that even the final, path of deliverance – as tragic a one as it may be – will be then closed – the destruction of the tyranny through external intervention as the result of its defeat in war. And the worldwide union, that many generations have fantasized about for so long, that has demanded so many sacrifices, will turn to its demonic side, its inescapability in this situation, if the supporters of these dark powers take charge of the guidance of this union.

Based on bitter experience humanity is now already convinced that not these social-economic movements (and which are patronized by naked reasoning), and not the accomplishments of science, are in a position to on their own lead humanity out from between a rock and a hard spot – tyrannies and world wars. Worse than this: the new social-economic systems entering into sovereignty,[11] clothe themselves in the mechanism of political despotism, place themselves as disseminators and fomenters of world wars. Science is transformed into their obedient servant-woman, and far more obedient and reliable than was the church for the feudal lords. The tragedy is rooted in scientific activity not being from the very beginning harnessed with deeply contemplated moral instruction. Everything was permitted for such activity, independent of the level of their moral development. It is not surprising that every success of science and technology is now turned to one side – against the fundamental interests of humanity. The motion of internal combustion, radio, aviation, atomic energy – all strike at the same time at the living flesh of nations. While the development of the means of binding all such technical achievements, those which allow the police regime to control the intimate life and hidden thoughts of each person, are used to erect an iron pedestal for the vampiric intensity of the dictator.

---

[11] The spread of socialism into many countries.

In this manner the experience of history leads humanity close to understanding this obvious fact, that dangers will be circumvented and social harmony attained not by the development of science and technology on their own, not by the redevelopment of government principles, not by the dictatorship of a strong person, not by the approach to the authority of pacifist organizations of the social-democratic type that are rocked by historical winds to right and to the left as a result of powerless scatterbrain idealism that extends all the way to revolutionary maximalism − but by the acknowledgement of the essential indispensability of one-sole path: the installation of some type of untarnished, highly authoritative institution over a worldwide federation of states, one that is immune to bribery, one that is a ethical institution, outside of the state and over the state, and this is because the state is secular due to its fundamental character.

What type of idea, what teaching will assist to create this style of government? What minds will build it and make it acceptable to the immense majority? By what means will general humanity arrive at an acknowledgement of such an institution and bring it to that height of governing over the federation of governments, and one that rejects violence? If it should accept the principle of gradual exchange of violence for something else to guide it, then what will it be in particular and what will be the consequences? And what doctrine can resolve all that will eventually surface, tied with the problems of their extreme religious complexities?

The present book strives to provide this, and at least in some measure answer these questions, although its general theme is much wider. While preparing for an answer, what is first to be done is to clearly formulate what this teaching sees as its most irreconcilable enemy and that this teaching is directed against it or him.

In the historical plan it sees its enemies in any state, party and doctrine that strived toward the violent enslavement of others and toward some form or other of a nation's installation of despotism. In the meta-historical plan it sees its enemy in one item: opposition to religion materializing in a tyrannical attitude, in the great torturer, who appears in the life of our planet in diverse forms. For this movement, of which I speak, and now when it is barely attempting to surface, and then, when it arises as a decisive voice of history, there will be one enemy: the drive toward tyranny and toward cruel violence, wherever it may appear, even within itself. The violence might be acknowledged suitable as a measure just in extreme unavoidable circumstances, only in an ameliorated form and just until that time when a higher institution, using means of educational improvement, will prepare humanity with the assistance of millions of highly-developed ideal minds and wills to replace force and have it done voluntarily with the dictate of an internal law – the voice of deep conscience, and the state changing into a fraternity. In other words, until the basic character of the state is finally transformed the living fraternity of all will not replace the soulless bureaucracy of state violence.

It is not absolutely necessary to suppose that a similar process will certainly take an immense interval of time. The historical experience of great dictators, with extraordinary energy and regularly capturing the populations of immense countries using one, intensely premeditated system of education and instruction, has irrefutably proven the amount of strength available in a lever when applied on this path of influence on the psyche of that generation. The generations are then oriented to be closer to what is presented as desirable for the dominating authorities. Nazi Germany, for example, connived to acquire what they saw as the effective generation. The issue is so obvious that nothing other than rage and disgust could summons its ideals within us. But not only its ideals, we must even reject its method in almost its entirety. But we must take the lever it unleashed into our hands and hold it tightly.

The age of the victory of broad religious enlightenment is drawing near, having decided a new method of seizure, one that is at present barely a noticeable instruction. Even if just a few dozen schools were placed under its supervision, a generation would be oriented in these concepts, capable of fulfilling the debt, not by compulsion, but with a good conscience; not out of fear, but from a creative impulse and love. Herein is confined the meaning of a person's ennoble education.[12]

I propose that this political and cultural international organization should have as its goal the reformation of the character of governments by the path of subsequent materialization of reforms that encompass everything. The decisive stage toward this goal is the creation of a worldwide federation of government as independent members, but with the purpose of having a special institution installed over the federation. I have already mentioned this: it is the institution materializing the control over government activities and guiding them with a bloodless and painless transformation from within. Particularly it is bloodless and painless, and its entire essence consists in this, and which is its distinction from revolutionary doctrines of the past.

What the structure of this organization will be, what it's appellation will be, seems to me too early in time and unnecessary to imagine. We will name it something conditionally in order not to repeat a verbose description every occasion it is referenced: a League consisting of transformed governments' characters. As far as its structure is concerned, then those who will take the responsibility of its organization will be more experienced and pragmatic than I am. They will be social activists and not poets. I can only say that the League – in the manner I depict it – must extend its branches into all countries, so that every branch will possess certain aspects: cultural, philanthropic, educational, political. This political aspect of each branch will be transformed – structurally and organizationally – into a national political party with the goal of worldwide religious and cultural reform. All of such parties will be connected and united in this League and by this League.

How in particular, where and among whom the installation of the League will occur, I of course do not know and cannot

---

[12] This refers to the concepts of ROSE OF THE WORLD, although still in an embryonic state.

know. But it is clear that the interval from its origin to the factual creation of the Federation of governments and the ethical institution over them must be examined as a preparatory period, the period when the League will devote all of its strengths to the promulgation of its ideas, the arrangement of its departments, the expansion of the organization, the education of the adolescent generations. and the creation within itself of that future institution that in time can be trusted in the role of a worldwide guide.

Its regulations cannot serve as an obstacle to the inclusion in the ranks of the League of people of diverse philosophic and religious convictions. What is definitely required is the preparation for an active participation in the materialization of its programs and the decisiveness not to violate its moral standards, accepted as though inscribed into stone.

In all the vicissitudes of social life and political struggles, the successes of the League must be attained not at the cost of any departure from its ethical codex, but particularly as the result of fidelity to it. Its reputation must be unblemished, unselfish, not subject to doubt, and authoritative, because the best strengths of humanity will flow into it and will uninterruptedly strengthen it.

Most likely the road to worldwide unification will lie at the foot of the staircase of diverse steps of international solidarity through the unification and merger of regional commonwealths. The final step at the top of this staircase is presented as the worldwide referendum or plebiscite: one or another form of everybody's freedom of expression. It is possible that it will lead the League to victory but just in the outlying countries. But what will follow is the historical progress of things. The unification of at least half the world's countries will complete the profound shift in the cognizance of the nations. A 2nd referendum may occur and perhaps even a 3rd, and in 10 years more or less the boundaries of the federation will coincide with the boundaries of humanity. Then the practical possibility for the materialization of the chain of wide measures that need to be taken for the sake of the conversion of the conglomerates of the government into a monolith will be revealed. It will be gradually transformed by 2 parallel processes: the external – political/ social/ economic; and the internal – educational/ ethical/ religious.

It is clear from all of this that the activists of the League and its national political party will be able to fight only verbally and with personal example, and only using those ideologies and doctrines that strive to cleanse the path of any of these dictators and not to support these dictators at their helm of authority. The League will see in the great Mahatma Gandhi and in the political party that he inspired, one of their historical predecessors, although he acted within a narrow national scale. Being the first government activist-ruler in the new history [of India] he confirmed a purely political movement for the basis of a high ethic and overthrew prevalent opinion, as if polity and morality were incompatible. But the national frames, within which the Indian National Congress operated, the League will expand to planetary boundaries, and its goals are the succeeding historical steps or order of steps, that can be compared with those steps that the great political party that liberated India installed for itself.

O, of course a few people will be found who will arise to confirm that the methods of the League are unpractical and unreal. Alas, as far as I am concerned we need champions of political realism. There is no immorality, no socialist depravity, that has not been covered by some pitiful fig leaf. There is no burden that is more dead, more mundane, than interpretations of political realism being a counter-balance to all that is celestial, inspired and spiritual.

Those who are unable to see the best in a person are those who will blame the League of the unreality of their methods. Their psyche is coarsened and conscience is decayed in the atmosphere of state arbitrariness. Those who have no foresight of what shifts in popular cognizance await us in the near future years join them. Trauma due to wars, repressions and violence of all possible types even at the present summon a wide movement for coexistence and for peace. Events that destroy the feeling of safety are constantly occurring and will occur, they will leave nothing of comfort and calm, undermining the roots of trust in existing ideologies and the order of things that they protect. The exposure of unheard terrors committed on behalf of the pompous facades of the dictator, the visual explanation upon which their temporary victories were erected and how they were paid, their superficial successes – all of this emaciates the soul like an extensively hot wind and which causes the resultant spiritual thirst to be intolerable. What do the believers pray for and what the unbelievers dream about in our age? It is about the alienation of the threats of great wars; about the routes to unification of the world without bloodshed; about the light-bearing virtuous person coming to head the united humanity; about the weakening of the violence of governments and about the growth of the spirit of fraternity. And assuredly we need to [pray and dream] to the highest degree that the world-encompassing liberal teaching – and which includes ethical and political and philosophic and religious – will convert the thirst of that generation into a national creative enthusiasm.

The circumstance that the concluding religious breakthrough in humanity – the Protestant Reformation – had in place 400 years ago, while the final religion of worldwide significance – Islam – counting some 13 centuries of existence, is often mentioned as a argument to the benefit of the opinion that the religious era of humanity has consummated. But of the potential possibilities of another religion as this one[13] should not be judged in the same manner as the final concrete forms that appeared such a long while ago, but instead whether the evolution of religion has now reached a point of deadlock. Does the possibility exist to combine religious creative thought with inarguable scientific theses? And likewise to add, in the presence of such an ideology, are the perspectives of contemplation of life's content pertaining to the new epochs being tarnished? Or is an actual and progressive influence of religion on [life's] content possible?

In reality, about 400 years have passed since the concluding concrete religious movement of international scope. But prior to the Protestant Reformation, similar movements did not occur for

---

[13] Referring to ROSE OF THE WORLD

a few hundred years. And why is this? Is it not clear that the assigned channel of ideological creative work of humanity during the concluding era has exhausted almost all of its spiritual and mental strengths? Materializing such aspiring progress, whether scientific, technical and social, creating such cultural treasures, as literature, music, philosophy, air and science of the preceding ages, it would be difficult for humanity to find within itself the strength to simultaneously create another universal religious system.

But exactly at the turn of the 20th century this epoch has appeared, when the apogee of great literatures and arts, great music and philosophy, has terminated. The sphere of social-political activity no more draws in any more special spiritual representatives of the human race, but actually less, even if extending itself further than it should. A gigantic vacuum of spirituality has formed, one that did not exist even 50 years ago, and now some hypertrophied science will fill the void without effort. If it is permissible to select a certain expression: colossal resources of human ingenuity just do not dissipate anywhere. The bosom of creative strengths is where the inter-religion for all humanity – predestined for birth – ripens.

Is it possible for religion – and not its old form, but that resultant religion by which the world is pregnant – to repel for the most part the threats of danger that hang over humanity: worldwide war and worldwide tyranny? Believe me, it was not even in a situation to repel the recent world war. If a 3rd [worldwide] war should flare, then this disaster, assuredly, will occur sooner than the League will be able to form. But its most impending task is the prevention of all wars, whose dangers will surface after the kernel of the coming inter-religion is formed, and this applies likewise to the prevention of worldwide tyranny. Can this religion attain the most harmony between the freedom of the individual and the interests of humanity, which only seems to be fantasized at the present stage of history? But this is just another aspect of its one and same very close goal. Will it be capable of developing on every side the creative capabilities that are inherent in a person? Yes, except for the demonic capabilities, that is, the capabilities of tyranny, torture, and its self-establishment at the expense of the balance of living entities. Does it require sacrifices of bloodshed for its triumph, as other movements of a worldwide direction? No, excluding these events where its propagators will have to testify at the expense of their own life, should this occur, to prove the validity of their ideas. Are its theses contradictory – not the philosophic doctrine of materialism (since it is contradictory in all points from A to Z), but by an objective and obligatory thesis of contemporary science? No, not in one letter or numeral. Is it possible to foresee in our epoch the establishment of its hegemony in such a regime where nonconformity will be prosecuted, when it will suppress dogmas of philosophy, science, art? But exactly the contrary will occur: from partial limitations of the freedom of thought in the beginning, then toward the unlimited freedom of thought. This is its destined path. So now what remains from the argument that religion is not capable of answering the essential questions of time, and even more, to pragmatically resolve them?

With full right and basis, such a reproach can be thrown not at religion, but, alas, at science. It is specifically the system that does not gaze at either to the right or to the left of the regions where contemporary scientific knowledge is outlined that is unable to provide answers to the most primordial, most elementary questions. Does a First Cause exist? A Creator? God? It is not known. Does the soul, or something like it, exist? And is it immortal? Science does not know this. What is time, space, matter, energy? Opinions about these items vary sharply. Is the world eternal and endless or, on the contrary, is it limited in time and in space? Science does not contain material for a concrete answer to these questions. For what reason should I do good, and not bad? Why don't I do bad if the opportunity is such that I will escape punishment? The responses are completely incomprehensible!

How can science be utilized in order to prevent the possibility of war and tyranny? I hear silence! How can social harmony be attained with the least amount of sacrifices? Mutually exclusive propositions are provided, similar only in one item: that all of them to the same measure are not related strictly to science. It is only naturally that upon such shaky, subjective, and definitely pseudo-scientific bases, a teaching of class, race, national and partisan egoism surfaces, which is exactly the deduction that is utilized as the justification of dictators and wars. A low level of spirituality is the distinctive trait of similar teachings. Subsequently, the sought-for ethical institution can be erected on the basis of not what is called scientific ideology – which essentially does not exist – but on an attachment to the spiritual world, on accepting the rays that pour from there and into the heart, intellect and conscience; and on the materialization of the covenant of activity and creative love in all regions of life. The moral level, fully corresponding to these enumerated signs, is called integrity.[14]

Yet another prejudice is also promulgated: the view of religion as a reactionary phenomenon due to its inherent substance, and especially the more in our epoch. But to speak of religion as reactionary or obsolete in general, without pertaining to its concrete forms, is just as thoughtless as to prove art in general or philosophy in general as reactionary. The person who thinks dynamically, who sees an evolving order of facts and processes, by which these orders are forms, he is able – in art as well as in religion and in any other region of humanity's activity – to circumspect the facets of reactionary and progressive forms. There are as many reactionary forms of religion that you want to encounter at your pleasure and even more than you would even want, but this does not have any application to that divinely-generated consummate religion to which this book is dedicated. Because in our century, there have not been and there are no more progressive goals, no more progressive methods, than those which are blended together with this religion.

During the previous century, under the impression of an aspiring progress in science and technology, the annihilation of art was prophesied. A hundred years passed and the blossoming

---

[14] The Russian word can also mean rectitude or virtue.

of art did not only not perish, but advanced in another aspect: the art of films. Thirty or 40 years ago, many in Russia seemed to feel that the annihilation of religion as the result of scientific and social progress was inevitable. And the success of religion did not perish, regardless of all the means taken against it as a result of those who were mobilized. It is particularly due to the influence of scientific and social progress that those who will implement the sole concrete and sole spiritual flower – ROSE OF THE WORLD – as a worldwide religious system, rather than a unification of scattered pedals, will be enriched.

What evolves from all that is mentioned above is a religious movement that includes a positive experience for humanity in its ideology and practice, and from the negative makes conclusions that demand much courage and rectitude in order to establish this on the paths of other currents of social thought. It is a movement that places as its closest goals the transformation of the state into a fraternity, the unification of the land and education of an individual as a cultured entity, a movement that will protect itself ahead of time from distortions of ideals and conduct with an undefeatable shield of the highest ethic. Such a movement cannot but be recognized as progressive, perspicacious, and creative for young people.

To use the shield of ethical conduct! But what would be the basis upon which such ethical conduct will be established? I speak of rectitude. But is not the rectitude of some entire social circle a utopia, and not just an individual one?

We need to be more precise as to what is here understood as rectitude. Rectitude is not solely the product of monastic asceticism. Rectitude is the highest step of the moral development of a person. The one who ascends to this summit is no longer virtuous, but holy. The forms of rectitude are diverse. They depend on time, place and human character. It can be generalized in the following terms: rectitude from the negative aspect is the state of a person who is stable and this ends only with his death. During this interval his will is free from the impulses of self-interest, his intellect is free from compulsive material interests, and his heart is free from boiling due to accidental and turbid emotions that humiliate the soul. From the positive aspect, rectitude is the penetration of active love toward God, people and the world when utilizing all the external and internal pursuits of a person.

Hardly can a psychological climate for the appearance of a moral environment and institution founded particularly on rectitude be perhaps prepared anywhere better than in a society that has been united with the hope of its materialization and so its meaning and goal is therein evident. So exactly the League needs to be such a society. Atheists can also surface among the number of its members. But the fundamental thesis of the League is the indispensability of a worldwide ethical environment that transcends the state. In particular it will solidify the most inspirational, creative, productive and gifted members in its core. An atmosphere of inexhaustible spiritual creation is characteristic of this core of energetic love and purity. This core consists of people who are sufficiently educated, in order to understand not only dangers that threaten each of us as a result of the hostile impulses of self-interest, but also the dangers of that excessive superficial understanding of religious-moral values that can lead to pious formalism, hypocrisy, mental obduracy, and sanctimony.

No one, other than the Lord God, knows when and where the first fire of ROSE OF THE WORLD will be ignited. The country – Russia – is only foretold. Tragic events are still possible which will complicate the consummation of this mystic act and will compel it to expand it to another country. This epoch – the decade of the 1960's – is only a conjecture. Destructive cataclysms are possible, and which will postpone this date into the next series of years. It is possible that the means by which the first flame will be ignited will not occur until the League transforms the character of government, but something else that presently is not yet ascertained by people. But whether it is there or here, in this country or another, earlier by a decade or later, the inter-religious church of the new eras that will encompass all humanity – the ROSE OF THE WORLD – will appear as the pinnacle of spiritual pursuit of the majority, as a religious council formed by people standing beneath a descending stream of revelation. So it will appear, surface, and enter the path of history.

I cannot use any of these words – religion, inter-religion, church – to explain with necessary precision what I mean. The series of its fundamental distinctions from old religions and churches in due course will compel new words to be created to apply to it. But even outside of this, we are presented with the task in this book to enter an expansive supply of new words into circulation. But here, in the very beginning, it is preferable to run not to these [obsolete] words, but instead to the descriptive definition of the distinctive traits of that which is to be called ROSE OF THE WORLD.

This is not an isolated or private religious confession, whether true or false. This is not likewise an international religious society similar to the theosophic, anthroposophic or Masonic, which for the most part are like bouquets consisting of various flowers of religious truth, eclectically picked from every available religious meadow of enlightenment. What is here is an inter-religion or pan-religion in this sense, one to be understood as an ecumenical teaching, directing attention to certain points of view of religions that have appeared earlier, during which all of them appeared as reflections of various formations of spiritual reality, various series of facts about other types of matter, and various segments of the planetary cosmos. This point of view encompasses *Shadanakar* as the whole and as a part of the divine cosmos of the universe. If the old religions are pedals, then ROSE OF THE WORLD is the flower, including the root, stem, cup and all its surrounding pedals.

The second distinction is the universality of the aspiration of ROSE OF THE WORLD and its historical solidarity. Not even one religion placed the task of the transformation of the social body of humanity in front of it, with the exception of Middle Ages' Catholicism. But even the papacy, persistently attempting to terminate the feudal chaos using dams of hierocracy, was not able to either weaken the exploitation of the have-nots by the haves, or decrease the wide reforms of social inequality, or raise the common welfare. Nonetheless, to blame the governing Catholic hierarchy of the time would be unjust. There were no material means yet, or economic or technical. It is not accidental that the world's evil affected time from its beginning and entirely to the new era, and was sensed as ineradicable and eternal. So Catholicism, essentially, and as did the balance of religions, just turned to the inner person, teaching personal self-perfection. But times have changed and material means are now available for the entire historical process. But it is not just ROSE OF THE WORLD that is able to now watch the social transformations (but not as though at the external that are destined to failure and not worth the effort), but to place them in an unbreakable bond with the perfection of a person's inner world. Now these 2 parallel processes which must complement each other.

Often we hear, "Christianity has failed." Yes, if all of this was in the past, this could be said, that it has failed in the social and worldwide moral application. "Religion has not failed," we also hear. Yes, if the religious creativity of humanity would take advantage of what is already created, religion in strictly the above-mentioned meaning definitely would not have failed. But while it is right to speak of this only in this manner, that the old religions could not achieve a substantial decrease of social evils, and because they did not allocate material means that were indispensable for this, and the absence of these means summoned their negative attitude to all similar attempts. This then prepared ahead of time a religionless stage of civilization. In the 18th century the socialist conscience awakened. The societal disharmony was finally felt and acknowledged as something unacceptable, insulting, and demanding defeat. Of course, this was interwoven with the fact that the material means earlier lacking were now available. But the old religions could not seem to understand this, did not want to utilize these means, did not want to head the process of societal transformation. And their most serious guilt is particularly this stagnation, this mental lethargy, this immobility and narrowness of conceptuality. Religion discredited itself with its historic perennial helplessness in this application, and the contrasting extreme that Europe fell into does not come to any surprise, and likewise other continents: the transformation of society by purely mechanical means with a complete rejection from the religious side of that process. There is no reason, of course, to be surprised at the outcome: shocks that the world has never seen, large scale holocausts, such that could never be described even if in a delirium. And even the possibility of such a decline of the moral level in the 20th century presents to this time a greater gloomy and tragic dilemma. A significant degree of responsibility falls on the old religions due to the depth and stubbornness of the previous religionless stage, due to the spiritual fate of millions of souls who, for the sake of the struggle for a just world order, placed themselves against religion in general and so uprooted the roots of their existence from the bosom of world spirituality. But true religious pursuit is its own type of social service, while true social service is at the same time – religious pursuit. No type of religious effort, even the achievements of a monk, can be isolated from the general, from work to the benefit of worldwide enlightenment. And every type of social activity, except demonic, can have an influence on increasing the amount of world benevolence, regardless of religious meaning. The heartbeat of the societal conscience, the effective social compassion and empathy, the inexhaustible practical efforts for the sake of transforming the social body of humanity – this is the second distinction of ROSE OF THE WORLD from the obsolete religions.

The 3rd distinction: its dynamic view. Religions, but not the foreign portrayals of meta-history, have already been: Judaism, early Christianity. But just in the distant past and during the short periods of their residency they attempted to spiritually comprehend the progressing historical process. During these short, half-forgotten epochs, the striking displays of the Book of Revelation remained hidden from the eyes of people by a veil of allegory and nebulous phrases. Symbolisms behind the images permitted any number of interpretations. So an original comprehension of the historical process was not sustained. The historical attempt was still small and narrow, the geographic periphery was removed, the mystical mind was not prepared for the attainment of an inner balance of the meta-historical and the extreme complexity of *Shadanakar*. But the appearance of ROSE OF THE WORLD preceded the era of the hegemony of science, at its very roots it shook their concepts of the world, nations, cultures and their fate. One more item preceded it: the epoch of essential socialist revisions and restarts, the epoch of revolution and planetary war. Both series of displays broke the psychological formations that existed motionless for many ages. In the field, dug by iron teeth of historical catastrophes, the seeds of meta-historical revelation fall. And the entire planetary cosmos is opened for spiritual viewing as an uninterruptible changing system of worlds, all having their own significance, turbulently carried to some blinding goal, inspired and transformed from age to age, from day to day. The series of impending epochs begin to surface, each in its own unrepeatable primordial form, interwoven with the struggles of the meta-historical principles in it. The aspiration of ROSE OF THE WORLD is to arise as the adopter, developer and interpreter of this comprehension. The conglomerate mystic mind of living humanity will comprehend the historical process in its past, present and future, in order to enter into its creative guidance. If it is possible to speak of some type or other of dogmas in its teaching, then these dogmatics are profoundly dynamic and multi-aspected, capable of further enrichment and development for its perfection in the prolonged future.

Out of this evolves also another, a 4th distinction of ROSE OF THE WORLD: the perspective of the consecutive spiritual-historical tasks that stand before it, fully concrete and having principally materialized. I will recount once more the nearest of them: the union of Earth's sphere into a Federation of governments having an ethical institution controlling it, the expansion of material sufficiency and a high cultural level of the populations of all countries, the education of generations in a noble manner, the unification of all Christian churches and free

Unia,[15] along with all religions, and directed toward a bright direction, the conversion of the planet into a garden, and the state into a fraternity. But this is a task definitely of the first rank. Its materialization will open the path to the resolution of tasks that are ever higher, to the spiritualization of nature.

And so, the inter-religion aspect, its universality, societal aspiration, and its solidarity, dynamism, ideology, and the subsequent resolution of worldwide-historical problems – these are the characteristics that make ROSE OF THE WORLD distinct from all the religions and denominations of the past. Its implementation being bloodless, the painlessness of its reforms, its goodness and kindness toward people, its waves of psychological warmth that expand into the surrounding regions – these are the characteristics that make it distinct from all political-socialist movements of the past and present.

It is clear that the essence of government, likewise the ethic structure of society, cannot possibly be transformed in a twinkle of an eye, knowing that an immediate complete rejection of compulsion is utopian. But this element will decrease in time and in the social sphere. Every discipline is arranged with elements of compulsion and comprehension, and it is upon the relationship between these 2 elements that one or another type of discipline exists. The majority percentile of compulsion, and with almost a complete absence of comprehension, is possessed by the disciplinary manner of slave-holding interests, prisons and concentration camps. And further, to the measure of the mitigation of the element of compulsion in disciplinary systems, the categorical imperative of inner self-discipline grows and replaces it. It is particularly due to having knowledge of this impulse that the new pedagogy is built. Addressing its principles and methods, like the methods of reeducation and rehabilitation of criminals, will occur later in this volume, in one of the final chapters. But it seems clear that already the stimulus of external compulsion will terminate faster than anything else in inner circles where ROSE OF THE WORLD is concentrated. Those

---

[15] Meaning the Uniate Church, or Roman Catholicism of the Eastern Rite.

people in particular who have dedicated their lives dealing with its problems and its ethic, and who now see no need of any external compulsion, will fill these inner circles. In particular, such people will materialize as its conscience, and if not them, then who will ascend the chairs of the Supreme Council?

Yes it is possible to reevaluate the educational significance of such social institutions, when those at the top of society guide it and provide what is worthy of it. Not those whose strong-willed principle is hypertrophied on account of other capable souls and whose strength is confined to an unintelligible attitude toward means, but those whose harmonic development of the will, intellect, devotion, purity of thought and profound life-long experience is combined with apparent spiritual gifts, those whom we call virtuous people. Very recently we saw an example of this: we saw a momentous year in India and the magnanimous Gandhi. We saw a earth-shaking scene: a man, not possessing any government authority, under whose authority was not even one soldier, not even one personal servant, who became the conscience, the religious and political leader of 300 million people, and just one silent word of his was sufficient for these millions to unite in a common bloodless struggle for the emancipation of their country, while any enemy who died caused a subsequent fast and mourning throughout all of India. It is easy to imagine how tragically the historical path of the Indian nation would have been distorted if – in place of this champion at the decisive minute – a person having the qualities of a one-sided tyrant, like a Mussolini or Stalin, someone with a domineering personality, a mastery of demagoguery and political intrigue, disguising his despotism with tirades about the national welfare! He would brilliantly play on the base instincts of the nation, on natural hate toward conquerors, on their envy of the rich. Then what waves of fire and blood would have flowed through India, consuming the fortresses of the highest ethical cognizance that thousands of years strengthened and which were cherished by the best of the sons of this great nation! And what tyranny would have arisen over the tortured country as a result, utilizing their inclination toward obedience that was inculcated into them due to centuries of servitude! Gandhi directed the liberating and edifying enthusiasm of the nation to another path. This is the first in the newest history as an example of this strength that gradually will replace the sword and whip of state authority. This strength is the nation's living trust of the person who proved his superior moral integrity, this is the authority of rectitude.

I foresee many objections. One of these is the following: Yes, this was possible in India, with its unique circumstances that will never occur again, with a 4,000 year religious past, with the ethical level of their nation. Other nations possess another heritage, and it is impossible for the experience of India to be transferred in any manner to any other country.

It is true that each nation possesses its unique heritage, and the heritage of India brought it to the point of becoming the pioneer upon this road. But almost every nation saw dictators and tyrannies of every possible shade in itself or alongside itself, with diverse ideological masquerades, and each nation could have become convinced that their blind authority was drawing their country into a dark abyss of catastrophes – one not drawn by an educated pragmatism, and not having to answer even by the demands of a nominal ethical level. But to have state guidance is an accomplishment, and a nominal moral level will apply little to it. Many nations are convinced what where political parties rotate instead of dictators, then also diplomats and generals, bosses and lawyers, demagogues and activists also alternate, like a kaleidoscope, some due to graft, others due to ideology, but not even one is capable of breathing a new, pure and fervent spirit into their life, to resolve the essential national problems. The result is that no one can trust anybody at all except themselves, and because not one of them even has a clue of what rectitude and integrity is. They are declining shadows, fallen leaves, carried away by the winds of history. If ROSE OF THE WORLD does not enter in time into the arena common to all humanity, the people will be dispersed by the flaming breath of conceited and ruthless dictators. If ROSE OF THE WORLD should appear, the [fraudulent leaders] will disperse and melt under the rising sun of this great concept, because the heart of the nation will entrust one virtuous person with more [authority] than a hundred contemporary politicians.

But its effect on the nation and its destiny will be even more potent and brighter if 3 supreme talents – rectitude, religious oratory and artistic ingenuity – will be coincidently residing in one person.

Many manifestations of religion pertained to its passing eras. One of such manifestations, and which is rather obvious, is the authority over minds by using statutory dogmas that are rigorously codified, logically and irrefutably expressed, and not subject to interpretation. The experience of the later centuries and growth of individualism brought to reality that what some person created was just their perception of the conditionality and oppression of any dogma. Subsequently, as non-dogmatic that any of the theses of ROSE OF THE WORLD might be, and no matter to what extent they are penetrated by the spirit of religious dynamics, it will still be very difficult for many to accept even them. As a result, many and many more will respond to its summons, but it will not so much be directed to the intellect, as much as to the heart, echoed in genuine compositions of literature, music, theater and architecture. Forms of art are spacious and have many aspects, more than theosophic aphorisms or philosophic deliberations. They leave more freedom for reflection. They present the opportunity for every person to interpret a teaching such that it is particularly more organic and more understandable for his individualism. Revelation flows along many channels, and art, if it is not the cleanest of them, it is the widest of them. For this reason all forms of art and a beautiful culture will clothe ROSE OF THE WORLD with sonorous and radiant covers. And so it is most natural of all for the person who possesses the 3 supreme talents to stand at the head of ROSE OF THE WORLD: the gift of religious eloquent, the gift of rectitude, and the gift of artistic genius.

Perhaps such a person will not arrive or not arrive soon enough. It is possible that he will not head ROSE OF THE WORLD, but instead a collective of the most worthy people. But if

Providence would direct such a great soul in our age – and it has already brought one – and the demonic powers were not able to estrange him, this would be a great prosperity for all the land, and since no one can deny that there is no greater and more radiant an effect on humanity than the effect of a genuinely talented orator who is installed as a seer and sage and raised to the height of worldwide guidance of social and cultural education. Particularly it is just such a person and only him who can be entrusted with such an extra-ordinary work that is unprecedented in history: controlling the ethics of all the states of the Federation and guiding the nations on the path of the transformation of these governments into a fraternity of all humanity.

O, we Russians have cruelly paid for unconditional trust shown to a strong person, who was accepted by many of us as a benefactor of humanity.[16] We will not repeat this mistake! Irrefutable signs do exist that will identify one person as worthy of a similar mission, and who is separate from one who is the evil genius of the nation. The latter was dismal; the former rejoiced in spiritual happiness. One strengthened his authority using executions and tortures; the other will not begin to attempt to use authority not even one day of his life, and when he does accept it, he will not spill any blood. One plants his personality cult throughout the land that is under his authority; to the other, such a veneration is repulsive and ridiculous. One is inaccessible; the other is opened to all. The latter's life is stormed by a ruthless thirst for existence and authority and he hides from imagined dangers behind impenetrable walls; the former is free of a life of temptation, and is calm in the face of dangers, because his conscience is clean and faith is unshakable. They are 2 antipodes, emissaries of 2 irreconcilable principles.

Of course, such a selected person in the Supreme Council would just be the first among equals. In all matters he depends on the cooperation of the majority, and his individual activities would be controlled by this majority. To attain such an

---

[16] A reference to Joseph Stalin

extraordinary post, he would have to pass a strict probation. A young person or elderly or aged could not be matched with such a rank. Temptations and struggles with passions must be long lived out. In regard to his actual selection, it seems to me that this would occur through one type or another of a plebiscite. Even during the years of the supreme preceptor's governing, the Council would still review all of his activities. His departure from the specified route would cause the authority to be transferred to another more worthy person. In general, all those tied with this question need to deliberate carefully on the matter, foresee dangers, weigh all decisions, and finally execute their resolution. But as long as the supreme preceptor will strictly follow the pre-assigned route, he will reside as the mystic tie between living humanity and the celestial world, the announcer of Providential will, the perfector and defender of billions of souls. It would not be frightening to combine the totality of religious and secular authority in the hands of such a person.

They will say: similar people only surface once in 500 years. But I say it is even greater: the personality of such a scale and possessing the sum of particularly such qualities, could never have been in the past. Einstein could not have appeared among the Maori of the 19th century; it would be a futile hope to find Dostoyevski, in the manner that we know him, among the subjects of Tutankhamun or Theoderic the Great. Then he would have possessed a different sum of qualities, and even then he would not have a possibility to display many of them. Such a person of whom I speak, even during the epochs of the recent past, could not have materialized the gifts entrusted to him, and his contemporaries would have remained in complete ignorance of the true scales and potential pertaining to him. It is only apparent that the necessary conditions are ascribed to the progressing present epoch. ROSE OF THE WORLD will initiate the process for the social and cultural atmosphere to insure that the supreme preceptor will have a chain of successors who are worthy of this crown.

They can also say: even all the enumerated talents are little for such an extraordinary activity. It is necessary to possess a wide, vigilant and practical political mind. Yes, and more. Such a minister will incur dealing with thousands of diverse problems. So is knowledge, experience and erudition required – economic, financial, legal and even technical. But the age of Aristotle has long passed; minds of an encyclopedia's scope are unimaginable in our era. And the activity of the person of whom I speak is likewise unimaginable if separate from the collective mind of the Supreme Council. The most profound minds will participate in it: persons sagacious in the vicissitudes of government administration, specialists in all branches of knowledge. It is not encyclopedic erudition and not secular business intellect that will be demanded of the supreme preceptor, but wisdom. A wisdom that understands people from the first gaze, that can decipher and grasp the essence of the most complicated questions immediately, and which will not even for a moment turn a deaf ear to the voice of conscience. The supreme preceptor must stand on a moral pinnacle such that love and trust toward him will replace any other methods of the practice of his authority. Compulsion, coercion of some other will, will be torturous for him. He will utilize such means only in rare circumstances.

And all of this is just one of many possible variations, although, in my personal view, it is the most desirable. Another will be presented in full: such is the guidance by ROSE OF THE WORLD, such is an attitude with legislative institutions and with the governing Federation, during which the principle of collectiveness will not be limited in any manner and not by anybody. The time is imminent to develop a constitution for the future, for the distant future, and not for us, but for the fortunate posterity who will have the responsibility to select one of the many variations.

But is this not a theocracy? I do not like the word – theocracy. Theocracy is divine authority. From the point of view of an atheist, to apply it to some type or other social and government institution is absurd. To the point of view of a believer – it is blasphemous. History does not recognize and cannot acknowledge a true theocracy. It is a hierocracy, the authority of the clergy, or the Pope or Dalai-Lama, that can be labeled an ecclesiastical state. But this arrangement of which I speak is directly opposite to every hierocracy: it is not just the church that dissolves into the state, swallows it and then in its name become dominant, but the entire conglomerate of governments, and the assemblies of churches gradually dissolve into the fraternity of all humanity, into the inter-religion church. And it is not the supreme hierarchs of the church that ascend the chair of its highest departments and legislatures that fulfill and control, but the best representatives of all the nations, all confessions, all social estates, all nationalities.

It is not a hierocracy, not a monarchy, not an oligarchy, not a republic, but something entirely new whose quality is entirely different from all else that has existed to this time. This is the worldwide national arrangement aspiring to the sanctification and education of the entire world's life. I do not know what it will be called at that time, but the essence is not in its appellation but in its substance. Its substance is labor in the name of the inspiration of the human, to inspire humanity, to inspire nature.

CHAPTER 2

ATTITUDE TOWARD CULTURE

Little by little the new attitude surfaces pertaining to all matters: the existence of ROSE OF THE WORLD would not have even a shadow of a meaning if it only repeated what was stated by others earlier. The new attitude towards it, the new comprehension summons literally all manifestations, from the greatest to the smallest: using the cosmic process and the historical process, the world's laws and the connection between worlds composed of different materialities, human attitudes and routes of personal development, governments and religions, the animal kingdoms and the elements. In short, it is all that we unite under the heading of culture, and all that we unite under the heading of nature. The new attitude applies to all matters, but this does not mean that every old attitude is devaluated or censured. In many situations such a point of view is indicated, where the various attitudes of the past can cease to contrast one another, but begin to supplement one another and must be read as a diverse series of aspects of one and the other or many realities. This is often changed, for example, with the investigation of obsolete religions and the realities that stand behind them.

In essence, this book is dedicated to this new attitude toward things: a similar problem that is extensively immense and complex is for this to be fluent and orderly in this chapter. The chapter has the heading, *Attitude toward Culture*, and the following, *Attitude toward Religion*, but do not expect from them a detail exposition, because all 12 sections of this work are saturated entirely with the new perception of diverse cultural spheres, diverse historical events, diverse religious systems, and likewise diverse kingdoms of nature. The initial chapters are equally valuable as somewhat of an introduction. They contain a brief exposition of certain fundamental principles.

The leading sphere of culture in our age appears to be science. The scientific method of knowledge claims the hegemony, for this reason the present chapter begins with the characteristic attitude of ROSE OF THE WORLD particularly to the scientific method. This method, extremely labor-consuming and summoning fiery odium from contemporary Philistines,[17] makes one principle distinct although it is alien to science: the principle of the perfection and transformation of the individual entity. The result of this is that the physical and ethereal skin of the individual becomes more pliable and elastic, more subservient to the will, than what we have at present. This route leads to such legendary phenomenon as the ability for the corporeal to

---

[17] This was term used in Russia toward narrow-minded individuals; in America we use the term – Neanderthals.

traverse through objects of the 3-dimensional world, movement through the air, passage through water, conveyance of immense distances in a moment's time, healing of the terminally ill and those born blind, and finally as the supreme pinnacle and exceptionally rare achievement – resurrection of the dead.

It is still unknown to us how to deal face to face with the laws of our materiality and the subjection of the lower laws to the higher. And if in the 20th century the majority of us will succeed in living an entire life, and not collide with irrefutable incidences of such or similar phenomenon, then the conclusion is not that such phenomenon do not occur, and not that they are categorically impossible, but just that the conditions of the non-religion era – cultural, social and psychological – interfere with the study and adoption of this method to such an extent (especially in the West and even more in the countries of the socialist frontier) that they reduce the quantity of such similar incidences to a few solitary ones. Truly certain incidences that were fateful for humanity and having a place about 2,000 years ago – we will speak of them later – are responsible in this respect, because they applied to not just a few isolated incidences, but they seemed to be unavoidable for humanity's multitudes on this route of comprehension and mastery of [religious] substance. In the future, the psychological climate of the non-religion era all the more and even more will accelerate along this route. Presently the adoption of this method is difficult up to a limit, while in some countries it is practically completely impossible. But there is no basis to think that this route will always remain slow and labor-consuming: the non-religion era is not infinite and we live at its conclusion.[18]

The psychological climate of the epoch of ROSE OF THE WORLD will particularly create the most pleasant of conditions for this method, as never before existed. But this is a matter of the distant future, and not for the near future. But until this actually becomes part of the present we have the obligation to utilize another method as a basis, something that is considerable

---

[18] Referring to the atheism of the Soviet Union's ideology.

less perfected and which will not lead us far, a type of government installed in several regions.

From this point on I will discuss the attitude of ROSE OF THE WORLD toward science and technology in the progressing historical stage. Science is accessible to all, independent of any person's moral stature. Sometimes it is just meagerly sprinkling facts and we try to conclude from them some consistency, and sometimes we do not understand their nature or direction, or do not know what impact it can have, or what discoveries of the future will have on the social structure. Not one person on earth is guaranteed that at any minute a hydrogen bomb, or some other even worse spectacular achievement of science, will not be thrown upon the Earth, upon him and his fellow citizens, by highly intelligent minds. Naturally for this reason, one of the first measures of ROSE OF THE World, after its entrance to control the activities of the state, will be the creation of a Supreme Education Council, that is, such a college that will dedicate itself to the ROSE OF THE WORLD through its inner circles. Comprised of individuals who combine the highest scientific authoritativeness with the highest moral stature, the Council will take under its control the entire scientific and technical activity, directing its work along 2 routes: planning and preserving.

All that pertains to the preservation of life's interests of humanity, its principles that pertain to every situation, is presented in a sufficiently clear manner, and we hardly need to stop here. What pertains to problems tied with the preservation of the interests of the animal and plant kingdoms, this will be dealt with in corresponding divisions of this book, those dedicated to the animal world and the worlds of nature, because this is hardly one sphere where the viewpoint of ROSE OF THE WORLD and the opinions of the majority of contemporary scholars cannot be reconciled. Nonetheless, this contradiction affects not just any sort of scientific conclusions, but just some of the parts of its practical methods, which not only in the eyes of ROSE OF THE WORLD, but also in the eyes of all any religious-moral teaching and even almost any humane person, are incompatible with the elementary demands of virtue.

Other than these purely methodological contradictions, there are no points of altercation and there cannot be between ROSE OF THE WORLD and science. No place exists for them to collide. Each is different from the other. Assuredly the circumstance is not accidental, that the scientific erudition of the majority of trained scholars of the 20th century does not interfere with the possession of personal devotion, does not interfere with them sharing and even creating brilliant spiritual systems of philosophy. Einstein and Plank, Pavlov and Lemaitre, Eddington and Miln, whatever their spheres of scientific research might have been, each one remained in his own manner a deeply religious person. It seems that I do not take into consideration any of the Russian scholars of the Soviet period into this class, some of whom were compelled to declare their materialism, not from philosophical reflection but in the light of entirely other principles that could be understood by everyone. Let us leave philosophy and polity at rest for the time being; in the purely scientific regions, ROSE OF THE WORLD does not confirm anything of what science has the right to deny. But this is different based on face value. Of those realities that ROSE OF THE WORLD confirms, science is meanwhile silent. But yet this is a short-term phenomenon. What ROSE OF THE WORLD aspires to resolve among problems that are social, cultural and ethic, it is impossible to imagine them colliding with factions of scientific authorities and any objections based on the essence of the issue.

It seems that then the very idea of science planning will not be the object of discussion, but the limits that surround planning and its practice. Some interest will not be lost in the special training of practice in planning and coordination of scientific work in certain governments of the mid-20th century. But its utilization will only occur with individual details, even though the Federation will be composed of many governments, large ones and small, even though each of them stands on a different level of economic development, formed of diverse cultures and possessing social-political arrangements. Some of these arrangements that differ for the most part due to their socialist and economic attitudes will be easier to entice into a common inevitable process of worldwide cooperation. Others that are adapted to the production of anarchy are drawn into it gradually. All of this during the initial period, and likewise with the very diverse cultural types, will create an extreme diversity of world economy cultural arrangements that will have an effect on one another. Even then, the obsolete national antagonisms will still be maintained for a long while. The balance and consensus of the needs of the individual nations and individual layers of the population will not immediately be provided, like those interested, for example, in the first order of development of these types and those types of branches of business that are here or there or the sales of their products somewhere.

A certain new psychological quality will be required of those who head the Scholar's Council and even ROSE OF THE WORLD, in order to rightly resolve these problems: a complete national impartiality, while natural, cultural-racial ties still reside. How much effort, what authority and even self-sacrifice will be required in order to weaken age-old antagonisms, for example: English – Arabian; Russian – Polish; or Armenian – Turk! What increase in better conduct will the Germans, English, Russians or Americans merit when they forget such animosity they created against so many nations. What educational means will be required in order to destroy the complexity of inherent self-interest that interferes with the ability of many small and middle-size nations to friendly deal with their neighbors and to cease fantasies of aggression dealing with their personal majesty on account of the majesty of others. But this is only one facet of the task.

Many western nations will have to face dealing with eliminating from themselves the residual traces of ancient feelings of their superiority over others. The Russian will have to deal with his country not being the crown of creation and that in many circumstances it is not better than many others. The Englishman will be compelled to execute a titanic internal work in order to sever themselves from the involuntary preference of the interests of Britain's residents over the interests of Indonesia's or Tanzania's residents. The French will be required to have the ability to accept to heart the interests of Paraguay or Thailand just as fervently as they do their own. The Chinese or Arabian will liberate their heart and mind from their inbred distrust toward Europeans – which they have justified for so many centuries and which is now obsolete – and learn to share what they have with the necessities of Belgium or Greece, and pay the same attention to themselves as to Laos or Sudan. The residents of the Latin American republics will have to separate from their custom of worrying and sorrowing only over themselves and accept participation in distributing their countries' recourses with the needs of Afghanistan, Cambodia, and even Siberian Yakutia. While the citizens of the United States will have to remember that they consider themselves Christians and that Christianity is incompatible with bestial hate toward any other race, and including the black. Difficult, difficult that this may be. It is clear that it is terribly difficult, but deliverance from war and tyranny can occur only through such a psychological self-redevelopment. And of course, not even one person can hope on the participation of worldwide planning departments in this work if he has not performed a similar procedure on himself.

The responsibility to learn national self-sacrifice will arise: not with your own blood, it seems, not with the life of your sons, but with currency. Because the especially wealthier nations will be presented with the obligation to a large measure to share their resources with the nations of the east and south, and to share them unselfishly, without any expectations of making a business profit from this assistance. To state this briefly, every person participating in the guidance of ROSE OF THE WORLD must have the feeling – first of all – of being a member of the cosmic whole, then being a member of humanity, and then only after all of this – being a member of your nation. It is not in the opposite manner, as has been taught and is being presently taught.

Because the general goal of ROSE OF THE WORLD is precisely that gigantic spiritual process that began millennia ago and ROSE OF THE WORLD is disclosed only in stages. So then the goal of this process is the dissemination of *Shadanakar*, while the nearest task of our epoch is for a person to be worthy of his material sufficiency, a simple life-long prosperity, and that an elementary moral relationship between people reside everywhere, not leaving even one person outside of your region. The thesis applying to this, that every person without exception must be secured a vocation, rest, leisure, serenity in old age, cultural access, utilization of all democratic freedoms, and a satisfaction with basic material and religious needs, will begin to aggressively materialize in life.

Not soon, but at least in the final chapters I will be able to expound on these concrete measures further, that system of additional reforms in the manner that I understand them, so these principles can materialize in flesh and blood. In the meanwhile my address will only concentrate on principles, so that the person who is unable to identify with these will not waste his time and strength in further reading, while the person who can identify with them will understand the inner spirit of ROSE OF THE WORLD before progressing further to deliberate on routes of transforming these ideals into a real life application.

Such is the principle in the relationship of ROSE OF THE WORLD to science and technology – to the extent that it is possible to provide understanding of this principle – not getting involved in meta-historical and trans-physical depth. And this must be the role of scientific method in the series of the impending epochs.

A few decades will pass. The progressing growth of the productive strengths will reach that level which we will rightly call the common aspiration. The conditions of life that are presently exploited by citizens of the advanced countries reside in the most barbaric corners of earth's sphere. The new attention of this extreme sum will be on peaceful goals, instead of it being presently squandered on arms, and will increase progress at an almost unparalleled speed. The period of general elementary training will occur in all countries even sooner. In the future the general intermediate education will be insufficient at its beginning. The intentions of the intellectuals will coincide with the intentions of humanity. The development of new and newer means of communication and their general accessibility, their practical comfort of use, will terminate the problem of international and intercultural distances. The length of the working day will decrease, releasing new reserves of time. Physiology will manufacture means that will assist the human brain to speedily and solidly recollect information earlier gathered. Leisure will begin to increase. And those questions that presently agitate the majority – the interests of business, the organization of production, the increase of products, factory technology, further perfection of life's comforts – will lose their importance. It is extremely likely that this will not be understandable and even strange to these generations, just as their predecessors were able to be carried away and consumed with the resolution of boring and plain problems. Supplies will arrive at the manufacturer having a higher quality, because the material basis of life will not be harmfully affected by any instability, but will be encompassing and completely solid.[19]

Technical and economic problems will cease to attract predominant attention. They will be resolved in collectives designed for that purpose, and no greater discussion will be concentrated on them than presently are applied to questions of the kitchen or the sink. Humanity's talents will turn in another direction, upon what the thirst for knowledge will dictate: love for all creation and the requirements of the higher forms of creativity and loveliness in art.

The thirst for knowledge was interpreted at one time as the discovery in travel across unknown seas, in wandering in undiscovered continents, but now it is possible with space travel and before the implementation of ROSE OF THE WORLD. But alien planets are inhospitable; after a few discovery expeditions these

---

[19] This is also Andreev's reflection on the poor quality of manufactured goods in the Soviet Union.

space flights will terminate. And even the thirst for knowledge will begin to change its direction. Systems of education and discovery will be reworked for humanity's potential to the extent that spiritual vision, spiritual hearing, and a profound memory will be implanted in every human's faculties, along with the capacity of the voluntary separation of the internal ethereal, intangible constitution of a person from his physical body. They will begin to journey into worlds of a different substance composition, those the levels that *Shadanakar* will unveil to them. This will be the age of Magellan's planetary cosmos, the Columbus' spirit.

So what system of views on individualism, on its value, on its rights and obligations, on the routes of its self-perfection, will promote the installation of a new psychological climate to speed the arrival of this golden age?

It is particularly in this fact that individualism maintains the same natural creative abilities and love as does God, and its infinite value is here contained. Its relative value is dependant on the stage of its ascending route, on the sum of its efforts – its personal and its providential – expended on its attainment of this stage, and to what level these abilities of divine creativity and love in life are displayed.

The earthly segment of the cosmic route of the ascending monad unveils itself at the stage at which its capabilities for creativity and love can and must spread into its surrounding natural and artificial environment, perfecting itself, that is, mastering in this environment the tendency of isolated self-confirmation of the parts and smaller parts on account of others. Evil is confined particularly in such a tendency, however it is expressed. Its forms and measurements are diverse almost to infinity, but its basis is always one and the same: an aspiration toward confirmation at the expense of the remaining and all that remains.

The ancient religions determined the relative measure of an individual's value based on the level of his observance of the written religious-moral code that was applied to him. These religions of an ascetic tint felt holiness was the supreme stage, understanding monastic service as its most immaculate form, next to martyrdom for the faith. As a result of this attitude, love was demoted to a second level. The monastic or martyr's achievement was accomplished not in the strength of love to people and to all the living, but in the strength of hunger for unification with God and deliverance from torment beyond the grave. Of course, I have here in view the prevailing direction, which is mastering your disposition, and not the forms of such surprising individual activists, the apostles of love, such as St Francis, Ramanuja or Milaraiba. No matter how intimidating this may seem to us, the threat of eternal torments of hell did not for the most part force the adherents of these religions to have an aspiration to illuminate laws of universal conduct, among them – the law of retribution or karma. Eternal retribution for temporal violation seemed to them a just act of Deity or in every situation – as in Brahmanism – an indisputable and absolutely inevitable law. Buddha as a light burned with the fire of compassion, but he taught only how to escape from the circle of the iron laws of the universe, and not how to illuminate and change them. What pertains to creativity, its inherent basis, is not at all fathomed, and there is even no understanding of it, but solely a concrete view of creativity, one without significance, with the exception of religious creativity in its narrow sense: ecclesiastical maneuvers, theology, preaching, temple construction, and the cult.

Other religions not inclined toward asceticism, such as Islam and Protestantism, have modified this ideal, expanded it, and along with this, reduced it, making it more accessible, more adaptable to the populous, summarized as the observance of a handful of commands in the attitude toward God, the state, near surroundings, family, and finally, to your own self. Now it needs to be repeated that neither one nor the other group has placed the religious task of society's transformation, and even more – nature, at the forefront. It is natural that similar tasks, but in an extreme simplified view, were placed finally as non-religious teachings. The reduced and contradictory ethical ideal was propagated, mechanically having united certain progressive characteristics with those that walked counter to the ethical minimum, and which for a long while seemed to be inarguable. They remembered the old formula – the end justifies the means – and fearing to expose it with truthful openness, began to take advantage of its practicality. In the presence of the characteristic, and the evaluations, of historical occurrences, their moral quality was ignored in full. Verdicts were issued based on whatever proceeded from the account of the general progressive or reactionary direction of the specific issue. That this brought justification to bloody incidences of many despots of the past did not seem to bother anybody, and even such scandalous massive slaughters as the Jacobite terror or the killings of the oprichniks.[20]

Many ancient achievements of social progress, like freedom of speech, the press, or religious evangelism, were discarded. The generations raised in a similar atmosphere gradually lost their very need of these freedoms, a symptom speaking more expressively than any tirades over the shocking religious repression of society. A realm of material contentment was displayed in front of them and was purchased at the cost of the prohibition of their religious freedom, at the cost of many millions of hecatombs of human lives and the discard of billions of souls to the lower regions of *Shadanakar*, whose divine patrimony was sold [by their traitors] for one swallow of lentil soup.[21]

I hope that this formidable lesson will not pass without serious consideration.

The teaching of ROSE OF THE WORLD is directed at the absolute value of the individual, at his divine primogeniture: the right to liberation from the club of poverty, from the club of aggressive societies, and towards prosperity, for all forms of freedom of expression and for the promulgation of such expression, for religious pursuit, for beauty. The right of a person to a safe existence and the use of the goods of civilization

---

[20] The mercenary police force of Tsar Ivan the Terrible.
[21] Referring to the event between Isaac and Esau.

is a right that is inherent to him, which on its own does not require his denial of either freedom or spirituality. But to confirm that as if some type of grave dilemma is confined here, that for the sake of attainment of all these natural benefits a person needs to sacrifice personal spirituality and social freedom – this means to lead people into deception.

The teaching will emphasize the obligation of the individual toward the subsequent expansion of that region to which his attraction is inclined, toward the growth, increase and illumination of what is created by his creative abilities. Creativity in this manner surfaces as a right and an obligation. To this time I cannot understand why this truly divine capability of a person has not encountered its obligatory attitude to itself in any of the ancient religions, except some forms of polytheism, and especially among the Greeks. It seems that only in Greece were they able to deify not only art productions, but the very creative element, particularly creativity, as in other forms of polytheism, and even crown great artists with apotheosis. It is sorrowful and strange that after the collapse of Hellenism, the creative gift ceased to attract the attention of religion, it was not comprehend anymore be ontological or metaphysical or mystic. Under the influence of the one-sided understanding of the Semitic idea that after 6 days of creation there occurred the divine rest of the creative spirit, so theological thought preferred to proceed on some tangent regarding the question of further creative activity of the one God, and the divine statement impressed in the Revelation of John – Behold, I create all anew – remained the sole ascension, the sole perspicuity. Then a completely suspicious attitude was installed toward human creativity, as though an arrogance into which an artist-individual could fall, and one more dangerous and ruinous than creative sterility.

The previous centuries of western culture – as wealthy the displays of ingenuity in all spheres of art, science and philosophy – taught us much. They taught us a reverent attitude toward human creativity, and respect of human labor. But in the light of this question, the religionless mood of these centuries promoted exactly what the ancient religions feared: that the person-creator became personally haughty because of his creative gift, as if he developed this gift within himself on his own. Nonetheless, this independence wove a nest for itself, not so much in the souls of genuine geniuses, and more in spiritual preachers, as much as in the series of second-rate activists of science and art. A series of special chapters in this present volume will be dedicated to a greater detailed investigation of these problems from the angle of the teaching of ROSE OF THE WORLD.

In every situation, creativity, as also love, is not an exclusive gift known only to those select. The select are known by their integrity, devotion, heroism, wisdom, ingenuity and talent. But this is just a revelation of the potential that is latent in every soul. The ocean depths of love, never-ending fountains of creativity, boil at the threshold of each of us wanting to create. Religion in its summation strives to destroy barricades, to allow living waters to flow here, into life. The creative attitude toward everything will be revealed in the future generations which this has educated, and the labor involved will not serve as a bridle, but as a revelation of the unquenchable thirst to create something new, create something better, create its own intentions. All followers of ROSE OF THE WORLD will take satisfaction from their creative labor, teaching this joy to children and adolescents. Be creative in all matters: in literature and construction, in exact sciences and planting of trees, in the decoration of life and in its ameliorations, in performing ecclesiastical ceremony and in the sacraments, in the love between a man and woman, in the fostering of children, in the development of the human body, and in dance, in the admiration of nature, and while playing.

Because every creative achievement, other than the demonic, that is performed on your own behalf and for yourself, is a divine accomplishment. This raises a person higher than himself, an admiration of his individual heart and the heart of others.

The majority of people move along a slow and wide route in the meaning of personal spiritual self-perfection. This road traverses weddings and childbirths, through participation in diverse forms of activity, through the fullness and diversity of life's impressions, through its joys and consolations. But there also exists a narrow road: it pertains to those who carry in their soul a special gift, one demanding intense self-restraint: the gift of holiness. Religious teachings that confirm their narrow way as the sole correct or transcendent are wrong. And just as wrong are those social or religious systems that deny it completely and impose obstacles in front of those who in particular feel they are summoned to such a route.

Hardly during the era of ROSE OF THE WORLD will there be monasteries. But there will be some, so that every person whose spiritual thirst impels him on this narrow path could work on disclosing within himself such capabilities of the soul, which are so necessary for many years of dedicated work in silence and solitude. If a person should proceed on this narrow path as a result of fear of retribution, or due to dreams of personal advancement, conceit, or monastic communion with God, then his victories will have no value. There is no Deity that will not gift a blessed visualization of His majesty as a reward to His faithful servants. The contemplation of the higher spheres is the exit of a person from himself and communion with the Sole One who encompasses all monads and constructs all peace. As a result, it is not spiritual egoism that will compel a person as a follower of ROSE OF THE WORLD to proceed on the narrow path, and not a thirst for individual salvation while at the same time having a cold indifference toward others, but the understanding that such gifts will be revealed while on the narrow path, and by which a virtuous and isolated person will help the world more effectively than a hundred living in the world, and which [gifts], after his death, will continue to have such strength, to the point that even potent demonic hierarchies will submit to its authority.

There is no necessity of any type in worrisome vows that accompany tonsure. There is no basis for condemnation and discredit of the person who departs from the path after the course of many years. The person who enters this path will first only commit to a temporary term: for 3 years, or 5 or 7. It is just after the successful completion of these stages that he, if he wants, will receive the right to commit to a promise for a longer interval, but even then the knowledge of irrevocability of the vow, or the suspicion of an irreparable error, will not worry or oppress him or cause despair or turbulent upheavals that he will not be able to live through. He will know that after this period he is free to return to the world, he is free to select another course of life, another vocation, he is free to have a family, children, and will not be subject to any censure or disregard.

I strove to promote the attitude of ROSE OF THE WORLD to scientific and outside-of scientific methods of investigation, to the individual, to his rights and obligations, to human creativity and work, now to the 2 fundamental views of the spiritual path: the wide and the narrow. In order to complement the presentation regarding its attitude toward culture, it would be proper to pause at its views on art, in the wide sense of the word. But this question has so many meanings and is important, and it is personally so close to me, that I decided to dedicate to it a series of chapters in one of the further parts of this volume. So, before proceeding to the question of the attitude of ROSE OF THE WORLD to other religions, I will just say a few passing words about the arts of the approaching era.

In the approaching era when the sun of the golden era will just begin to again shine upon the clouds over the horizon, what are the distinguishing traits of the type of art that people will create that are compatible to the spirit of ROSE OF THE WORLD?

It would be naive to attempt to foretell or chart the diverse artistic directions, genres, schools, stylistic fashions, that will cause this sphere of culture to sparkle at the conclusion of the passing century. But it seems to me that a certain all-encompassing style – and one not exhaustive of course – of all trends of art will be defined. The creators of this art will not avoid illumination of sorrowful and horrible facets of the world that earlier occurred. They will consider it cowardly to forget about the bloody roads of history, about the reality of the terrible and infra-physical layers of *Shadanakar,* about their ruthless laws restraining innumerable crowds of unfortunate people in the shackles of inhuman torture, and about those massive terrifying failures of the community human-spirit that were promoted and prepared by the strengths of the God-resisters and which materialized in a history almost inescapable, and which will only terminate with the subsequent movement of the golden age. But this high level of realization will not serve as an obstacle to their love of the world, the land, it will not reduce their joy, but on the contrary it will promote whatever nature, culture, creativity, community service, love, and friendship births! Should such knowledge of hidden dangers that threaten the person you love weaken the fervency of love? There will occur marvelous creations still not achieved pertaining to the fullness and affirmation of life, of purity and joy.

In the channel beds of all the arts, those that already are and those that will soon arise, there will surface sincere people similar to drops of rain reflected in the sun's rays, and the compositions of these future creators will deal with love, and pertaining to many more facets than ours, with adolescents, the joys of domestic family life and social activities, and about the expansion of humanity's comprehension, about the progression of the limits of knowledge, about the *stikhials* that draw into a friendship with people, about the daily close association of the friends of our heart that are still invisible to us. But little will be mentioned of what will agitate people of these epochs and what we are not able to acknowledge.

It seems to me that such art, with its male aspect of fearlessness and its female aspect of overwhelming love, sagacious joy and kindness toward people and the world, and with an acute knowledge of its dark recesses, can be identified as translucent realism or meta-realism. All will rejoice over such art and the talent of such individuals will be lauded, and even if they only possess one such specialty: a beautiful feeling, wide periphery, depth of thought, acute vision, purity of heart, and happiness of soul.

The time will arrive when the ethical and aesthetic level of society and even activist artists will become such that any need of any limitations will fall to the side, and freedom of artistic expression, literature, philosophy and science will reach its fullness. But meanwhile, until the moment when ROSE OF THE WORLD accepts control over the governments, and the epoch of this ideal level arrives, several decades must pass.

Initially, when national antagonism and racial prejudices are still not obsolete, and aggressive organizations still manipulate these prejudices, it will be necessary to implement proscriptions on any propaganda dealing with animosity between one or other groups of the population. Later control will still be preserved over books and teaching materials that polarize scientific and philosophic ideas. It seems to me that control over works of fiction will require some minimal control, to protect the bookstores from a flood of tasteless literature. Of course, more than all, an unconditional prohibition will be placed on pornography.

So not to place too much emphasis on the difference in understanding between culture and civilization, I can state that culture is nothing other than the common volume of humanity's creativity. If creation is a supreme, precious and sacred ability of a person, his display of the divine prerogative of his spirit, then there is nothing on earth – and there can not be – anything more precious and sacred than culture. Such a culture common to all humanity is just beginning to surface.

The atmosphere of ROSE OF THE WORLD and its teaching will create the preconditions so the dream of culture would be the legacy of every mind. And this would allow at least a limited number of individual comprehensions to grasp the entirety of its esoteric complexity. Then the spirit of this concept, and not the literal, will gradually become accessible to almost everybody.

CHAPTER 3

ATTITUDE TOWARD RELIGIONS

So often we utilize the word *truth*, and how seldom do we attempt to define this understanding. We do not get annoyed, however, that we repeat in essence Pilate's question,[22] and attempt to discern this understanding to the extent of our strengths.

We call *truths* – the theory or the teaching that in our view expresses an unadulterated or undistorted conceptualization of some type or other object of knowledge. The precise meaning of the word *truth* possesses an unadulterated expression of some type or other knowledge in our mind. But as many objects of knowledge exists in the world, this many truths can also exist.

But objects of knowledge are learned from external sources, and not internal to ourselves. Subsequently, the truth about some object of knowledge that we learn from outside of our self must be acknowledged as relative truth. Absolute truth is the reflection of this object of knowledge that is acknowledged within our self as some type of object. Such a knowledge is principally possible only when the contradictions between objective and subjective are removed; when the subjective of knowledge is identified with the objective.

Absolute universal truth is the unadulterated reflection of some knowledge of the great universe that is acknowledged within yourself. Absolute private truths are unadulterated reflections of some part of the universe, parts that are acknowledged within yourself.

It is natural that absolute truth of the great universe can surface only in the cognizance that is commensurable to its subjective knowledge, one that can identify with the objective, that can learn of things not only from the external, but from the internal. Such subjective knowledge is called absolute, God, Sun of the World.

---

[22] John 18:38

God within Himself as the object of knowledge is known only to Himself. His absolute truth, as the absolute truth of the universe, is accessible only to Him.

It is clear that any private truth, as small as may be the object of knowledge, is only accessible for us in its relative variation. There can exist several or many variations of private truths: the personal or individual diverse facets of one private relative truth. Under this condition, small scale objects of knowledge of – in comparison with the subjective – are reflected in the comprehension of a series of related objects that are similar or completely identical. If it were not this way, people would be deprived of the ability to understand one another in anything at all. But the more the objective knowledge is compared to the subjective, the more variations it summons. Relative truth of the universe and relative truth of deity births as many individual variations as there are those who accept such objects.

So it is clear that all of our truths are – strictly speaking – just approaches to truths. And the more meager the object of knowledge, the better it can be grasped by our comprehension, and it reduces the gap between its absolute truth and our relative truth pertaining to it. Nevertheless, the proportional scales of subjective and objective do have a limit, the lower of which is where the gap between the absolute and relative truth begins to grow. For example, the gap between absolute truth of some kind of elementary part and our relative truth about it is exceptionally great. Between the absolute truth of the universe, the absolute truth of deity, and our relative truths about it – the gap is immensely large.

As shown above, absolute truth is the legacy of only the omniscient Subject. If the representatives of the ROSE OF THE WORLD had pretensions at some time to claim the absolute truth of its teaching, this would be just as groundless and absurd.

But the affirmation that all teachings or one or another teaching is false is just as groundless and foolish. There exists no such thing as a completely false teaching and it cannot. If some opinion should surface that is deprived of some fragments of veracity, then it could not be a teaching that should be transmitted as representing something correctly. It should remain as the personal property of the person who first advertised it, and this occurs, for example, with philosophic or pseudo-scientific conclusions of certain mentally ill.

Religions differ between themselves, not in the strength of the veracity of one of them and the falsity of the balance, but according to 2 other coordinates. And particularly, first, due to the diverse steps of its ascension to absolute truth, that is, in conformity to the decrease in them of the subjective, epochal element. This stadial difference can be conditionally called a vertical difference. Second, they are different due to the fact that they speak of different things, reflect different categories of objective comprehensions. This series of difference is a segmental difference, and can be conditionally called a horizontal difference. Both forms of differences must not be removed from view even for one minute in the investigation of the question of the attitude of ROSE OF THE WORLD to other religions.

In the development of science we observe an uninterrupted process of the accumulation of relative parts of truths and their perfection and refinement. At the subsequent stage, what is usually rejected is not a series of facts accumulated in the past, but just those whose interpretations are now obsolete. In circumstances where an old series of facts are now subject to doubt and rejected is relatively rare, and this has occurred, for example, with alchemy. But unfortunately, in the history of religion, other circumstances dominate. In place of successive changes or replacement of deliberations that are not subject to the question of spiritual facts, we see more than often, as at the subsequent stage of religious development, a significant series of earlier attained relative or abstract partial truths rejected, and then our own, a new series of them, with the inclusion of some number of the old, are passed off as though absolute. This observance is very correct when pertaining to the replacement of pagan religions by monotheistic systems.

It is clear that our preservation of similar customs under the conditions of the expanding periphery of the 20th century should lead us, the majority, to the creation of still another denomination. The entrance into religion of the scientific method would be, of course, an insolent error, and just as illegitimate as the infiltration of methods of painting into the sphere of science. But an adoption of the good attributes of scholasticism, rather than their rejection, and this being a reinterpretation of the series of accumulated relative truth acquired long ago, is now long overdue.

Of the hundreds of possible examples I will select one for the time, and an extremely obvious one: the idea of reincarnation. This concept profoundly penetrates Hinduism and Buddhism, and has some esoteric presence in Judaism through the Kaballah. It is rejected by orthodox Christianity and Islam. Is it proper then to think that this concept – an idea that is not generally accepted – represents a racial or stadial-cultural aberration of the Indian cognizance? The matter is that during the coordination of concepts of various religions, it is necessary first of all to learn to sieve the primary issues from the secondary, the common from the private. What is common or principle of any concept is contained in the kernel of the idea, what has persevered with extreme persistence throughout the ages. Thrown into the field of various cultural environments, it provides different shoots, diverse variations of the subject concept. If the teleological direction in general has a place in history, then of course, this direction must have an affect first of all and particularly on the existence of such persistent religious kernels widely scattered among the millions who confess the knowledge of the basic idea.

The kernel of the idea of reincarnation consists in the teaching of the specific *I* who is completing its cosmic induction, or some known segment of it, through the stages of subsequent existences in our physical world. All the balance of things, such as the ethereal-material nature and structure of the reincarnating entity, or the extent that the reincarnation depends on the law of karma, the expansion of the principle of reincarnation likewise applying to the animal kingdom, or the rejection of such an expansion – all of this are just variations or diverse forms of the basic concept.

The fallibility of these religious dogmas consists, for the most part, not in their content, but in their pretensions that their law – confirmed by dogma – possesses a general, universal cosmic significance, while this fact – confirmed by their dogma – must be confessed by all of humanity, as though without this there is no salvation. All that is expounded leads us to the recognition of the genuineness of that religious experience what was cast as the idea of reincarnation. Yes, such a route of induction has a place. Based on principle, there is nothing unacceptable for Christianity or Islam in the essence of this idea, except perhaps for the fact that nothing was produced and transmitted to us by the founders of either Christianity or Islam, but this does not prove anything, since we know that the Gospels and Koran do not include everything that was possibly stated by their relative founders.

Nothing decisive is concluded from any of this basis indicating that the route of reincarnation is as though the sole possible and only real route of the construction of an individual's spirit. Refining this direction in order to reach this type of route, the cognizance of the Indian nation, as often as this occurs in similar situations, absolutized its revelation and became deaf to the acceptance of other types of routes. The exact same occurred with the Hebrew and Arabic nations, but in an opposite manner: accepting as truth this other route of induction, where incarnation in the material stratum occurs just one time, the cognizance of these nations justifiably absolutized this other type of route. This now promotes an environment where the diverse meta-cultures of humanity can in general adopt one or another type of route. The result was that disagreement – and one that seemed to be irreconcilable – appeared between these 2 categories of global religion. In reality though, both these antagonistic ideas of truth, in their own form, fixes concretely 2 of the possible types of route, and nothing is required to remove this contradiction, except the rejection of this attitude of pretension from each side to the universal exclusiveness of their concept.

So one of the historical reasons of the perhaps irreconcilable contradiction between religions consists in the unjustifiable coerced absolutism of some or another thesis. And here is another reason:

One of the fundamental dogmas of Christianity appears to be, as this is well know, the teaching of the Triune Deity. The founder of Islam rejected this dogma, suspecting traces of polytheism in it, but the primary reason being his personal religious experience did not include a position indicating a similar truth. But it is hardly worth it in the 20th century to repeat the argument of Christian theologians who during their own era proved and explained the essential difference between the dogmas of the Triune Deity and polytheism: this is so elementary that we need to only suppose that presently among Islamic thinkers we will not find any who will insist on what they consider to be an erroneous confirmation, after ascertaining the questions of Christian confessions. What pertains to the second argument – that the religious experience of Mohammed did not contain any confirmation of the Triune Deity – means that it is inconsistent logic. No general experience of any type can sustain the confirmation of all true ideas that have earlier appeared during the progress of humanity's collective increase of divine knowledge and secular knowledge. Every personal experience is limited; only the wisdom of the Omniscient has the ability to grasp the entire sum of truth within Itself. As a result the circumstance that Mohammed in his religious experience did not undergo anything that would confirm the thesis of a Triune Deity, must on its own not serve as an argument for the refutation of this idea, even in the eyes of Orthodox Islam adherents. Instead of providing the creed, "The Prophet, having recognized the complete singularity of God, is convinced of the falsity of the teaching of the Trinity," this statement should be more correctly stated as, "The Prophet, having recognized the complete singularity of God, did not however receive any indication of the Triune indivisible Deity." It is fully natural that

Christian divine teaching does not only not possess any objections against the Islamic teaching of God's singularity, but completely coincides with it. At least it complements this thesis with the idea that with its two thousand year sustainability and its expansion with billions of adherents, the concept indicates the veracity of its basis. So to what will this contradiction between these 2 primary dogmas of these 2 religions lead us? Will it not be to an arbitrary and improperly measured denial of one of them, and even if there is no positive data to prove the positive experience of either one?

Now we will look at a second historical and psychological reason that has inculcated a disagreement between tenets: the wrongful denial of an alien affirmation only on the basis that we do not utilize the positive data dealing with this question. Pathetically there is no end to the number of disagreements based exclusively on this logical and gnosiological incompatibility.

We will bring to investigation one more observation that is known to all: Islam (Sunnism) and Protestantism reject the validity of the cult of saints. Almost all the balance of religions accept it and in one or another form materialize it. The objections of this cult are based on a person not needing intercessors of any kind between them and the Deity, and that spiritual honor and prayer is being offered not to God, but to those who were humans – sinful creatures, and this leads to deification of that person. But what specifically does this famous tenet mean, "A person has no need of intercessors."? If they have no need of the person who is proclaiming this thought, then where does he get the right to speak on behalf of others, even for all humanity? Who authorized him? It is not the billions of peoples who, in almost all countries, in almost all religions, sense the living daily need in such intercessors, which has caused the existence of the cult of the saints to be psychologically possible? If we do not test such a necessity in something and begin to disdain all those who have tested their need for this, treating them like fabricators, greedy liars or stupid ignoramuses, then what will we prove by this, except our own ignorance?

The 2nd assumption is the wrongful attribution of divine veneration and prayer to those who were people. But divine veneration – in the monotheistic sense – is not offered them: nobody equates them with God. The thought that this occurs is absurd, and people who were raised in Christian countries consider this to be unforgivable stupidity. True that in Hinduism the idea of the avatar – the incarnation of Vishna in human form – does exist, but they are avatars, and not saints. The saints are admired as those who have overcome their humanity, they have become the materialization of God's will, as messengers of the celestial world. Protestantism rejects categorically the understanding of sainthood. But now surfaces quickly a debate over portions of the issue, rather than its essence. It seems that Luther and Calvin, rejecting the ascetic monastic concept, did not reduce the significance of secular virtue, although they understood it, from the one side, wider than Catholicism, and from the other side, somewhat reduced. Mohammed, dying, forbid his adherents to turn to his spirit in prayer. This displays the purity and sincerity of his thoughts, but it contradicts the fundamentals of a general religious-ethical representation of the world.

So if rectitude, as a person's supreme self-sacrifice on behalf of humanity in the name of God, is a faultless and unselfish service to Him, if it is this way, then no way should you imagine that a righteous soul after its termination is just resting in some inactive state of bliss. With all the strengths of its soul, among them also those that are only revealed after death, the righteous will materialize assistance to the living and those lower in rank in order to raise them higher. This concept is so natural, just like an adult helping a child. No doubt this would have been known by prophet Mohammed. We need to suppose that certain extremes, superfluous items, in the cult of the saints that he observed among Christians, agitated him to prohibit his disciples from installing anything like this. It is possible that he thought that this prohibition would balance the circumstance, that it was not absolutely necessary to mention the names of deceased righteous in prayer, so as to have to provide them invisible assistance. One way or the other, every teaching is decisively confirming the truth of spiritual immortality and a high moral law. It is only in spite of logic and personal principles that a person can suppose that as if the spirit of the saint in his post-mortem state is inactive and indifferent to those presently alive. The rejection of the cult of the saints is logical only from one point of view: the material. But from another side, to install the absoluteness of the cult of the saints as generally obligatory is also not a valid action.

Prolonged stages do occur in the soul's journey, even in the route of an entire nation when they are genuinely not in need of any intermediaries. This is when the soul – consciously or unconsciously – feels that the strengthening of its self-confidence, stability, freedom, spiritual volition, excludes the possibility of turning to someone else, other than to God Himself, for assistance. So what is our basis and what right do we have to bind such an individual to participate in the cult of the saints?

A significantly immense complexity substantiates the fundamental contradiction between Christianity and other religions is the affirmation of the deity of Jesus Christ as a dogma, his veneration as an incarnation of one of the hypostasis of the Triune Deity. It is known to everybody that the balance of religions either agree with the recognition of Jesus as a prophet in series with other prophets, or either ignore him and often just energetically reject his providential mission. Christianity, for its side, depends on the words of its founder, that no one proceeds to the Father except through the Son. As a result, the possibility of salvation is denied to all those who are non-Christians.

I have the impression however that we would escape much misunderstanding and coarse condescension of ideas if we were to pay attention to all of Christ's statements that have been transmitted to us, while asking ourselves: Is Jesus speaking in this particular situation as an individual, as a concrete historical figure who lived in some or another country from this time to that time, or is the voice of God which he hears within himself being transformed by his mind and through his lips into human words? Every passage spoken by Christ demands investigation particularly in this range: is he speaking at the subject time as a messenger of the truths of the spiritual world, or as a human? We cannot – or should not – imagine Christ at every moment of his life speaking as a messenger and never as a human. Hardly can we subject to doubt that in his sorrowful announcement on the cross, "Father, father, why did you abandon me?" this was a torture impressed upon him during one of those minutes when he, Jesus, a human, had to live through a tragedy of sensing abandonment, a tragedy that ruptured the tie between his human *I* and his divine spirit? But it was the person of God the Son, the worldwide Logos, which they assumed was speaking to them during his teaching expounded at the Last Supper. All of his words, all the sermons of Christ preserved in the Gospel, need to be subjected to this type of division into 2 categories. It is completely obvious in this incident that his words dealing with the statement that no one approaches the Father except through the Son, needs to be understood not in a condescending, narrow, restrained and ruthless meaning, that as if not even one human soul – except the Christian – will be saved, but rather in a majestic, truly spiritual, cosmic meaning, that every monad needs to be immersed fully and unconditionally into the depths of God the Son, who is the heart and demiurge of the universe. And it is only through this all-consuming act that it returns to its source, to God the Father, incomprehensibly identifying itself with Him and the entire divine Triune Deity.

One of the visible activists of the religious-philosophic community in India once stated a very profound thought, saying that, "The wisdom of the Hindus, meekness of the Buddhists, courage of the Islamists, all of this is derived from Christ." Apparently, his understanding of the name in this specific application, of course, is not the historical figure of Jesus, but the Logos that is expressing itself from within Jesus Christ predominantly, but not exclusively. In my opinion of this, the road to this point of view stumbles along in this idea and upon which Christians can arrive to a mutual understanding of the many currents of oriental religiosity.

I think likewise that certain expressions that have been inculcated into Christian theology are almost mechanically repeated by us and at the same time they appear unacceptable for other religions, and so they need to be reviewed and refined. How for example should the word *incarnation* be understood in its application to Jesus Christ? So should we now imagine that the Logos of the universe was clothed with the composition of·the subject human flesh? Can we allow a concession that by the way of teleological preparation from generation to generation there was created a corporeal instrument, and individual physical organism, a human brain, that is capable of containing universal Intellect? If it is this way, then we need to suppose that Jesus yet during his life possessed omniscience, even though this does not correlate even with the facts of his history based on the Gospel and his personal addresses. Is not this disproportion of scales intolerable for us: the convergence of the category of the cosmic in this finite sense with the category of the local-planetary narrow human mind? And it is beyond tolerance not because it transcends the limits of our intellect, but on the contrary, because in it the product of contemplation on the defined, long-passed cultural stage is overwhelmingly obvious, when the universe as we understood it was a billion times smaller than it is at present, when the possibility of the firm atmosphere and terrible hail from the stars to be torn from this hook upon which all of it hangs seemed to us to be a reality. Would it not be more precise as a result to speak not of the materialization as a human of the Logos in the substance of Jesus Christ, but of It expressing Itself through him, now by means of the great divinely-engendered monad becoming the Earth's planetary Logos? We call Jesus – the Word. But know that who is speaking is not an incarnation, but particularly [the Logos] expressing itself in verbal speech: God does not materialize as a human, but expresses Himself in Christ. Particularly in this sense, Christ is truly God's word. And if it is so, then one more obstacle between the agreement of Christianity with certain other religious currents is removed.

I only briefly touched on 4 intra-religious disagreements. With the exception of the latter one, the remaining are founded on an incongruity of the spiritual experience of their great visionaries, from an insufficient crystallization of ideas. Such contemplators viewed the subject from different points of *Shadanakar*, each contemplator viewing the subject topic from a different corner and so seeing its different aspects. We can conditionally call such disagreements – contradictions in a horizontal direction, understanding from this perspective the validity of both points of view and their imaginary, and not actual, contradiction.

Another example. From the time that Christianity and Islam began to exist, they continued to struggle against what they identify as paganism. Over the course of centuries humanity has been plagued with the notion – and perhaps its own type of axiom – that monotheism and polytheism are irreconcilable and incompatible. Researching this, as to why and how this occurred, just leads us far off the path. The essence is something else. On what basis do the religions having a Semitic root, that affirm the existence of spiritual hierarchies and even during the Middle Ages elaborated teaching regarding them – angelology and demonology – even to the most petty items, limit the diversity of these hierarchies with only these few that were included in the systems developed in the Middle Ages? Is there even a shadow of validity in their categorical rejection of every encounter of spiritual hierarchies? There are decisively no bases for this, except for the fact that the Gospels and Koran are silent on this topic.

Particularly in view of insufficient basis for groundless rejection the church during the initial centuries of Christianity did not so much reject the gods of the Olympic pantheon, as much as identify them with demons and evil spirits of the Semitic canonic texts. This occurred as if the recognition of the veracity of the existence of the hierarchy of nature, the great spirits that have become national guides, could shake the singularity of God – creator and constructor of the universe, the source and culmination of the worldwide stream of life – more than the recognition of His other beautiful offspring – Angels and Archangels, and likewise demons, which are all located in the canonic instruction of the Bible.

It is a pity that the olden incomplete understanding was not explained to this time: from the ancient polytheism nothing remains now for a long time, but the embittered, narrow intolerance – deprived of all wisdom – appears every time when it is forced to expound its conclusions to Christian churches, or at least those that speak in its name, based on the attitude of Hindu, Chinese, Japanese and Tibetan systems. The other 2 religions having a Semitic root are just as much intolerant. Here at face value is the typical evidence of the diversity of religion in a horizontal direction: not contradicting one another in essence, not having an altercation of one against the other in the vast unseen spiritual cosmos, however Christianity and Hinduism, Buddhism and Islam, Judaism and Shintoism, speak of various items, of different spiritual regions, of different segments of *Shadanakar*. Human limitations interprets this as a contradiction and pronounces one of its teachings as the truth, while the balance are false: "If there is only one God, then the other deities are imposters; such are either demons or a game of humanity's imagination." What infantile thinking! There is a sole Lord God, but many deities [gods]. By using either capital letters or small letters to signify the proper understanding of these words in the Russian language should be sufficiently clear in speaking of their various or relative capacities that are attributed to the words god and deity in both situations. If the repetition of these words in their difference meanings scare someone, then they can be replaced with words from polytheism, such as: great spirits, great hierarchs. But nothing will change. The use of the word spirit can in a series of narratives lead to misunderstanding, because many of these deities [gods] are not spirits, but mighty entities possessing a corporeal materialization, although others may have a trans-physical level of existence.

All of these disagreements between religions that are based on misunderstandings bring to mind one comparison that I read in some religious literature. It was about several travelers who climbed up the same mountain but from different sides, and they studied its various slopes, each one from the side he was climbing, and when they descended they began to argue about which of them had actually seen its correct structure, but others just had their imagination since they were not paying attention, but just climbing absent-mindedly. Of course, each of them ascertained the mountain was as it seems to them from the slope they were climbing, while the testimony of the other travelers — viewing it from their side — was fallacious, absurd and they were just not paying attention. In the same manner the first conclusion that evolves from a confrontation of the intra-religious disagreement consists of a route to estrange or discredit the others that were likewise based on somewhat of a plain misunderstanding, or on an incompatible objective religious comprehension in the different series of experience, that is, a contradiction in the horizontal direction.

But not only polytheism, but also animism and animitism,[23] were not invalidated by indeterminate, accidental or objective manners that surfaced in the cognizance of original humanity; the trans-physical reality still pervaded regardless. Providence particularly is still providence because it never abandoned nations and races to the whim of fantasies and illusions, without any possibility of approaching the higher reality. Not God, but a sinister, malicious power would have been recognized as true, guided humanity if we were to imagine that for tens of thousands of years original humanity was obstructed of any possibility to live something spiritually or at least, other-worldly, to become involved with something other than the physical world or personal phantasmagoria.

---

[23] or, pra-animism

DANIEL ANDREEV

This disagreement that deals with the confirmation of the thesis about the *arungvilta·prana*[24] by the most ancient of confession, and its rejection by the oppression of the majority of recent religious teachings, can be examined as a stadial disagreement, a disagreement in the vertical direction, the disagreement between diverse stages of religious comprehension. But here we collide with that error, that invalid approach to that alien experience – with which we earlier became familiar – discerning the question about Islam's rejection of the cult of the saints or the concept of the Triune Deity. And here under all these arguments, those that have resulted in an opposition to ancient revelation, there lies that same naïve train of thought: there is nothing mentioned in the authoritative canonic texts about the *arungvilta·prana*, so this must mean it does not exist. Such a train of thought, in the least measure, is dangerous, because in such a situation the conclusion is to deny the reality of not only the *arungvilta·prana,* but also radio waves, and sub-atomic particles, and many of the chemical elements, and galaxies, and even for example, the planet Uranus, because all of the canonic texts are absolutely silent about them.

The following is also explained in this manner: the decisive necessity to take into account that which was not considered during the epoch of the formulation of the ancient, classical – if this is the proper term – confessions; the experience of the original comprehension of spirit, and likewise that which could not be considered due to the progress of things; the experience of the evolution of religion over many centuries in all the continents; the experience of world history and the experience of science. The material of these series of experience teaches us to approach all dogmas and theses dynamically, to be able to understand every thesis as a link in a chain of religious-historical development and to be able to stratify it into 2 or even into 3 strata. The very deepest stratum is the fundamental idea that contains the relative private truth. The next stratum is the

[24] The impersonal, imperceptible substance of an alien materiality spilled into *Enrof,* overflowing from body to body and securing the possibility of individual organic existence. (definition by Daniel Andreev)

specific coloration, formulation, detail of the idea in that measure where its individual, racial or epochal aspect is justified, because particularly this and only this racial or epochal arrangement of soul provided the possibility for this nation in general to absorb this idea. The very external, 3rd stratum is the husk, an aberration, the inescapable turbidity of humanity's comprehension, through which the light of revelation needs to penetrate.

Subsequently, the experience of all the stadial developments, among their number the polytheistic, animistic, and others, must be liberated from its external stratum, from the husk, and be newly grasped and included in the world ideology of religious culmination. Of course, the principle of such work is here hardly noticed, systems of criteria are needed for an immense modification, and even in general such a review of religious legacy is a colossal task demanding the simultaneous effort of many and even more. At the present time there are not any cadres for this work, not to mention all the other unavoidable conditions to overcome. But if this task is great, then the sooner that the initiation and preparation of the work begins, the better. We should not underestimate the difficulties, but all the criteria exists to anticipate that, with the conditions of a good will, with the energy and initiate of the leadership, the crevasses and pits that presently separate all religions will gradually be backfilled, and even though every religion will preserve its originality and singularity, but a certain spiritual union, a certain type of integration, will in time be able to unite all teachings of the right hand.

It is well known that many Japanese who profess Christianity also presently remain faithful to Shintoism. This annoys the devout Catholic or Protestant, and even the Orthodox, because he cannot understand how this is psychologically possible, and even senses something as though scandalous in this display. But this is possible without any kind of scandal and is even completely natural because the experience of Christianity and the experience of Shintoism are distinct in the horizontal direction. They deal with different concepts.

Shintoism is a national myth. This is one aspect of the world's religious revelation that is directed to the nation of Japan and only to it. This is a psychological consciousness, or better said, a trans-physical reality, that is raised over the Japanese nation and only upon them and is displayed in its history and culture. Answers to questions of a cosmic, planetary or general human character cannot be found in Shintoism, such as those regarding the Creator of the world, the evolution of evil and suffering, the routes of cosmic institution. It speaks only of the meta-history of Japan, of its meta-culture, of its hierarchies, its national leaderships, and of the heavenly council of illuminated souls – those particularly of Japan – who have ascended to the higher worlds of *Shadanakar*. The syncretism of the Japanese, that is, their simultaneous profession of both Shintoism and Catholicism, or Shintoism and Buddhism, is not a psychological paradox, but on the contrary, it is the first indication of how to consummate the experiences and truths of various religions and between individuals in a harmonic manner.

Of course, before the materialization of integration between Christianity and other religions and cultures of the right hand occurs – and this is just one of the historical tasks of ROSE OF THE WORLD – the natural precedent is to accomplish a unification of all Christian denominations. The preparation of this unification, pertaining to the areas of theology, philosophy, psychology, culture and organization, will be spearheaded by ROSE OF THE WORLD with indefatigable inspiration. Until the unification of Christianity occurs, until the Eighth Ecumenical Council (or several preceding councils) examines the entire scope of ancient dogmatics and supplements it with a new series of theses founded on the spiritual experience of the previous thousand years, until the supreme authority of the unification of Christianity sanctifies the theses of the teaching of ROSE OF THE WORLD, until this time these theses can, of course, be professed, affirmed, preached, but must not be cast into final, unconditional and unalterable forms that are to be recommended for profession by all Christians.

Rose of the World sees its supra-religiosity and inter-religiosity in this unification of Christian denominations and in the further integration of all religions of the world for the sake of a common concentration of all strengths for the improvement and perfection of humanity. Any religious exclusion of its adherents is not only alien, but will also be impossible. The wisdom of Rose of the World teaches a commitment toward the culmination of the highest ideals in all nations

The building of Rose of the World assumes a series of concentric circles. Those who are not adherents of any religion of the right hand, who are outside the general church, are not included. Those who have not yet attained a comprehension of the supra-religious unity will have a place in the outer circles. The middle circles will contain those less active, less creative, from among the adherents of Rose of the World. The inner circles consist of these who have established the meaning of their existence in a cognizant and voluntary concept of divine creativity.

Let the Christian enter the Buddhist temple with apprehension and reverence: for thousands of years the oriental nations, separated from the centers of Christianity due to deserts and mountain ranges, attained the truth about other edges of the celestial world through the wisdom of their teachers. The sculptures of supreme sovereigns of other worlds and great messengers speaking to people of these other worlds sparkled through the smoke of incense. The western person did not approach these worlds. Let his intellect and soul be enriched by the knowledge that is here preserved.

Let the Islamist enter the Hindu temple with a peaceful, clean and austere feeling: these are not pseudo-deities that stare at him here, but conventional images of great spirits that understood and passionately loved the nation of India, and it is appropriate for other nations to accept this testimony with joy and assurance.

And let the devout Shintoist not ignore the imperceptible building that serves as a synagogue, or have neglect and indifference toward it. Here is another great nation that has enriched humanity with the most profound of values, preserving their experience regarding these particular truths which the spiritual world revealed to it and to no one else.

ROSE OF THE WORLD can be equated with an inverted flower whose root is in heaven, while the pedal bowl is here, among humanity, on earth. It's stem is the revelation through which the spiritual sap flows, sustaining and strengthening its pedals – the fragrant choral of religion. But other than the pedals, it also has a pith; this is its individual teaching. This teaching is not a mechanical combination of more or less high theses of various theosophies of the past. Other than the new attitude toward religious legacy, ROSE OF THE WORLD materializes the new attitude toward nature, toward history, toward the destinies of humanity's cultures, toward their tasks, toward creativity, toward love, toward the routes of cosmic ascension, toward the subsequent illumination of *Shadanakar*. Although distinct activists of the past spoke of it, but through religion, through the church, it will be in the future accepted and professed first of them all. In other situations this attitude is new. The attitude of ROSE OF THE WORLD appears to be new in an irrelative sense, because it has not been related by anyone ever in the past. This new attitude evolves from a new spiritual experience, without which only a plausible and unproductive religious eclecticism would be possible, and this would be in place of ROSE OF THE WORLD.

But before we pass to the content of this spiritual experience, to the fundamentals of this teaching, first I must explain the routes that the soul must take in order to acquire this experience, and the methods by which we can easier or faster facilitate this acquisition.

Book II

About the Meta-Historical and Trans-Physical Methods of Comprehension

Chapter 1

Certain Specifics of the Meta-historical Method

A commonly known expression is – religious feeling. This expression is incorrect. In general, religious feeling does not exist, but what exists is an unobservable world of religious feelings and encounters, infinitely diverse, often in contrast one with another, different and accordingly each having an emotional content and a direction according to its objective, a strength, tone and, to add, its color. The person who is deprived of individual religious experience cannot even suspect the width and diversity of this world. He can only make conclusions about it based on the testimony of others. Such testimonies, due to the absence of personal experience, almost always are accepted with distrust, with prejudices, with an inclination to interpret them not in relation to the affirmation of the witnesses, but in relation to dogmatics of a irreligious system.

The diversity of the world of religious feelings corresponds with the diversity of methods of religious comprehension. To expound these methods signifies writing a fundamental investigation based on history and the psychology of religion.

Any similar task does not pertain in any respect to the task of the present book. The intention to provide an understanding at least of certain methods of religious comprehension is one of the components that enter into the task of this book, and particularly those methods that, as it seems to me, have a considerably greater creative significance toward the current historical stage.

A most sorrowful mistake would occur if someone was to suspect the author of this book of pretensions for the role of being a founder or initiator of some great convention – historical, cultural or social, the creation of what is here designated by the appellation – ROSE OF THE WORLD. Actually all is completely otherwise. ROSE OF THE WORLD can appear and be displayed only as the result of the simultaneous effort and an immense number of people. I am convinced that not only in Russia, but in many other boundaries of the world, this process is occurring, with the initial progress, it seems, in India and America. Although presently local for the most part, this grandiose reality is being thrust into humanity's cognizance. Initially a cognizance of an individual, then hundreds, in order that later it would become the legacy of millions. Yes, perhaps right now, here at this very minute, people that still know nothing about one another, often separated by immense expanses and national boundaries, or at least separated by the walls of several houses, often encounter and experience agitating bursts of comprehension, contemplate the trans-physical height and trans-physical depth, and some of it will integrate into them, each one according to his relative personal ability and arrangement of his soul, to express it or at least approximately reflect this experience in the composition of literature, paintings and music. I do not know how many, but as much as I can see, some quantity of people already stand in this stream of revelation. And my task is to express it in the manner that I particularly have, and only this.

Subsequently, the address here will not go in the direction of a scientific formation of thought and knowledge, and not even artistic, but of an understanding that requires some reevaluation of occurrences that have dominated Russia over the previous 40 years.

I suppose that a serious commencement of researchers, those standing on the highest level of contemporary physiology and psychology, into the immense amount of apocalyptic literature, into autobiographical testimony of religious authors and some religious activists, those having experiences of a similar type, unprejudiced instruction and fluency in the material dispersed in the efforts of comparative religious studies, will all lead to producing a scientific method, upon which basis a foundation of religious gnoseology, and in part a meta-historical comprehension, will succeed in being laid. A person can also imagine the commencement of scientific-pedagogic practices, placing as its goal the possession of the mechanism of this comprehension, to provide individuals – those who have up to this time passively accepted this process – the ability to summon it and direct it, even if in part. But all of this is a matter of the distant future, and not the near future. What is only undoubtable for the time being is that the diversity of this process depends on both objective and subjective comprehension.

We should not embrace what is too immense to embrace. I can here speak just of that variation of process that caused an altercation in my personal life. I will get to that point where I will need to proceed in a manner that will increase the autobiographical element in this book, although I personally would prefer to avoid this element as a result of certain other circumstances. Now the center of attention will be 3 views of religious comprehension: meta-historical, trans-physical, and ecumenical. Nonetheless, it is impossible to draw a fully distinct border between them, but this is also not needed.

First of all: how is the term – meta-history, specifically to be understood?

Sergei Bulgakov, although not the sole Russian thinker that placed this problem on its edge, states, "Meta-history is the noumenal[25] side of that universal process, where one of its sides is revealed to us as history." I have the impression however that the application of Kant's terminology to the problems of this series can hardly help the explanation of the essence of the matter. The understandings of noumenon and phenomenon were developed for other trains of thought, summoned by other philosophic needs. The objectives of meta-historical experience can only be wedged into a system of this terminology by someone like Procrustes.

Another invalid association of meta-history is with any type of form of the philosophy of history. Philosophy of history is particularly history; meta-history is always mythological. Whether this way or the other, the term *meta-history* is utilized in the present book as having 2 meanings.

First, as a conglomeration of processes lying meanwhile outside the field of vision of science, outside its interests and its methodology, flowing into those strata of another form of existence which, being submersed into other currents of time and into other forms of space, often shine through or penetrate processes that we accept as history. These other-worldly processes are bound in a tight manner with the historical process, and they define it to a significant degree, but by no means are they simultaneous with it and with greater fullness are they disclosed on the routes, in particular, of that specific method of comprehension that is proper to be named meta-historical.

The 2nd meaning of the word *meta-history* is the teaching of the processes of another form of existence, the teaching, it seems, not in a scientific sense, but particularly in the religious.

This process itself, or at least the variation with which I am familiar, does not have even the least relation to scientific forms of comprehension. I will repeat and underscore this. It consists of the following 3 phases.

The first phase consists of a momentary inner act completed without the participation of the subject's will and, it would seem,

---

[25] The term noumenon is used in the philosophy of Immanuel Kant.

without visible preliminary preparation, although of course, in reality such a preparation, just flowing along the threshold of consciousness, must have a place. The content of this act impacts as a lightning strike, but the experience encompasses immense bands of historical time, although undivided as far as knowledge is concerned and inexpressible in any words, and they are great historical phenomena. The form of such an act manifests as something beyond measurement, saturated by dynamic-effervescing images over a minute or hour, when the individual senses himself like the person who, after a long residence in a quiet and dark room, would be suddenly thrust under the open sky in a turbulent storm overwhelming him with its immensity and potency, almost blinding him and at the same time filling him with a sense of encompassing happiness. The individual earlier had no clue of such a fullness of life or the very possibility of such a fullness.

Synthetically they embrace entire epochs simultaneously, the entire – if I can express it this way – meta-historical cosmos of these epochs with the great principles battling during them.

It would be a mistake to suppose that these images have an definite visible form. No, the seen element is included in them as perhaps also the audible, but their comparison to these elements, for example, is like the ocean compared to a spring that enters and becomes part of the larger body of water. To provide a conceptualization of this encounter is extremely difficult due to the absence of several precise analogies with something else that is more known. Experiencing this imposes a tremendous effect on the entire psychological composition of the individual. Its content so much transcends all that was earlier found in the circle of the individual's knowledge, that it will for many years sustain in him the spiritual world that was encountered. This will become for him his most precious inner legacy.

So is the first stage of meta-historical comprehension. It seems to me admissible to call it meta-historical illumination. The result of this illumination will continue to be preserved in his psychological depth, preserved not as a memory, but as something living and continuing to live. Over the years and gradually from that initiation, additional distinct images, ideas and entire concepts will rise into his circle of cognizance, but they will for the most part remain deep inside of him, and the one who encounters this knows that no other concept will ever be able to sway him from this cosmos of meta-history now disclosed to him. These images and ideas become the object of the start of the 2nd stage process.

The 2nd stage does not possess the monumental character as does the first: it presents itself as a certain chain of states, a chain penetrating weeks and months and appearing almost daily. This is the inner contemplation, an intense impact, a concentrated gaze – sometimes joyful, sometimes painful – in historical forms. But not introverted or isolated, but blended with a 2nd meta-historical reality that stands behind them. The expression – gaze, I utilize here conditionally, and with the word – form, I interpret this not only as a seen manifestation, but as synthetic manifestations including the seen elements at least to the extent that the contemplator can in general have a manifested shape that can be seen. Under the circumstances it is imperative that due to the content of similar contemplation there would exist displays of strata of matter of a different dimension in a significant quantity. It is clear that the physical organs of sight and audio are unable to perceive them, but certain others having the composition of our structure do, but usually separated as though a sound-insulating wall against the zones of daily comprehensions. And if the first stage of process was distinguished due to the passive state of the individual, placed as though an involuntary spectator of a stunning spectacle, then in the 2nd state it is possible. To a known extent, it is the guiding activity of the personal with which often, for example, make the choice of one or another object of contemplation. But often, and especially during productive times, images flare deliberately.

It seems to me that I can name this 2nd stage of process particularly as – meta-historical contemplation.

The picture generated by such an image is similar to a sheet upon which are clearly portrayed individual figures and perhaps their general composition, but other figures are foggy, while some intervals between them are empty space. Other parts of the background or separate accessories are entirely absent. Now appears the need to explain the vague connections, filling the empty wandering gaps. So the process advances to the 3rd stage, considerably freer from the effects that are outside the personal and outside the intellectual principles. It is clear because particularly during the 3rd stage considerably more errors occur, incorrect importations, too many subjective interpretations. The principle handicap consists in the inevitable distorting effect of intellect, and it is obviously almost impossible to completely separate from this. What is possible is something else: having caught the inner nature of meta-historical logic, this provides another opportunity to reconstruct the effort of the intellect in a proper direction.

This 3rd stage of process is naturally named – the meta-historical intelligence. In this manner, meta-historical illumination, meta-historical contemplation and meta-historical intelligence fix the definitions of the 3 stages of that route of comprehension of which I speak.

I will stipulate the possibility of yet another type of condition that represents the diversity of the state of the first stage. This is an illumination of a special type that is connected with experiencing the meta-historical principle of demonic nature. Some of them possess immense potency and a wide sphere of activity. This state, which would be correctly named – the infra-physical rupture of the psyche, is very painful and for the greater part is saturated with a feeling of self-induced individual terror. But just as in other situations, a stage of contemplation and intelligence will follow subsequent to this condition.

* * *

My books, written or else composed in a purely poetic plan, are built upon personal experience of meta-historical comprehension. The concepts that appear as the torso of these books are derived in their entirety from this experience. Where did I acquire these forms? And to compile these books, who inspired me and how?

What right do I have to speak with such assurance? Am I able to provide some type of guarantee to the originality of my experience? Now, here, in one of the preliminary parts of the book *Rose of the World*, I respond to these questions, to the extent I can. There is nothing at all for me to gain anyway, so I will strive to keep this at a minimum. But of course, a short account of what, where and when, and under what circumstances the hours of my meta-historical illumination occurred and how I encountered them will enter into this minimum.

The first event of this type that played an immense role in the development of my inner world, in many ways a very defined role, occurred in August 1921, when I was not yet 15 years old. This happened in Moscow, toward the end of the day, at the time when I much loved to aimlessly wander the streets and pointlessly fantasize. I stopped at a parapet in one of the city squares that surrounded the Cathedral of Christ the Savior, one that overlooked the shore [of the Moscow River]. It was a marvelous view that opened over the river, Kremlin and the region beyond the river, with its dozens of church bells and cupolas of many colors. It was about 7 o'clock and the church bells were summoning parishioners for matins. The incident of which I speak opened in front of me or it was over me. It was some turbulent, blinding, unattainable world that enveloped the entirety of the historical reality of Russia in an awesome unity with something of disproportionate size that hovered over it. Many years I was nourished by icons and ecclesiastical concepts, and now gradually I was floating away from them into a circle of special cognizance. Intellect for a long while could not compare with all this, trying to create new and newer designs which somehow had to harmonize the contradictions of these ideas and interpret these images. The process quickly entered a stage of meditation, bypassing that opportunity for my contemplation of the event. This construction seemed to be flawed as my intellect could not access the same level of the ideas impressed by the event, and so it required another 3 decades saturated with supplemented and profound experiences for me to properly understand and explain the abysmal depth that was unveiled to me in my early youth.

The second incident of this series that I encountered was in Spring 1928, in the Church of the Intercession at Levshinski corner. I remained after Easter matins in the church. This liturgy, which begins about 2 o'clock in the morning, was special, as popularly known, due to the recitation once a year of the First Chapter of the Gospel of John – In the Beginning was the Word. The gospel passage is repeated by all priests and deacons participating in the service, from the different ends of the church, in order, verse by verse, in various languages, those utilized and those obsolete.[26] This early liturgy is one of the pinnacles of the Orthodox – and in general Christian – calendar of worldwide services. If matins can be compared with the sunrise that occurs at the ends of the liturgy, then it is a genuinely spiritual noon, full of light and worldwide joy.

The inner event of which I speak occurred was completely different from the first in its content and in its tenor. It was much wider and as though connected with the panorama of all humanity and with the encounter of worldwide history as a single mystical current. Through the celebratory movements and sounds that were being performed in the liturgy in my presence, it gave me a sensation of that higher realm, that heavenly world, where our entire planet is presented as the great temple and where eternal liturgies of enlightened humanity are performed without interruption in an unimaginable majesty.

In February 1932, during the period of my short-term service at one of Moscow's factories, I became sick at night, running a high fever, and I had a certain experience where, of course, the majority did not notice anything except my delirium, but for me it was awesome in its content and unconditional in its conviction. The essence of this experience I designated in my books and will designate here under the expression of the Third *Yuitzraor*. This is a strange and entirely not a Russian word, but I was not the one to invent *Yuitzraor*, but it was thrust into my cognizance at

---

[26] Meaning, in both modern Russian and Old Church Slavonic.

some time. The meaning of this gigantic essence is very simply, it can be rather compared with the monsters of the ocean depths, but incomparably more massive in size. I would define it as a demon of a great and majestic stature. This night remained with me for a long while as one of the most torturous encounters that I have known in my personal experience. I think that if I was to accept into utilization the phrase – infra-physical outburst of psyche, then this encounter would fully apply.

In November 1933, I accidentally, and I mean particularly completely accidentally, entered one church at Vlasyevski Lane. There the akafist of the venerated Seraphim of Sarov was being performed. No sooner did I open the entrance door that immediately a warm wave of descending choral singing rushed into my soul. A state that is extremely difficult for me to explain, much less in writing, enveloped me, An overwhelming power forced me to my knees, although I earlier disliked having to worship on my knees – a psychological immaturity motivated me to earlier suspect that something servile was contained in this maneuver. But now standing on my knees seemed insufficient. And when my hands laid on the worn rug that had been trampled by thousands of feet, some type of secret door of the soul swung open, and tears of a blessed ecstasy burst unrestrainedly from me, incomparable to anything at all.

And I need to truly say that anything following this encounter no longer was very important to me, whatever they might call the ecstasy or rapture. The content of these minutes was my ascent to the heavenly Russia, enveloped by the *Sinklit* of the illuminated spiritual streams of an other-worldly warmth, pouring from that concentrated source which justly and precisely possesses the appellation of the heavenly Kremlin. The great spirit that at some time traversed our world in the figure of Seraphim of Sarov, and who is one of the most brilliant lamps of the Russian *Sinklit*, approached me and knelt to me, covering me, just like with an epitrachelion, under his priest's stole emanating rays of light and a joyful warmth.

During the course of almost an entire year, and until this church was closed, I attended the akafist of Seraphim of Sarov every Monday and – amazingly! – I relived this state each time, again and again and with unweakening potency.

* * *

At the beginning of 1943, I was part of the movement of the 196th Infantry Division across the frozen Ladozhski Lake, and after a 2-day walk over the Karelian Isthmus,[27] we arrived late that night into the besieged Leningrad. During my walk through the unpopulated dark city to the area of troop disposition, I experienced a condition that in part reminded me of the earlier one in my youth at the Church of Christ the Savior that had the same content, but the embellishments were not at all the same. I was as through propelled through a specific environment at the front that night. At first I passed through its translucence, and then I absorbed it into myself, it was decorated austerely and gloomily. Its insides became dark and it sparkled with contradictory, irreconcilable principles, and its stupefying size and a roaring immense monstrous demonic entity impressed me entirely with terror and anxiety. I saw the 3rd *yuitzraor* clearer than at any time before. And only the fluttering brilliance from his enemy that was approaching preserved my intellect from irreparable rupture. This entity approaching is our hope, our joy, our defender, the great spirit national guide of our homeland.

Finally, I experienced something similar in September 1949, in Vladimir, but by now fully free from metaphysical terror, besides it was at night, in a small prison cell as my sole comrade slept, and several times later in 1950-1953, also at nights, in a common prison cell. The experience collected on this route of comprehension was insufficient for *Rose of the World*, but the very movement along this route brought me to the point that finally I seemed capable to consciously absorb the effect of certain providential powers, and the hours of these spirit encounters became more of a perfected form of meta-historical comprehension, than what I just described in writing.

---

[27] between the Gulf of Finland and Ladozhski (Ladoga) Lake

Relatively often many have experienced the exit of the ethereal body from its corporeal edifice, when it is resting in deep sleep and it journeys along other strata of the planetary cosmos. But returning to its mundane mentality, the traveler does not preserve any accounts or recollect what he saw. With the immense majority, what is preserved is only deep in the memory, obliviously separated from cognizance. The depths of the memory are anatomically located centrally in the brain, and this is the storehouse where recollection of the pre-existence of the soul is located, and likewise here are its trans-physical journeys, similar to what I have mentioned above. The psychological climate of certain cultures, and the religious-physiological practice over many centuries, the direction to this side, as for example, in India and the regions of Buddhism, are capable of weakening the barrier or obstacle between the depths of memory and consciousness.

If we were to sever ourselves from cheap skepticism, we cannot but turn our attention to this, particularly in these regions. Often it is possible to hear, even from the most plain of people, confirmations that the sphere of pre-existence is not displayed as completely closed in their cognizance. In Europe, those initially raised in Christianity just put this problem off to the side, and then when they study secular or non-religious science, it is only a rare few who take the individual effort to weaken this barrier between the depths of memory and consciousness and can make use of it.

I need to say completely directly that such strengths were not unveiled to me personally, and for the plain reason that I did not know how to approach the matter and I did not have any guides. But in their place there was something else to which I was obligated, and probably to the strengths of the invisible executors of providential will, and particularly this was a small cleft, as if a narrow slot in the doors between the depths of memory and consciousness. No matter how unconvincingly this might be declared to the overwhelming majority, still I have no intentions of hiding this fact, that even though they were weak and fragmented, but for me they were conclusive testimonies of bursts from the depths of memory that were disclosed in my life from childhood, and which increased during adolescence and continued through the 47th year of my life[28] when it finally illuminated the days of my existence with a new light. This does not mean that as though there transpired a complete release of the capacity of my memory's depths, to reach this is still far away in the future, but the significance of the images, from wherever they were given me, became for me so tangibly clear and the images of these occasions were so distinct, that their quality and focus distinguished them from regular memory or recollection, and opposed to the tactics of the imagination, they were indisputable.

So how can I not condescend with gratitude before destiny, which led me through a complete decade under these conditions (those that are discredited by almost everyone who has not experienced them)? But it was not at all completely easy for me, but which, together with these others, they served as a potent means to the revelation of the spirit-organs of my existence. It was particularly in prison with its isolation from the outside world, with unlimited spare time, and with the one and-a-half thousand nights[29] that I spent in vigilance, lying on a cot with other sleeping comrades, it was particularly in prison that the new stage of meta-historical and trans-physical comprehension began for me. The hours of meta-historical enlightenment were frequent. The long series of nights turned into a solid constant set of contemplation and meditation. The depths of memory was sending into my consciousness more and more distinct images, illuminating the events of my personal life and history and contemporary events with a new meaning. And finally, when awakening in the morning after a short but deep sleep, I knew that day that what I saw were not arbitrary dreamings, but something else entirely, they were trans-physical journeys.

If similar journeys occur through demonic strata and so without a guide, but under the influence of sinister tendencies of

---

[28] This would be 1953, the year of Daniel's final series of revelations.

[29] the 5 years of his initial incarceration, up to the death of Joseph Stalin.

the individual soul or due to the treacherous summons of demonic principles, a person, awakening, does not distinctly recollect anything, but what evolves from the journey is a pulling, deceptive, sweetly-spooky sensation. From this sensation, like from some poisonous seed, only such activities can then grow, those that will bind the soul for a prolonged period after its death to these worlds. Such wanderings occurred to me in my adolescence, such activities that caused the further revelatory route of my life on earth to draw me further and further from these frustrations and into an abyss, and I had no merit to stop it.

If this descent occurs with a guide, one of the brethren of the *Sinklit* of the country or the *Sinklit* of the world, if it has providential meaning and significance, then the traveler, awakening and feeling on occasion that same sweetly-spooky tempting sensation, at that time he will recognize his deception. Besides this, the deception will acquire a balance in his recollections. This is the understanding of the awesome meaning of the existence of these worlds and their genuine appearance, and not just the façade. Due to the plane of his vigilant state, he does not attempt to return to these lower strata by means of a moral collapse, but transforms the acquired experience into a object of religious, philosophic and mystical intelligence, or even making it the substance of his artistic creations, in addition to possessing an indispensable cautionary meaning.

During the 47th year of my life I remembered and understood some of my trans-physical journeys that occurred earlier. Up to this time the recollections of them carried a character that was nebulous, fragmented, vague, and the chaotic partial-images could not be arranged into anything completely assembled. New journeys in part remained in the memory as distinct, as dependably trustworthy. My person as an entity was in turmoil due to sensing these partially revealed secrets, and as a result no dreamings or fantasies remained in my memory, and only the most significant revelations.

An even more perfected view of such journeys through the planetary cosmos is the exit of the ethereal body. It is the journeys with a great guide through the series of ascending or descending strata, but with full protection of the vigilant consciousness. Then, having returned, the traveler brings recollections that are even more indisputable, and exhaustive. This is possible only in the circumstance if the spirit organs of sensory perception are widely expanded and the locks from the depths of memory are removed forever. This is genuine spirit-vision, and this, of course, I did not encounter.

I had however the great opportunity to converse with some of those long dead and who now reside in the *Sinklit* of Russia. I am almost unable to approach this with a pen, for me to fully relive their genuine close proximity to me and which caused me to shake. I am unable to relate them to you by their names, but they were so close to me that they embellished the tune of my individual senses, something that cannot be repeated. The encounters occurred during the day in a people-filled prison cell, and I had to lie on my cot with my face to the wall in order to hide the stream of tears that testified to my happiness. The close proximity of one of the great brethren caused a strong and rapid beat of my heart and put me in a condition of solemn veneration. My entire substance greeted still another with a warm, kind love, as a precious brother seeing right through my soul and loving it and providing me forgiveness and comfort. The approach of a 3rd dictated to me the need to get on my knees in front of him, as before a magnate who is incomparable above me when he enters, and his closeness was accompanied with an austere sensation and extraordinary acute attention. Finally, the approach of the 4th produced a feeling of rejoicing happiness, a global happiness, and tears of ecstasy. I want to have doubt in much of this. There has been much in my inner life of which I have been suspicious of their trustworthiness, but not in these encounters.

Did I actually see them during the time of these encounters? No. Did they actually converse with me? Yes. Did I hear their words? Well, yes and no. I heard them, but not as an audible sound. It was as though they spoke from somewhere in the depths of my heart. Many of their words were especially new to me, appellations of the various levels of *Shadanakar* and the hierarchy. I repeated these appellations in their presence striving to vocalize them with sounds of my physical speech as close as I possible could, and I would ask, "Is this correct?" I had to refine some of these appellations and names several times, and there were some of those that more or less did not possess any exact sound that I could fine. Many of these alien words spoken by the great brethren were accompanied by displays of bright light, but this was not a corporeal light, although they can be compared in some circumstances with strikes of lightning, in others with the sun's glow at sunset, in a 3rd group with moonlight. Often these were not even words in that sense, but were as if entire chords of phonetic phrases and meanings. It was completely impossible to translate such words into our language, so I had to figure the meaning of them and to guess at the pronunciation of the syllables. The conversation concluded not in distinct words, but in questions and answers, in entire phrases expressing very complex ideas. Such phrases, not separated into individual words, as if sparked, sealing my comprehension on a gray sheet of paper, and with an extraordinary light illuminated what was nebulous and unclear to me, what pertained to my question. Soon these were not even phrases, but immaculate thoughts transmitted to me directly, bypassing words.

So the route of meta-historical illumination, contemplation and intelligence was supplemented with trans-physical journeys, encounters and conversations.

The spirit of our age will not hesitate with the question, "So what the author calls experience can be sufficient for his own self as subjective. But can this have any great objective significance other than an experience of a patient in a mental institution? Where is the proof?"

This is strange. Do we need to approach every display of a spirit-life, every display of culture, with the demand of proof? And if not to every one, then why particularly to these? Since when do we demand factual proof from an artist or composer of their musical inspiration or artistic imagination? So there is no proof in the region of religion and in part meta-historical experience.

Without any proof the experience of another will be believed by the person whose psychological formation is a echo of the former. He does not need and will not accept proof. But if the person, to whom all of this is alien, should receive proof, he will not accept it anyway.

But up to this time meta-historical comprehension has been enriched in reality by just a handful of diverse varieties in the sphere of religion. It is interesting to note that in the Russian language the word *revelation* in the literal sense equally means the same as the Greek *apocalypse*. But each of these 2 words seems to have a special shade of meaning fastened to it. The meaning of the word revelation is more general. If we do not isolate ourselves in a narrow frame, we will have the opportunity to include in the quantity of historical events the revelations of such incidences as the visions and ascensions of Mohammed and even the enlightenment of Gautama Buddha. Apocalypse is only one of the forms of revelation. Revelation pertains to the destiny of nations, realms, churches, cultures, humanities, and of those hierarchs who in these destinies display themselves as especially active, immediate and direct, such as the revelation of meta-history. Apocalypse is not so universal, as ecumenical revelation. It is lowly on the hierarchical ladder. It is more private and is situated closer to us. But particularly the result of this is that it answers to the burning questions of destiny thrown into the oven of historical cataclysms. Apocalypse plugs the fissure between the attainment of universal harmony and the dissonance of historical and personal existence.

As is well known, only and barely a few nations in a few ages were blessed with the wealth of such a revelation. Apocalypticism sprouted in the midst of Judaism, it appears, near the 6th century B.C. It enveloped early Christianity and beyond this maintained its presence in the Judaism of the

Middle Ages, sustained by the fiery atmosphere of its messianism.

In Christianity, in part in the east, the apocalyptic form of knowledge was completely lost already by the beginning of the Middle Ages, and then suddenly flared in a dull, flickering, smoky flame during the first century of the great Russian schism.[30] This is not the place to insert an analysis of the complex and innumerable reasons for this damaging event, but it is impossible to not note its tie with the anti-historicism of religious comprehension and world of religious feelings that stops our attention at the Byzantine ecclesiastical fathers and actually strikes at the representatives of Russian Orthodoxy, even among the most prominent, those in whom there is no doubt of rectitude and the highest of spiritual experience. Anti-historicism stands just like an absolute canon of religious thought. It is instructive to remember the irresolvable conflicts between official anti-historicism of the Russian ecclesiastical ideology and the inherent, congenital irrational draw toward the apocalyptic form of comprehension, toward meta-history, in the religious and autobiographical compositions of secular Orthodox writers and thinkers: Gogol, Khomyakov, Leontev, Dostoyevski, Vl. Solovyov, and Sergei Bulgakov.

Speaking of the meta-historical method of comprehension, I unnoticeably migrated to the trans-physical: the journeys and encounters I have described pertain in part still to the spheres of trans-physical comprehension. Know that I already said that very seldom can these manifestations be precisely classified.

Perhaps some will declare their amazement. Why in place of the generally understood word – spiritual, do I often utilize the term – trans-physical? But the word – spiritual, in its strict meaning validly pertains only to God and to monads. The term – trans-physical, applies to everything that possesses tangibility, but a different one than what is ours, it applies to all worlds

---

[30] This would be the 17th century with the breakaway of the Old Believers or Old Ritualists

existing in the spatial expanses having a different set of coordinates and different dimension of time. Trans-physical, in the sense of an objective comprehension, I understand as the entire unification of such worlds that are outside of dependence on the processes that proceed them. Such processes tied with the formation of *Shadanakar* comprise meta-history; those tied with the formation of the universe comprise meta-evolution. The comprehension of meta-evolution is a universal comprehension. The word – trans-physical, in the sense of religious teaching, signifies the teaching of the structure of *Shadanakar*. Objective meta-historical comprehension is tied with history and culture; the trans-physical is tied with the nature of our stratum and other strata of *Shadanakar*, while the ecumenical is tied with the universe. In this manner, such apparitions, those that I called trans-physical journeys and encounters, while independent of their content, can pertain either to a meta-historical category of comprehension, or to a trans-physical, or to the universal.

After this medium-length discussion, there is nothing that impedes us to proceed to an investigation of the 2 remaining categories of religious comprehension, but I suppose, only in their varieties with which I am acquainted.

CHAPTER 2

SOME DISCUSSION ON THE TRANS-PHYSICAL METHOD

It would seem that the attitude of people towards nature is infinitely diverse and individual, while sometimes it is internally antinomian. But if we were to investigate the evolution of this attitude through the general history of culture from the initiation of writing to our days, it is possible to disclose some of its types, or better said, phases. I will permit myself here and very simplistically, in the most general characteristics, to note 3 or 4 of the very important phases in the manner that I conceive of them. This is not an original picture of how this attitude has changed in culture and throughout the centuries, but just some crude sketches and quick ones in order to bring the reader inside the problem, instead of creating for him a historical perspective of this question.

The earliest phase is characterized by the cosmos seeming to be extremely miniature, while Earth is the sole residential or inhabitable world. As a result, this world, other than our physical stratum, possesses a material basis alongside other strata that also have one, but their material basis is of another nature and of other qualities than ours. First is the approach to the trans-physical reality of *Shadanakar*. All of these strata, likewise ours also, are deprived of further development. They are created once and for all, and are populated by good and bad entities. For these entities, the human is the center of their interests, and to add, is the bone of contention. The human himself does not realize nature as something lying outside of him and does not place it as contradistinctive to himself. The individual manifestations of nature awaken, of course, one or another feelings – fear, satisfaction, reverence; but nature as a whole, as is obvious, is almost not accepted or is just accepted on a purely esthetic plane. The cultures of antiquity fundamentally pertain to this phase, and likewise certain cultural forms of the Orient of much later origin. Polytheism is characteristic of the first phase from a religious perspective.

Typical for the 2nd phase are those monotheistic systems that either ignore nature, not displaying any interest toward it, or are hostile to it. The growth of individualism causes the impression that a person can attain self-perfection. Nature does not submit signs of development, it is direct and static, it is amoral and arational, it resides within the authority of demonic powers, and that part of the human entity that possesses the identical substance of nature demands either its enslavement by spirit, or it will become enslaved by the demonic.

This is a phase struggling against nature. Christian and Buddhist and Hindu nations traversed it. Judaism, as long as it coincided with its national religion, remained in it. The latter, just as with the Islamic nations, did not so much struggle against nature, as much as pass alongside it. The Semitic feeling of nature in general is meager.

The 3rd phase is tied with the era of the reign of science and with the impoverishment of the world of religious feelings. Having inherited from Christianity this principle of a struggle against nature, the person of the 3rd phase frees it from religious meaning, rejects the domination of natural elements in their individual state, and substantiates nature as strictly utilitarian. First, nature is an object of rational – scientific – research. Second, it is a gang of soulless powers that must be subjected for a person's use. The physical periphery immeasurably expands. The knowledge of structure and laws of our stratum attain a head-spinning depth. This is the value of the 3rd phase. But in vain do natural scientists expound about love toward nature. Intellectual love can only be experienced if pertaining to the products of the intellect: it is possible to emotionally love an idea, thought, theory, scientific discipline. So can you love physiology, microbiology, and even parasitology, but not a lymph, not a bacteria and not a mosquito. Love toward nature can be a manifestation of the physiological order, can be a display of esthetical order, and finally, of the ethical and religious order. It cannot just be a manifestation of one order, like an intellectual. If individual specialists of natural science love nature, then this feeling has no tie of any type either with their specialty, or in general with the scientific method of the study of nature: this feeling is either of the physiological or esthetical order.

Perhaps nothing so evidently illustrates the narrowing of the gap between humanity and the elements over the past century as does the evolution of clothing. The coat and hat, which crucially accompanied every cultured person, even on a summer day, are just now utilized depending on climatic conditions. Fifty years ago it was considered inappropriate to leave the house without gloves. Now they are only used in cold weather. In place of formal coats and starched shirts, considered proper with our grandfathers even with the temperature at 90 degrees, short sleeves with open collars have won over our life. Instead of wearing high boots, now they are replaced by slippers and even bare feet. Women have liberated themselves from nightmare of corsets, and now in the summer take strolls in short skirts and blouses that are open at the top, while long dresses are reserved for quality occasions. Children, whose forefathers, when they were same age, decorously in public and even in July, wore their school jackets with a cap on their heads, now run about barefoot in shorts.

The man of the global city is now so distant from nature to such an extent he does not even begin to miss its warm environment and return to it, and almost unconsciously. This instinct of a natural love toward nature has dissipated. With this accumulation of recent historical experience, the soul now possesses the kernel of a totally new attitude toward nature. This is the 4th phase.

And so we have 4 phases of the attitude toward nature: the pagan, ascetic, scientific-utilitarian, and instinctive-physiological.

What is the attitude toward nature from the side of that ideology that lies as the basis of the ROSE OF THE WORLD's teaching?

This question is wide ranging, but it seems to me not difficult to conclude what the primary importance consists of in this attitude. Know that the acceptance of ROSE OF THE WORLD is distinct first of all due to feeling the transparency of the physical stratum, experiencing the translucent strata of the trans-physical through it, having a fiery love of this experience and cherishing it diligently. This feeling envelopes the sphere of culture and history and pours over into meta-historical teaching. It applies to the sun, moon, star-filled sky, and forms the foundation of the ecumenical teaching, that is, the meta-evolutionary. It grasps all earthly nature and finds its expression in the teaching about the *stikhials*. The teaching of the *stikhials* appears as a branch of a greater general teaching about the structure of *Shadanakar* – the trans-physical teaching.

No matter how much the ancient concepts of the *stikhials* – the spirits of the elements in the widest meaning – are turbid due to secondary impurities brought in by the limited human imagination and mind, no matter how many aberrations might distort the pantheons of polytheistic religions with their images of native deities, truth still lies at the very base of these beliefs.

But of course, we need to attain and venerate the worlds of the *stikhials* in a completely different manner than how this was accomplished by the nations of antiquity. The experience of succeeding stages since then has enriched us, expanded knowledge and sharpened our mystic deliberation. The primary distinctions of our belief in *stikhials* compared to the beliefs of the ancients consists in the following:

The ancients anthropomorphized their concepts of the elements of deities. We no longer feel the necessity to attribute to *stikhials* a form that is human-like. The ancients looked at these worlds not knowing what they were, but that they were once and for all instituted and unchangeable. We provide for ourselves an account in the fact of their evolution, although it is unlike the evolution of our organic world, and we will strive to attain its routes.

The ancients were able to live through the connections with the separate strata of the *stikhials*, but vaguely differentiated them one from another, while they had no clue at all about the instituted routes of these monads. Personally speaking, they did not possess a clear concept of the immense number of these strata. The immense number of the mutual tie of these strata and routes instituted for the monads residing there becomes for us the object of trans-physical comprehension. The ancients were not in a condition to sketch for themselves a general picture of the planetary cosmos. We can more precisely differentiate every stratum and include it with all of its specific distinctions and specialties in the general panorama of *Shadanakar*. The ancients could not reconcile belief in these worlds with belief in the sole One. For us, there is no contradiction of any type between both these beliefs.

And I need to add one more thing to our spiritual obligations in regard to the *stikhials*. The ancients envisioned them in their propitiations and eulogies, and this is all. We will aspire to materialize our connection with them in preparation of participating in their recreation and creativity, to attract and incorporate their benevolent participation in our life – the possible paths to this will be shown in the subsequent chapters – and, finally, in our personal assistance of the bright *stikhials* and in the effort of enlightening those in the dark.

This attitude toward nature combines the pagan attribute of life's happiness, the monotheistic spirit-inspiration, and the width of the knowledge of the scientific era. All of these elements are transformed into the supreme union of a personal spiritual experience that births the consummate religion.

The promulgation of the deception that every religious ideology is malicious to life occurs because it substitutes all the treasures of our world with the other-worldly treasures. Such a generalization is no more legitimate than, for example, the affirmation that as if the art of painting leads a person away from the world based on the attitude that this was purpose of painting in the Middle Ages. What is hostile to life is the religious creed of a defined phase, and even this occurs in its extreme presentations. The attitude toward the world of which I speak does not lead away from the world, but teaches to love it fervently and with altruistic love. It is not contradistinctive to these other worlds, but embraces all of them as one majestic beauty, as a pearl on the chest of the Deity. Do we like a crystal lamp any less because it is transparent? Will we love our world less as a result that other worlds penetrate through it and pervade it? For the person who feels this way, yes, this life is good and death just may not be an enemy, but a good guide, if the life that was worthily lived in the world precedes the transfer into the other worlds, and these are not less satisfying, wealthy and beautiful forms of worlds, but more.

So how? By what route does a human attain this penetrating perception of these worlds? Does it come independently from the efforts of our will as a fortunate gift of fate, or perhaps it is something that is consciously inculcated into our selves and over several generations?

Until the unifying efforts of the majority of people are directed toward such instruction, the joy of the penetrating perception of the worlds remains, in reality, up to the mercy of God, and in order to receive it there is no need for us to exhaust a lot of strength. It is only our invisible friends of the heart, the carriers of providential will, who with long extended efforts disclose in one or another of us the means for such a perception. But often, more often, it is disclosed to those of a narrow band. And this type of disclosure is sufficient so that the penetration through the physical world would now begin, and so the happiness attained is comparable to a blind person receiving his sight.

To summon this process is completely arbitrary — within yourself or in another — it is hardly possible, and at least at the present. We can work in this direction to the extent that in each of us or in our children this effort would proceed to greet the effort of the Providential powers, so that in the mental-physical formations a tunnel would as if be dug simultaneously from both sides: by us and by the friends of our heart.

The colossal task of such pedagogues at the present can only be predicted as one of the tasks of the future cultural era. There is a need still for immense preliminary work in training and in the categorization of experience. I will further deal with this in more detail in a latter part of this book. Right now I will just communicate some indispensable information about 2 or 3 possible variations of this method. These variations and many others are not here stipulated, but they can be, it seems, included and to help one another.

There is one prerequisite or precondition, and without which any efforts of any type in this direction will produce nothing. This is the individual preparation of the person to achieve the state for this crystal receptacle to penetrate through him, and which we call nature. This means that this process is accessible to anyone who will himself allow the possibility of the existence of the worlds of the *stikhials,* and even for maybe children, if this assurance of the *stikhials* and love toward nature from their earliest years is inculcated into them by their elders. It is natural that the person who early denies the existence of these worlds will himself not squander time and effort on similar experiences. And if he should even think to exert some effort later, even considering it an experiment, he will not achieve anything, because his individual disbelief would have continued to extend into any acquired results, and he would attribute these results to self-inducement or something in that category. A step forward becomes a step backward, or standing still.

So if the required inner condition is right in front of our face, we need to worry over the creation of unavoidable external conditions. It is easy to guess that the address is directed to these periods, maybe a month and-a-half twice a year, when the contemporary person is freed from work or earning a living and can permit himself to isolate himself in nature. I think that conditions are best in summer, because particularly with summer, when the sun stands high, the development of growth and exposure of the surface of the ground and the bodies of water, the activities of the *stikhials* increases several times over on account of the impact of their new and newer strata. I am not talking about the situation that usually occurs particularly in summertime when residents leave for a vacation, that is, even for a month to have the opportunity to commune with nature. Although, and I need to say this directly, that a month is not enough time to get very far, and a 2-week vacation for any type of effective experience is almost worthless. I will also stipulate that for some of us the winter nature is individually closer, and in such circumstances, of course, it all depends on a person's predisposition.

Perhaps someone is waiting for me to provide more details in regard to a daily regimen. I prefer to ignore such trivial recommendations. So what is the important task? To enter deeper into nature to the extent possible, into the life of the elements, and not to enter to ruin nature and not as just an inquisitive spectator, but as a son who is returning home after many years of roaming in some foreign land. In order to accomplish this task, one individual will naturally do it his way, and another will do it their way. I do want to state the conditions that particularly have helped me personally.

Having selected for the interval a certain place that is beautiful and desolate of people, it is possible to first of all escape the dirt of our soul and mind and all the trivialities of daily mundane worries. It is necessary to weaken this connection with the big city, be less dependant on the radio and strive as much as possible to avoid newspapers. It is indispensable to simplify your life, wear as little clothing as possible, and completely forget about wearing shoes. Bathe 2 or 3 times a day in a river, a lake or sea, finding a suitable place for this, where you can remain for the interval with nature, one on one. Read such books that you can apply to a peaceful, altruistic mood and for the time will promote the movement of your thoughts into the depth of nature. Science literature is not very useful during such times because it turns your direction towards complex issues. It is best to avoid subjects that are technical or scientific. It is good to reread classics of literature or children's books. If you bring your children, it is a good time to play games with them and have lengthy and edifying conversations with them. I hope I am not scaring anybody with my recommendations, but I would also add to the above, a regular diet that is a minimum of meat and fish and with as little alcohol as possible. Do not even think about hunting or fishing.

In such an environment you can begin roaming; but I do not want to call this strolling or hiking. These will be walks to consume the entire day, from dawn to dusk, or for 3 or 4 days while spending the nights in the forests, while wandering the roads outside local villages and the trails between fields, through meadows, preserves, villages, farms, through slow moving fords across rivers, and on occasion meeting others and having shallow conversation. Also spending the nights at a campfire along a river, or in a field, or maybe in a barn. I stayed away from all types of machines or operating equipment, and especially transit, lest I take advantage of it instead of walking. After my roams I would return to my room in the local village for a few days and listen to the roosters and the children and the people in the streets, and read literature with some depth in it, and then again depart into the wilderness.

Of course, some of the local populace considered me a vagrant, lazy, because they would be working in the fields, while I would be hiking or camping. But this did not affect me because they did not know my situation. Since I felt I was right, I ignored their opinions.

But all of this is a direction toward the external environment. It is possible to squander an entire summer involved in forests and fields and return with nothing. The external conditions need to be supplemented with some endeavors of the mind and senses. So of what does this consist?

A person gradually becomes accustomed to perceiving the noise of the forest as an ocean, the wave of the grasses, the soar of the clouds and flow of the rivers, all the voices and movements of the visible world as something alive, so then he profoundly meditates upon, and has a friendship with, all of this. This feeling will increase and gradually envelop all the days and nights, and will displace all other thoughts and feelings, invariable taking control. It is like being thrown face down, lowering your head lower and even lower into the sparkling, rocking depths with its quiet light, an existence immemorial, beloved and native. The sensation of such a consolation, a wisdom-filled rest, will devour even an infinitesimal crumb of triviality. It is good during such days to lie, oblivious to time, along a river bank and aimlessly watch the water flowing, while the sun reflects on its surface. Or else, lying somewhere in the middle of tall grass, to hear the organic noise of a pecking woodpecker. You must believe that the *stikhials* of the *Liyurnas* are happy over your presence here and speak with your body as it descends into their flowing substance; that the *stikhials* of *Faltora* or *Arashamf* are already singing to you songs with the rustling leaves, the hum of bees and the warm respiration of the wind. You will walk along the water-filled meadows, fragrant with the fresh cut hay, at evening on the way home from a long hike, and the quiet fog will begin to surround everything. This is a good time to remove your shirt and allow your warm body to interact with the fog covering the meadows.

This experience of life is possible not only in central Russia, but in the native landscape of any other country, from Norway to Ethiopia, from Portugal to Philippines and Argentina. The details will only relatively change. The chief item is to create this simplicity and levity outside of yourself and repeat such intervals every year if at all possible. Some will think, "This is stupid." As if we do not make use of available sources out of which appear fog, wind, dew. As if we do not know the mechanics of the formation of rain, or the growth of rivers. But all of this contributes to a natural derivation of the elements of nature and as supplemented by science. But this will not interfere with the teaching of the *stikhials*, upon which all of these mechanical processes are dependent.

Learning of the elements of nature as a mechanism occupies meteorology, aerodynamics, hydrology, and a series of other sciences. But this must not and will not interfere beginning at the time of the crystallization of the teaching of the *stikhials*, those comprehensions that are utilized by these mechanisms.

Personally with me it began during a 1929 sweltering summer day near the small city Tripolye in Ukraine. I was happily exhausted after a several-mile roam over open fields and along streams and windmills, and which allowed me a wide open view at the bright-blue branches of the Dneipr, and at the sand covered islands between them. I climbed to the top of a neighboring hill and suddenly was literally blinded. In front of me, not stirring under the descending waterfall of sunlight, a sea of daisies spread out further than my eye could see. At this very second I sensed that an invisible ocean of some kind of rejoicing living happiness was oscillating over this majestic scene.

I walked to the very edge of the field and with a pounding heart, I pressed 2 leafy daisies to both cheeks. I watched in front of me, at these thousands of agrarian suns, almost gasping for breath due to love toward them and toward those whose joy I was feeling at his field. I felt something strange. I felt that these invisible entities with joy and with pride are leading me as a distinguished guest, as if to their marvelous celebration, something like a mystery play[31] and feast. I carefully took a couple of steps into the thick growth of a field of daisies and, closing my eyes, heard their contact and their summoning rustle was softly heard and flaming divine heat surrounded me.

So it began at this point. True, I recollect the encounters of this type that pertain to the earlier years, as a child and adolescent, but they were not so enveloping. But those earlier and later, not occurring every year, but sometimes it was several times just in one summer, they occurred in the midst of nature and absolutely when I was alone. These were strange minutes when I was intoxicated with joy. They appeared for the most part where behind me was 50 miles that I walked on foot, and when I unexpectedly entered some spot that was unknown to me, and which impressed me with the abundance of foliage freeing growing. Entirely, from head to toe I was embraced with ecstasy and agitation. I climbed through wild growths, through marshes warmed by the sun, through thorny bushes and finally threw myself onto the grass to caress it with all my body. What was most important was that during these minutes I unambiguously realized how these invisible entities loved me and penetrated through me, whose existence was mysteriously connected with the foliage, water, and meadows.

In the following years I spent the summer for the most part in the regions of the Bryansk forests and much occurred to me there, and which recollection comprises the delight of my life. But I especially love to recollect my meetings with the *stikhials* of *Liyurna*, those which I at the time thoughtfully named – souls of the rivers.

Once I took the initiative for a individual excursion, over the course of a week roaming the Bryansk forests. It was very dry. Strands of dark blue gloom extended the plumes of the forest fires, while white smoke-filled clouds slowly moving rose often over the massive pine groves. In the interval of several hours, I

---

[31] Also Miracle Play, a theatrical exhibition with a Biblical event as the topic.

had to wander down a hot dusty road, not noticing a fountain or a stream. The intense heat, suffocating, as though in a greenhouse, caused me intense thirst. I did have a detailed map of the area, and I knew that soon I should come across a small stream, and one so small that on my map it did not even have a name. And so it was: the character of the forest began to change, the pines gave way to maple and alderwood. All of a sudden the red-hot road burning the soles of my feet turned downward, and in front of me was a green marsh of tall grass. I ran out of the grove and saw about 20 feet ahead of me the long-awaited river curving. The road crossed at this ford. What a pearl of the universe! What a charming child of God that was able to meet me here! It was only a few footsteps wide, covered entirely with low-laying branches of ancient willows and alders. It meandered following a exact course along a green depression.

Throwing my heavy knapsack on the grass and removing all my outer clothing, I entered the water to the chest. And when my warm body was immersed into this cool pool, and the ripples of the shade and sunlight shined on my shoulders and face, I suddenly felt some kind of invisible entity grabbing my soul with such an immaculate joy, and from where I could not ascertain. But it was with such amusing happiness, that as though it loved me already for a long while and was waiting for me for a long while. It was entirely as though the most subtle soul of this river. All meandering, all vibrating, all lightheartedly, all consisting of coolness and light, worry free laughter and kindness, evolving from joy and love. And when, after my soul's long stay in its soul, and my body in its body, I lied down on the bank under the shade of overhanging branches and closed my eyes. I felt that my heart was so freshened, so washed, so cleansed, so blessed, as much as it could possible be since the first days of creation, at the dawn of time. And I understood that what occurred with me at this time was not a normal bath, but a genuine bath in the supreme sense of this word.

Maybe someone would be willing to say that he was passing the time in forests and bathing in rivers, and he strolled through forests and fields, and he, standing in a nice breeze, experienced the state of being one with nature, but however, he did not feeling anything similar to these *stikhials*. If a hunter was to state this, there is no reason to be impressed: the *stikhials* see an enemy and hazard in this destroyer of nature, and there is no better means of demobilizing them than to take away the weapon from them when they are in the forest. But if it was not a hunter to say this, then let him attentively remember the weeks of his life in the midst of nature.

It is impossible, of course, to ahead of time define the length of the stage of this immersion. The interval depends on many circumstances, both objective and personal. But sooner or later that first day will arrive when you will sense the entirety of nature in a manner that this is the first day of creation and the land is in a state of bliss in its paradisiacal beauty. This can occur at night at the campfire, during the day in the middle of a rye field, in the evening sitting on the warn steps of a porch, or in the morning on a dew-filled meadow. But the contents of this interval will everywhere be one and the same: a head-spinning joy of a first-class cosmic enlightening revelation. No, this does not mean that the inner vision has opened. You will not yet see anything other than the ordinary landscape, but you will experience its multiple layers and saturation with all your substance through the spirit. For the person who traverses this first enlightening revelation, the *stikhials* will become more accessible. He will more frequently hear such types of entities, those not having a name in our language, but the soul now has the ability to draw near to these marvelous entities for entire days at a time.

But the essence of the first enlightening revelation is identified with another, a higher. It pertains not only to a trans-physical comprehension, but also to one that for me is impossible to find any other appellation, except for the ancient word — ecumenical. In specialized literature this type of condition is elucidated by many authors. William James calls it the breakthrough of cosmic comprehension. From its manifestations, it can possess a very diversified spectrum among different people, but the encounter of a cosmic harmony remains its essence. The method that I describe in this book is capable, to a known extent, to make this minute get closer, but this is not a reason to hope that such joys will remain regular guests in the house of our soul. From another side, this condition can grasp the soul and without any conscious expectation of it to occur. Such an incident is described, for example, in Rabindranath Tagore's *My Reminiscences.*

It is easy for a person who has not just once experienced the feeling of general harmony in the midst of nature to conclude that this was the same as what I describe. But, no. The burst of cosmic immersion is a event of colossal subjective significance that can only occur a very limited number of times in the life of a person. It occurs suddenly and unexpectedly. This is not a mood, not a consolation, not a happiness, this is not even a overwhelming joy. This is something that is far greater. The event itself will not so much have a tremendous effect as much as will the recollection of it. On its own it contains such a bliss, that to correctly speak of the connection with it, it is not a shock, but an illuminating revelation.

The content of this consists in that the universe – not the world only, but particularly the universe – unfurls as though in its own higher plane, in this divine spirituality, which penetrates and envelopes it, removing all tormenting questions regarding suffering, struggle and evil.

In my life this occurred on the night of a full moon, July 29, 1931, in these Bryansk forests, along the shore of the medium size Nerussa River. Normally I aspire to be alone when I am with nature, but on this occasion what happened was that I was a participant in a small common excursion. There were just a few of us, young adults and adolescents, and one of us was a novice artist. Each of us had a knapsack on our shoulders filled with provisions, while the artist also had a traveling album for sketches. All we wore were pants and shirts, while some even removed their shirt. We walked in tandem as the Negroes walk along the animal trails of Africa, without speaking and quickly. We were not hunters, not scouts, not explorers searching for something to dig from the ground, but plainly friends who wanted to spend the night along a campfire at some popular reaches of the Nerussa.

Like the sea, as far as we could see, the pine forest turned into a broad-leaved forest, as this always occurs in the Bryansk forests along low flowing rivers. Centuries-old oaks, maples, and ash towered, and aspens surviving with their sturdiness and height, appearing like palms with their crowns at a head-spinning height. Willows had their branches reaching over the streams. The forest stepped up to the river precisely with loving cautiousness. The wilderness silence was broken only by our barely noticeable footsteps, a few footprints we left. We followed paths left behind by lumberjacks or woodcutters, who would cut wood for the winters and haul them into Chukhra or Neporen on sleds.[32]

We reached a local swimming area before the evening hours of a hot, cloudless day. We swam long, then gathered brush and started a campfire about 6 feet from the quietly trickling river, under the shade of 3 old willows, and we cooked for ourselves an ordinary meal. Darkness set. From behind the oaks the low July moon shined, completely full. Little by little the conversations and the stories ceased, the comrades one by one fell asleep about the crackling campfire, while I remained vigilant at the fire, quietly waving a tree branch like a large fan to defend myself from mosquitoes.

And when the moon entered into my direct vision, and the overhanging branches of the willow tree lighted a pattern on the ground from the light, the hours that will remain in my life as the most beautiful of them all began. Breathing quietly, throwing myself on my back on a pile of straw, I heard how the Nerussa was trickling, not behind me, but just a few steps from me, but it was as though directly through my personal soul. This was the first extraordinary incident.

Solemnly and silently all that existed in the world, all that could exist in heaven, trickled right through me, poured into me. It was a bliss that was barely endurable for a human's heart,

---

[32] Local villages

and I felt as though uniformly constructed balls were slowly rotating, while floating in a world-wide round dance, but through me. And all that I could imagine or contemplate, was embraced by a joyful single unity of myself. These ancient forests and transparent rivers, people sleeping at the campfire, and other persons, and nations of close and distant countries, city mornings and noisy streets, churches with sacred images, seas incessantly agitating, and the steppes with its waving grasses, all was really and actually in me the entire night, and I was in them all. I laid there with my eyes closed. And beautiful, white stars, and not at all like what we always see, but larger and brighter, also floated from with the entire global river, as white watery lines. Although I could not see the sun, it was just the same and it also flowed somewhere close to my periphery. But it was not its radiance, but some other light that I have never seen before, that penetrated all of what there was, all that floated through me and at this time soothing me like a child in a cradle, with an all-satisfying love.

Attempting to express in words all that I encountered cannot be done because language is too lacking and insufficient a manner. How many times I have attempted by means of poetry and artistic prose to transmit to others what occurred with me that night. And I know that any attempt of mine to do so – and this is also one more – will never provide another person to understand the true significance of this event of my life, not its scale, not its depth.

I aspired with all my strength to summon this encounter again. I created all those external conditions as they existed back in 1931 when this happened. In the subsequent years I even spent the night at exactly the same spots and on the same dates. But all was in vain. The next occasion that it did occur was 20 years later and just as unexpectedly, and not on a full moon night, but in a prison cell.

O, this was only the beginning. Yet, this was still not that enlightening revelation after which a person becomes something else, something new, enlightened in that higher concept, as the great nations of the Orient define this word. That enlightenment is the most sacred and most secretive, the spiritual eyes now unleashed.

But my responsibility is to share with others what is the best of what we possess. My best is that I traversed the routes of trans-physical and meta-historical comprehension. This is why I write this book. In the 2 preceding chapters I showed, in the manner I could, the most important landmarks of my inner path. What is further will be an exposition of what I learned about God, about other worlds and humanity, while upon this path. I will strive not to return to the question as to how I was able to gain this knowledge. The time is now to speak of what I understand.

CHAPTER 3

THE STARTING CONCEPT

1. THE MULTI-STRATIFIED STRUCTURE

As is well known, our physical stratum, the understanding of which is equivalent to the understanding of the astronomical universe, is characterized by having space defined by 3 coordinates, while time, within which it exists, has one. This physical stratum in the terminology of the *Rose of the World* possesses the appellation of *Enrof.*

In the arena of contemporary science and in the arena of contemporary philosophy there still continues an argument whether *Enrof* in space is infinite or finite, whether it is eternal or limited by time, and likewise whether *Enrof* envelopes the entire physical universe and whether it encompasses all forms of existence with its form

The understanding of the multi-stratification of the universe lies at the basis of the concept of ROSE OF THE WORLD. Each stratum is understood as possessing a specific material world, whose materiality is distinct from any other of the number of spatial coordinate worlds, or any of the other number of time dimension worlds. Along with this coexists, for example, a contiguous strata, whose space is measured by using 3 coordinates, but time is measured not with just one, as it is with us, but with several dimensions. This means that in these strata time passes via several concurrent or parallel rates or different speeds. Events in this particular stratum occur synchronically in all of its time dimensions, but the center of the event is located in one or 2 of them. To tangibly fathom this, of course, is not easy. The residents of such a stratum, although active for the most part in one or 2 time dimensions, but exist in all of them and comprehend all of them. This synchronistic existence provides a special sense of the fullness of life, one of which we are not aware.

(I will jump ahead of my exposition and now add that the greater number of time coordinates united with the least number – one or 2 – of spatial dimensions, is a source of torture and suffering for the residents of such strata. This is similar to realizing the limit of your means, a burning sense of helpless malice, while recollecting deceptive possibilities that they are not in any position to utilize. A comparison in *Enrof* would be the torture of Tantalus,[33] or the inability to bite your elbow with your teeth.)

With rare exceptions, as with *Enrof,* as the number of time dimensions increases, so does the number of spatial dimensions increase proportionately. It seems that there are no strata in *Shadanakar* having over 6 spatial dimensions. Of the strata in the *bramfatura*, the number of time dimensions that can be achieved is an immense quantity: 236.

Strata and entire *sakualas* are different from one another and so is the character of the manner they occupy their spatial expanse. By no means do they all possess cosmic expansion, as does *Enrof.* No matter how difficult this is to imagine, the spatial expanse of many of them terminates at the boundary of their solar system.

---

[33] A Greek figure of mythology doomed to eternal torture in hell.

Other are more local: they are as if confined within the limits of our planet. There are also several that are connected not with a planet in its entirety, but just with some part of its physical formation or a fragment. Nothing similar to a sky exists in such strata.

Being connected to each other with common meta-historical processes, possessing for the most part as though a pair of hostile spiritual poles, all the strata of each celestial body comprises an immense, tightly-mutually-acting system. I already mentioned that such system are called *bramfaturas*. The general number of some of this is limited to just a single one, while others have a quantity of several hundred. Other than *Shadanakar*, the general number of strata at the present is 242,[34] and which includes the solar system consisting of the *bramfaturas* of the sun, Jupiter, Saturn, Uranus, Neptune, the moon, and likewise some satellites of the larger planets. The *bramfatura* of Venus is still in an embryonic stage. The remaining planets and satellites are desolate within their own strata, just as those in *Enrof*. These are the ruins of perished *bramfaturas*, discarded by all the monads, and will never be recognized as a *bramfatura* ever again.

The *bramfatura* of Venus is still in its embryonic stage. The remaining planets and satellites are just as dead in their strata as is the one here in *Enrof*.[35] These are ruins of perished *bramfaturas*, discarded by all the monads, and they will never be recognized as a *bramfatura* ever again.

The systems of materiality having many strata, to a certain stage are analogous to the *bramfaturas*, but are incomparably more colossal, enveloping certain constellations, for example, the majority of stars of Orion, or the systems of binary stars with their many planets, or the star Antares. There are still other greater colossal systems of the galaxy and the entire universe. These are macro-*bramfaturas*. What is known is that macro-*bramfaturas* exist with an immense quantity of strata of diverse

---

[34] The list compiled by the translator at the beginning of this volume actually indicates a total of 248.

[35] Earth's moon.

materialities, up to 8,000. What we have in *Enrof* is an extreme material destitution, an emptiness, as nowhere else found in the macro-*bramfatura*.

It is easy to understand that macro-*bramfaturas* are located beyond the reach of even the greatest of human souls that now reside in *Enrof*. Except in rare unique premonitions, no one otherwise is able to directly acquire any concrete information regarding them. Such information is occasionally transmitted to us from the supreme spirits of *Shadanakar*, immeasurably greater than we, through the intercession of the invisible friends of our heart. But even such communication is extremely difficult for our perception. So it was almost impossible for me to understand the awesome and sorrowing news that there exists a material stratum in the macro-*bramfaturas* of our galaxy, and this is a place where time does not exist. It is like a hole in time, although movement does continue. This place is the torture chamber for great demons, the realm of pitch-black eternity, but not in the sense of endless prolonged time, but in the sense of the absence of all time. Such an eternity is not absolute because time can still be introduced there, and particularly this is one of the tasks of the immense cycles of cosmic initiation. Because with the introduction of time the liberation of those incarcerated in this galactic hell of great torture will be possible.

Molecules and certain forms of atoms enter into the composition of the tiny system. This is the micro-*bramfatura*. Over time there are very few of them in existence that will ever vanish or perish. However, these are relatively complex worlds, and we still must not let out of our view that the elementary particles are living entities, and some of them possess a free will and a complete rational faculty. But communication with them, and even should it be a person and direct intervention into a micro-*bramfatura* is factually impossible. Not in any of the strata of *Shadanakar* and not at the present time is even one entity capable of doing this. For the time being this is beyond the strengths of even the planetary Logos. It is only in the macro-*bramfaturas* of the Galaxy that spirits are sufficiently equipped with unimaginable power and majesty that they are capable of simultaneously descending into many micro-*bramfaturas*. To accomplish this such a spirit must preserve its individual quality and then simultaneously be incarnated into millions of the infinitesimal worlds, appearing in each of them with their entire fullness, although this just might be for an infinitesimal interval of time.

This entire time I am still discussing, one way or another, the material strata, because spirit strata as strata do not exist. The difference between spirit and materiality is more stadial than principle, although it is only God who creates spirit and which emanates out of Him, while materiality is created by monads. Spirit in its primordial or immemorial form has no shelter or crust that we can possibly identify with matter. It exists as a substance that we cannot exactly, but at least with our first approach to understanding, identify with a refined form of energy. Only God and monads – the infinite number of divinely-born and divinely created higher *I* entities that are indivisible single spirits – are spiritual. They differ from each other due to the level of their congenital potential scale. The monad that is raised to a high level can be here or there and in many spots of the universe all at the same time, but it is not omnipresent. The spirit of God is truly omnipresent. He resides even where no monads at all reside, for example, in the ruins of the *bramfatura* that all the monads have discarded. Without God nothing can exist, and even including what we call dead physical matter. And if the spirit of God would discard that, it would cease to exist. It would not transform into another form of matter or into energy, but completely vanish.

2. THE EVOLUTION OF EVIL – GLOBAL LAWS – KARMA

If the myth of the rise and fall of Lucifer is examined in the light of applying to the spiritual history of *Shadanakar*, it will lose its meaning. No events of any kind in the meta-history of our planet, those that could be reflected in the events of this myth, have ever occurred. But something else did occur once a very long time ago, and the recollection of this remains preserved in several other myths, although somewhat distorted, for example, in the tale of the revolt of the titans. But we will discuss this in more detail in another chapter. As far as the legend tied with the rise and fall of Lucifer is concerned, these events occurred sometime back in the universal plane, it transcends all categories of our mental capacity and on a scale of the macro-*bramfatura* that encompasses the universe. What did occur was transmitted into a myth by visionaries of antiquity during that particular epoch's planar human understanding. The understanding of that epoch was scaled down, while the scale of our conceptualization expanded it immeasurably. And if we now want to catch the immortal and valid kernel of this myth, its original concept, we must disdain all the inclusions appended to it over these many epochs, and remain just on the one central fact that it will affirm.

It is natural that the comprehension of even the sages of these eras was far from the present conceptualization of the size and structure of the universe, and so far away that the knowledge of the universe that percolated into their cognizance, owing to the strengths of the invisible friends of their heart, was compressed and squeezed into the small box of their empirical experience, even though they had a strong mentality, but it was not enriched or refined. Nevertheless this task is not even difficult for the person today who attempts to express it in human terms and understanding, although it is just an echo of the universal secret of the rise of who is called – the Dawn. Such an attempt would consist of 2 stages: first, an exploration in the ocean of our expositions of particularly those who are closer than others to reflect on this reality that is beyond our bounds; second, an exploration in the ocean of our language of such word-combinations that have the capability to at least somewhat reflect, in their order, these dodging expositions.

But such a work is tied with the organic growth of individualism and its ecumenical experience. It cannot be forced due to some personal drive. I feel myself to just be located at the beginning of such a work. For this reason I am unable to say anything about universal events of this order, except to openly ascertain something factual that occurred in the past: at some prehistoric depth of time some spirit, one of the greatest that we call Lucifer or Dawn, expressing this integral essential freedom of choice that every monad possesses, apostatized from his creator for the sake of creating another universe according to his own individual intent. A large number of other monads, great and small, attached themselves to him. Their creation of another universe began within these regions. They attempted to create worlds, but these worlds emerged as unstable and so collapsed, because, once they were established, the apostatized monads were rejecting the concept of love as a result of their conduct in this matter, while love being the sole unifying and cementing principle.

The universal plan of Providence leads a large quantity of monads to a higher unity. To the extent that their ascension along the levels of existence formed, their unification was perfected and love toward God and among themselves grew among them even more. And when each of them is immersed into the Sun of the World and creates for Him the materialization of a consummate unity of the highest degree, this evolves into a merger with God without the loss of your indivisible identity.

The universal intentions of Lucifer are contradistinctive. Each of the monads that attached themselves to him only posses a temporary confederacy and have the potential of being his sacrifice. Every demonic monad, from the greatest to the smallest, cherishes a dream – to become sovereign of the universe: pride dictates to each that particularly he – that one – is potentially greater than all the others. A categorical imperative is what guides this type, and it is expressed to a certain degree by the creed: there is *I*, and there are those that are not *I*, and all the not *I* must become *mine*. In other words: all and each must be devoured by this one sole, absolutely self-affirming *I*.

But God forgoes Himself. The principle of defying God strives to consume everyone. This is why it is, first of all, vampiric and tyrannical, and this is why the tyrannical tendency is not only inherent to any demonical *I*, but comprises its integral character.

This is why the demonic monads unify for a temporary duration, but due to their essential nature, they are contending not for life, but for death. This contradiction is disclosed with their group grabbing local authority, and a mutual struggle begins and the strongest will win.

The tragedy of the demon's progress is that the cosmic struggle is stipulated by the fact that the Lord creates new and even more new monads, while the demons are incapable of creating even one, and so the relative increase in strength is successively never in their favor. New apostasies are not occurring and will not any longer occur. This is an absolute guarantee and I am deeply sorry that the exceptional difficulty of this problem does not allow me to find the necessary route of understanding for this, to explain it somewhat intelligently better. In any case all the demonic monads are from a very ancient emanation or evolution, all of them are longtime participants of the great rebellion. True this occurred also later and does occur at present, although not apostasies but something rather externally similar: the highly-conscious, developed entity, or even an entire group of them, temporarily place themselves in a position opposite to Providential will. But this selection of the defiance of God occurs not just with a monad, but with the lower *I*, the intrinsic limited comprehension. For this reason its God-defying activity traverses not the spiritual world, but the corporeal worlds that are under its authority, and their will is now demonic, subject to the law of retribution. In this manner the revolt appears doomed to begin with, and any participant now enters onto a prolonged route of redemption.

Gradually, over the progress of the struggle, the failure of the attempts of demonic powers to create a personal universe became understood to all of them. Continuing to create distinct worlds and applying extreme efforts to simplify their existence, they at this time placed in front of themselves another goal: to possess the worlds by using already existing powers or those presently created by Providence. From this time forward, their new goal was not a destruction of worlds, but particularly their possession. Yet the destruction of the worlds would be the eventual result of such a conquest. Deprived of the unifying principle of love and creativity, and just cemented by the contradictory principle of violence, the worlds cannot exist for much of a long period.

There are galaxies that are in the process of self-destruction. And when astronomical observations of extragalactic nebulas comprise a prolonged period, the process of these catastrophes are viewable by science. Perished and perishing planets do exist: Mars, Mercury, Pluto, are the ruins of *bramfatura*. All the monads of light were banished from these systems that fell to demonic sovereignty, and what followed was the consummation of this catastrophe, and demonic hordes surfaced as uncomfortable wanderers in the universal expanse of outer space searching for new objects for their intrusion.

But there are macro-*bramfaturas* and entire galaxies that cannot be invaded because the invaders do not possess such strength. Within our galaxy, the system that is completely freed from demonic principles is Orion – a macro-*bramfatura* of extraordinary spiritual light. Whoever will gaze at the great nebula Andromeda through a reflecting telescope will see with his own eyes another galaxy that has never experienced any demonic invasion. This world, from beginning to end, is ascending a growing bliss in steps. In the middle of millions of galaxies of the universe, such worlds are few, but it is a pity that our galaxy does not enter into their number. The powers of the insurgent that were discarded downward a long while back from the macro-*bramfatura* of the universe led a non-stop, persistent struggle against the powers of light in the worlds of our galaxy, and which struggle has acquired a million forms. The arena of the struggle surfaces as *Shadanakar*.

It became such an arena still in these distant eras when in *Enrof* the earth presented itself as a partially-molten sphere, while the other strata of *Shadanakar*, counted in the amount of single digits, were only created by the great hierarchies of the macro-*bramfaturas*. There was no law of mutual gorging there. In these worlds, among the entities that are presently known to us under the general appellation of angels, there reigns the principles of love and friendship among all. There was no law of death. Each person traversed from stratum to stratum by the route of material transformation, freed of suffering and without any possibility of returning to a previous lower status. However in these worlds, at the time only possessing a 3-dimensional expanse and subsequently almost the same type of corporeal density as *Enrof,* there was no law of retribution. Mistakes made were restored with the help of higher powers.

Flashes of recollections of this were raised from the treasuries of the deep memory and into the cognizance of ancient sages, but abridged and simplified by their limited comprehension; this brought the legends of paradise lost to crystallization. In reality, it was not paradise, but the most beautiful dawn, and not the one over the earthly *Enrof* that was still deprived of organic life, but over the world that is now called *Olirna,* that then shined and was preserved in the memory of those few human monads, those who did not appear in *Shadanakar* until much later as a majority, but they began their route beginning at a time that we would consider long before antiquity, and not in *Enrof,* but in the angelic *Olirna.* This fraternity of the pre-angelic caste can be called, in a popular sense, humanity's first *Shadanakar.*

The great demon, one of the confederates of Lucifer, was thrust into *Shadanakar* with smaller hordes. Its name was *Gagtungr.* This was a prolonged and obstinate struggle and he was only able to win a partial victory. He did not succeed in banishing the powers of Light from the *bramfatura,* but he was able to succeed in creating several demonic layers and transform them into inaccessible citadels. He was able to succeed in interfering in the process of the emergence and development of life in the earthly *Enrof* and place his seal on the animal kingdom. The planetary laws that helped the powers of Light begin the creation of organic life in *Enrof* were clandestinely distorted: to falsely and criminally ascribe laws of mutual gorging, vengeance and death to the Deity.

"God is light and there is no darkness of any type in Him." Salvation only evolves from God. Joy only emanates from Him. Grace is derived only from Him.

And if global laws infuriate us due to their cruelty, then this is because the voice of God is exalted in our soul against the ingenuity of the great Torturer. The mutual struggle of demonic monads, the victory of the stronger, and not the one who is right, and the overthrow and discard of the defeated into the nether-regions of torment – this is the law of luciferic powers that was inscribed upon the face of the organic world of *Enrof*, expressing itself in the law of the struggle for survival. Every suffering of an entity, every pain and torment of his exudes an emanation – both here in *Enrof* and there in the post-mortem world. Every feeling of his, every agitation of his psychological nature likewise exudes an identical and comparable emanation. Such emanations of malice, hate, avarice, animal and human brutality, penetrate into demonic strata, and supplement and append with itself the loss of life's strengths among various classes and groups and residents. But these emanations are barely sufficient to complement the loss of powers that particularly the separate demonic confederacies have lost. As a result the emanation of suffering and pain – this is called *Gavvakh* – is capable of inundating gigantic hordes of demons of almost all forms and frames. In essence, *gavvakh* is their sustenance.

Supporting its paw on the laws of *Shadanakar, Gavvakh* distorted them in order for them to birth and multiply suffering. It made them burdensome, cruel and intolerable. It prohibited the law of transformation to reside in *Enrof.* Operating on both sides of the struggling principles, death emerged and it became the law. It prohibited the principle of general friendship. Operating on both sides by using their strengths, mutual gorging emerged and this became the law of life. And eventually the demonic powers intervened into the life of other layers of *Shadanakar,* those through which entities now passed, although

166

once they were incarnated as humans in the earthly *Enrof,* these layers were turned into worlds of retribution where torturers would reign, sustaining themselves on the suffering of martyrs.

Among the various forms of *Gavvakh*, the one that has a connection with the extract of corporeal human blood has a special significance. When the blood of people and animals pours from the organism, during the initial minutes of this process, it generates a burning emanation of special strength. This is why certain classes of demons are very interested in this, not so much in the death of living entities of *Enrof* and in the post-mortem suffering of their souls, as much as particularly in the exit of blood from the entity. But the shedding of blood alone in history did not occur and does not occur without our oblivion to the influences of these blood-suckers[36] of our realm. And the blood-spilling sacrificial offerings in certain ancient cults were horrible, not only as a result of their cruelty, but because they were by no means sustained, of course, by their deities, but particularly by these demons.

A new layer was created and a principle was founded for the new humanity by having the planetary Logos, the first and supreme of the monads of *Shadanakar,* supplement the powers of Light. *Enrof* was set aside for the animal kingdom. The new layers were populated by titans, who had a similar outline as us, but much more immense and majestic. In the world resembling *Enrof,* only while it was still early dusk, their radiant figures moved along a background of blue-gray, lead-colored sky, along the slopes and curves of the empty mountains, and filling them. The humanity of titans numbered several thousand. As long as they were deprived, the birth of new ones was not connected with the union of the 2 older in any manner. But the *Gagtungr* managed to summon them to a rebellion against Providence. Their concept consisted in they being the seed and kernel of a new global principle, a 3rd one, that would rise and oppose both God and demons. They thirsted for the absolute freedom of their *I,* but they hated the cruelty and malice of the demons. The

---

[36] Lit: vampires

rebellion concluded when the powers of *Gagtungr*, utilizing the law of retribution, drew the souls of the titans into deep regions of torture. Their torture was there prolonged over a million years, until finally with the help of Providential powers, they succeeded in escaping their captivity. Now the majority of them accomplish their route among humanity, blending their stature and personality with the general background, although their coloration is now not so dark. Their creativity is noticed by a gloomy recollection of their rebellion against God, as though scorched by an ancient fire and which consumed their strength. Their spirit is distinguished from demonic monads by their impulse towards Light, contempt toward anything vile, and a thirst for divine love.

During the final millennium before Christ, the potency of *Gagtungr* was so great that in the strata of many meta-cultures of humanity, the temporal character was taken away from retribution. The exit from the torture regions was silently closed and all hope for the residents in torment was removed.

This law of retribution, the iron law of moral implications and results, those results that can appear during the course of life, but in all their fullness appear after death and even in subsequent incarnations, can be called by the Hindu term – karma. Karma is a kind of an equal-effect of 2 contradistinctive wills, like for example, the law of death and the law of the struggle for survival. If demonic powers would not encounter constant obstacles from the sides of their enemies, the laws would be more difficult, because the demonic goal of the laws is to birth *gavvakhs* and to paralyze the emergence of the souls of Light that crossed over to them. The law also possesses another facet, this is its purging significance. This is the remnant of the most ancient of the bright antecedent laws of the peace-making beautiful hierarchies. The goal of these hierarchies and all the radiant powers of *Shadanakar* is the amelioration and enlightenment of laws. The goal of the demonic laws are their greater weight load. The intent of Providence is the deliverance of all designated for sacrifice. The intent of *Gagtungr* is the drive for all to be a sacrifice.

Divine humanity of the subsequent global period will be a benevolently voluntary unification of all in love. Diabolic humanity will be an absolute despotic tyranny, and it is obvious that it will not escape the progressing period.

The cosmos is the course installed for monads. The anti-cosmos is the worldwide union of rivals and gangs of damaged bright monads that are taken captive in the worlds over which demons rule. These captives had their most sacred attribute taken away from them: freedom of choice.

Gagtungr is not intimidated by the disproportion of its scale to the scale of Lucifer in the universe. He, as with all demonic monads, understands his smallness as just a stage. Blind faith in his unlimited growth and victory is inseparable from his *I*. So do any of these monads believe in their coming macro-galactic triumph, no matter how small they are at the present time and what submissive place they may hold in the hierarchy of the rebellious. As a result, any of them, and *Gagtungr* included in this number, is a tyrant not only in the ideal sense and not only at the present moment, but in each stage to the extent that any authority is permitted those somehow attaining this stage. Tyranny summons such an overwhelming allocation of *gavvakh* as no other principle of leadership will. The *gavvakh's* attachment increases the amount of demonic potency. If the demon begins to supplement the storage of its powers on account of the inclusion of other psychic emanations – joy, love, self-denial, religious veneration, ecstasy, happiness – this would cause a rebirth of his essence and so he would cease to be a demon. But particularly this is something he does not want. And by using tyranny, only by using tyranny, he can restrain the centrifugal strengths within the demonic hordes that are subject to him and keep them from leaving.

And this is why often in meta-history – and also as reflected in history – acts of apostasy occur with the reverse revolt of individual demonic monads against *Gagtungr*. Similar revolts supported by the powers of Light cannot occur, because any of such monads are potentially the same type of planetary demon. If it should become stronger than *Gagtungr*, it will become an even greater torturer than he. We must not, however, forget that occurrences of revolts of individual demonic monads against *Gagtungr*, such as the one mentioned above, are rare, but many revolts are against the demonic administration in general. Such revolts are nothing else other than the return of demonic monads to the Light, and it is clear that assistance of Providential powers are provided them in the amount they need it.

But the insatiable drive toward universal domination comprises the source of the only joys that *Gagtungr* understands. He encounters similar joys at every occasion when the smallest part of any victory seems to him a step forward, approaching his terminal goal. These victories consist in the enslavement of other monads or their souls, the demonic – whether semi-confederate, semi-slave, or bright – to become prisoners and the object of his torture. As much as the *Gagtungr* can envision the cosmic future, he pictures himself as some kind of a sun, around which innumerable monads rotate in a concentric circle, then one after another collapsing into him and being consumed, while gradually the entire universe will arrive at this state of rotation around him, plunging into him, world after world, into a monstrously inflated hyper-monad. But his demonic mentality is powerless to envision any further. The least of these monads are incapable of picturing even such an apotheosis. Due to stable belief in their terminal victory over the universe, they concentrate their will and thought on closer and easier attainable stages.

3. REGARDING THE QUESTION OF THE FREEDOM OF THE WILL

There exists a certain prejudice, a certain special mental condition, which is inherent in our era within a considerable quantity of people, to the extent that over the past 4 decades it was diligently inculcated into the cognizance of many nations. This is a specific train of thought that leads the thinker to a conclusion that sprouts and grows with the course of time into an axiom, into a dogma: that as if religion deprives a person of his freedom, demanding a blind allegiance to higher powers, that places him in total dependence on them. But if they are advertised as only illusions, then in reality the dependence on secular human institutions strengthens those that strive to exploit the ignorance of the masses. This is of what religious enslavement consists, and from which humanity is liberated through science and materialist philosophy.

To debate this deliberation means to compose a complete dissertation that places the refutation of the bases of materialistic philosophy as it goal. Such dissertations are long already composed, and if they are not sufficiently known at this time in Russia, then the reason is in the circumstances that have an attitude not so much toward philosophy, as much as toward politics.

As far as a confirmation is concerned, as if every religion demands subjection to higher powers, there is no doubt that some religious doctrines actually preach predestination and a factual absence of a person's freedom of will: this is a fact, and I least of all am inclined to start defending any religious preferences without my own investigation. However to propagate this illusion, applying it to all religion in its entire validity, is not such a large step in comparison to confirming, for example, that global fictional literature is reactionary due to its inherent nature, but the justification of this depends on the individual reactionary writers and the individual reactionary schools.

I wanted to quickly explain the invalidity of such an accusation in its application to the concept of ROSE OF THE WORLD.

First of all, I permit myself to express my perplexity: there is no science or philosophy of any type, and among them also the materialistic, that does not debate the fact of the dependence of human will on many substantial reasons. Particularly the materialistic philosophy especially insists on a special dependence of the will on factors of an economic series. And nonetheless, no one seems to be annoyed by this humiliation of a person to any natural and historical unavoidable situation. No one wails about a person's enslavement to the law of gravity, the law of the preservation of matter, the law of evolution, the laws of economic development, and etc. All understand that in the framework of these laws there remains sufficient room for expansion for the materialization of our will.

Meanwhile, the genuine concept does not add even one new factor, or a supplement, to the enumerated sum of factors that define our will. The matter is not in their number, but in their interpretation. No matter how immense or infinitely diverse are the items integrated with the expression – higher powers, they have an effect on our will, but not so much by the route of supernatural intervention, as much as with the assistance of those very series, those laws of nature, evolution, etc., which we are conditioned to count as objective facts. These series of facts to an immense degree define our consciousness, and not only consciousness, but also the subconscious and the hyperconscious. Out of these evolve the voice of conscience, responsibility, instinct, and others, which we hear from within ourselves and that define our conduct. Such a mechanism is the tie between the higher powers and our will. True, there sometimes is a place for revelations that subjectively can seem to be a violation of the laws of nature by the higher powers. This is called a miracle. But where such apparitions actually occur, and that do not just seem to be aberrations, any arbitrary violation of natural laws by higher powers does not actually occur, but the display of these powers is through a series of other laws that are still not disclosed to us.

That which in part seems to us to be a monolithic, plain, inseparable mover of our conduct, for example, the conscious, in reality presents itself as a very complex result of various series. Basically the conscience is the voice of our monad. But its access to the sphere of our cognizance is predicated on the effect of other influences: external circumstances, such as some kind of incident that serves as a motivation or impulse in order for us to hear the voice of this monad. This is the display of Providence, the effect of the powers of Providential nature.

In this manner a person's choice is predicated on 3 series of powers: the Providential powers, utilizing the laws of nature and history for their goals, as instruments, and gradually enlightening them; the demonic powers, utilizing the same laws but in a manner to burden the person; and the will of our personal monad, providing voices of the heart and intellect to the periphery of our cognizance with the help of Providential powers.

So, will we consider the laws of nature and history as just mechanical, impersonal unavoidable incidences, or as an instrument of these or other living, personal, spirit entities composed of some other substance? With this in mind, the degree of our freedom does not decrease and does not increase. Subsequently, the degree of freedom of a person's choice from the point of view of the concept of ROSE OF THE WORLD is no less that from the point of view of materialism, but the series that defines its factors are contemplated differently and more precisely discrete.

And if the materialist does not insult the limitation of our freedom due to the completely impersonal and insensitive laws of nature, then how can he humiliate us with the limitation of the freedom of our will due to Providential powers? It is only the demonic powers that can insult the limitation of the freedom of our will. Yes, this will insult, but know that these same powers, these primordial enemies of ours, are restrained, and our entire goal is to reform and restore them. And we will cease to endure this insult only when we become inaccessible to their influence. The evolution of global life leads the series of entities from a minimal level of freedom to expansive forms. (The voice of a monad in the incipient cognizance of a microbe hardly attains to anything, and its conduct is defined for the most part by demonic powers acting through laws of nature as through its instinctive mechanism.) The higher animals already are considerably freer than a microbe, the amplitude of their arbitrary activity is much wider. With a person it grows incomparably.

Opposers of religion such as this [materialist] direct our attention to the requirement of a denial of personal will, requiring a submission of our will to Deity. But they are right with this attitude of some religions of the past. But ROSE OF THE WORLD is not a religious teaching of the past. It is a religious and societal-ethical teaching of the future. ROSE OF THE WORLD does not demand any kind of submission of the will to God's, because what is valuable is that the person attains personal perfection voluntarily, and not compulsively.

The demand for servile subjection of the will to Deity will not echo from the sanctuaries of religious consummation. From it there will emanate a summons toward community love and to the freedom of Divine creativity.

The Lord is an immutable and inexpressible supra-supreme aspiration. He is a spirit-creating authority acting in all souls, not ever ceasing even in the depths of demonic monads and directing worlds and worlds, from the micro-*bramfaturas* to supra-galaxies, for which reason He transcends perfected benevolence, and transcends supreme holiness. The higher the step of each *I*, the more his will coincides with the creative will of the Lord. And when it [the soul], having started its cosmic route with the simplest form of living material, traverses the level of the human, the demiurge of the nations, the demiurge of the planets and stars, the demiurge of galaxies, then through God the Son, it is immersed in the Father and his will fully becomes concurrent and harmonic with the will of the Father, his strength with the strength of the Father, his image with the image of the Father, and his creativity with the creativity of the Father.

Divine creativity is the bright creation of all monads of an ascending stream of the universe, from a person, from the *stikhials* and enlightened animals, to the demiurges of the galaxies, the giants of unimaginable majesty. This is why we so often here incur the word – demiurge, which is hardly utilized in ancient religions. The demiurges are all who create for the glory of God, from love of the world and its primordial Creator.

He is absolutely good.

He is omnipotent, as an ancient theologian ascribed to Him. And if He is omnipotent, then this makes Him answerable for evil and the sufferings of the world, so He is not good. It would seem that it is impossible to exit from the circle of this contradiction.

But the Lord creates out of himself. All the monads that proceed out of His depths are inseparably an essence and quality of this depth, and one of them is absolute freedom. In this manner the divine creativity itself limits the Creator: it defines His omnipotence using this trait, behind which lies greed and the might of His creation. But freedom is freedom because it includes the possibility of diverse choices. And in the existence of many monads, [freedom] is defined by their negative choice, their selfish conceit, their apostasy. Subsequent to this is what we call the evil of the world, subsequent is suffering, subsequent are cruel and merciless laws, and subsequent to this is that these evils and sufferings can be overcome. Laws preserve the world from its conversion into chaos. Even demons are forced to come to account with them so the world would not revert to dust. This is why they do not discard laws, but use them for purposes of oppression. Laws are blind. But they [the demons] can become enlightened, but not in the blink of an eye, not through a miracle, not through some external intervention of Deity, but through a prolonged cosmic route of the apostatized monads exhausting totally and finally annihilating their evil will.

God possesses all-encompassing love and an inexhaustible creative force combined into one. All that lives, and the human is included in this number, approaches God through 3 divine qualities that are inherent to him: freedom, love and divine creativity. Freedom is the condition; love is the route; divine creativity is the goal.

The demonic monads are free, just as all are, but their love is deeply damaged. With them it is directed exclusively inward: the demon loves only himself. And as a result the entire potent storage of love residing in its spirit is concentrated on this one facet: the demon loves himself with such great strength, and it is a love of himself that no human is capable of possessing.

The capability of creativity cannot be discarded by the demonic monads. But divine creativity does not extract anything from them, except some limited animosity. Every demon creates only for his sake and for his own credit.

A human's creativity is transformed into divine-creativity from that minute and in the measure that its overwhelming creative impulse is directed by the effort of his will and belief, and not to attain these or other egoistic goals, such as personal credit, satisfaction, material success, cruel applications, or harmful teaching; but only for a service of God in love.

Particularly 3 words – freedom, love and divine-creativity – define the attitude of ROSE OF THE WORLD to art, science, education, marriage, family, nature and even to all religions having an application to the elements of life, such as its prosperity, structure and beauty.

5. THE DIVERSE MATERIALITY OF A PERSON'S STRUCTURE

Among the numerous levels of *Shadanakar* is a multi-dimensional world where human monads reside – the indivisible and immortal spiritual sole one, the higher *I* of persons. Created by God and only by God, while some, and only a few, are mysteriously born of God, they enter *Shadanakar* clothed in a supra-subtle material, and it would be more correct to call it energy; this is a substance penetrating the entire *Shadanakar*. Every individual spirit entering our *bramfatura* is inevitably clothed with it. The world where our monads reside has the name *Iroln*.

The creative effort leading to the enlightenment of the universe is the task of each monad, except the demonic. (There are no demonic monads among persons.) Human monads materialize this effort in the lower worlds that are subject to their enlightenment creativity, creating their material claddings for themselves, and through these claddings they have an effect on the environment of comparative layers.

First of all the monad creates a *shelt* from matter of five-dimensional space, then an astral body from matter of 4 dimensions. Both of these claddings are often summarized in our understanding under the word – soul. *Shelt* is the material receptacle of the monad with all of its divine qualities and it closest appurtenances. It is not the monad itself that is remaining in the five-dimensional *Iroln*, but it is particularly the *shelt* that manifests as that *I*, which begins it journey through the lower layers. The *shelt* is created by its own monad. It accepts the participation of the great *stikhial* – Mother-Earth – in the creation of its astral body. In the creation of astral bodies, it accepts the participation of all the entities of *Shadanakar* – people, angels, *daimons*, animals, *stikhials*, demons, and even the great hierarchs, but only when the [demons] descend into those layers that are inaccessible to the astral body. This body is the highest instrument of *shelt*. The capabilities of spiritual vision, audio, smell, profound memory, ability to travel, ability to communicate with *sinklits*, *daimons*, *stikhials*, angels, and the ability to feel cosmic panoramas and perspectives, is concentrated in [this body].

Furthermore, the Mother-Earth, productive due to the spirit of the Sun, creates an ethereal body for the incarnated monads: without it, any life at all is impossible in the 3 and 4 dimensional worlds. And when the *shelt* with all of its claddings, including the ethereal, discards its very external, short and temporal, physical body – the final of its receptacles – in *Enrof*, then only a corpse remains in *Enrof*. The physical body is created by angelic hierarchies for our behalf; they create the very material and the great *stikhial* of humanity, the *Leeleet*, which sculptures a series of posterity for this three-dimensional material. The effect of this monad in this activity, and through its *shelt*, consists of it providing individualism to the subject link of the posterity.

So is consummated the process of descent; now begins the process of ascent.

The physical body can accept a monad just once, or over and over, or many times. The ethereal body can be recreated only in case the subject bearer, now fallen under the law of retribution, is compelled to fulfill a course through the cycles of places of great torment. While in the ascending course the ethereal body accompanies the subject bearer through all the worlds of enlightenment until it fully reaches the *zatomises* – the residences of enlightened humanity, the heavenly cities of meta-culture. Such a body is composed of a life-providing substance, not just one that is applied universally, but diverse in all the three-dimensional and four-dimensional worlds. Recollecting the most ancient of revelations of humanity, it would be most correct to call it *arungvilta-prana*.

The astral body accompanies the subject bearer higher, including the *sakuala* of the Supreme Obligation, but it is only the *shelt* that can go higher, since it is enlightened to the end and merged with the monad into a single item. Then the monad discards the *Iroln* and, now clothed entirely with a refined *shelt*, it enters the staircase of the highest worlds of *Shadanakar*.

In subsequent parts of the book, the subject will deal with all of these layers, many of them will be described, to the extent possible. But I am sorry that I am not in a position to expound in more detail on the questions of the mutual activity of these diversely-clothed monads, of the function of each of them, and about their structure.

6. META-CULTURE

The structure of *Shadanakar*, a colossal problematic whose time to pass is very soon, will remain in remembrance in its very basic features, unless it provisionally adapts the essentials of being a supra-nation, and having a meta-culture and trans-myth.

The term – supra-nation, is understood as the collection of nations unified as a common, compatibly created culture, or else as a distinct nation, if its culture was created by it on its own and has attained a high degree of brilliance and individuality.

This means that fully isolated cultures do not exist; all are mutually connected. But each culture is fully individual in its own manner and, disregarding the influence that it may have on another, in its own fullness it remains the legacy of only one supra-nation, the one of its creator.

The understanding of supra-nation cannot necessarily be brought into the present concept if it did not possess, in line with the historical, likewise a meta-historical meaning. But its meta-historical meaning is that the originality of a supra-nation is not limited by its cultural sphere in *Enrof*, but is explained likewise in many layers of other forms of material as an ascending, as well as descending, series. So we must not forget that the supra-nation is understood as the collection not only of those individual characteristics that pertain to it at present, not only our contemporary, but very many of those that pertained to it earlier, even as far back as the dawn of its history, and those in its post-mortem stage that have affected and now affect its trans-physical layer. The supra-nation is tied with all of this.

A staircase of strata rises over humanity, a general one for all supra-nations, but over each of them these strata change their color, their physiognomy, their content. There are such strata that apply distinctly to one super-nation. The issue likewise applies to the demonic worlds of the descending series, existing as if under the supra-nations. In this manner, the significant portion of *Shadanakar* consists of distinct multi-stratified segments. The layer of *Enrof* in each of such segments is occupied only by one supra-nation and its culture. These multi-stratified segments of *Shadanakar* carry the name meta-culture.

Every supra-nation possesses its myth. This myth is created not just in the infantile period of its history, but also at the opposite. And just as the traditional use of the word – myth, does not coincide with that meaning that is applied here, it is necessary to carefully explain the meaning that I have applied to this word.

When we speak of a regimented coordinated system of ideally saturated forms incarnating some type of all-encompassing international teaching, and which found its expression in traditions and culture, in theosophemes and philosophemes, in memorable literature and in sculpture and arts and finally in a moral codex, we speak of the myths of great international religions. Four such myths exist: Hindu, Buddhist, Christian and Islamic.

When we speak of a regimented coordination system of ideally saturated forms defined in their relationship to *Enrof,* to the trans-physical and spirit worlds from the side of one supra-nation of some kind, of a system that overflows into a defined religion, and of a system which plays a very significant role in history of the subject supra-nation, we speak of the national religious myths of distinct supra-nations. Such myths are the following: Egyptian, ancient Iranian, Hebrew, ancient Germanic, Gallic, Aztec, Inca, Japanese and some others.

When we have in view a world of forms that are ideally saturated and likewise perhaps connected, although not very tightly, with the ideas of a religious and moral association, but not arranged with an organized system and just reflecting the general moral, trans-physical, meta-historical or ecumenical truths tied particularly with the obligations and realities of that culture, we have before us a general myth of supra-nations. Such myths are the following: Roman Catholic, German Protestant, Russian [Orthodox].

And finally the last is the 4th group – the general national myths. These are the myths of individual nationalities entering into the compositions of a supra-nation, but having created within itself its private and very local system that is not very regimented and not necessarily identified with any specific religion. As examples the following can be provided: the pagan groups, the Slavic tribes, Finnish tribes, Turkmen tribes, and likewise the myths of certain isolated and disconnected tribes of India. In essence, all of them contain highly developed systems of morality, but otherwise do not possess any acute aspects.

We will not apply the word – myth, as having any other definition in the history of culture.

In this manner the 3 final groups of myths pertain to specific distinct cultures. The first group are the myths of international religions, tied mystically with such strata of *Shadanakar* that lie above its segmented members, called meta-cultures. It seems to me that the understanding of the national-religious myths are acceptable without difficulty. The general myths of the supra-nations need to have a pair of supplementary definitions for clarity. This definition is inductive.

The general myth of the supra-nation is the sum of its concepts regarding the trans-physical cosmos, its participation in its subject culture, and each *I* entering this culture. The concepts that this culture structures is poured into the mold of a cycle of religious-philosophic ideas, a cycle of artistic images, a cycle of societal-ethical understandings, a cycle of government-political institutions and, finally, a cycle of generally national, life-possessing norms that materialize in ceremony, in the daily mundane arrangement of existence, in customs.

But the staircase of the layers of *Shadanakar* do not end where the segments of meta-culture are consummated. Further, five-dimensional and six-dimensional worlds arise, that likewise have received their cloudy reflection in the myths and religions of humanity. In this sense, the appellation of – trans-myth, is applicable to many of these strata. But in a more narrow and more higher sense the word – trans-myth, is applied to a special *sakuala*: the system of worlds with five-dimensional space and with an immense number of time coordinates. These are the 5 grandiose, beautiful and transparent pyramids, as though shining from the inside and out with sun-like brilliance, and which are hanging perfectly over *Enrof.* Not only *Enrof,* from there but the heavenly regions of meta-culture also seem to be profoundly low, in the dusk. These worlds are the higher aspects of the 3 (and not 4) great international religions, and the 2 religions that are almost annihilated due to their national isolation as a result of a series of historical reasons, but they still possess remnants of their earlier brilliance.[37]

---

[37] The pyramids are further described in the text.

BOOK III

Structure of *Shadanakar.*
Worlds of the Ascending Series

Chapter 1

The *Sakuala* of Enlightenment

I do not know where and when I will die this time, but I know where and when I died the previous occasion before I was born in 1906 for a life in Russia. Of course, this knowledge does not have common significance and can only interest those who are capable of bearing it with trust in my witness and who in the process feel a karmic connection with my destiny. But my knowledge of certain stages of the route between my previous existence and the progressing, based on my objective interest, is wider. I can and must explain of their existence from what I was able to gradually remember. Nonetheless, it is better not to say what I was able, but instead, what they helped me remember.

I often met people who possess the same type of a profound revelatory memory, but not one of them decided to speak about this. Even a vague thought of any attempts to impress these recollections into a written form has not even materialized with any of these people. Their guilt for not doing this was the conviction that this would only summon ridicule once people understood what was being related, and subsequently causing them psychological embarrassment, and prejudice from people they do not even know, and there is no way to actually prove any of it.

For a long while I looked at the matter in the same way, and yes, even now I pursue a similar attempt, but not without some hesitation. But all that I narrate in this book, categorically all of it, has just as much a source that is unsubstantiated, so I do not see any more of a basis to be silent particularly of the revelations of my profound memory. Either I should not start this book at all, or else, once starting it, I have to speak of everything, and disregard fear of repercussions. What strengthens me is my hope that the readers not believing me will discard my book after the first few chapters, but just those people who have an acclimated inclination toward my exposition will pursue it further.

My previous death occurred about 300 years ago in a country that had another type of meta-culture at its head, one very ancient and mighty. My entire present life, from earliest childhood, wearies me with homesickness, a lonesomeness for this ancient homeland. Maybe, it is so consuming and deep because I lived not just one life in this country, but 2, and therein very satisfied ones. But departing from *Enrof* 300 years ago, during my entire route through *Shadanakar*, initially I felt liberated from a destiny of any redeeming post-mortem descents into the depths of these strata where places of torture unfold, lasting sometimes entire centuries or even millennia, where those confined deal with the karmic knots with which they tied themselves during life. Initially I was able to untie these knots while still in *Enrof*, with prolonged torments and bitter deprivations atoning for those crimes and errors I committed while a young man. And so the first time I died with an unburdened soul, although from a religious point of view this country was truly fated to await a post-mortem horror. But I already knew that due to my exclusion from the caste system and my 40-year life among the outcasts, I was able to redeem all. Death was easy and full of hope.

This was my declared hope and such did not deceive me. Regarding the first hours, even regarding the first few days of my new existence, I was not allowed to remember, even to this time I cannot. But however, I remember a few localities of that new stratum where subsequently I resided for a long while.

There is one meta-culture for everyone. This stratum, however, is very diversified. In the ancient tropical, immense meta-culture, which twice enveloped my life, it was similar to its nature in *Enrof*, but softer, without the extremes of its cruelty and majesty, and without raging tropical rains and devastating arid deserts. I remember how the white towering clouds, in extraordinarily powerful and triumphant forms, hung almost motionless over the horizon, billowing up to the apex of the sky. Nights and days rotated, and all these gigantic radiant towers stood high over the land, hardly changing their features. But the sky itself was not blue or light-blue, but a green-blue. And the sun there was more beautiful than the one we have. It was as if it played with various colors, slowly and waveringly changing them, and now I am not able to explain why the light from this origin of coloration did not cause the same color on the objects upon which it shined. The landscape remained almost the same, but the prominent colors were green, white and gold.

There were rivers and lakes. There was an ocean, although I did not have the chance to see it. Once or twice I did stand on the shore of a sea. There were mountains, forests, and open ranges that reminded me of our steppes. But the growth of these zones was almost transparent and so light, just like the forests in the northern regions of *Enrof* during late spring, when leaves just begin to cover them. The crests of the mountain ranges, and even their slopes, seemed to be just as tranquil and semi-transparent, as if all of this was the ethereal flesh of those elements that composes the physical body we know well in *Enrof*.

But birds and fishes and animals were not aware of this stratum. People remained as its sole inhabitants. When I say people, I refer not to that type which is just like ourselves residing in *Enrof,* but the type that we will become after death in the first of the worlds of Enlightenment. Finally, I was then assured that the comfort which we absorb into our thoughts from old religions regarding meeting our close ones – is not legend and not a deception, as long as what we do in life does not draw us into the bitter regions of redemption. Some close friends met me, and the joy of association with them again became the content of entire periods of my life in that stratum.

It is very ancient, even when angels resided there long ago, before the creation of humanity, and it is called *Olirna.* This musical word seems to me an appropriate appellation, and with credit to those who named it. Association with close friends did not consist of any kind of discredit, bitterness, trivial worries or misunderstandings, as we would defile this here. This was an ideal relationship, in part due to our conversation, but for the most part in silence, which is characteristic here with association with the few with whom we were united, and especially if it was a profound love, and especially in profound minutes.

In *Enrof* we were completely free of any worries regarding sustaining our existence, this had such a negligible effect. Because the weather was not always the best, we still needed shelter but only the minimum. It seemed to be this way in *Olirna,* but not necessarily in other meta-cultures, but I do not remember in detail. The most beautiful of plants was our food, and we drank directly from springs and streams, and they each had a unique flavor, if I remember correctly. Clothes in *Enrof* were beautiful, vivid, a light gray but still radiant, sewn out of wool, silk or linen, and it seems that our body actually created its own clothes, but it is an ethereal body that we here will not even recognize. But in the worlds of Enlightenment and in *Enrof,* life cannot exist without such a body.

As for me, all of the initial time spent in *Olirna* was saturated with worry over those still remaining in *Enrof.* I left behind children and grandchildren, and the old lady – my wife there, and all of my valuable possessions, for which I violated the laws of the caste system and became an untouchable. This severance from them contributed to my constant alarm of their fate. Soon I learned to see them as cloudy figures wandering through thorny trails of *Enrof.* And then after some time passed, I finally met my wife again, and she was just as young as she was early on, but more beautiful. Her journey in *Enrof* was consummated several years after mine, and now the joy of our meeting was not clouded in any manner.

New methods of revelation and senses for perception opened one after another within me. Not those senses of sight and audio, which in the ethereal body completely coincide with their relative organs of the physical body. No! These senses of sight and audio acted from the first minutes of my residency in *Olirna*, and it was particularly due to them that I was able to perceive *Olirna*. But that which we call spiritual vision, spiritual audio and profound memory; that which majestic sages strive to unveil in *Enrof,* that which is revealed there but just by a few among the many millions – is that which in *Olirna* is revealed gradually to each person. Spirit vision and audio destroy the barricades between many strata. The lives of those whom I left behind on Earth, I perceived particularly through these new senses, but not distinctly, but I still perceived them.

I was much consoled by the flowering nature; I had not seen in *Enrof* such beauty before my eyes even. But it is strange that I did not lack anything in such a nature, and soon I realized why: it was the diversity of life. Sorrowfully I remembered the singing and chirping of birds, the buzz of insects, the wave of fish, the beautiful forms and unconscious sagacity of the higher animals. Only here was there explained to me how much our association with nature, the animal world, means for us. However, those who knew more than I, impressed on me hope, that the ancient, nebulous fantasy of humanity about the existence of strata where animals become educated and highly intelligent is not a fantasy, but a premonition of truth. Such strata exist, and in time I will enter them.

Later on, and actually very recently, they reminded me of certain zones in *Olirna* that possess all the meta-cultures. They spoke of regions that were similar to rolling steppes. Those in *Enrof* who were excessively conceited or vain, whose karmic bundles were untied, but whose soul was narrow and tight, are located here for some interval. Now among the transparent quiet hills, under a majestic sky, nothing interferes with them restoring the damage done; they accept and absorb the rays and voice of the cosmos and moving the boundaries of their expanding *I.* They also spoke of the zones of *Olirna* similar to mountainous regions. There in the valleys labor those who could believe, but only after death, and they sense this here. From the valleys they gaze at the mountain summits, but not in the manner that we see them, but in a spiritual glory. The omnipotent spirits that reign there pour their strengths into streams of contemplation. And the capability of the soul paralyzed with unbelief is opened there, during the days and years of a direct view and vision of the complexity and diversity of the universe and the triumphant majesty of other worlds. But so much of this I do not remember so distinctly and perhaps because I was just a visitor there, but this information is accurate to the extent that I understood it, and subsequently it is reliable.

Other than association with people and enjoyment of nature, time passed at work on my own body: the necessity is to prepare it for transformation, because the route from *Olirna* into the next, the higher world, lies not through death, but through transfiguration. And I understood that the verses of the Gospel that narrate about the ascension of Jesus Christ somewhat allude to this event. The resurrection from death changed the nature of His physical body, and with the ascension from *Olirna* it will transfigure a second time together with the ethereal body.

Ahead of me, as for all the remaining, awaits the transfiguration of just the ethereal body. A transfiguration similar to what, at some time in the past, the apostles saw with their personal vision when they penetrated into the *Olirna,* but they did not attain penetrating the worlds that hang higher. Otherwise how could the evangelists express the transfer of the Savior from *Olirna* there, except to just call this event His ascension to heaven? And I, raised in an austere Brahmanism, began to remember how the Christian myth, so unfathomably full of truth, astonished me.

And the figure of the great traitor,[38] which for a long while I accepted as just a legend, became for me a reality. I discovered that he now resides here in solitary isolation, on a deserted island in the middle of seas of *Olirna*. Initially he was discarded downward by the burden of his karma, and one unrepeatable due to its severity, and the worst of any crime committed any earlier or any later. This traversal through places of torment prolonged over 16 centuries. Not having seen any person this entire interval, he was finally raised from there by the One whom he betrayed on earth, but only after the One who was betrayed attained such incredible spirit power after his death, and which was so needed for this event, and which no one else was able to attain any earlier in *Shadanakar*. Raised by the powers of light higher and higher traversing the stages of purgatory, he was able to redeem his betrayal and finally attained *Olirna*. Not yet associating with its residents, he prepares himself on this island for further ascension.

I saw this island from a distance. It is rough. Within it are gorges with steep and frightening cliffs, whose summits are all inclined in one direction. The summits are sharp. The color of the cliffs are very dark and black in between. But no one in *Olirna* sees Judas at all. His prayer at nights, emanating from the island, is all they know about him. In the future, when the kingdom of the one who is called antichrist is established in *Enrof*, then Judas will accept a great mission from the hand of the One he betrayed. He will again be born on earth and will fulfill it and suffer martyrdom in the end at the hands of the prince of Darkness.

But to explain by what specific efforts my personal transformation was attained and what individually consummated at this very moment with my body, I am not able. Now I have the strength to recollect only what occurred at that time before my eyes: a large assembly of people, maybe a

---

[38] Judas Iscariot

hundred, arrived to accompany me to this high route. For someone from among those living in *Olirna* to attain transformation is always joyful for that person and for others.

This event is surrounded by celebration and festivity and a happy mood. Apparently the event occurred during the day, at what appeared to be the top of a hill and, as always in *Olirna*, under the open sky. I remember how rows of human faces turned toward me started to little by little fade and then as though fade completely into the distance. But in reality, what was actually seen, was me departing from them as I rose over the ground. In the distance, along the horizon, I saw and to this moment a semi-transparent mountain ridge, as though constructed from chrysolite. Then I noticed that the mountains began to radiate an amazing glow. Shaking rainbows collapsed, crumbling along the sunset. From the dusk, marvelous lights of various colors emanated, and the brilliant majesty of sun could not over-shine them. I remember the feeling of encompassing beauty, an ecstasy and amazement incomparable with anything. When my gaze was directed downward, I noticed that the crowds that accompanied me were not there, the entire landscape was transfigured entirely, and I understood that the moment of my transfer into the higher stratum was accomplished.

I was informed ahead of time that my stay in this stratum would be very short, because all those passing through it do so in a few hours, but during these hours this entire stratum – and its appellation is *Fayir* – will be consumed with joy over me having attained it. This was a great celebration prepared for every ascending soul, but not for just human souls, but for the souls of other monads of *Shadanakar* that rose through the stages of Enlightenment, and even the higher animals.

In its popular meaning, *Fayir* is the limit of the route. Beyond it they can consummate an incarnation in *Enrof,* but only with an assigned mission. In the future however, apostasy and rebellion is not excluded, even premeditated betrayal of God or treachery is not excluded, but never will blind dissent be possible. What will be excluded forever and ever from the number of possibilities is that paralysis of spiritual understanding that appeared in the psyche of the living and changed its variations, shades of color, and names during diverse ages of *Enrof.*

I saw a crowd of entities and their twins and triplets of illuminated figures. They appeared here from much higher strata, moved by the feeling of mutual joy. The feeling of mutual joy is a quality of the enlightened but possessing incomparably greater measure and strength than ours. Every soul attaining *Fayir* births this festive feeling, the same that millions already possessed that passed through earlier. How can I express the state that enveloped me when I saw assemblies of the enlightened in festive celebration when I, a nobody, attained this world? It was not just a gratitude, not just a joyful motivation, not just an agitation, but it would be sooner similar to a bliss-filled upheaval when the dead in *Enrof* devote themselves to unrestrained and soundless tears.

I do not remember the minute and form of my transfer into the succeeding stratum. The incredible encounter of *Fayir* summons a profound exhaustion and as though a softening of all the textures of the soul. And all that I can here reassemble from what I encountered in the succeeding station of the ascent can be reduced to being in one state that seemed to last a very long time, perhaps even entire years.

It contained a bright radiant tranquility, with an abundance of light as we will have, the topic of activity arises, not about rest, but about movement, and not about calm. But we do have this in *Enrof.* But it is not this way everywhere. Even the very word – bright radiant – is not as precise as it should be. Because the shine of *Nertis* is radiant and at the same time it is inexpressibly soft, the glamorous gentleness of our nights with a full moon is here united with the shining easiness of the high autumn skies. If we could compare ourselves to a child being rocked on his mother's knees after many months full of insults, suffering and undeserved bitterness. This female cordiality is spread throughout, even into the atmosphere, but with special warmth it radiated from those who surrounded me, like a caring feeling with inexhaustible love for the sick and weak. So was the state of those who entered before me into the higher strata and those who descended from there into *Nertis*, to those, as myself, whose purpose is to install cordiality, love and happiness.

Nertis is the country of great rest. Unnoticeably and insensitively, without any effort from my side, except the pinnacle of the work of my heart, my ethereal body slowly changed here, becoming all the lighter, penetrated by spirit and more obedient to my wants. This is our type of body that will appear in the *zatomis*, the heavenly countries of meta-culture and particularly occurring in *Nertis*. And if I was able to see one of my close associates remaining in *Enrof*, he would understand that this is *I*. He would grasp the unexplainable similarity of the new figure with the one with which he was familiar in the past, but he would be shaken to the depths of his heart with the other-worldly brightness of the transfiguration.

What is preserved from the past? Features of the face? Yes, but now they eternally shine, with an extra-terrestrial youthfulness. Senses of the body? Yes, but on the sideburns 2 soft-blue flowers will shine, which are the organs of spiritual audio. The forehead seems to be decorated with a magic, shining jewel, which is the organ of spiritual vision. The organ of profound memory that is located in the brain will remain invisible. So these changes were invisible, and occurring within the inner organs of the body, because all the senses created earlier for the tasks of nourishment and education were abolished or else changed at the root, and made capable for new tasks. Nourishment now became a process similar to breathing, and the supplement of corporeal strength was accomplished on account of the adaptation of the bright emanations of the *stikhials*. Reproduction, as we understand it, does not exist in any of the worlds of the ascending series. There exists another manner, and I will describe it when I reach the chapter on the heavenly Russia.

Over the course of a long time I began to perceive all that was residing in me, a joyful growth of strength, as though releasing my hidden and long-awaited wings. It is not necessary to understand me excessively literally. The topic is not about unfolding something that would remind you of wings on some flying creature of *Enrof*, but of the emergence of the ability to have an unhindered movement in all directions of four-dimensional space. The following was also a possibility for me: the immobility I had previously also calmed me, but the possibility of flight transformed my nebulous fantasy into something concrete, new perspectives that were now revealed to me.

From the friends of my heart I discovered that my residence in *Nertis* was nearing its conclusion. It seemed to me something similar to a cradle, and as if I was resting in it and it was slowly rocking up and down, but with each motion it seemed to be ascending higher. This movement generated a taste of even greater happiness, and into which I must now enter. And I understood that I now was located in another stratum – in *Gotimna*, the final of the worlds of the *sakuala* of Enlightenment.

In *Gotimna* there were as though colossal flowers, but their size did not deprive them of surprising softness, and inside of their pedals were 9 more flowers. I did notice the construction of 2 of them: one was a sky-blue color, while the other had a gold tint. These immense flowers of *Gotimna*, and there were entire forests of them, would bend down and then back up, rock back and forth, with a sound of an undefined rhythm, and their oscillation causing the softest of music, one never fatiguing and always peaceful, like the sound of a breeze through a forest, but filled with a saturation of meaning, warm love and the inclusive participation of each of those living there.

With easiness and calmness we moved about, and in a manner not even comprehendible of any entity in *Enrof*, as if swimming in any of the 4 directions of space between these singing flowers, or slowing down and conversing with them, because their language was now understandable to us and they understood us. Here on these sky-blue fields or under immense, quietly sparkling golden pedals, those who entered *Gotimna* from the *zatomises* visited us, and in order to prepare us, their younger brethren, to enter the succeeding station of our route.

Gotimna is called the garden of supreme destinies, because here the destinies of souls are foreordained. In front of me is a junction of paths: it appears to every person who enters this stratum. Once the selection is made it is impossible to change the long centuries that will be spent in one of the many worlds that are here chosen. I could freely select one of the 2: either an ascent into the heavenly India, the end forever of the route of reincarnations, and its exchange for the route of an ascending transfiguration traversing strata of a different form of matter; or else the other one, which also consists of several that exist in *Enrof*, but not as the result of bundled karma, since it was unbundled, but as a means of materializing the tasks to which only I was assigned, and with which I was entrusted, and which I freely accepted.

And although the word – mission, in the Russian language echoes of scholasticism and is deprived of poetics, I will utilize it as I proceed further to denote specific tasks to be accomplished in *Enrof* and which are entrusted to distinct souls. The difficulty of the responsibility is that whoever accepts the mission grows a number of times, since the mission is always connected, not only with the destiny of its executor, but also with the destiny of very many souls, with a destiny applying to those before life and after death, and often with the destiny of entire nations and the entirety of humanity. So whoever abandons his mission deliberately or as the result of weakness or lethargy, awaits a retribution and redemption in the deepest and frightening of strata. This does not mean that the person who traverses the *sakuala* of Enlightenment is incapable of any further fall, betrayal, or a moral backslide on earth. What is impossible is only a blind failure based on lack of knowledge of the existence of God. But if the executor of the mission becomes a soul slumbering at the bottom, under rays of *Nertis* and *Gotimna*, he can be awakened at the darkness of night of *Enrof*, and will be led to the side or downward. If such disappointments do not affect the essence of his mission, Providential powers will raise him from any collapse, so the mission will somehow or other be accomplished.

Revealed in front of me was the opportunity to withdraw backwards, to the region of another meta-culture that was to this point unknown and alien to me, still relatively young, but with an immense future. Something rather agitating, turbulent, gloomy, emanated from this immense, multi-layered mass, nebulously accepting or pulling me from a distance. The assignment that I accepted was supposed to have a relationship to the great task evolving far beyond the boundaries of this meta-culture and with the responsibility in the distant future to encompass the world. Already, thousands of souls were in preparation for participation in this task.

So I selected this opportunity in particular. I now understood that I placed upon my shoulders this burden, and which would be prohibitive for me to discard. So from the *Gotimna* of India I was transferred to the *Gotimna* of Russia. There I was supposed to finish preparing for the execution of my mission, which my *I* accepted from above. But withdrawals, acts of rebellion and betrayals were still possible even after my bright lives, because even then the soul that falls asleep can awaken in the light of the sun. I noticed such withdrawals during my own route long after *Gotimna*. However the opportunity to throw light on this will occur in other chapters of this book. Now is the time to discuss the *zatomises*, the heavenly countries of the meta-culture.

CHAPTER 2

THE *ZATOMIS*

The pinnacles of meta-culture, called *zatomises*, to a certain degree are coincident with geographic contours of relative cultural zones of *Enrof.* The space of all *zatomises* are 4 dimensional, but each of them is distinctively individual due to the number of time dimensions that are specific to it. The material structure of this *sakuala* is created by one of the angelic hierarchs – one of the Monarchs. The *zatomises* themselves are slowly assembled through the compatible powers of the hierarchs, heroes, geniuses, saints and people of periphery, capable of handling the creativity of national populations, until the supra-nation that they are constructing is independently installed in history. And later when its historical route is consummated the millions of its immortal monads continue their ascent from one height of global comprehension and creativity to another.

The founder of each of the *zatomises* will be one of the great person-spirits.

The panorama of these strata brings to mind our own nature, but from a great distance. Rather, the sky with its clouds seems to be closest of all to the landscape of the *zatomises*. Zones are integral with the location of our oceans and seas, as if bright dense fogs, easily penetrating and shining. These are the souls of the sea *stikhials*. The rivers of *Enrof* are in direct relationship to their souls, with a formation of inexpressible beauty, and to describe them as shining fogs is insufficient. Their plant life is little similar to ours, but these are the souls of the *stikhials*, of which we will speak later. While on this topic, I feel I need to mention that the souls of some of the *stikhials* that are between incarnations are residing in the *zatomises*.

The higher humanity – the *sinklit* of the meta-cultures – is our hope, our joy, support and reliance. People of integrity, some sages and heroes enter here immediately after their death in *Enrof*, quickly traversing the worlds of Enlightenment. We have no reliable history of the suppressed majority of souls: they migrate into the population of nations, not leaving behind a trace in any chronicles, or traditions, except in the memory of those who knew them or heard of them from living witnesses. These are inconspicuous heroes of our life. To think otherwise, that is, to imagine the *sinklit* of meta-cultures in view of some assembly of famous figures would significantly prove that our morally-mystical mentality still sleeps a deep sleep.

Others, especially those who possess special gifts, even those who fall after death into the depths of purgatories, rise from there by the powers of Light, their term shortened due to their redeeming purification, and then they enter the *sinklit*.

Not only some of the artistic geniuses, but still more of the sages and heroes, and people of integrity – all have their karmic bundles untied in *Enrof*, where they redeem the burden of their crimes, and death widely opened the gates for their entrance into the *zatomises*.

Death encountered others when they were unprepared for the higher stages, yet still heavily burdened. They have the obligation to right from the beginning traverse the series of stages to the highest purgatories, highest meaning – relative to the horrible sphere of magma and the center of the earth, but the lower are relative to ourselves on the surface.[39] Many thousands of such souls having finally attained *Gotimna*, do not select new descents into *Enrof*, but work and struggle in the fraternities of the *zatomises*.

A 3rd group did not burden their souls in *Enrof* with any type of falls, but on the contrary. Although all of their periphery, the expanse of their knowledge, their cosmic awareness, grew after *Olirna*, they are still insufficiently enough. The route from *Olirna* signified for them the beginning of a journey, often a long one, and even prolonged perhaps for centuries, until they finally become capable of observing the tasks and wisdom of *Sinklit*. As a result, such souls do not redeem themselves between the final death in *Enrof* and entrance into *Sinklit*, but they only expand and enrich themselves.

The route of reincarnation in general is not an ecumenical law, but the vast majority of the portion of monads move nevertheless following this route. They already experienced a series of births in other nations of *Enrof*, in other meta-cultures, even in other millennia and in other ends of the world, and many traversed their route up to the human cycle in other realms of *Shadanakar*. Their *shelts* endure perhaps even longer then the substance of the plant and animal kingdoms. Others knew about

---

[39] The higher the purgatory the closer to the center of Earth; the lower the purgatory the closer to the surface of Earth.

the incarnation of the titans in humanity during prehistoric times, among the pre-angelic entities or the *daimons*. The recollection of this garland of birth is preserved in their profound memory, and the volume of the spiritual personality of such monads is especially great, their ability to retain memory is far reaching, their future wisdom is distinguished by its special width. The bearers of the higher gifts of artistic genius – to which several chapters in another part of this book is dedicated – all possess a similar garland of incarnation behind themselves. And also the opposite: the people of integrity of the Christian meta-cultures, in contradistinction to the people of integrity of certain eastern meta-cultures, know, and the majority anyway, another route of ascent: the route leading into *Enrof* occurred just once, but the result of journeying through other strata of such higher worlds that unfold in front of them, the memory of this burns in their souls like a star, and its rays – during their sole life in *Enrof* – untangles all the snares of darkness in their heart.

The activity of the *Sinklits* are considerably diverse and so wide that it is far beyond our vision, and for most of us it is just incomprehensible. I can direct our attention to 3 of its facets: assistance, creativity, struggle.

Assistance is toward all who have not yet attained *zatomis*. Angels of gloom, the superintendents of purgatories, would not release their sacrifices, not for more centuries and centuries if it were not for the incessant efforts of the *Sinklits*. The magmas and terrifying worlds of the earth's core would retain the sufferers in their entirety until the 3rd global period (at the present we are approaching the end of just the first period). Those residing in *Enrof* would be surrounded by almost an impenetrable shield of spirit-darkness if it were not for the *Sinklits*.

The other facet is the creation of independent [artistic] treasures, whose significance will never perish. However, spending time viewing the *Sinklits'* creations and attempting to understand it should be at a minimum as far as we are concerned.

The 3rd facet of activity of the *Sinklits* is somewhat more understandable: their struggle against the demonic powers. We can say that their struggle is occurring corporeally, but of course, their weapons are just not able to actually collide with the weapons of *Enrof,* because their composition are of a different category. They depend on the perfection of mastering their personal abilities in order to resist those to whom they are directed. However his general principle of warfare is characterized by this volitional concentration of emanations that paralyze the enemy. It is impossible for the brethren of *Sinklit* to undergo any catastrophe in war. But the 2nd is possible: in case of [the enemy's] defeat, this will result in their prolonged captivity in demonic fortresses.

The landscapes of the *zatomises* are arranged in a manner that is barely similar to ours, and especially because residences as we know them, do not exist there. Certain institutions have assigned a special purpose, and they are for the most part utilized for the communication of the brethren of the *sinklit* with other worlds and with the spirits of other hierarchs. The buildings where association occurs in its highest forms with the monads of the *stikhials* are called *sheritals*. The brethren of the *Sinklits* can descend into the worlds of the descending series entirely to the magma and rise to exceedingly high strata that are designated as the Higher Aspects of the Trans-Myths of Global Religions.

In each *zatomis* a transformed language dominates that is compatible with the country of *Enrof,* and one that is not just spoken, but a language communicable via light. It would not be improper to apply to this language the concept of a vocabulary. But I need to mention that the vocabulary is considerably different than ours and is relative to something else, comparatively more wealthy in its storage of comprehension.

Alongside these languages of the meta-cultures there exists a language common to all strata, entities and hierarchies, and is derived from them. The speed and easiness of learning different languages here at the present is incompatible to the means of this process in *Enrof.* This occurs without any effort at all and on its own. The common language adopted by the *zatomises* is called the language of the *Sinklit* of the World, but this is not entirely precise: the *Sinklit* of the World, which was earlier addressed, knows such forms of communication that have absolutely nothing in common in any manner with any vocal language. But the brethren of the *Sinklit* of the World, descending from their heights to the *zatomises* of the meta-cultures, arranged the creation of a sole language of the *zatomises*, and only this language is tied with their assignment.

Among the *zatomises*, there reside other entities other than the *Sinklits*: future angels. These are the most miraculous of all the creation of God, and if we remember the sirins and alkonosts of our [Russian] folklore, we can approach a representation of those creatures that decorate life in the *zatomises* of Byzantium and Russia; a representation of the entities that are to become sun-emitting archangels. Different entities reside in other *zatomises*, and which are no less beautiful.

I have now reached the point of numbering the *zatomises*. There are 12.

Mayif – is the most ancient of the *zatomises*. It is the heavenly country and *sinklit* of the Atlantic meta-culture. It existed in *Enrof* approximately from the 20th to the 9th millennia B.C.

Leenat – is the *zatomis* of what is called Gondwana. We need to understand that this appellation does not refer to the prehistoric and ancient continent that resided in the Indian Ocean, but the meta-culture that had its centers in Java, Sumatra, southern Hindustan, and some cities that now lay at the bottom of the ocean. The era of the existence of the Gondwana culture was over 6 millennia B.C.

Ialu or *Atkheam* – is the *zatomis* of the ancient Egyptian meta-culture. It eclipsed the Atlantic with its scale and majesty. This culture created an immense *sinklit* and blinding *zatomis* during the terms of its historical existence.

Eyanna – is the *zatomis* of the ancient Babylonian-Assyrian-Canaanite meta-culture, apparently during the 4th millennium B.C.

Shan-Ti – is the *zatomis* of the Chinese meta-culture existing in *Enrof* from 2nd millennium B.C. Its significance increased when Confucius created his immemorial moral codex and raised the moral level of the nation.

Sumera or *Meru* – (I do not know which of the names is the more correct.) is the *zatomis* of the Indian meta-culture, the most omnipotent of all the *zatomises* of *Shadanakar*. In ancient mythology the summit of Mt Sumera was crowned as the city of Brahma, and on its slopes cities dedicated to other deities of Hinduism were dedicated, but the heavenly India was not limited by their number, and at the present encompasses an area far greater than the geographical India.

Zervan – is the *zatomis* of the ancient Iranian meta-culture including Zoroastrianism. Their monotheism is not precisely defined, nevertheless it is a religion of high moral and ethical standards.

Olymp – is the *zatomis* of the ancient Greek and Roman meta-cultures.

Nikhord – is the *zatomis* of the Hebrew meta-culture, but the lower stratum of the *sinklit* of Israel. The founder of *Nikhord* was the great person-spirit Abraham.

Rai (Paradise) – is the conditional appellation of the *zatomis* of the Byzantine meta-culture. It is similar to the balance of *zatomises* of the Christian meta-culture, and this is one of the ladders that leads from various side to the supreme and highest world called the heavenly Jerusalem. It is nothing other than the Supreme Aspect of the Christian Trans-Myth. Paradise is an ancient and powerful stratum, and exists to some extent in Russia. It founder was the great person-spirit who resided in *Enrof,* John the Baptizer.

Eden – is the conditional appellation of the *zatomis* of the Roman Catholic meta-culture, one of the ladders that leads to the heavenly Jerusalem. Several other nations also belong to this meta-culture although they have different ethic roots, such as the

Poles, Hungarians, Czechs, Irish and Serbian. The founder of Eden is the great person-spirit who resided in *Enrof*, the apostle Peter.

Monsalvat – is the *zatomis* of the meta-culture of western and northern Europe, North America, and likewise Australia and some parts of Africa. It is geographically the largest of the *zatomises* and contains the most members.

Zhunfleiya – is the *zatomis* of the Ethiopian meta-culture, which two thousand years materialized its existence in exceptionally bad historical and geographic conditions, as a fragment of Christianity between two hostile oceans – Islam and the primitive pagan Negro tribes. This meta-culture was unable to achieve even one-tenth of its potential.

Dzhannet – is the *zatomis* of the Mohammedan meta-culture. Islam is unique from all the other religions of the world because the Supreme Aspect of Trans-myth is absent from it, meaning in the very highest of the *sakualas* there is no world that is particularly connected with Islam.

Sukkhavati – is the western paradise of Amitabha Buddha. This is the meta-culture connected with northern Buddhism which is called Mahayana. It dominates in Tibet and Mongolia, while in Japan and China it coexists with *Shan-Ti* and with the national Japanese *zatomis Nikisaka*.

Aireng-Dalyahu – is the most marvelous *zatomis* that is still little known among us in Russia – the Indo-Malayan meta-culture. It separated from the meta-culture of Indian about the 5th century, and encompassed the Brahman and Buddhist kingdoms of Java, Indo-China and Ceylon.

The *zatomis* of the Negro meta-culture. Sadly, I know almost nothing about it and not even its name. What is known is that it is relatively young and still very weak. After the suppression of the Sudanese culture and its religion, the Negroes for a long while lost the possibility of the resurrection of their meta-culture.

Arimoiya – is the future *zatomis* of the general meta-culture connected with the appearance and reign of the future inter-religious ROSE OF THE WORLD. The materiality of *Arimoiya*, as with other *zatomises*, is created by one of the Angelic hierarchies

– the Dominions. The great person-spirit that was incarnated on Earth as Zoroaster is the guide of its development and whom I decide to conditionally designate with the expression of – great architect.

The Heavenly Russia or Holy Russ is connected with the geography of the three-dimensional stratum that approximately coincides with the area of our country. As far as I know the number general population that now resides in the heavenly Kremlin is about half-a-million.

Now I need to briefly list the 15 *zatomises* of this second *sakuala*.

Nambata – is the *zatomis* of the Ancient Sudanese meta-culture. It developed under bad conditions and extremely slow, or to say this better, it smoldered in the valley of Niger, in the region of lakes Chad and Kordofan from the 9th to the 5th millennia B.C.

Tzen-Tin – is the *zatomis* of the pra-Mongolian meta-culture. It is pra-Mongolian not in the ethno-graphic sense, but in the territorial. Its population belongs to the yellow race, but anthropologically, and even spiritually, it is closer to the nation of Gondwana than to later Mongolia. It settled in northern China and the Amur region in the 4th and 3rd millennia B.C.

Pred – is the *zatomis* of the Dravidian meta-culture. It carries this appellation conditionally since nationalities of various ethnic roots became part of it, and in some respects it is close to the *Sumera*.

Asgard, or often incorrectly called by its more popular appellation of *Valgalla* – is the *zatomis* of the Ancient German meta-culture, and which had a growth parallel with the historical stratum of Christianity. Its catastrophic end occurred in the 20th century.

Tokka – is the *zatomis* of the ancient Peruvian, meaning pre-Inca, meta-culture, that historically developed in the centuries just prior and after Christ.

Bon – is the *zatomis* of the ancient Tibetan culture that was destroyed by Buddhism, although some of its elements organically migrated into the culture of Mahayana.

Gaouripur – is the *zatomis* of the small Himalayan meta-culture that very early separated from India, but with great possibilities. It was particularly here that at one time the brightest centers of Buddhism flared. Here in the bosom of this teaching those meta-historical processes flowed and which created out of it this religion in its fullest meaning: a teaching that was not just moral, but also trans-physical and spiritual.

Yunkif – is the *zatomis* of the Mongolian meta-culture and which immediately became the spoils of an unusually potent *yuitzraor*. Its catastrophe occurred in the 13th century.

Ieroo – is the *zatomis* of the ancient Australian meta-culture, and which has existed in complete isolation from the balance of humanity in central Australia for 2,000 years. Eventually the society declined into a slave state. The meta-culture perished as a result of the extreme activity of demonic *stikhials* – the spirits of the desert and impassible overgrowth of brush.

Taltnom – is the *zatomis* of the Toltec-Aztec meta-culture.

Kertu – is the *zatomis* of the Yucatan-Mayan meta-culture.

Intil – is the *zatomis* of the Inca meta-culture, and whose destruction in *Enrof* saved the world from greater dangers, as strange as this may seem.

Daffam – is the *zatomis* of the [American] Indian meta-culture that resided in the region of the Great Lakes.

Lea – is the *zatomis* of the Polynesian meta-culture that perished as a result of its extreme geographical dispersion. Some remnants still molder in the Hawaiian and Tahitian and other archipelagoes.

Nikisaka – is the *zatomis* of the Japanese meta-culture and which was seriously wounded twice: by Buddhism and then by the European culture, and as a result was not able to achieve its potential. Shinto is essentially the religion of *Nikisaka*, the Japanese *sinklit*.

Chapter 3

The Middle Strata of *Shadanakar*

Before attempting to draw a picture of the panorama of demonic *sakualas* that possess such a colossal significance for the trans-physical and meta-history of *Shadanakar*, and likewise the *sakuala* of the *stikhials*, some of which with demonic principles are tightly connected, it is expedient to provide an understanding of several *sakualas* of the ascending series, as though subsequent to the *sakualas* of the *zatomises*. These *sakualas* are considerably diverse, but all together they compose the middle strata of *Shadanakar*.

It is natural that the higher the hierarchical strata are located, the more difficult their comprehension, and the less analogy with *Enrof* can be found in the landscape, and in the figure and form of the entities that reside there, and in the content of their life. Nine-tenths of all that is seen, or one way or another realized, remains incomprehensible, and in the majority of situations we have to limit even the elementary facts by using standard expressions, but not attempting to hide their validity or their profound meaning. As a result the present chapter does not offer to the reader almost any prospects, except for an emaciated assessment of some *sakualas* and the strata that compose them.

At this point I need to explain my use of the word – egregore, as opposed to its use in Hinduism or any of the other esoteric literature. I understand the egregores to be other-materiality forms evolving from certain mental attributes of humanity and which influence larger groups. Egregores are deprived of spirit monads, but temporarily possess a concentrated volition and something equivalent to consciousness. Every egregore has its own arbitrarily assigned government. These entities reside in a stationary status and are non-aggressive. The majority of egregores do not participate in the struggle between the demonic and Providential powers of *Shadanakar.* Nonetheless there are some who will migrate to the demonic camp.

With their fall, egregores disappear and the equivalence of their consciousness dissipates into space. They do not experience this as any suffering.

As much as I can speak about the landscape of these strata, the region of the *sakualas* of the egregores are characteristic of yellow rolling hills.

The 7 strata that compose this *sakuala* can be listed in the following sequence:

Zativ – the egregores of primordial tribes that die together with either the absorption of the tribe into some nation, or with its physical dissolution. Located here were the egregores of the most ancient cultural-political institutions of humanity, but which now have dissipated into space.

Zhag – the region of egregores of the governments. Located here are the egregores of certain mature societal-political contemporary institutions, for example, the party of the Indian National Congress.

Foraoun – the egregores of the churches. These are formed from those dark-ethereal emanations of the multitudes of the population that are members of churches, and just anybodies, those not attaining any rectitude of the soul that would apply to their respective religious institution. Such possess secular intentions, material interests, greed, ambitious drive, and in general are from the class of those that the ecclesiastic fathers called – people of the world. Often these egregores are a large brake pedal and heavy load on the ascending path of the church. Eventually the egregores of ROSE OF THE WORLD will be located in *Foraoun.* This is inevitable, since the inter-religious church of the future will be composed of not just saints, but of hundreds of millions of people who presently reside at various stages of the route.

Yudgrogr – the egregores of the anti-churches, the masses comprising the warring political parties of the new era.

The next stratum whose name I do not know is populated by egregores that are born out of the mental activity of the demonic population of the *shrastras*.

Likewise I do not know the name of the stratum that belongs to the egregores that appeared as the result of the mental activity of the world of the *daimons* – that second and brighter humanity. A few words will be said about them in later pages.

The last of the strata of the egregores is named *Tsebruemr*. Is it still empty. In time it will be the egregores of the arriving anti-church, where the demonic quasi-religion of the generation of *Gagtungr* will materialize. They will be the kernel and bases of the arriving diabolic humanity at the conclusion of the first Eon.

In the *sakuala* consisting of 3 or 4 dimensional spatial strata with an immense number of time coordinates, there resides another higher humanity of *Shadanakar*. It is regretful that my knowledge of it is extremely meager. The majority of questions that appear while contemplating on them remains a wide problem for me, it is too complex of a panorama of *Shadanakar*. This humanity is named the *daimons*. It is traversing the route of development, one similar to ours, but its beginning occurred far earlier than ours and consummated far more successfully than ours. It is obvious that the defining factor of this situation is that the mission of Jesus Christ was disrupted in *Enrof* almost at its initiation by the powers of *Gagtungr* and only signified a partial victory, but in the world of the *daimons* it will completely consummate. Chronologically this was consummated much earlier than when Christ was incarnated as a human in the person of Jesus. His victory in the world of the *daimons* alienated the most difficult of obstacles that were loaded by the *Gagtungr* on their ascending route, and to the present time these objects are far distant from us. Any sacrifices occurring due to their installation has been avoided many times. The appearance of societal disharmony among them has long not existed, and strengths are directed toward a spiritual and ascetic self-perfection and for the assistance of other strata, and also in part the humanity of *Enrof.*

The *daimons* are winged people, their figure being partly similar to angels, but from which however they are distinct by the fact that they exist in 2 genders, and many others as well. The basis stratum of their residency is compatible to our *Enrof,* and possesses the name *Zheram.* Nature, similar to ours, is installed there to the level of a high artistic and cultural perfection, by which the mechanical civilization is inspired through inner wisdom regarding the strengths and strata of *Shadanakar* and the development of high capabilities and their personal domain. The *daimons* are aware of all aspects of the humanity of *Enrof.*

The retribution of the *daimons* liberates them from post-mortem descents into the demonic worlds beginning at the time of the consummation in *Zheram* of Christ's task. But the multi-stage *sakuala* of purgatories is known due to experience, although it is forgotten by the majority of us. For them a sole stratum is reserved, its name being *Yurm,* where several of them enter a purgatory after death. A world of enlightened *daimons,* their heavenly country is created for them, named *Kartiala,* and it is parallel to the *zatomises* of our humanity. From there an ascent to the *sakuala* of the supreme Obligation is revealed and finally one to the *Sinklit* of the world.

Among the many tasks that rise in the presence of the *daimons* of *Kartiala* in regard to the many worlds of *Shadanakar,* one consists in their active participation in the struggle against the *yuitzraors* and the *shrastras* of anti-humanity. Another is the influential creative activity directed toward the creators of our artistic culture. Only blindness due to materialism can force a person right passed its innumerable witnesses from the side of our poets, writers, musicians and philosophers. The majority of the *daimon*-influencers who fulfill their task depart from those whom they have influenced. Often they receive a dual-unity, a very rare occurrence and very complex to explain.

Not rare are those incidences when human *shelts* intertwine into their garland one incarnation in the world of the *daimons*. Such an incarnation provides them the ability to strengthen the bright aspiration of their soul.

But in the *sakuala* of the daimons there resides also another race having a lesser census, and which remains behind in their development and are as though under their guardianship. The history of its appearance in these worlds is not entirely clear to me. It seems that these specific *daimons* at some time in antiquity went astray from the route, losing their wings and imposed damage and harm upon themselves while on the road of personal redemption. These wingless entities are almost indistinguishable from humans.

Here I approach the fact that will inevitable summon an outburst of denial and even agitation in almost every person reading this book. But if a person cannot discard words from a song, then these concepts cannot be discarded from this book. And so these entities, which I discussed as being a lower race of the *daimons*, can in part be defined as meta-prefigures of certain heroes of global literature and art of *Enrof*. Regularly the intuition of the artists of *Enrof*, due to their personal qualities and at least for sure their ingenuity, will mature in *Zheram*. So one or another of these entities will start to contemplate and come to the realization of its reflection in the art of the humanities. This reflection becomes as though a magic crystal that concentrates people's emanations and then releases them at times of creative stimulation. These emanations, ascending into *Zheram*, provide strength to the meta-prefigure for development. If such a reflection is not created, the development slows and in some situations, the meta-prefigure, perhaps, will have to even discard the *sakuala* of the *daimons* and begin its slow route to *Enrof*.

After such revelations, as strange as they may seem to us, such as the world of *Fongaranda*, other revelations tied with the *sakualas* of the angels will unveil and assuredly will appear familiar and even regular. There are 2 such *sakualas*. The first is the lower consisting of 3 strata, and so has the appellation: the Angels of the Lower Circle. In essence, this appeared first during the time of the humanity of *Shadanakar*, when those residing in the strata were composed of a more solid material, although they were not in *Enrof*. This era preceded the era of the titans. We are not presently in a position to understand or meditate on the content of their life in the enlightened worlds, but can only grasp this side of their activity that has a direct bearing particularly on us. The first of these strata is occupied by cherubim, guardians of the persons who bear bright missions. They are particularly guardians, and not so much influencers: these are the *daimons*! From childhood we hear of guardian angels, and it is not our fault we thought that such an angel stood behind the right shoulder of each living person. But their figure is genuinely such as tradition depicts them, and the landscape of their world is among the attractive colors, those we have no capacity to absorb, but they remind us of pink and lilac from a distance.

Another stratum has a white-gold shade penetrated by sheaves of light, and it belongs to the seraphim, the guardians of certain fraternities of humanity: churches, religious communities, some charity organizations, and a very few cities where the spiritual integrity and moral purity has a special significance in the eyes of the Providential principals. Epochs have occurred when the seraphimic guard surrounds some city, because one or another of some meta-historical event is occurring there or one or another trans-physical process is being accomplished, and this demanding special assistance or protection. After all is concluded, with the change of epochs, the seraphimic guard departs. So it was with Kiev when under Prince Vladimir the Great, or with Moscow under Princes Daniel and Ivan Kalita, and several times with Jerusalem, Rome and many other cities. In a rare situation when the seraphimic guard does not leave the city and remains over the course of many centuries, then it transforms into Varanasi, a city of colossal meta-historical importance. Of course, from the narrow, tunnel vision of the Christian point of view, expositions of this type do not summon anything except misunderstanding. The figure of the seraphim is similar to angels with 6 wings.

The *sakuala* consummates with the world having the appellation of Thrones, whose figure is similar to our vision of archangels. The color of their residence is a blue-green penetrated with rotating sheaves of light. The thrones are the guardians of nations. There are many of them. The spiritual formation of each nation is guarded by an entire regiments of these shining entities.

Moving on to the 2nd *sakuala* – the Angels of the Higher Circle – I am deprived of the possibility to make its understanding easier, although I use a bare visualization of figures, as in the preceding. I can only say that here is the residence of the bright hierarchies of immense power, particularly those who are the creators of the material 3 and 4 and 5 dimensional strata of *Shadanakar*.

The first that proceed are the Astrals, known in Christian mysticism by the appellation of Authorities: these are the creators of the materiality of *Enrof*. After them are the Powers, the creators of the materiality of the *sakuala* of the *daimons*. And then the Dominions, the creators of the materiality of the worlds of Enlightenment (other than *Olirna*). The *sakuala* of the Angels of the Higher Circle is crowned by the world of the Principals, the creators of the materiality of the *zatomises*, and then the Archangels (what the sirins, alkonosts and gamayuns of paradise, Eden, *Monsalvat*, *Zhuenfleia*, and holy Russia, turn into), all the *zatomises* of Christian meta-culture. They create the materiality of the world of the Supreme Obligation. The materiality of the most angelic worlds, as also the materiality of the higher strata of *Shadanakar*, are created by the hierarchies of the meta-*bramfatura*.

I know that what I have expounded is completely incompatible with the traditions of Christian angelology, disregarding the common appellations. I am sorry, but this is how it is. But I do not compose this of myself, and cannot insert changes until such time that the one sole Logos will indicate so, and it is to It that I fully entrust myself.

211

The exposition has now reached to the *sakuala* of the Supreme Obligation. These worlds are common, applying to people, angels, *daimons*, *stikhials*, and even enlightened animals. But my knowledge of these latter is very dearth, so not to discuss them any further.

I am not even assured in the name of the first of them; it sounds something like *Yusnorm*, but I cannot seem to be able to pronounce it more precisely. The rotation of the planet around its axis occurs here also, and from what I can see, night likewise exists there, because I vaguely remember an overwhelming beauty of a bright fog occurring, and as if directly in front of me, the creating womb of our universe was first unveiled and clearly enough for me to see. This was the *Astrafair*, the great center of our galaxy, hidden from us in *Enrof* due to dark clouds of a cosmic material.

I saw the distribution of innumerable stars, but not as the type we have: these were not stars, but *bramfaturas*. Not just shining points, but systems of concentric spheres shining from within each. When your gaze stops at any one of them, it becomes larger and clearer, and seems to get closer to you. Right now it seems to me that all of them slowly rotated, having a harmonic sound and echoed against each other in polyphonic voices. But perhaps it now seems to me to be this way because of the impression upon me of the harmony of the spheres that arrived close to me, not externally, but due to secular tradition. In any case, the harmony of just these emanated through sound waves of an unimaginable choir, vibrating here and around me, and moving me from such depths to such heights that I could not comprehend or fathom by just looking.

This also reminded me of a stratum that earlier appeared to me as an all-encompassing temple, predestined for the place of humanity's eternal divine liturgy.

O, but not just humanity! Here was the presence, it seems, of millions of entities and I do not know how many, really, but over half of them were not human and should not have been standing with them. Here were enlightened souls of the *stikhials* and the enlightened souls of animals, here were marvelous *daimons* and angels of various circles. When we read in the Apocalypse of the prophesy of highly intelligent animals that surround the altar of another world and who perform their ceremony,[40] this perhaps is a symbol, but this is also a notation of the reality, that reality, that existed long before the era of the author of the Apocalypse. So the *Yusnorm*, as the ecumenical temple, is the materialization of the concept particularly of that great person-spirit who during his previous incarnation as a human on earth was the Apostle John the Divine.

And if there were millions there petitioning,[41] then the number standing at the throne of the Temple were in the thousands, because each who attained the *sakuala* of the Supreme Obligation becomes, in *Yusnorm*, one of those attending, and who then is replaced by the next.

Yes, the elements of speech is utilized in the liturgy, but this is in an unpronounceable language of the *Sinklit* of the world, where the words are not plain distinct sounds, but as though mental musical cords, while others materialize at this time as bursts and showers of light. The elements of movement occur in this liturgy, a heavenly reflection of a sacred dance. But since there are 5 dimensions in *Yusnorm*, the movement occurs not in a horizontal direction as it is with us, but in all 5 dimensions of space. The elements of light and color also participate as elements of the liturgy, but it is not possible for me to provide a meaning to the colors, and which are beyond the basic 7 colors that we are able to see.

The Worlds of Supreme Obligation are remnants among the *zatomises*, the *Kartiala* of the *daimons*, and the *Khangvilla* of the enlightened animals – from the one side. While from the other side – the worlds of the Higher Trans-Myths of the Supreme Religions. The *Gridruttva* is oriented over *Yusnorm*, that white chamber where the great plan of creation of humanity is developed. After it follow: *Alikanda*, similar to a flower's

---

[40] Rev 4:6-7
[41] Rev 7:9

receptacle; *Tovia*, similar to foam or dew covering a white garden, or falling snow; and *Ro*, immense singing crystals, and their echo is most beautiful composition of music in *Enrof* and *Olirna*, among the *daimons*, and even in the *zatomises*.

These 3 strata are the residences of humans' monads, all of them reuniting with their assigned restored souls. The arrangement of the structure of *Shadanakar* attained finally that grandiose *sakuala*, and the best manner for me to describe such overwhelmingly ponderous spectacles, as these worlds are, and it is only proper to call them the Supreme Aspects of the Highest Religions, their most immaculate trans-myths.

And as much as I can remember, just a part of the colossal and beautifully majestic *Iroln* pertains to this *sakuala*: this is the location of the monads of persons prior to their union with their assigned souls. This is the first world to which the individual spirit of each person is released in his eventually entrance into *Shadanakar* from the Father's bosom It is similar to a constant traversal and return of a number of suns. But it was not clear to me. It seemed to me that this world did not have 5, but had 6 spatial dimensions, yet it was not actually included in the sakuala of the supreme Obligation, although I still list it there.

Higher along the hierarchical staircase of *Shadanakar* there are arranged, one after another, the *sakualas* of the cosmic invocations. What does this mean? Over the course of many millions of years of history of *Shadanakar*, the active effects of other *bramfaturas* had and have a place. Some of them are more potent than ours, or stand ahead of ours in their development, or finally, they correspond to ours in their sizes and steps of ascension, however their location in the spatial expanse is not so far from us. Subsequently they are very mutually active with *Shadanakar*. The materiality of the worlds of invocation was created by the bright powers of other *bramfaturas*. They reside there as the most supreme of entities, and without effort they encompass all of the cosmic spatial expanse. They are migrants from other *bramfaturas*, great helpers and friends of the bright powers of *Shadanakar*.

I cannot specifically state anything about several of the *sakualas* of the worlds of invocation, except for some of their names. So for example, there exists the sakuala of the invocation of *Orion*. *Orion* is the system of the *bramfaturas* of gigantic power, completely liberated from demonic principals. It plays a colossal role in the life of the galaxy. Of course, reciting the appellations of the 10 strata of which this *sakuala* consists will only cause disappointment in the reader. Since I do not know whether these names are appealing: *Yumaroyya, Odgiana, Ramn, Vualra, Leegeya, Fianna, Eramo, Veyatnor, Zaolita,* and *Natolis.*

Regardless of the dissimilar conditions that reign in the physical strata of Jupiter or Neptune, when compared to our conditions, we need to accept the thought that many of the planets and their satellites possess *bramfaturas*. Jupiter is likewise in our stratum, in *Enrof,* and is populated by highly intelligent creatures, but they are so distinct from us and they live in such conditions that are inconceivable to us, since in the plane of *Enrof,* no communication of any type exists and never will. However, communication does exist in the five-dimensional strata of both *bramfaturas*. The elite of Jupiter and its satellites created within *Shadanakar* 2 strata of its invocations, then one stratum was created by Saturn and its satellites, then one by Uranus and one Neptune. All of them compose the *sakuala* of the planetary invocations.

There are 3 strata that occupy a special place: *Eeora, Akhos,* and *Gebn*. These are the sakuala of the invocation of the transformed planet *Daiya*, and which no longer exists in *Enrof.* This planet rotated at one time between Mars and Jupiter. A very long time ago, the efforts of its demiurge banished all the demonic powers from it, and to the *bramfatura* of its satellite that opposed it. *Daiya* then entered the 3rd eon, meaning that it was physically transformed and disappeared form the global Enrof.

The satellite was subject to a catastrophic collapse, and the asteroids are its remnants, while the demonic hordes were scattered into the special expanse.

There are 9 strata that compose the sakuala of the solar system. Again, these are just appellations: *Raos, Flermos. Tramnos, Gimnos, Aryer, Nigbeya, Trimoyya, Derayn,* and *Eeordis.* And there are 4 appellations of the strata of the invocation of the center of the Galaxy: *Grezuar, Maleyn, Virueana* and *Luevarn.*

To the list of the *sakualas* of invocation there is just one more system, and which would be proper to be called a *bramfatura,* although it is included in *Shadanakar.* It possesses five-dimensional and six-dimensional strata. This is the *bramfatura* of the moon.

I do not exactly know when the development of lunar humanity – the selenites[42] – concluded in Enrof, but in any case, this occurred an extremely long time age, almost a million years back. But what development occurred there at more than just a slow pace, although there was a significantly short period of time between the time organic matter appeared on the surface of the moon to the appearance of highly intellectual creatures, in comparison to our evolution.

The tragedy that affected the selenites was their defeat by *Boglea,* the female lunar demon.

The following were the stages of the religious and cultural descent of the selenites: diabolic humanity, inbreeding, and ruin due to their technological overload. Progressive lack of spirituality brought the selenites to a barbaric state and they were unable to deal with their overwhelming industry and so they perished from cold and famine. But it was *Boglea* who was working behind the scenes all this time in the world of the lunar *bramfatura.* The moon for some extremely long time resided in an independent semi-isolation, hostile toward the powers of Light and somewhat toward *Gagtungr.* But toward its latter

---

[42] based on H.G. Wells, *The First Men on the Moon*

history, there occurred a compromise and even treaty and union between them and the planetary demon. The purpose was the consolidation of powers to banish the principal of Light from *Shadanakar*.

Then *Boglea*, this blue-gray deceiving and enticing demoness, constructed her own special stratum – the lunar hell, where she intended to discard all the sacrifices of the struggle, with the agreement of *Gagtungr*. Some of these sacrifices were even subject to a further descent to a more terrifying realm: thrown from *Shadanakar* into the wastelands of the Galaxy.

Then the 3 remaining strata of the lunar *sakuala* resisted the world of *Boglea*. *Soldbiis*, one of the visible *zatomises* on the surface of the moon, is the world of the residence of many enlightened, but it tragically fell behind. Its final incarnation in *Enrof* occurred during the epoch of the lunar diabolic-humanity and inbreeding. This world was then directed during a later period for its eventually restoration and gradual enlightenment in *Soldbiis*.

Another world is *Laal*, the lunar elite. Very many selenites from this stratum rose even higher, to the Elite of *Shadanakar*. And finally the 3rd, the brightest of the lunar worlds, *Tanit*, the residence of the lunar goddess.

If we could apply a subtle analogy to what we feel during nights of a full moon, then we will be convinced in the presence of the following components of our experiences: First is the premonition of harmony, which is the effect of *Soldbiis* and *Laal* on us. Second is the subtle homesickness for the celestial regions: this is *Tanit* summoning us to it. Third is the gravitational pull toward sexual dissipation; this is the temptation and pressure of *Boglea*. She is afraid of the sun and always recedes from it to the unseen back side of the moon. As a result the emanations of *Boglea* are so weak during a full moon that they hardly affect us.

This exposition of the structure of *Shadanakar* has finally reached such a grandiose *Sakuala* and which forced me to describe them in these formidable definitions, as worlds of what would be called the Supreme Aspects of the Highest of Religions, their pure trans-myths.

Many years ago, long before the Second World War, when I was still very young, I had a vision of an unexplainable, beautiful image that persistently remained with me: it was as though visible from an infinite distance, a bluish pyramid constructed of crystal, through which the sun was shining. I felt its immense significance, waves of grace, strength and beauty emanated from this shining concentration, but I could not understand the meaning of this image. Later, even with my limited human comprehension, I thought this was a refractive reflection of the Global *Salvaterra*. What a childish thought! The person whose soul touches the reflection of the Global *Salvaterra* will have integrity and be prophetic. And then it ended, and such a reflection did not have any tangible aspect at all.

Several years pass from the vision and then just recently it was explained to me, its essence, that this pyramid was not alone, but with it there were matching others, and 5 in all, but a 6th will never be in *Shadanakar*. There was just one blue of them all. The balance were of other colors, and it is impossible to say which of them was the prettiest. At the same time, none of they actually had any similarity with any other geometric shape. As I could comprehend them, they were particularly gigantic crystal pyramids, and it seems that each of their shapes had a relative profound meaning.

One of the pyramids struck me, one smaller in size, but it was impressive because of its other-worldly whiteness and symbolized the superlative trans-myth of the religion that I personally never could identify with any of the number of global or higher religions: the trans-myth of Zoroasterism. My lack of understanding this has still not dissipated. To this time I cannot explain what manner this localized religion, and which historically was long ago extinguished in *Enrof*, and as it seems to me, was not so much a wealthy mythology, as much as one that reflected a colossal reality and was the only one that professed it. This pyramid is called *Azur*.

Another pyramid, likewise not as large in comparative scale, but it seemed to me to be golden. This is the superlative aspect of Judaism, that aspect that leaves the anti-Christian irreconcilability of its earthly twin far behind and below it. This is that golden world of heavenly glory that slid into the visions of the great mystics of Kabbala and in the premonitions of the prophets. But the Talmud, which took so long and so hard to create, is just dust of the valley for the sovereigns of the celestial heights. The name of this golden pyramid is *Ae*.

The gigantic pyramid, whose color reminds me of lilac, is the superlative aspect of the Hindu trans-myth. This complex world consists of layers, and the outermost of its layers is the terminal goal of the Vedanta and Yoga, the higher layer of the *Sinklit* of India. There is a reference to this in Hindu philosophy having the name *Niruddhi*.[43]

Another layer is *Eroyya*, and if I can describe it in the following manner: although many reside in these worlds who were once people, but here they are only guests.

The final layer of the lilac pyramid is *Shatrittva*, the residence of many hierarchies of the Hindu pantheon. In other places I will speak of the images that are contained in this pantheon.

No less great is the green pyramid, which consists of 2 layers of worlds of the superlative aspects of Buddhism. The first of the 2 layers of the green pyramid is Nirvana. The 2nd layer belongs to Dhyani-Bodhisattvas, the hierarchs that materialize as the leadership of the people of the Buddhist meta-culture.

The blue pyramid, which has been avoiding me for 20 years, is the heavenly Jerusalem, the higher trans-myth of Christianity. This is what stands behind all the confirmations of the Christian teaching, which are common to Catholics and Orthodox and Lutherans and Abyssinians and to the future followers of ROSE OF THE WORLD. Although I call it – confirmation, this is not precise, because this is the one that is for all. The heavenly Jerusalem is the superlative layer of the

---

[43] One of the 8 Ashtadikpalaka

sinklits of Christian meta-culture, but all of this is still not the church. The church is the superlative worlds of *Shadanakar.* And before this exposition draws close to them we need to first turn back, and deeply below, into the fire and gloom, because without an understanding of the awesome and terrifying demonic *sakualas*, who reside also in their potency, it is impossible to properly mentally approach the superlative strata of *Shadanakar.*

BOOK IV

STRUCTURE OF *SHADANAKAR*:
ITS INFRA-PHYSICAL FORM

CHAPTER 1

BASICS

One of the facts where religious comprehension to this time has not provided itself an account consists in the Truine state of the One Entity, and which is ascribed to God, that it is as though repeated or reproduced in some of the monads that He has created. One important statement consists namely in a distortion of the intrinsic mystery of the Deity, one that is turned inside-out due to repetition by these great demonic monads: its Truine state. The fact that Lucifer also consists of an indivisible triune unity is something beyond my ability to discuss, since it immeasurably transcends all possibility of our understanding it, and we are hardly able to acknowledge much more about him except for the fact of his existence, the fact of his fall at some primordial time, and still one more fact: their constant struggle against God's activities.

The essence of *Gagtungr*, the great demon of *Shadanakar*, disregarding his gigantic scale in comparison with us, under the best of conditions, perhaps can be understood to a considerably greater degree. What is primary is that its triune state is clear, although the reasons for this triune existence, its evolution and goal – if there is a goal – remains undisclosed to us.

What is obvious first of all is that right here in front of our face some kind of scandalous parallel exists with the Most Holy Trinity. But the question of the essence of the Divine Triune Unity – virtually not the most profound of problems of theology – can be at least somewhat touched in another part of this book, so I will not deal with it here.

I can only say that the *Gagtungr* strives to resist the first hypostasis of the Divine Truine Unity with its own first person – the great Tormentor [*Gisturg*]; resist the second hypostasis with his second person, which more precisely is characterized by the appellation of the Great Whore; and resist the third hypostasis of the Triune Deity by using the antipode named *Yurparp*, who is the materializer of the demonic plan. In some sense he can be labeled the principal of form, this is that facet of the great demonic entity which is unveiled in the life of various strata of *Shadanakar* as the principal actively reconfiguring their intentions to be consistent with the intents and goals of the Tormentor, the principal of reformulation. The great Whore – her name is *Fokerma* – is the facet of the demonic entity that is drawing and sucking souls and destinies into the orbit of the *Gagtungr*. The first person, the *Gisturg*, the great Tormentor, is the final and deepest spot of the demonic *I*, the carrier of the highest [demonic] will, authority and desire.

His body is indescribably ugly, as the spiritual eyes of some people viewed him, those who penetrated into the dark realms of *Digm*, the world of his residence. As though lying spread upon the turbulent lilac ocean, with black wings that stretch from one horizon to the other horizon, he raises his dark-gray face to the zenith where his ultra-violet glows flare and swing. Woe to that person upon whom the *Gagtungr* focuses his stare and the person who meets his stare with opened eyes. Of all the people who were bearers of the dark mission, and who later were thrust into *Digm*, only one – Torquemada – found strength within himself to remember the name of God at his final moment. The balance of monads became slaves of the devil for countless centuries.

Other than *Gagtungr*, other select criminals are also found in *Digm*: monads of some persons who merged with their demonized *shelts*, and also so many souls of certain entities of a demonic nature, among their number are the great *igvies*, the dark guides of anti-humanity that have already finished their route through the various – and more tangible of the material – strata. Here they plot and plan their struggle against God. Here they prostrate themselves in front of *Gisturg*, and have enjoyment with their closeness to the great Whore, and commune with the dark crevasses of knowledge by viewing the face of *Yupatr*.

Shadanakar also possesses an even lower demonic stratum. This is the multi-dimensional *Shog*, whose materiality was created by great demons of the macro-bramfatura. Potent streams of inspirational addresses and invocations of powers for the struggle against God flow here from the depths of the universe. And not one entity, except *Gagtungr*, can enter this stratum. A few however, and only for a minute or so on rare occasions, are able to see it from a distance. During these minutes they need to receive a lamp of indescribable light that will shine at the zenith of *Digm*, and which is not like a sphere, but like a pulsating arch stretched from one horizon to the other, and this light is somewhat comparable to violet. This is the anti-cosmos of the galaxy, the point of concentration of the potency of Lucifer himself. On occasion the arch as if bends toward itself and into itself from the ends, and the powers of Lucifer pour into *Shog*. Then *Gagtungr*, absorbing them, raises his wings toward the black sky. This is the little we have of a recollection of those who have seen *Shog* from the outside. The appearances and forms of this world from the inside are far beyond our transcendence.

Nevertheless there does exist in *Shadanakar* other strata from which the anti-cosmos of the galaxy can be viewed, although from a different aspect. The anti-cosmoses of all the *bramfaturas*, including the *Shadanakar* in that number, are 2-dimensional: they are like an endless flat plane. All of them overlap each other in one and the same stack. It can be called the demonic axis of the galaxy. In order to understand this easier, I would like to bring as an example a certain conditional spatial model. Let's take a book and place it vertically on its spine, open it and then shuffle the pages, and then mentally expand each page infinitely in its 2-dimension flatness, with each page on top of the other. All of the flat pages overlap each other at the corners, but all are in one vertical stack and inside the spine. The cosmic similarity of this stack of flat strata is the demonic axis of the galaxy, its anti-cosmos. Naturally it can be seen by any entity that is residing in any of its 2-dimensional flat worlds, including its corresponding strata of *Shadanakar* in its number.

This specific 2-dimensional strata of *Shadanakar* is often named hell, but this term here is not entirely proper. This stratum is not a purgatory of human souls in their post-mortem state, but the residence of the majority of demonic entities of our planet. This can be called the anti-cosmos of *Shadanakar*, but this is also not entirely precise, because the divine cosmos resists not just this stratum, but all the demonic worlds. This [anti-cosmos] specifically emerges as the chief demonic citadel. Its present name is *Gashsharva*.

The entities that reside there can be considered being in a state of incarnation, if a person should want to. Nevertheless, the understanding of incarnation in general is extremely relative. The monads of these entities are always located high in *Digm* and *Shog*; their *shelts* maintain their existence between incarnations, for the greater part, at the one-dimensional Bottom of *Shadanakar* – in a world of terror.

Gashsharva is the nucleus of the system created by demonic powers of *Shadanakar* as a counter-weight to the divine cosmos as its expected replacement. Not just deprived of any festivity, and a morose place, this world for any person could not but seem to be scary. Its large number of time coordinates, while having to deal with only 2 dimensions of space, creates a distinctive spiritual stuffiness. For every monad, the process of the entrance of its *shelt* into this world is tormenting. It recollects the reaction of a body that is securely compressed in a tight iron corset.[44] The less the spatial coordinates, the denser the materiality of the world. However the atmosphere of this world is nonetheless similar to air, while the soil is more solid than any other material of *Enrof*, and the scenery is flat and uniform. As far as the foliage is concerned, I cannot think of anything equivalent to it. The source of light consists of self-emitting creatures and some artificial items. For some reason, blue and green light does not penetrate here, but in their place are 2 different infra-reds. One of them I will conditionally call infra-violet, and because to separate it from ultra-violet, which is something else. But the diffusion of the infra-violet light emitted caused it to be very dense and dark and at the same time an intensive lilac color.

The anti-cosmos of the galaxy is seen from *Digm* as a lamp emitting a completely unimaginable and untransmitable light, and from *Shog* in the form of titanic, flaming and pulsating infra-violet flashes traversing across the zenith. From the *Gashsharva* it appears as if part of the horizon, emitting a steady infra-violet shine from the infinite reaches of space.

All the residents of *Gashsharva* are bound together under the tyranny of *Gagtungr* and along with this possess something like a union of common interests. They hate the *Gagtungr*, but of course, it is not as if God is with them. Here the superintendents of the lower purgatories, magma and nucleus, reside – the 3 *sakualas* of Retribution.

The demons that are the superintendents of the purgatories are called angels of gloom and this appellation corresponds entirely to their composite figure. They possess certain human characteristics, but have wide wings of amazing beauty that emanate purple and scarlet colors when they flutter in a majestic manner. Being the superintendents of the lower purgatories,

---

[44] Daniel Andreev wore an iron corset due to his spinal deformity.

they supplement the loss of their vital strengths by sucking the *gavvakh* of people who are drawn into the purgatories as a result of their karma. Glancing at these purgatories from *Gashsharva*, they find there a lower density atmosphere, and where it is difficult and uneven to fly as a result, as though in short hops or zigzag, but it still is possible.

The other residents of *Gashsharva*, being the superintendents of the magmas, who are called *rifra*, are completely deprived of human features. More than anything, each of them is similar to a moving ridge of hills. They have something that seems to be a face, but it was very blurry.

Perhaps the person reading this book will discredit me for insufficient descriptions, or else because I am faithful to the Christian tradition. But particularly, I do strive to banish any games with my imagination from these pages, and the more impoverished the fantasies, the better. As far as the Christian tradition is concerned, what remains here is not what I personally prefer, but what has received confirmation through my spiritual experience. The forms of certain entities proclaimed by Christian demonology have received such a confirmation. No matter how strange this is, creatures that look like notorious devils do actually exist, and you can imagine them even with a tail and horns. They reside in *Gashsharva* and sustain themselves with their questionable pleasures of being superintendents of the nucleuses, the *sakualas* consisting of the more terrifying purgatories of *Shadanakar*. In general there is some truth in many of the legends that we approach with a laugh, or in the best of circumstances, if we look at them symbolically, we really should understand them completely literally. Sometimes a test of our intellect in such modern times is truly backbreaking.

The circle of *Gashsharva's* residents are bizarre and variegated. I know also about potent demons from among them that are of the female nature, and I am conditioned to call them *vogleas*. They are giants. In the history of humanity they often enter the scene as those who increase the number of sacrifices and who instigate anarchy. We need to here completely forget how they look since they are monsters of our world. Their hide is immense, wrapping around them like cords and still undeveloped; it is black and purple. Every nation possesses a *voglea*, but it seems, just one. In any case there is only one in Russia, and she is very ancient. The term of their incarnation in *Gashsharva* – if you can count this as an incarnation – appears to me to be for many centuries.

At one time these creatures resided on the surface of the land, but not in *Enrof*, but in their region of somewhat high density and which is similar [to *Enrof*] from a distance. Created by *Gagtungr* at the very beginning of the *Shadanakar's* history, this stratum has long ceased to exist. The external forms of the demonic entities in this world were frail and in general somewhat alien. But they could not consider themselves masters there; they were compressed, compacted by their light. Under his influence, their nature is supposed to change; it was to stop being compatible to their demonic substance. Right now in *Gashsharva*, they are provided a difficult life, but nonetheless they are left to themselves.

There are also other creatures that nest there, but I do not know about them. What is known is that some of the people who did reside in *Enrof* at one time, now reside there and they are assigned special dark missions. Otherwise, here they hardly suffer, but they do have another task. In *Gashsharva* they worriedly prepare themselves using the powers of *Gagtungr* for their incarnation in humanity in subsequent order.

Often someone will have to descend into *Gashsharva* using the power of Light. These descents are torturous, but they are summoned due to unavoidable necessity with the demanding circumstances of battling against the armies of *Gagtungr*. The residents of *Gashsharva* watch their enemies penetrate into their realm, but they are helpless to interfere with their invasion.

The demonic base includes still one more world: this world possesses one-dimensional space and one-dimensional time. This is the Bottom of *Shadanakar*, the place of suffering of the demonic *shelts* and several people, those who possess the dark missions noted above.

The Bottom came on the scene at the very beginning of the creation of our *bramfatura* through the powers of *Gagtungr* and the dark powers that are even more potent than he. Its materiality is the most dense of anything possible. The materiality of *Enrof* to a certain degree is similar to it, but only if in the center of stars or in such monstrous bodies of our galaxy such as white dwarfs. It is difficult to imagine how in similar conditions it would be to somehow have any movement or motion. However it does happen at the bottom of *Shadanakar*, but for the conscious creatures it is torturous to an excruciating degree. This causes a need for them to summon effort to sustain their vital strengths, because otherwise the creature will be drawn into this crevasse that leads to a place that is even more sorrowful: the Bottom of the Galaxy.

All of this will now help me to finally explain the details as pertaining to the understanding of their incarnation. The demons, incarnated in *Gashsharva* or in certain other strata having 3 and even 4 dimensions, after death are submerged to the Bottom where a new body awaits them, the most dense that is possible. Such are the laws of karma turning the 2nd edge against the demons.[45] The emanations from their suffering at the Bottom supplement the loss of the vital strengths of *Gagtungr*. Can they really rebel against the law of karma? But during the time of their incarnation in all the other strata, particularly this law is utilized as a source for strength for their life. To rise against it means to reject the *gavvakh* as nourishment, it means they place themselves opposite the entire demonic camp, the entire anti-cosmos, that is, to cease being demons.

Every *bramfatura* of our galaxy contains a Bottom, except for those who are free of demonic powers. Subsequently, such *bilge water* is in the millions in our galaxy. Similar to this, as the two-dimensional cosmic smoothness of many anti-cosmoses or *Gashsharvas* slide along a common plane, so do all the cosmic

---

[45] Referring to the concept of a double-edge sword.

planes of the galactic *bilge waters* slide into a single vanishing point. This point is located in Antares. This star is not just incidental, since it is otherwise named the heart of the scorpion, and has served in many mythological tales of antiquity and the middle ages as the personification of malicious and even diabolical powers. The immense planetary system of this star is the concentration of the hordes of the galaxy that struggle against God, their residence is in a 3 dimensional world. This is also the titanic meta-*bramfatura* of the demons, the anti-cosmos of our Milky Way to the extent that this anti-cosmos generally enters the *Enrof.*

I already mentioned that the *bramfaturas* where the demons were defeated are not eternal, and the great planet-satellite of the star Antares, dormant at the bottom of *Shadanakar* at present will soon dissipate, but another will take its place. The one that was in dormancy during the epoch of the creation of *Shadanakar* perished millions of years ago.

In outer space, the star Antares can be seen in late spring and summer low along the southern horizon, and many well remember its bright pulsation of a wine-red radiance. From the bottom of the *Shadanakar,* not the sun or any other celestial bodies are seen, nothing, except the motionless Antares, upon which the Bottom is hung at one end. From there it appears to be infra-red. At the opposite direction of outer space, this one-dimensional world slowly subsides as it approaches the surface of the earthly sphere. At that end nothing is visible at all. Here lurks the fissure to the place deprived of time, the Bottom of the Galaxy.

As I mentioned earlier, not only the Bottom, but also all the worlds of the demonic base entered into existence during the period that the physical body of *Shadanakar* was cooling. Before the appearance of organic life in *Enrof,* the activity of *Gagtungr* succumbed to attempts to create a stratum on the surface of the earth for residence of the demonic powers, and when this failed, then it attempted to strengthen and develop *Gashsharva* and other strata connected with the strata beneath the crust, with the magmas and core of the planet. When organic life appeared in *Enrof,* [*Gagtungr's*] activity was directed to occupying the animal kingdom, and this partially succeeded and so caused laws to be loaded upon the demiurges. In summation, the result of the activities of both these powers served as the basis of the formulation of those laws of nature and karma which are presently in effect.

*   *   *

Religions having a Semitic root possess an inherent drive to place responsibility for the cruelty of laws on the Deity. It is no surprise that this has not summoned protest, and even its cruelty has not even plainly been acknowledged, or at least the cruelty of the laws of retribution. Due to a tranquility incomprehensible to us, even the saints of the Christian meta‑cultures have reconciled themselves with the fact of the eternal suffering of sinners. The absurdity of an eternal sentence for some temporary crime has not upset their thinking, while their conscience seems to be satisfied with the idea of immemorial infallibility of the concept, meaning no exit to the imposition of these penalties, and this is likewise not understandable. I have the impression that intellect and conscience have circumvented this assessment a long while back. It seems to us to be a scandalous thought that as if this law, in the form that it exists, was created by divine volition.

Yes, not one hair will fall without the will of the heavenly Father, and neither will even one leaf on a tree shake. So we should not understand this in the sense that the entire global law in its totality is the display of God's will, but that the institution of free wills, which the entire universe possesses, is sanctioned of God. As a result of the existence of large amounts of free wills what occurs is the possibility of apostasy of some of them. The result of this apostasy is their struggle against the powers of Light and their creation of the anti‑cosmos that is installed in contradistinction to the cosmos of the Creator.

CHAPTER 2

THE WORLDS OF RETRIBUTION

During the epochs of primordial societies, the demonic powers were occupied with resisting the deceleration of their development and with the preparation of the strata of their trans-physical magmas and cores for the acceptance of millions of souls of future humanities. Somewhat later, already during the historical eras, *shrastras* and *sakualas* of the *yuitzraors* were created. The majority of purgatories appeared during even later epochs.

I begin this exposition of the worlds of retribution with purgatories because they are closer to us than others. They are commensurable with the understandings to which we are accustomed, and in the circumstances of the descending route after death, the descent begins particularly with the purgatories. In the majority of circumstances a person is limited to the purgatories.

The purgatories of the various meta-cultures somewhat differ from one another, and even each of them will endure some significant changers over the course of centuries. They were also constructed at different epochs. In the meta-cultures of antiquity, including the Byzantine, they were not common. More precisely stated, in their place were inescapable worlds of irredeemable suffering. Echoes of mystic knowledge of these irredeemable purgatories is clearly heard in the majority of ancient religions.

The most ancient of purgatories belongs to the Indian meta-culture. Particularly this *sinklit* was first in the history of humanity to attain such a potency of Light, and which was unavoidable in order to serve as an obstacle to the powers of *Gagtungr* that wanted to turn certain redemptive post-mortem strata into a sakuala place of suffering. The Indian meta-cultures inherited the original purpose of purgatory from the ancient humanities of *daimons* and titans. Later, certain strata f the Hebrew, Christian and Islamic meta-cultures were transformed into purgatories. The decisive significance pertaining to these was the resurrection of Jesus Christ, his descent into the demonic worlds, and what occurred subsequently over the course of a series of centuries: the struggle of Christian *sinklits* against the demons over the amelioration of the law of Retribution. A victory in this struggle was not attained in the Byzantine meta-culture. The hostile camp surfaced as invincible to opposition. The conclusion of this struggle was the Byzantine meta-culture severing itself from *Enrof.*

I mentioned earlier in passing of the multi-significance of this circumstance, that Byzantine Orthodoxy did not accept the concept of purgatories when it appeared in the western Church.[46] With such terrifying perspectives of eternal torments awaiting the sinful soul [in Catholic purgatories], we need to find the flammable substance contained in ascetic extremism that ignited the Byzantine religious spirit to the very end of its history. Yes, right before the eyes of the Byzantine seers, this eschatological depth unfolded with all of the extremes of its demonic cruelty. So we should not be amazed at the desperate excesses of asceticism in this country,[47] but rather sooner note that all the meta-cultures that do not recognize purgatories do not necessarily maintain such excesses.

In the Russian meta-culture the first sheol was created in the 12th century, and it was a place of suffering transformed by the powers of Christ. In the course of time it somewhat changed its appearance, and the karmic bundles that the dead brought with themselves into this world were also modified. Nevertheless, the mechanical facet of the effect of the law of Retribution remains, of course, unchanged, always and everywhere. It consists in that a violation of the moral law causes and imposes a burden upon the ethereal body of the criminal. As long as he is alive, the burdened ethereal body

---

[46] Roman Catholicism
[47] Specifically Russia with its number of monasteries, hermitages and convents.

remains as though on the surface of the three-dimensional world. During this time the physical body plays the role of a round life preserver for the drowning. But just as the tie between them is severed at death, the ethereal body begins to submerge deeper and deeper, from stratum to stratum, until it reaches the point of balance with the surrounding environment. This is why it is mechanical. But there are entities that follow after his positive activities: the preservers of karma. This is a totally special category. Among the diverse forms of the demons of *Shadanakar*, they are migrants.

When the demonic hordes of the planet *Daiya* were banished distant of its *bramfatura*, to the *bramfatura* of its satellite,[48] then the satellite was subsequently annihilated and transformed into a collection of dead fragments – asteroids, and its demonic residents were dispersed into the global expanses of space seeking a new harbor. Some of them entered *Shadanakar*, concluding somewhat of a deal with the powers of *Gagtungr*. These entities are highly intellectual, but possess a cold-like-ice sphere of sensation. They likewise have no concept of hate or love, malice or compassion. They assumed the responsibility of the work of the mechanism of karma, supplemented the loss of their vital strengths with the emanations of the psychological torment of those people who – after their life in *Enrof* – were compelled to descend into *Skrivnous*, *Ladref*, and *Morod*, the higher strata of the purgatories. The size of these entities is immense: they are partially transparent and gray, like discolored glass; their bodies are rectangular. But the *Morod* creatures, and no matter how strange this is, have a similarity to the snouts of guard dogs, with protruding ears and sharp penetrating eyes. They enter into struggle against the powers of Light only when these powers exert the effort to ameliorate the laws of karma and the transformation of the purgatories.

The first of these purgatories is named *Skrivnous*. Here is a picture of a godless world and godless society without any embellishments. The landscape is colorless, just a medium gray,

---

[48] Meaning, its moon.

and the ocean is motionless, without a wave. The stunted foliage, low growing bushes and mosses remind me of some of the steppes of our tundra. But at least the tundra during spring is covered with flowers. The ground of *Skrivnous* cannot grow even one flower. Valleys that look like immense troughs serve here as the residences of millions of the populace of those who were once people; they are shoved in between medium high, but unscalable embankments. *Skrivnous* knows no love, or hope or joy or religion or art. The place has never seen a child. The endless labor is interrupted just for sleep, but sleep is deprived of any dreams, and their work is deprived of any creativity. Some type of immense scary creation lurks on the other side of the embankments. Time to time they throw piles of objects from there, which soar through the air into the compound. Each of these objects is the item on which they need to work, whatever each one finds: they do not have much for tools and everything is always dirty and broken. They work and sleep for the most part in long buildings that look like barracks, internally divided with barriers about waist high.

The residents' bodily design continues as entirely human, but specific traits are washed out and smoothed. Their faces look like pancakes and almost completely identical one to another. Nevertheless, the memory of their existence in *Enrof* is not only preserved in the soul of the residents, but gnaws at them like a dream of paradise lost. Of all the torments of *Skrivnous*, the one most persistent is the boredom due to their inescapable slavery, and this causes their work to be tedious due to the absence of any perspective, any kind at all.

Not only do they have an absence of perspective, but one nightmare that eternally hangs over them is the sole actual exit from that place. This exit consists of a box in the distant ocean that looks like a black ship that is speedily and silently sailing toward shore. Its appearance throws the residents into a panicky terror, since not one of them knows if he is insured from being swallowed by the outside darkness of this prison. [The ship] gathers a few of them, those whose burden of karma dooms them to suffering in worse depths of the strata, and the boat sails away. Those incarcerated in this boat prison do not see the route accomplished. They only feel its movement when the ship's horizontal direction changes to a spiral descent, as if the ship is drawn into the whirlpools of Moskstraumen.

The redemptive sufferings are limited in *Skrivnous* for those whose conscience is not defiled by memories of any grievous faults or crimes.

The succeeding stratum is similar to the preceding, but it is darker, as though it has cooled at some uncertain foggy gloom at the edge of eternal night. There are no buildings here or crowds of people, however each senses the invisible presence of many others: traces of movement similar to the impressions of footsteps gives away their presence. This purgatory is called *Ladref* and tens of millions experience a short interval of residency here. This place is the result of little belief, pertaining to those who did not possess sufficient strength for spirituality to penetrate into the substance of their person and ameliorate their ethereal body.

Those who are destined for further descent perceive it subjectively in this manner: it is as though they fall asleep and suddenly awaken in a different place. In reality, it is demonic entities – the materializers of karma – who transfer him during a period of oblivion into another current of time dimensions, even though the number of spatial coordinates remains at 3, and this remains unchanged in all the sheols.

The person redeeming his karma surfaces in the center of some complete gloom where a weak phosphorescent light from rare equivalents of foliage emanates only upon the ground. The landscape is not deprived of gloomy beauty in a few places due to a few illuminated cliffs. This is the final stratum where still something exists that we can generally call nature. The subsequent strata will be qualified as only urban landscapes.

Absolute silence reigns here in *Morod*. Every person who sojourns in this world does not perceive the existence of other residents and is assured of only his own total isolation. The melancholy state of great abandonment envelopes him like an iron armor or corset. It is vain to dream, pray, call anybody for assistance, or seek. Each one is doomed to solely associate with his individual soul. But the soul of the criminal, for this soul whose memory is defiled due to crimes committed while on earth, there is nothing more frightening than isolation and silence. Here each person comprehends the meaning and scale of the evil he accomplished while on earth and drinks the cup of terror to the bottom as a result of his crimes. From this endless dialogue with himself, the unfortunate person is not distracted by anything, not even by the struggle for survival. Because there is no struggle here of any type: food is abundant and surrounds him, provided by certain forms of plant life in the ground. Clothes? In the majority of strata, and including *Morod* in that number, the ethereal body on its own exudes a covering of a specific weave, and which they possess in lieu of clothing. And if in the worlds of Enlightenment it is beautiful and radiant, then in *Morod*, and due to the damage that pervades the creative abilities of its residents, they are only permitted to exude one made of ethereal scraps. Nevertheless, similar squalid rags clothe the astral-ethereal creatures that are being redeemed in *Ladref.*

The person who is unable to cleanse his conscience in *Morod* now awaits not a descent into the succeeding stratum, but a sudden and horrifying collapse into it. This is similar to a crevasse into which the unfortunate one will unexpectedly fall and which will suck him down: first the feet, then the torso, and finally the head.

Now my narrative has reached *Agra*, the stratum of black fogs, between which are scattered, like islands, black reflections, similar to a mirror of the great cities of *Enrof.* This stratum, as with all the purgatories, does not possess any connection with the cosmos. As a result there is no sun here, or stars or moon. The sky is perceived as a dense lid, under which a constant night is shrouded. Some things do shine on their own: the ground dimly shines, but of a blood red color. This is the only one color that dominates the region. We in *Enrof* are unable to perceive it, but the impression that it provides seems to remind me of a dark scarlet. It seems that this is that invisible light which in physics is called infra-red.

I am a little bit, and just barely, familiar with infra-Petersburg. I remember that there was also a large – but black like Indian ink – river, and buildings emanating a blood-red glow. This is similar to the illumination of our holiday nights, but an eerie comparison.[49]

The external figures of the ones who fall into this world, to a certain extent, have a figure like gnomes: the human design is preserved, but the form is ugly and misshaped, and their growth is stunted and their movement is slow, with no corporality to their body. Deprived of clothing, their body does not exude anything. What reigns is a vulnerable nakedness. One of the torments of *Agra* is the sense of helpless shame and contemplation of personal destitution. Another torment is that here begins the first experiences of a acerb remorse for those in similar circumstances, and he now becomes aware of his share of accountability for their tragic destinies.

The 3rd torment of these unfortunates is fear. With its presence in *Agra* it births other entities of a predatory demonic nature. They are called *vogleas*. Due to fear of them, the poor gnomes hide in corners or creep under buildings, where they are hardly able to breath, to get away from the *vogleas*. To die in *Agra* means to be eaten, or better said, to be sucked inside a *voglea* through its porous hide, in order to then reappear even lower, in *Buistvich* or in the frightening *Rafag*.

Later I saw that the *vogleas*, a large number of them, but only part of the total, were intellectual, and that the crude, gloomy civilization by which *Agra* is distinguished, is particularly their creation. Mechanical equipment, by which to ease labor, they practically did not have. They piled some kind of material by hand, similar to gigantic tree trunks (like those in California), and then made buildings out of them, and each piece of this material, when solidly attached to the next, began to shine with a pale scarlet color, but almost not having any

---

[49] The Northern Lights of the Arctic.

outward radiance. But why there was a connection between the buildings of humanity's cities in *Enrof* and those erected by the *vogleas* in *Agra* remained unknown to me.

They did not possess a language of sounds, of course, but they did have something like a language of gestures. They build buildings, as I noticed, in order to hide in them from the short drenches of rain that occurred every minute. The rain was black.

One more thing was also certainly strange, and this is that with the *vogleas* they do not have 2 genders, but 3. Each gender breeds its gender by using the middle gender, but the female gender still raises the offspring.

In a few places in this civilization there are scattered, like islands, silent buildings with no reflection. The *vogleas* do not even get near them; as I was able to see, there was something about them that was invisible that bothered them. Such buildings were erected in the same places as Isaac[50] and certain other churches of Petersburg. They were the sole refuges from the *vogleas*, where the persecuted *Agras*, and even for a short period, can sense some security. Who erected them? When? From what material? I do not know. Hunger did not allow these unfortunates to hide in these shelters, but rather herded them in the search for even edible fungi, since all the land was covered by the foundations of these joyless city.

If their heavy karma does not cause the person who falls into this place to become a sacrifice of the *vogleas* and he does not wake up in one of the subsequent worlds of the descending series, earlier or later he will be sentenced to a transformation for an ascending route. Having concluded his redemption he gradually corporeally changes. He increases in growth, the features of his face again develop, and they reminded me of the features that he possessed earlier, and now the *vogleas* will not dare to approach him. The transformation itself will occur with the help of brethren from the heavenly Russia: they descend into *Agra* and they surround the one who finished his probation. Some gnomes will also be present at this event, but only those

---

[50] The Cathedral of St Isaac in the center of St Petersburg.

who will likewise be raised from this place in the same manner. But for the meanwhile they watch from all sides at what is occurring, and it seems to them that as though the brethren of the *sinklit* raise the freed person on their wings or in the folds of their radiant coverings. The *vogleas*, seized with a mystical agitation and fear, watch this event from a distance, but they are not in a state to understand anything.

The staircase of ascension is not closed in front of any demonic monad, even in front of any *voglea*. But for a similar conversion there is a need for such an acute and clear comprehension, one that almost never happens here.

Sometimes something different occurs here: in places the landscape will change its form and here will appear shining spots similar to large algae-filled ponds. Something like decaying foliage is in them. This is how *Agra* illuminates the next lower stratum called *Buistvich*. Everything there decays, but it never entirely decays. It is a state where live decaying matter is combined with spiritual lethargy, and this is the torment that *Buistvich* imposes. In *Buistvich* the bundles of their karma are untied, those whose souls were loaded by the attraction to doing nothing enlightening during their corporeal life, having not accomplished anything to as if counterbalance a mundane life. Here the captive gnaws on a pessimistic repulsion toward himself, because his ethereal body is transformed into something like fecal matter. No matter how disgusting or how detestable this is, *Buistvich* in essence is nothing else but the *vogleas'* toilet.

Here begins the corporeal torment in addition to the psychological: the ability of the captives to move is extremely limited, and likewise their capability of self-defense is also restrained. But self-defense is essentially indispensable for any of them, because alongside them reside the souls of frail demons in the form of humans and clothed in dark-ethereal bodies and who are residing here during an interval between 2 incarnations in one of the demonic worlds. Here they have an appearance of insect-humans and they are about the size of cats. In *Buistvich*, they slowly and little by little eat alive those who were once people in *Enrof.*

Beyond *Buistvich* is the purgatory having the name *Rafag.* Here the residents rid themselves of the karmic results of their treachery and mercenary commitment to tyranny. *Rafag* is a torment of uninterruptible self-emaciation. There is nothing to compare such a condition in our stratum, except for suffering due to cholera. This is the final stratum, and the landscape, looking at it although from a distance, reminds us of our cities. But shelters, like those that are scattered in *Buistvich* and *Agra,* are not found here. Any intercession of humanity's prayers do not penetrate as far as *Rafag.* The place is so deep that just the powers of the *sinklits* and the supreme hierarchs of *Shadanakar* can reach this place.

The angels of gloom dominate over the 3 final and even lower purgatories.

The first of these strata is *Shim-Bieg* and it appears as a slow flowing stream, moving along an indescribable gloomy world confined under a high lid. It is difficult to understand the origin of a lifeless and colorless partial-light. The meager rain sprinkles on the streams, causing small bubbles to form on its surface. And it is not just the lack of clothing that tortures the souls here, but the souls themselves in their degrading ethereal bodies are similar to smoky-brown pieces. They bounce back and forth, clinging to whatever they fall on, as long as they do not fall into the stream. Not only does fright weary them, a more intense torment consists in their sense of shame, and which in no place does it attain such intensity as in *Shim-Bieg.* This burning lonesomeness for the genuine body they possessed earlier in a soft warm world reminds them of their joyful life on earth.

Here compassion increases as a result.

The mouth of the stream seems to draw even closer. And the stream itself, and this entire tunnel-vision world, terminates there in the manner the subway tunnel terminates when it reaches the next subway station. But the waters do not fall into nothing: they and the shores and the lid – all of it seems to dissolve into a gray barren desert. No body can survive there, and you cannot even notice there any environment or soil. Only one thing does not die away there: the spark of self-consciousness. This purgatory is called *Dromn*, it is a nightmare of horrible non-existence.

And if in *Shim-Bieg* those who are responsible for the death of many human beings, even though this pertains to the death of criminals whose death sentence they signed, or against whom they acted as an informer or traitor, are still redeemed, those who reside in *Dromn* are those who, in our eyes, violated the law incomparably less. Yes, the mathematics of karma are strange mathematics. Those drawn into *Dromn* are not criminals, not murderers, but the karmic result is due to their active unbelief, a militant rejection of spirituality, and an effective campaign promoting the fraudulent concept of the mortality of the soul. This mystery of this amazing, disproportionate penalty, as it would seem to us, is due to that all of these volitional acts done during their life in *Enrof* were as if plugged and nailed tight in the respiratory channels of the soul. The consequence now surfaces as an even worse heaviness of the ethereal nature than that which would exist as the result of separate crimes if they were to be considered on an isolated basis, each on their own.

For the captive of *Dromn*, it seems that nothing exists anywhere, and not even himself, and it is particularly this way because this is how it was during his own life. And even with the greatest of effort he will hardly be able to soon come to grips with the striking fact of the imperishable self-conscious *I*, even here, in absolute desolation, as opposed to his intellect and sound mind. Realizing this he will begin to vaguely understand that all could have been otherwise, if he did not himself choose this state of non-existence or half-existence.

But the boredom of the volitional abandonment, embellished by this residency in *Dromn*, little by little begins to yield its place to alarm. The *I* feels it is drawing him somewhere, as though down and obliquely, and on its own he as a dot is being expanded into a stretched figure, thrust toward some bottom. The absence of any sense of orientation does not allow him to understand whether he is falling slowing or if he is thrown at some great speed. Only an inner sensation cries louder than any proofs of logic that he is moving not upward and not sideway, but particularly downward. Now below a rose-colored space is recognizable. After a few moments this light can even seem joyful to the falling person. But then the chilling speculation of what it might be penetrates the unfortunate I: he realizes that he is unstoppably descending into a burning hot, quiet sea as if made of iron. The acceleration of his descent rapidly increases and he approaches the red-hot surface of *Fukabirn* and submerges into its center. In addition to the burning corporeal suffering the torment consists of particularly the terror of a descent into eternal tortures, a descent that is characterized as inescapable and irrecoverable.

Fukabirn is the final *sakuala* of the purgatories. Now begins the *sakualas* of the trans-physical magmas. These local worlds coincide with three-dimensional space, but they have other currents of time with belts of fiery hot things in the mantle of the planet. Let me repeat and underscore: in all the meta-cultures, except the Indian, the sufferings of these worlds did not have an end until Jesus Christ accomplished his liberating descent into them, and which in ecclesiastical tradition is called – the descent of the Savior into hell. From this moment it became possible for all the powers of Light, although it would demand immense efforts, to liberate the sufferers from these abysses after a properly-defined term, the length determined as necessary to untie the bundles of their personal karma.

The first of the magmas is *Okruis*, the slimy and sticky bottom of *Fukabirn*.

From *Dromn* no old fragments of any type remain from the *shelt* that covers the body, so here begins the formation of a new corporeal entity. In *Okruis*, its construction reaches its end, and there is nothing remaining that would even distantly remind it of a human figure. It is now a somewhat spherical shape created from live infra-metal.

So what is the purpose of the torments of *Fukabirn* and *Okruis*? Why? First, there are few sufferers here. In *Skrivnous* and *Ladref*, millions anguished; here are only hundreds, maybe even a few dozen. The persecution and conviction of a philosophic enemy, sentencing the innocent, the torture of defenseless people, imposing affliction on children – all of this is redeemed through suffering here, in *Okruis* and *Fukabirn*.

Here those undergoing anguish recollect distinctly the religious instruction they heard on earth and of what they were warned. Corporeal torments are felt subjectively here as retribution, but they already begin to recognize the dual nature of the law and that the person responsible for its cruelty is not God, but the demonic powers. Their perception of it becomes clear: here is the materialization of the Providential side of the law, its ancient basis that was created by the demiurges long before the discard of *Gagtungr* into *Shadanakar*. To clear perception, to clear the conscience, the growth of spiritual hunger – is that facet of the law of retribution which the bright powers withheld from the dark powers, and because of this facet this law did not become an absolute evil.

The infra-physical composition of magma is very similar to its physical composition. Their captives initially preserved freedom of movement, but for the meanwhile there is no need for activities to support their existence. They absorb strength from the surrounding environment in a mechanical manner. All of this pertains also to the 2nd of the belts of magma – *Gvegr*, which is portrayed as a fiery red-hot motionless environment.

However I did want to bring to mind that suffering in *Enrof* – no matter what kind it is – will mitigate post-mortem torment, and mainly in the sense of shortening its term, but never in the sense of its intensity. The term of the redemptive punishment of the soul after death is defined, basically, by the scale of the sufferings of those they sacrificed as a result of their actions in *Enrof*. The massive character of crimes incurs a lower descent into the strata of retribution. *Okruis* can be exchanged for *Yukarvayr*, *Gvegr* for *Propuilk*. The matter is such that corporeal torments started in *Fukabirn* and growing in *Okruis* and *Gvegr*, reach their apogee in the subsequent stratum named *Yukarvayr*: this is the turbulent magma. Here those who corrupted high and bright ideals are redeemed, those who need to answer for the distortion of the trans-physical routes of thousands and millions. Here are also those who are guilty of practicing those vile acts that we in our dry emaciated language call sadism, that is, such conduct where the suffering of others does not just cause a feeling of pleasure, but that the undue pleasure was completely clearly understood by the perpetrator at that time and so he again and again committed this atrocity on others.

Fortunately, time is here speeding by much faster and ahead of us comes *Propuilk* – solid magma, the world of the redemptive sufferings of the masses of executioners who are guilty of the murder of armies and who are the torturers of national populaces. They are deprived of any freedom of movement. Their body is as though encased in a solid container, pressuring them on all sides. The worst of all corporeal punishments they suffer here is still not comparable to the suffering of their soul. Here is also a burning repentance and such a despair for God, one that they cannot possibly incur in any of the higher strata. Fortunately, only a few descend as far as *Propuilk*. Do we need to say that here exist such creatures like Ezhov[51] or his confederate Beria?[52] It is surprising that here, and not too long ago, that Maluta Skuratov[53] completed his term of anguish here, while of the western meta-cultures, [Maximilien] Robespierre and [Louis Antoine de] Saint-Just, and several of the inquisitors of the 16th century, still have not loosed their karma.

The *sakuala* of the magmas concludes its strata with the one possessing the name – *Erl*. This is the super-heavy magma. Here the corporeal sufferings are subdued in comparison to the spiritual torment. The *Erl* was created for the retribution of those who are, as we would call them in our legal language, recidivists. These are the ones who have once already ended in the magmas and were subsequently redeemed and then returned

---

[51] Nikolai Ezhov, minister of National Committee of Internal Affairs (head of Soviet secret police).
[52] Lavrenti Beria, minister of KGB of the USSR.
[53] Henchman of Tsar Ivan IV the Terrible.

to *Enrof,* but there again committed horrible crimes and were sentenced back again, so they are now here.

So the magmas end.

Further down begins the *sakuala* of the worlds corresponding to the physical core of the planet, typical for all meta-cultures.

The first to which we arrive is *Biask,* the infra-red caves, the most pale of the scarlet color of the nether regions, if we can thus define the staircase of strata from *Fukabirn* to *Biask.* The human form here changes and they now appear as a head with 4 legs. As a result of this they are deprived of the ability to speak, and even then there is no one with whom to speak. Each of the inmates is isolated from the balance of the world and sees only his tormentors, particularly those who appear as, and this may be strange, notorious devils. Sitting here in *Enrof,* a person can laugh all he wants at the belief in the existence of such horned ugly creatures, but it is not worth even to have your mortal enemy to have a close friendship with them.

But because the sacrifices that fall into *Biask* number in all about a dozen, the devils, having need of their *gavvakh,* a large number of them, well they beat the *gavvakh* out from their sacrifices with all their means, however a manner they can think of. The sacrifices of *Biask* are those who corrupted morals in *Enrof.* Such crimes are deemed very severe because they cause greater karmic harm for thousands of human souls. Even executioners, by whose hands hundred of persons physically perished, did not cause such damage as those of whom it is said in the Gospel, "Whoever leads astray even one of these little ones who believe in me, it would be better if they were to hang a millstone on his neck and drown him in the depths of the sea."[54]

Lower than *Biask, Amiutz* opens its jaws: it consists of vertical ravines. They hang in them completely helpless and some are stuck to keep them from falling. But since the crevasses lead to *Gashsharva,* the unfortunate seems to be hanging straight over a nest of the demonic powers of

---

[54] So does Daniel Andreev render this verse from Matt 18:6.

Shadanakar. Here are those who combined deliberate sadism with immense crimes.

But the vertical ravines of *Amiutz* also contain side caverns that are dead ends. This is the *Etrech*, the planetary night, continuing from the beginning of the installation of *Shadanakar* to the end of the existence of our planet in *Enrof,* that is, to the consummation of the future eon. There are only a few who were assigned here, for example, Ivan the Terrible. And further there is one more stratum, a really special one, and it is solely for Judas Iscariot because of what he did. It is called *Zhursch*, and no one has ever, except for Judas, entered this stratum.

It is clear, of course, that we are unable to create for ourselves even a remote visualization of the sufferings that are endured in the strata of the core.

So now the descriptions have reached the final of the strata – the cemetery of *Shadanakar.* Somehow I was not successful in hearing exactly the pronunciation of its appellation. At one time it seemed to sound like *Sufel,* but at other times it seems that the more correct was *Sufetkh,* but I am still not sure. Those so obstinate in their evil are released here from the lower places of suffering. Their shells – what remains of their *shelts* – are here discarded by monads. Monads fall from *Shadanakar* in general in order to begin everything all over again in other and new regions, times and forms. And this is much better than to collapse through the Bottom of *Shadanakar* to the Bottom of the Galaxy: but the monads go no further from here and cannot escape cosmic time.

But the *shelt* that is alive possesses self-realization, although it is a lower *I.* In *Sufetkh* it can hardly move, gradually expelling the last remains of its vital strengths. This is that very Second Death that is mentioned in the Holy Scriptures. The spark of consciousness smolders to the end and the measure of its torment increases beyond its perception by the demons. To this time no one from the Light has been able to enter here, even the planetary Logos. The *Sufetkh* can been seen on occasion by the brethren of the *sinklits*, but not from inside, but from neighboring strata. Then they can differentiate the desert, over which stands the pale-violet sun of *Gashsharva* – the anti-cosmos of *Gagtungr*.

Fortunately, during the entire history of humanity there was assembled hardly a few hundred monads who fell into *Sufetkh*. Of them only a few left any trace in history, because all the mature monads descending are drawn into *Gashsharva*. In *Sufetkh* are those who are not needed in *Gashsharva*. Of all the historical figures I know of only one – Domitian.[55]

I well know that the humanitarian cognizance of our age would want to view a completely different picture than these that I have displayed in this chapter. Some will be frightened because my testimonies display to them excessive recollections of popular figures, and the source of which is historical Christianity. Others will be shocked at the barbaric severity of the laws and tangible character of the terrible torments in these places of sufferings. But first I am prepared to ask, "Did they actually seriously think that the teaching of the fathers of the church would not contain anything except games to scare the imagination?"

And those who are agitated by the severity of the laws can only answer in one way, "So must we work toward their enlightenment!" Of course, with intellectual customs of the humanitarian age it would be easier to gain an understanding not of the tangible torments, but of the psychological: gnawing of the conscience, melancholy due to the impossibility of love, and such items. Essentially it is the great criminals of history who are subject to tangible sufferings for the most part. At the same time, each of us has the volition to exert effort to ameliorate the severity of the penalty for violating these laws.

---

[55] Titias Flavius Caesar Domitian, Roman Emperor. 51–96 AD.

CHAPTER 3

SHRASTRAS AND *YUITZRAORS*

I now approach a description of the worlds that have for humanity and its history and for the entirety of *Shadanakar* an especially new meaning, such that particularly these worlds were created by the demonic powers as direct weapons for the materialization of the global plan of *Gagtungr.*

There are actually 2 categories, 2 *sakualas* of the infra-physical strata, tightly connected together.

I mentioned a little already about how each of the meta-cultures includes a specific anti-pole to its *zatomis*, a special citadel of its demonic powers where as if the sacred cities of the *sinklits* are reflected inside-out through black mirrors. This address will deal with the *shrastras*, the residences of anti-humanity.

The *shrastras* are various regions of a single, three-dimensional spatial world. Each of them possess, however, its own unalterable number of time coordinates (dimensions). The circle of *shrastras* are meta-geologically connected with the lower strata of the earth's core and includes a compensating series of ledges. It is located opposite the dark dual antipodes of *Eyanna, Olymp*, Paradise, *Monsalvat*, heavenly Russia, and the balance of *zatomises*. The compensating series of ledges, equally projected as mountainous masses on the surface of the ground, have their peaks and crests turned toward the center of the planet.

In *Enrof,* these regions are lifeless and dead, they contain basalt and lava and nothing more. But it is not this way in the four-dimensional world. Closer to the center, under them lies a scarlet-colored desolation, blazing turbulent waves of light and heat of a dark-orange illumination. There are 2 equally-acting forces of attraction on the under side of the crust: one draws toward the thick crust and the other to the center of the earth (please note that the understanding here of *up* and *down* are not the same as ours). In the underground orange-scarlet sky, infra-violet and infra-red lights that are almost black motionlessly stand. So do *Gashsharva* and the places of suffering of the earth's core perceive the region. These multi-millions of societies and these monstrous hierarchies live in the rays of these moons and strengthen their citadels. In our eyes they manifest themselves as great autocracies, government tyrannies, and the impersonal or faceless vampires of global history.

So what type of nature is this? What type of landscape reigns in this underside of the world? There is no blue or green light here. The vision of the residents is not able to perceive these colors and these are the only 2 that our eyes are unable to perceive. The place also possesses something like plant life, but it is dense and awesome: clusters of massive deep-scarlet bushes, while in some places, separate from the others, there are flowers made from a flickering flame. The contour is very uneven. Scattered in these expansive desolate areas are lakes and seas made of white and pink lava. The entire landscape has its unique and original geo-urbanistic character: gigantic cities of multi-millions of population; while in infra-Russia, for example, the chief city is connected almost with the entire compensating ledges of the anti-Urals, while another corresponds to the Caucasus, while at the present more cities on the compensatory ledges of the mountains of Kazakhstan and Tian-Shan are being created. There are also cities here and in the lowlands, but there are further depressed since these regions for the most part are filled with lava.

Anti-humanity consists basically of 2 races or species very different from one another. The primary of the 2 races is the smaller in number, but they are highly intellectual creatures, moving about the circle of reincarnations in the *shrastras*, where the assume a four-dimensional form, somewhat remindful of ours. This is a body corresponding to ours physically, called *karrokh*. It is constructed of the materiality of these strata, created by the higher demonic hierarchies. The residents of the *shrastras* possess a pair of upper limbs and a pair of lower limbs, but with a different number of fingers and toes. Other than this they are equipped with protrusions that are used for flight and made of skin. The have red penetrating eyes pointing in various directions from their cylindrical heads. They have a mouse-gray skin and an extended tunnel-shaped mouth that would generate repulsion in a person. But these creatures possess an acute intelligence, they are creators of a high civilization, and in some respects are advanced beyond us. They are called *igvies*.

The *igvies* appeared first in the *shrastras* of the Babylon-Assyrian meta-culture. A another race existed in the more ancient *shrastras*, the ancestors of the present *raruggas*, of whom I will speak later. But I do not fully understand the actual evolution of the *igvies*, the matter is having to deal with strange occurrences that the intellect is unable to absorb. Although among people there are no monads that are demonic by their inherent nature, but there were occurrences, nonetheless exceptional and rare, when a person on his distant route voluntarily became an *igva*. Other than the desire to do this, what it requires is a colossal clarity of cognizance and a unique development of special abilities. So was the founder of anti-humanity, an individual, completely real, residing in Uruk and Babylon, where he was a priest of Nergal,[56] while behind him he had a long chain of incarnations in more ancient cultures and also in the humanity of the titans.

The *igvies* evolved from the union of this [monad-person] with *Leeleet*. She is capable to often acquire – but very rarely and just at the will of *Gagtungr* – a female figure in the more solid worlds. When she appeared in Babylonia, what people saw occur was the following: it was as though she just appeared out of nothing and nowhere. Three people saw her: the future father of the *igvies* and 2 others. One of them went out of his mind and the other was executed. This entity, for whose sake she accepted a translucent physical figure, united with her through his astral, and later his ethereal, body. She then descended, completely enveloped in a flame of fire, to the desolate infra-physical

---

[56] A deity worshipped in ancient Mesopotamia.

stratum where she ejected the first *igva* couple from her uterus. The progenitor of this race did not incarnate any more, not in the *shrastras* or in *Enrof.* Now he is in *Digm* and his involvement in the construction and materialization of the demonic plan is very considerable.

The *igvies* possess a verbal language of one-syllable word structures. Among our languages, it seems to be phonetically closest of all to the Chinese, but because of the tunnel shape of their mouth, sounds similar to *o* and *ou* dominate among the vowels.

On occasion they wear clothes, but more than often they walk about nude. The overwhelming intellectuality of these creatures emasculated their sexual drive. The manner they breed is similar to humans, but more offensively. They sexually intercourse while walking with no need of privacy, since they are deprived of any sense of shame. The feelings of love, loyalty and sympathy do exist but in an embryonic stage. In place of a family they have short-term unions, and for raising their offspring, they hire competent nursemaids. They have a servile sense of morality.

Their society consists of 2 classes: the higher intelligent, into which enter scholars, engineers, priests and, if this is the proper word, administrators. The balance are subject to them and conduct themselves only in the manner they are guided. Nevertheless, such guidance is austere and provided by those who are called – great *igvies,* a group of priest-emperors that seem to inherit this rank successively through generations, and also by the *yuitzraors* who reside in the neighboring stratum.

Almost unlimited and factual sovereignty is held in each of the *shrastras* by the great *igva.* The *shrastra* realm is not a monarchy and of course is not a theocracy; it is a satan-cracy. The principal of dynastic inheritance of authority over the *igvies* is so strange. The successor is selected and prepared for decades, an entity of impressive rationality and perception and foresight. The great *igvies* possess an immense clarity of comprehension. They are capable of perception as far as the anti-cosmos of the galaxy, and *Gagtungr* himself invokes them constantly. After death the great *igvies* ascend directly to *Digm*.

It would be incorrect to say that at face value the *shrastras* possess science and technology that is at least equivalent to ours. More likely, it is our science and technology that is superior to the science and technology of the *igvies*. Other conditions and laws of these strata are defined differently than we do ours. The content of their sciences and the methods of their scientific research and principals of technology is similar to ours. True, they are far from advancing beyond us in this region, likewise many of us would consider their customs and other attributes to be magic and sorcery. But they do utilize the concepts of the gear, wheel and internal combustion. They have ships to sail on their lakes made of infra-lava. How barbaric this may seem to us, the *shrastras* have long practiced regular races, and even their tourist industry is highly developed, but not with recreational goals, but for educational purposes. They even have an aviation industry, even though the *igvies* are capable of motion with great speed, with the ability to balance themselves upside down on their heads and even sit on ceilings and wall like flies.

Science provided *igvies* the possibility to penetrate to the surface of the ground. But in their infra-physical stratum this surface is dead and desolate, just as with the surface of our moon. But just as the spatial expanse of the *sakuala* of the *shrastras* terminates at the edges of the solar system, there are no stars in their sky. But the *igvies* see the sun and planets, although in a different manner than we do. The temperatures in the *shrastras* is very high, and for us it would be intolerable, and for this reason the sun that appears to the *igvies* as a vague infra-red spot only radiates a bare warmth and which is insufficient for them. Regardless of all the measures taken for their self-defense, those taken against famine, the *igva*-pioneers on the surface of the ground suffered cruelly. This surface is still little suitable for their existence, just as the inner regions of Antarctica for us. However they do have in view some type of adaptation of the surface for their use, but this will occur in their personal stratum and not in ours.

It is their most cherished of expectations, a dream that unifies them, to expand their sovereignty to all the strata of *Shadanakar* with the help of the *yuitzraors* and *Gagtungr*. They are supposing that the great God-opposer of the coming era, who is residing in *Gashsharva* while in the process of preparation for his birth in the midst of humanity in the near future, will create in *Enrof* a creation that is semi-human and semi-*igva*. This will initiate a new race of *igvies* in our stratum and they will breed quickly, as do fish. Their intent is to gradually replace people, to transform the surface of the earth into a residence of diabolic-humanity.

Igvies move along a circle of incarnations in the *shrastras*, while in the intervals they remain in one state as follows: their *shelt* together with their astral falls to the Bottom (since incarnation is impossible in a super-heavy body without an astral), while they are carried through the magmas and *Gashsharva*, barely touching them. During this descent their ethereal bodies rapidly scatter into droplets.

Incidences of enlightenment among the *igvies* is rare and only on an individual basis, and as a result of course, there occurs a change with them after their death. All of them, except for a few of the great *igvies*, have an inside-out understanding of God, as though he is a global tyrant, more terrifying that *Gagtungr*. They have heard about Christ from their great *igvies*, but their perception of him seems to be more of an anti-christ, as though a rebellious and extremely dangerous despot. In general, all is turned upside down regarding this topic. Because of this it is only natural that their religion primarily consists of an ascetic demonism and whose veneration ascends to *Gagtungr*.

The *igva* civilizations are enhanced by science and technology; it includes several branches of art. In front of a grandiose cone-shaped temple in *Druekkarg*, the principle city of the Russian anti-humanity, one that looks like a mountain but hollow inside, there hangs a monstrous sculpture: a pre-*igva* riding a *rarugga*.

What serves as an obstacle to the development of art is the orientation of the *igvies'* psyche and their weak emotionalism. The representations they create are actually ugly and distorted, and all of their art seems to follow this trend; our aesthetic critics would consider such art as tasteless.

However what is more developed among the *shrastras* is architecture. Cities are constructed from buildings of super-human measurements, but their geometric shapes are bland. In part they look like the sides of a cliff, hollow inside and faceless on the outside. Pyramid-shaped buildings shine with a façade of red, gray and brown colors.

And there in these cities, music blares, and for the most part it is noisy. Our ears would consider it cacophony, but on occasion it will rise to a level of rhythmic tunes that would even entice some of us. Another role in life that the *igva* plays is dance, if this word is permitted to be used when applying to their promiscuous bacchanalia. And their demonism, combining strikingly lunimous effects, their deafening sounds from gigantic musical instruments, and ecstatic soaring through the four-dimensional spare, transforms the masses into insanity. Such scenarios draw the angels of gloom while the energy vibrations nourish *Gagtungr*.

There are other creatures that reside in the *shrastras* other than *igvies*, who are aboriginal to this inside-out world – *raruggas*, an ancient species whose figure is remindful in part of centaurs, in part of angels of gloom, but more than all, of mesozoic pangolins[57] who are able to fly. They rise into the air but not in the manner as did the pterodactyls of *Enrof* with their bat-like wings. The *rarugga's* wings are immense and their length is about the height of a tall person. Due to the law of gravity in *Enrof,* it would not be possible for such massive creatures to fly here.

Their similarity to pangolins is not accidental; *raruggas* are these pangolins. After prolonged incarnations in the bodies of an allosaurus, tyrannosaurus, and pterodactyl, some of them, those

---

[57] Anteaters

having more of a predatory appearance, entered the route of further evolution in the infra-physical strata. Over the course of millions of years they attained a level of intellect, but this intellect was still very far from the acute intellectuality of the *igvies*. As a result their corporeal strength and unbelievable emotional flare modified their psychological attitude such that after a prolonged struggle for control of this stratum, the *igvies* were forced to reconcile with a tight coexistence with *raruggas*. Soon between the 2 races an original *modus vivendi* was instituted and which evolved into a union. Now the *raruggas* are something like an educated cavalry of the *shrastras*, their army. The *igvies* themselves participate in wars only in extreme situations, their effort more directed to guidance and technology. The retarded brains of the *raruggas* are still not developed enough to deal with the tasks of military science. But their unsurpassable blood-thirstiness, their militarism and fearlessness is an indispensable condition for their victorious wars in this stratum. The ancient traditions of infernal winged horses is an echo of the existence of the *raruggas*.

There are 2 types of war on the back side of the world. In earlier history these satan-cracies were reduced significantly, either due to mutual competition or armed warfare. Of course, not all the wars of humanity occurred here in this gloomy world, but ours did unconditionally. During the course of the worst of these wars, some *shrastras* endured catastrophic changes and even annihilation. Now it is more complex: the higher demonic institutions concentrate all their effort to weaken peace between the *shrastras*. The reason for this is very complex and will be gradually explained later. Truthfully, the irreconcilable struggle progresses not between *shrastras*, but between *igvies*, *raruggas* and *yuitzraors* on the one side, and the *sinklits* of the *zatomises*, angels, *daimons* and even the demiurges of the supra-nations, on the other.

After the meta-culture consummates the cycle of its existence in *Enrof*, its *shrastra* incurs dim and melancholy days similar to a constant agony due to hunger. *Gagtungr* no longer needs such *shrastras* and they are discarded to their own arbitrary volition.

But the life of the *shrastras* are tightly woven with the existence of a completely different species and scale of demonic entities, whose strata comprises the neighboring *sakuala*. And even though neighboring, it is mutual active with the *sakuala* of the *shrastras*. *Igvies* and *raruggas* are still not in a position to migrate into these strata, but the residents of the neighboring *sakuala* – the *yuitzraors* – are able to enter and do enter, or better said, slither, into the cities of the *igvies*.

These potent entities play a role in history and meta-history that is just as immense as they are physically immense. Even if the head of one of these creatures was to appear in the center of Moscow, his tentacles would reach as far as the sea.[58] They move place to place at a fascinating speed, and possess the ability to speak, but they are also somewhat smart. Their evolution is complex and in a dual manner.

Each birth of an *yuitzraor* appears in the world as the offspring between *karossa*, the local and national materialization of *Leeleet*, the International Aphrodite of humanity, and the individual demiurges of the supra-nations. In the majority of meta-cultures, these entities were born due to the will of the demiurges as defenders of the supra-nations from external enemies. First they appeared in the meta-culture of Babylonia: its demiurge attempted to use its offspring to resist the militarist egregores of Egypt and Media, which threatened the very existence of the Babylonian supra-nation. But the *karossas* carry the cursed seed of *Gagtungr*, the result of when he in deep antiquity inseminated the ethereal body of *Leeleet* with distinct national-cultural expressions of their specific meta-culture. And the seed of *Gagtungr* predetermined that the first *yuitzraor*, from its beginning, will fulfill the will of its demiurge, so then it was quickly reborn as the trans-physical carrier of the great and powerful empire of Babylon. His aggressiveness caused an altercation with the demiurges of the other supra-nations, and at least to the point of they defending their countries in *Enrof.* These measures consisted of the birth of similar entities who

---

[58] This would be the Baltic Sea, about 400 miles away.

would be capable of resisting the *yuitzraor* of Babylon. In this manner, these monsters appeared in the Iranian and Hebrew meta-cultures, and later in all the others.

The propagation of these extremely aggressive and deeply unfortunate entities occurs by means of something that is remindful of gemmation. They are asexual. Each offspring immediately becomes a mortal enemy of its parent and the potential to become its murderer. So did the dynasty of *yuitzraors* evolve in the meta-cultures, and they would succeed one another after the murder of the parent and the heart eaten. In the majority of meta-cultures there simultaneously exists just one *yuitzraor* or else a *yuitzraor*-parent with one or several offspring who lead a despairing war against the father. The most monstrous scenes of meta-history is the struggle between *yuitzraors* and their annihilation of one another.

Over the course of Russian history, three reigning *yuitzraors* have succeeded each other, but before the one perished, his offspring appeared and who was allowed to devour the parent's body. A different situation was created in the European meta-culture: there existed simultaneously several dynasties of *yuitzraors*, and this circumstance birthed immense historical consequences for the entire world, since the presence of several similar dynasties hindered and continues to hinder the unification of the European supra-nation into one corporate body. So the reason for all the great European wars and the 2 recent world wars.

The *yuitzraors* reside in a desolate world that is similar to hot tundra, it is divided among separate zones corresponding to the boundaries of the meta-culture. Each *yuitzraor* is allowed to enter not just the neighboring zones (of course only if they defeat the neighboring *yuitzraor*), but also the *shrastras*. He floats into it like a mountain of fog. The *igvies* and *raruggas* tremble at hearing his voice, as though in the presence of a sovereign or despot, but along with this they see in him a great defender who is against the other *shrastras* and against the powers of Light.

The *yuitzraors* can vaguely see *Enrof*: the people and our landscape is blurry and imprecise, but they love our world with a fiery and unquenchable passion. They want to incarnate here, but they cannot. They see *Gagtungr* from a distant and tremble like slaves. They consider the great *igvies* as having limited authority and as nothing more than fulfillers of their will. In reality the great *igva* sees higher and deeper, knows more and strives to utilize famine, militarism and the power of the *yuitzraors* in the interests of anti-humanity.

So what supports the vital strengths of the *yuitzraors*? The mechanism of this process is very intricate. The *yuitzraor* emanates gigantic quantities of its personal psychic energy that penetrates into *Enrof.* The unconscious region of a person's psyche accepts it and so it materializes in the middle of humanity's societies in the form of complex national-state feelings. This veneration of your state (not your nation or country, but particularly the state and its potency); living a life as a participant in the grandiose activity of the sovereignty, cult of Caesar or leaders; a fiery hate of its enemies; a pride in the materialistic success and external victories of your state; patriotism, militarism, blood-thirstiness, and military fervor – all of these feelings surfacing in the regions of human subconsciousness can grow, inflate and hypertrophy, and all due to the inclusion of *yuitzraor* energy.

These series of energies with their bequeathments enrich those people having this particular attitude. This causes a psychological manipulation of the population that results in psycho-emanations, and these descend through the earth's crust and penetrate into the neighboring infra-strata and release what appears to be a liquidy dew on the ground of the *shrastras*. The *igvies* then gather it for the *yuitzraors* – and which is their primary obligation – while any extra they eat themselves.

It is very possible that I am simplifying or not completely correctly expounding the mechanism of this process. But essentially it is the nourishment of the *yuitzraors* though the psycho-emanations of the population, and these emanations are connected particularly with the emotions generated by the state government. This is not only a most serious fact, but is the reason for innumerable catastrophes.

Igvies are not permitted entrance into the strata of the *yuitzraors*, but they see it from the outside, vaguely, like shadows. If they can stealthily enter, they observe the struggle between the *yuitzraors* and the demiurge, both with all their strength striving to pour more of the nourishing dew into the enraged carcass of a demon. But watching this, they do not see the demiurge because he is invisible to them and utilizes this unseen potency and radiance to struggle against the demon, to attack him with sensations of terror and malice. They know that the defeat of the *yuitzraor* will subsequently cause the annihilation of the state formation in *Enrof*, the ruin of the entire dynasty of *yuitzraors* or else the destruction of the *shrastras*.[59] So is the destruction of the warring governments of the subject meta-cultures predefined, and in every case for many centuries.

There still remains a few words to be said about *Druekkarg*, one of the *shrastras*.

Its principle city is encircled by a citadel, consisting of several concentric rings. *Navna* languishes in one of them, she is the Ideal Conciliar Soul of Russia. During the era of the 3rd *Zhrugr*,[60] her situation worsened: a solid lid was installed over her. Now her radiating voice hardly penetrates anyplace; she is a bluish color light on the surface of cyclopean concrete walls, and which is invisible to the *igvies* and *raruggas*. But those outside of *Druekkarg*, just the believers in Russia and the enlightened in the heavenly Russia, hear her voice. Who is she, *Navna*?

This is the one who unites Russia into one nation; who summons and draws the separate Russian soul higher and higher; who inspires Russian art with a unique fragrance; who oversees the immaculate and supreme female images of Russian folklore, literature and music; who births in Russian hearts a nostalgia for a lofty predestination and obligation for Russia – all of this is *Navna*. What makes her conciliar is that nothing from

---

[59] Some of this indirectly pertains to the death of Joseph Stalin, and is further discussed in Book 11, Chapter 3, *The Dark Shepherd*.
[60] Joseph Stalin

any Russian soul that rises to *Navna* enters into her or is preserved by her or blends with her, if she finds anything in it of a personal *I*. This can also be said in the following manner: a certain category of spirit-energy that each person possesses, and which enters into the living organism of the nation, resides in *Navna*.

Navna is the bride of the demiurge of Russia and the captive of the *Zhrugrs*.

The *Zhrugr*, as with the balance of *yuitzraors*, is unable to have offspring, except occasionally the gemmating *zhrugrits*. But something remotely similar to a wedding between it[61] and the *karossa*[62] of Russia having the name of *Dingra* consists in him sucking the soul out of individual Russians, or more precisely, their *shelts*, and while they are asleep he throws them into the uterus of the *karossa* of *Dingra* where they are transformed, mutilated and spiritually emasculated. We perceive the result of this as a mental rebirth of those of our fatherland who became active builders of this citadel.

---

[61] the *Zhrugr* is male
[62] the *karossa* is female

BOOK V

The Structure of *Shadanakar*: The *Stikhials*

Chapter 1

The Demonic Stikhials

There are 4 *sakualas* among the number of the diversely-significant and diverse materiality strata that compose *Shadanakar* that are connected with those that we call the *stikhials* of Nature. How are they connected? By what means?

Among the number of the diversely significant and diversely materiality strata that compose *Shadanakar*, there are 4 *sakualas* that are tied with what we call the *stikhials* of nature. How are they tied? Using what?

Here we touch on a thesis whose exposition is subject to some difficulty. The matter is that the meaning and significance of certain zones of the three-dimensional world that we perceive by our 5 senses is sufficient enough for what we need, for example, the snow-capped mountains formed out of gneiss, granite and other rocks, and covered with solid ice and glaciers that encompasses us. But the three-dimensional zone is only a partial sphere or the outer sphere relative to another zone that is conditionally expressed as also a partial sphere, but possessing a different number of spatial coordinates. The snow-capped ridges, lifeless, uncomfortable and plantless in their dead majesty is only one of the 2 partial spheres or 2 strata of a tightly connected system. The other partial sphere, or better said, its other stratum, has different dimensions. This stratum appears as a country of incarnated spirits of tremendous majesty. It is called *Orliontana*.

Particularly the irradiation of *Orliontana* through the crust of a three-dimensional object summons an impression of royal tranquility, potency and brilliance. *Orliontana*, watched with a spiritual vision, are the mountain peaks in spiritual glory. The summits that are accessible with our physical eyes are no more than the production of the power of these entities – the *stikhials* of *Orliontana* – over millions years of years of formation. When the human soul, carrying within itself the consequences of a prolonged existence in a condition of unbelief, now is isolated in *Olirna* in the middle of these semitransparent mountains, it is particularly the vision of the stratum of *Orliontana* that promotes the removal of the final traces of blind insulation and stagnancy in the psychological entity and communicates to the human soul an understanding of the multi-stratification and spiritual majesty of the universe.

But in contradistinction to *Orliontana*, the majority of strata of *stikhials* are local, that is, their spatial expanse does not extend to cosmic proportions. In fact, it is deprived of even an extension to the end of the solar system, which the worlds of the *shrastras* even possess. This is why there is no heaven in the majority of these strata. The strata of the *stikhials* are like their own category of oasis, between them is desert. There are definite boundaries to separate them one from another, as with the *shrastras*, and this is due to them having different numbers of time coordinates.

Stikhials are called monads who have traversed their route of installation in *Shadanakar* primarily through the kingdom of nature. Meanwhile we must not forget that humanity is also one aspect of the unique form of the kingdom of nature. It is particularly the *stikhials'* powers, which simmer there and without which their existence would be unthinkable, that express this aspect of it. So it is no wonder that such *stikhials* do exist, which are tied not with nature (in the general sense of the word), but with humanity, with the intrinsic aspect of its *stikhial.*

Chapter 2

The Bright *Stikhials*

I am exhausted with numbering new and newer strata, with the introduction of new and newer appellations. Now only a few remain ahead of me: the review and structure of *Shadanakar* nears its end.

I am so happy that I have completed our descent into the demonic worlds and that now in front of us are the strata of beautiful creatures, ones that for a human are unconditionally pleasant and welcoming. But to describe the bright ones, and more so those on our side, is always significantly more difficult than the dark or monstrous.

Particularly shining and sparkling in the exalted *Flyauros* are the monads of the bright *stikhials* that draw their *shelts* from there, similar to rays, to the *zatomises*, in order to there concentrate around themselves an enlightened material: these are their souls clothed in astral covers. During the interval between incarnations, these souls remain there. When they are incarnated in the worlds of the bright *stikhials*, in their proper order they concentrate around themselves a materiality that is a more dense substance, an ethereal. Particularly these worlds are listed in this chapter. Not one of the bright *stikhials*, except for the *stikhials* of *Arashamf*, is unaware of an increase in quantity, and is unaware of incarnations in *Enrof.* Each of them independently clothes itself with a weave of a four-dimensional world: this is the incarnation that no longer needs to increase its number. But after the chain of incarnations, every *stikhial*, in place of their succeeding death, relives a transformation leading to *Fayir* and *Yusnorm*.

The European tales of elves are not at all tales: this is the stratum of the residence of small well-mannered and mesmerizing creatures that resemble elves, and which they actually are. So can we call this stratum: country of the elves.

The higher and thin stratum of the earthly crust, where the seeds and roots of plants take cover, has its corresponding trans-physical world – the marvelous country of *Darainna*, the region of good spirits. It is interjected with roots and seeds. Its landscape appears to be enchanted, and its seeds and roots quietly shine with the most gentle shades of light blue, silver and green colors. Surrounding each seed is a living aura that softly radiates. The residents of *Darainna* are tiny creatures, similar to white hats, with smaller hats as a head and as wings. Their higher and lower members protrude out from them. They float through the air by waving their wings in a orderly manner. This is also their manner of speech, the manner they communicate with one another, and they hover over the seeds and roots as over a cradle. They are familiar with the secret process [of growth] and thanks to which every tiny seed grows into a large tree. If it were not for their help, the dark powers would gain access to these cradles and long ago would have transformed the surface of the ground into impassible growths to scare anybody: vampiric and predatory and ugly equivalents of weeds and thorns.

Going deeper into the ground of *Darainna*, finally you will reach *Ron* or *Kattaram*.

Along the ground of the forests, the area of mosses, grasses, bushes, and all that we call undergrowth, is the corresponding stratum named *Murokhamma*, while the residence of the *stikhials* of the forests is called *Arashamf*.

No, they are not wood nymphs. Perhaps such creatures did exist, but I am not aware of them. The *stikhials* of *Murokhamma* and *Arashamf* do not look like humans at all, and not even do any of the creatures of this stratum. The souls of the individual trees reside in the *zatomises*. There they are intelligent, tall, handsome and smart. The brethren of the *sinklits* associate with them as much as they can, and for the purpose of mutual exchange of ideas, feelings and vital experiences. But in *Arashamf,* they are clothed with an ethereal body and are submerged into somnolence. Each *stikhial* of *Arashamf* passed through a number of incarnations. For many of them the general sum of years of their existence in *Enrof* can be quantified as a huge amount, nearing a million. The landscape of *Arashamf* is remindful of greenish non-burning flames, quietly fluttering and emitting a nice fragrance. Some of the residents are kind, like people of integrity, and are well-disposed toward us. They are patient, tranquil and prudent. On occasion among them is something like a festive occasion: they cling to one another, all on the same side. The entire ethereal forest transforms into a quietly overflowing flame with all of them bending down to one another and then rising. Their choir's voice sounds like psalms or praises. Occasionally the stratum *Murokhamma* will also participate; it has the appearance of being the same type of greenish environment, but much thicker, darker, warmer and happier.

Every person can easily remember how summer evenings or spring days would cause calm breezes to kiss the ground. They would kiss the ground with its grasses, meadows and roads, trees, surface of rivers and lakes, and people and animals. These are the *stikhials* of the stratum called *Vayieta*, they rejoice over life. They rejoice over us and foliage, waters and the sun; they rejoice over the cool, hot, soft, hard, bright or halfway dark ground. They fondle it and caress it. If we should have the opportunity to see *Vayieta* with our own eyes, it would seem to us that we were immersed into a place greenish, fragrant, with waves bouncing back and forth, crystal clear, cool and warm and principally alive and smart and joyful for us.

When a person shoves his face into the grass of a flowering meadow to escape the heat of a hot day, it is due to the sweet smell emanating, and the breeze across the warm soil, and the leaves encircling your head, and hearing the winds through the pine trees, and the light and warmth hovering over the meadows

– these are the *stikhials* of *Vayieta* playing and being idle together with the children of *Faltora*, the region of the *stikhials* of meadows and fields. Not even one cloudy thought remains in us and it would seem that this is paradise once lost, the dust of vital cares soars with the souls of immaculate respiration and, other than an all-consuming love toward nature, we are not in a condition to experience anything else.

Through the running waters of peaceful rivers the world shines truly with an inexpressible enticement. A special hierarchy resides here, from a long time back I was accustomed to call it the souls of rivers, although now I understand that this expression is not exact. Every river possesses such a soul, unique and irreplaceable. We see its eternal stratum of an eternally flowing body as the current of a river; while its genuine soil is in the heavenly Russia or in another heavenly region if it flows along the grounds of another culture of *Enrof*. But the internal stratum of its body, the ethereal one, which it permeates with life and where it materializes almost with complete self-realization, is located in a world that is merged with ours and called *Liyurna*. The bliss of its life consists in that it uninterruptedly provides for both streams of its meandering body of a large river, and then to the sea. And so its body never dries, gushing and flowing from source to mouth.

It is impossible to find the proper words to express the enticement of these creatures, such joyful, laughing, pleasant, polite, and peaceful, and there is no human kindness that can be compared with their kindness, except for maybe the kindness of the most bright and loving of some parent's daughters. And if we should be so fortunate to perceive *Liyurna* with body and soul, to immerse our body into the river's current, our ethereal body into the current of *Liyurna*, our soul into its soul shining in this *zatomis*, you will exit to the shore with such an immaculate, enlightened and joyful heart, the type a human has not possessed since the fall due to sin.

Vlanmim, one of the higher strata and the region of the *stikhials* of the sea, has a similar but partial effect on the human soul as does *Liyurna*. The landscape of this world is a bright-blue, with a rhythmic wave-filled ocean that is a soft-bright and ravishing blue that does not exist in *Enrof*, while its waves do not cause any foaming, but milky-white and azure bubbles similar to large flowers instead. Such flowers scatter and dissolve in front of your eyes, scatter and then again dissolve.

The *stikhials* of *Liyurna* have a female nature, while the *Vlanmim* are male, but this has nothing to do with reproduction, although the unification of the river with the sea is an expression of the love of the *stikhials* of both these worlds. *Vlanmim* is also capable of making us more wise and pure, but the place is susceptible to the effect from below of the gloomy *stikhials* of the ocean depths – the *Nugurt*, and this can be very severe. Its effect is noticeable on the psychological orientation and even physical figure of a person.

In the final strata, nonetheless, there are still noticeable signs of the others, the *stikhials* that are not bright: the *Nugurt*, as well as the *nibrusts* and *Duegguer*, the *stikhials* of the large port cities.

Over the lands and seas stretches *Zoongoof*, the region of the *stikhials* of the atmospheric moisture; they create clouds, rain, dew and fog. *Zoongoof* is not separated by a defined boundary from *Eerudrana*, the region of the *stikhials* whose activity is manifested in *Enrof* with storms and often hurricanes. Both of these strata overflow into each other, as do their entities.

If during a light freeze the soft snow quietly falls or if the trees and buildings stand white with frost, almost exuding a festive joy which we experience, all of this testifies to the closeness of the marvelous *stikhials* of *Nivenna*. The wild expanses, flawless, inexpressible immaculacy, this is *Nivenna*, the region of the *stikhials* of frost, falling snow, and the landscapes covered with fresh snow. Frolicking in an other-worldly happiness, just like we imagine elves doing, they cover the beloved land with their bridal veil. This is why such a joy of life penetrates us when myriads of soulless white stars quietly descend all around us. And why, when we look at trees or city parks covered white with frost, do we experience a sensation that unites us with festivity and calmness, a gush of vital strengths and ecstasy, reverence and infantile excitement. And the *stikhials* of *Nivenna* love especially those of us who have preserved eternally such a childlike principle in the soul; they greet him and motivate him to play with them. Running in the snow, causing muscles to flex and blood to circulate as they play in the snow or ride on skies from the mountains, all of this is what these *stikhials* enjoy.

Neighboring *Nivenna* is the severe and overcast *Akhash*, connected with the polar regions of our planet, the stratum of the Arctic and Antarctic *stikhials*. *Akhash* possesses cosmic reaches, and the Milky Way can be seen there. Here at corresponding times of the year the boundaries of both polar zones move toward the tropics.

Just as *Akhash* possesses cosmic reaches into space, the next 2 and final strata of *stikhials* also possess this: *Diramn*, tied to the stratosphere of the ocean belts of the lower temperatures, and *Sianna*, the world of the high temperatures and which encompasses the atmosphere of our planet at high altitudes. The residents of these *stikhials* are so immense and so strange compared to our psychological constitution, that to understand them is a matter that is extremely difficult. They are bright, but reflect a fiery formidable light. Only those who have entered exceptionally high altitudes of spirit are able to access their realm.

So are the *sakualas* of the Smaller *Stikhials*. They are small, but of course not in comparison to the size of people, since many of them are considerably stronger than an individual person, but in comparison with the *sakualas* of the others, the ascending staircase of the Supreme *Stikhials* alongside the original planetary deities. These are the potentates. The small stikhials joyfully tremble at their respiration. The majority of them are beautiful, tall and congenial entities of inexpressible majesty. But it is almost impossible to say anything about the landscapes of these strata, just as with the figure of these great entities, each of them has the ability to simultaneously be at several different spots of their stratum.

The King of the Blessing Wings is *Vauimn*, the incarnated spirit of the ocean atmosphere, he expands his sovereignty from the distant limits of the atmosphere to the very deepest abysses. His brother is the King of Life-Giving Waters,[63] *Ea*, and he has another name *Vlarol*, and he was honored by the Greeks under the name Poseidon, and the Romans under the name Neptune. Both spirits stand on an eternal guard at the sources of life in all the earth, not only in *Enrof*, but also in many other *sakualas*. Both are ancient, and just as flawless, as are the water and air.

The 3rd of the brothers is more ancient, the King of the Fiery Body, *Povurn*. Similar attributes are contained in the nether-world deity of Pluto or the Hindu Yama of ancient beliefs. This terrifying potentate of the underground magmas is not the servant of *Gagtungr*, although his transformation awaits him, it seems last of all, at the end of the 2nd Eon.

There is also a 4th great brother, but the youngest of them, the King of All Animal Kingdoms, *Zaranda*. He is incarnated in a stratum of a different materiality. The tragic history of the animal kingdom in *Enrof* placed a deep wound of global sorrow on his person. And no matter how historians attempt to explain the enigma or symbolism of the Egyptian sphinx, meta-history will always see in it the emblem of the one who combines within himself the nature of a great beast and the wisdom of superior humanity.

There are 7 supreme *stikhials*. Two divine sisters share between themselves the remaining regions of omnipotence: *Estira*, the Queen of the Eternal Garden, the mistress of the plant life of the kingdom of *Shadanakar*, and *Leeleet*, the International Aphrodite of all humanities.

The significance of *Leeleet* in our existence is immeasurably great. Just as with all the supreme *stikhials*, her world of residency is incomparable with any of our forms and is indescribable, but her personal figure is beyond visualization. Her body made of another materiality is omnipresent in her

---

[63] meaning fresh water, as opposed to salt water.

stratum, and just on rare occasions does she allow an image, but which can only be perceived by a person's spiritual vision. Although I do not know the mechanism of this process, what I do know is that without the participation of *Leeleet* the formation of even one body is impossible in the worlds of corporeal materiality, with the exception of the animals whose form is developed by *Zaranda*. In all the other kingdoms, this activity is executed by *Leeleet*: she formulates the series of generations, just as in the humanity of *Enrof*, so with the daimons, and in the demonic worlds, including the *raruggas* and *igvies* and the residents of *Duegguer*. Every body constructed from another materiality, created with her direct participation in the dark worlds, is *karrokh*.

This is why she has earned the merit of the entire appellation of being the sculptor of our flesh. As a result, her existence and operation is unbreakably connected with the region of human sexual sensations; and she or her *karossa* is involved in every act of human sexual intercourse. While the embryo is maturing in the uterus, she is always there.

At one time during the deepest of antiquity, this *stikhial Leeleet* became the spouse of the Principle Angel, that magnificent Spirit who later became the Logos of *Shadanakar*. This occurred during the era of the creation of the angelic strata, and *Leeleet* became the progenitress of this first humanity. But *Gagtungr* succeeded in penetrating *Leeleet's* world and as a result her refined material body received a certain demonic element. This was a catastrophe. From this point the entire series of posterities that were created through her, whether this was in the worlds of the titans, *daimons*, or humans, have received some of this element. Hebrew mysticism knows the term *Eytzekhore*, the seed of the devil in a human.

The primary and final of the supreme *stikhials* is the mother of all the remaining, and not just them, but also all that exists in *Shadanakar*: every *stikhials*, every animal, person, *daimon*, demon and even the great hierarchies. The never insufficient bosom, she is the creator of all the ethereal bodies of all creatures, while she participates along side each of their personal monads in the creation of their astral bodies. She has this quality of an inexhaustible warm love toward all, even toward demons: she worries and sorrows over them, but forgives. All call her *Mati*, even the angels of gloom and the monsters of *Gashsharva*. She loves them all, but she respects the excellent and superior hierarchies of *Shadanakar*, and especially Christ.

The sun impregnates her, and in *Enrof*, in her personal inexplicable world, the great and blinding spirit impregnates her. She perceives people, their psychological state, their inner image. She hears, she responds to the requests of our heart, she answers through nature and love. Yes, may her name be blessed! We can and we must pray to her with great humility:

May the beautiful moon, the daughter of heaven and earth be blessed, and may the sun bless you 3 times. All of us at one time or another resided in your immaculate viscera with our future body and our future soul, together with the entirety of *Shadanakar*. O, great God, the bringer of light! You were glorified in the temples of Egypt and Greece, on the shores of the Ganges, on the ziggurats of Ur, in the country of the setting sun and in the distant west, on the smooth mountain slopes of the Andes. All of us love you, and the evil and the good, the wise and dark, believers in different ways and non-believers, those who can feel your heart that is immeasurable in its goodness, and those who plainly rejoice in your light and warmth. Your blinding Elite already created in *Shadanakar* a staircase of brilliantly shining strata and along it flows a cascade of spiritual blessings, lower and lower, into the world of angels, into the world of *stikhials*, in the world of humanities. The beautiful spirit, the conceiver and father of all corporeal creation, the visible image and likeness of the Sun of the World, the living icon of the Sole, allow me to adhere to no one but yourself. Let me be an unheard voice bringing universal praise to you. The shining one, love us.

CHAPTER 3

ATTITUDE TOWARD THE ANIMAL KINGDOM

We often do not even consciously notice that our point of view toward all existing creation has become for us something like a second *I.* It seems that all in the world is evaluated in terms of solely how and to what extent it can be useful for a person. But if this historical-cultural provincialism has seemed to us now for a long time to be barbaric, and was led into some political theory and calling itself – nationalism, then the cosmic provincialism of humanity will now seem to be just a joke to our posterity.

A new attitude and ideology is arriving. Part of it is that the human is an entity in a grandiose series of other entities. He is more perfected than others, but is also more meaningless than most of them, and each of these creatures has an autonomous and inherent value, and regardless of its usefulness for a human.

So how can we define this value in some concrete situation? What criteria should be select? How can we develop a hierarchy of value?

It is possible to constitute first of all that the value – whether material or spiritual – of some object – whether material or spiritual – grows together with the sum of the effort that was expended in order to make it what it is. Of course, when we apply this same principle to the value of living organisms, we are easily convinced that it is impossible for us to determine the amount of such effort toward their creation. But something else is possible: it is possible to determine the highest step on the cosmic ladder that this organism has attained, which criteria is easier for us to utilize. The development of intellect and capabilities of a human, which distinguishes him from animals, demands an unbelievable amount of effort, both from his side and from the strengths of providence, and much more effort than was earlier expended on the evolution of animals from their simplest form to the highest of animal forms. This becomes the basis of formulating a cosmic hierarchy of value, to the extent that we can understand it. Now we can conclude that the value of infusoria has a lesser value than an insect, while the value of an insect is less of a value than a mammal, while this class of creature is far from the value of a human, although the value of a human is comparatively small with the value of an archangel or demiurge of a nation, while its value, and as a result of its immense scale, is lost along side the value of the Sovereigns of Light, the demiurges of the galaxy.

If we were to take this principle and isolate it, we can make the conclusion of a human's factual impunity in regard to all that stands below him, since his value is higher, meaning, nature has provided him the right to utilize their lives as however he may find it useful to do so.

But no ethical principle must be viewed in isolation, since it is not self-sufficient and independent. Rather, it is part of a general system of principles, defined now as the existence of *Shadanakar*. The counter-weight of the principle of spiritual value can be called the principle of moral obligation. This principle is still not acknowledged in those stages below the human and even in the earliest stages of humanity's development. Now we are in a position to formulate it with precision to a sufficiently significant proximity. This is the concept: beginning with the level of a human, the obligation of creatures relative to those standing below them grows to the distance that they ascend higher on the evolutionary scale.

This obligation was placed on the original progenitors of the human race in regard to the animals that they tamed and domesticated. But this did not consist of the human feeding and sheltering them, as this is just a plain exchange. It was an obligation toward them in a base, material sense, and not in a ethic sense, and because in exchange for the food and shelter the human provided the animal, he would take work and milk, and hide or wool, from the domestic animal, and even take its life, even though such is not in proportion to what was provided to the animal. The ethic obligation of the original humans consisted in having to love the animal that they domesticated and utilized. The ancient horseman had a close attachment to his steed; the shepherd did not just worry over his flock, but tended to their safety; so the peasant and hunter who loved his cow or dog. All of them fulfilled this ethic obligation. This elementary obligation remained the typical norm with humanity until our days.

All entities, including infusoria, possess what we conditionally call a *shelt*, a subtle crust or covering over the soul, created from an alien materiality and by the immortal monad for itself. No material existence of any sort is possible without a *shelt*, since no existence of any sort is likewise possible without a monad. But the monads of animals reside in one of the worlds of Obligation – in *Kaermis*, and their souls accomplish a prolonged route along a spiral ascension through a special *sakuala* consisting of several strata. They are incarnated here in *Enrof*, however almost none of them execute any post-mortem descent. The law of karma is still in effect for them, but it is of another form: untying their karmic bundle only occurs in *Enrof* over the route of their innumerable incarnations in various categories, but with extreme slowness.

Based on the initial concepts of Providential powers, *Enrof* was designated particularly for the animal kingdom, for the large numbers of monads who descended here with their *shelts*, in order to enter a great creative work: the enlightenment of the materiality of the three-dimensional world. The interference of *Gagtungr* distorted this intention, tangled the route, corrupted their destiny, and stretched the term to some frightening length. This was attained at the very beginning primarily by subjecting organic life in *Enrof* to the law of mutual gouging or survival of the fittest.

It is simply enchanting how playful almost all the infant offspring are of all the animals. And this just not only pertains to baby wolves and baby lions, but even piglets and hyenas summon a joyful and touching feeling in us. But then the demonic principle or instinct surfaces in an animal at the minute that it has to struggle for its life, that is, succumb to the law of survival of the fittest. If it were not for *Gagtungr*, all of the present wild beasts would be dancing and praising God, and they would become more beautiful, intelligent and sagacious in *Enrof*, as they were intended.

His activity caused a sharp rupture between the 2 halves of the animal kingdom. He was able to success in demonizing one half very strongly, placing the spiritual development of these animals at a very low ceiling, so that they could not exist in any other manner than at the expense of other animals. In general, the principle of viciousness or ferocity is demonic based on its own nature, and in no matter in what creature we might find it, meaning, that the demonic powers are already inherently operating within them.

The other half of the animal kingdom were designated as sacrifices of the first. The principle of ferocity was not instilled into this half, and this is obvious due to their nourishment being foliage, vegetation, and their only manner of safety or escaping danger is by hiding or flight, and this also horribly contributed to the tardiness of their mental development.

The goal of the enlightenment of three-dimensional materiality continued to stand right in front of the Providential powers. But since the animal kingdom surfaced as incapable to do this, at least for the foreseeable future, some short internal of time and prerequisites were implemented that would allow it to sooner and more successfully deal with this task. What was allocated to some was the character of progression, quickly dashing forward, much like jumping from a trampoline. Yet for others, this springboard operated in the opposite manner with the development of monkeys, a tragic form or regression. As a result, our jump from animal to human was at the cost of the cessation of development of an innumerable quantities of other species of creatures.

The more vicious an animal, the greater its demonization. Of course, this demonization is limited by their *shelts* and the higher density of the materiality of their covering, but it is unable to deal with their monad. But the demonization of the *shelt* can reach a horrifying stage and summon the worst of consequences. Sufficient is the recollection of what occurred with many of the forms of the class of reptiles. The mesozoic era is distinguished because this category of creatures, which attained such a gigantic sizes, was severed in half: one half remained vegetarian and acquired in the future the possibility of development in other strata, and now possesses its own specific material world called *Zhimeira*, where brontosauruses and iguanodons have passed through innumerable incarnations and now reside in a state that is obviously highly intelligent, and they have become well-mannered and unusually gentle creatures. The other half are the gigantic synapsids,[64] predators who evolved in other strata toward the opposite direction. They long lost their physical body, while instead possess a *karrokh*, and they reside as vicious creatures in the *shrastras* in the form of *raruggas*.

Zhimeira, the present residence of the better part of the animals of the pre-historic geological era, is already vanishing, but the residents are being transferred to a much higher stratum. There also exists 2 other strata that are completely filled with billions of creatures: *Eesong*, the world of the souls of the majority of animals that presently exists, through which they pass as a sparkle during the intervals between their incarnations; and *Ermastig*, the world of souls of the higher animals. After death a few of them also reside here, but for a longer time than do the ones in *Eesong*, before continuing.

There is still another world where the assigned souls of many are located. Such are clothed in enlightened bodies, beautiful, but they are not the most intelligent, however they possess a high level of common sense. This world is *Khangvilla*, the highest among the *sakualas*, that they must eventually attain in order to rise higher, to *Fayir*, *Yusnorm* and *Kaermis*.

O, the vile traces of the footsteps of *Gagtungr* are visible even in many of the strata of the animal kingdom! He was successful enough to pressure certain *shelts* of animals, impose

---

[64] The Russian word also applies to pangolins and lizards.

violence upon them, and one without analogy in our stratum. He crushed them and pummeled them, and then gathered the individual parts and created collectives from them. Such individual *shelts* of many of the lower animals have a short-term existence in their collective *shelts*, as for example the majority of insects, including worms, flies and bees. The world of the collective souls of insects and simple forms of such species is called *Nigoida*. Some of them, true, but for the time being just a few, do rise higher to *Khangvilla*, and there become prettier and smarter. In general, *Khangvilla* is the great independent and general *zatomis* of the entire animal kingdom, and from them the enlightened animal souls rise through *Fayir* into *Yusnorm*, where they start participation in the eternal divine service of *Shadanakar*.[65]

I have an incidental note to provide in regard to the resolution of a trans-physical and eschatological dilemma dealing with the animal kingdom. But this should be sufficient enough to understand the intent of the complexity of this problematic, and more than it was for the thinkers of the religions of antiquity. The simple statement that animals are not cognizant of sin, does not resolve the essence of the matter at all. If we were to understand sin in this context as to their open sexual conduct, then truly animals are not cognizant of sin as here understood, since they are inherently psychologically deprived of a sense of embarrassment, meaning a lack of shame. But from another side, the understanding of sin is immeasurably wider than just the sexual region. Malice, cruelty, unjustifiable and unrestrained anger, bloodthirstiness, ferocity – all are sins of the animal kingdom, but yet we still do not have any data so to determine the extent that these or other animals are cognizance of these actions or whether they know that they should not be performing them. So this does not resolve the question of the presence or absence of such prohibitions. Of course, it would not be foolish to conclude that law is only effective if a creature has

---

[65] This is an allusion to the animals of Revelation chapter 4, 5 and 6.

comprehension of actions. (The law of gravity was discovered by Newton, but all and everything has been subject to it regardless.) So do animals have a sense of some higher law, or not, or sense it in some feeble manner, or not at all? It does not matter: causality is causality, while karma is karma.

To the amount I understand this, a hungry lion that kills to satisfy his hunger does not carry personal guilt, since for him, such behavior is a necessity, but it is the prehistoric guilt of all predators of his class or category that bears the guilt. The satisfied tiger, who attacks a victim solely for the purpose of satisfying some personal urge to kill and main, bears a personal guilt, because he was not forced by inherent design or instinct to kill another, becoming his sacrifice. A wolf defending himself from an attack by a pack of dogs, and killing one in the process, is not personally guilty, but he is guilty as the representative of a predatory species, whose ancestors at some time in prehistoric eras made the choice to proceed in this direction. This is a type of original sin. But the fed and domesticated cat who is playing with a mouse solely for reasons of recreation is guilty due to original sin, and its own personal also, since there is no real necessity to do this. But people will say that I am forcing human applications and even legal laws to the behavior of animal worlds, and which do not apply. But the understanding of guilt is not just a legal definition, but also trans-physical, meta-historical and ontological. In the various kingdoms of nature, the understanding of guilt changes when applying to the various hierarchies of the development of the organism, and so it is not definitive that the reality of the concept of karma should only apply to humans and not to them also.

It seems that the dominating contemporary view toward animals consists in 2 contradictory principles: the utilitarian and the emotional. The animal world is also divided into categories dependent on its attitude toward humans. First of all we have domestic animals. We care for them, and if it is an animal we love, like a cow, and it becomes ill, we weep over it. But if it stops giving milk, then the owner leads it somewhere and butchers his beloved animal to use it for meat to feed himself and his family.

The 2nd category is a significant part of wild animals, including fish. We do not domesticate them, we do not expend worry over their condition. We just kill them hunting or fishing and use them for food. Third are the predators and parasites. We care less about them and kill them should the occasion arise, and not worry about it. And if we could define a 4th group, this is a certain part of the wild animals, and especially birds, those that destroy other harmful creatures. As far as other creatures are concerned, like reptiles and amphibians to crows and magpies, they are often captured for scientific experiments, or plainly for recreation: children throw rocks at them, but for the most part they are just ignored.

It is only apparent that I have been speaking of the attitude toward animals in Europe and America and many countries of the Orient. But with India it is a completely different picture. Brahmanism, as we all know, from a long while back has proscribed the consumption of animal meat, and implemented a factual sustenance of milk and plants. Even the manufacture of articles from hides and skins is considered sinful and unclean, while is some areas a cow and other certain animals are declared sacred. In my opinion, what they have done is right.[66] It is good for a nation to rise to an understanding of something that is the conscience of the entire population and not just something in the mind of a few individuals. So what ideal, what ethic, can we implement, those who have confessed Christianity for so many centuries.

There was one incident in my life which I would like to share with you here. This is difficult. The matter is that a few decades ago, I executed this knowingly, even deliberately, an ugly, vile action pertaining to one animal who is in the category of man's best friend. This occurred because at the time I was passing through a certain stage, or better said, a zigzag of an inner path, toward a higher level of darkness. I decided to practice, as I at

---

[66] Daniel's previous 2 incarnations as a resident of India needs to be considered in his conclusion.

the time expressed this – a ministry of evil – an idea not fully developed in its stupidity, but which enveloped my imagination and inclined me toward a chain of actions, one more torturous than the other. I wanted to know, finally, if there was in the world some type of action, no matter how base, vile and inhuman, that I would not perform it particularly as the result of my weak character and no resistance toward cruelty. I have no mitigating circumstance as an excuse, that I was a thoughtless child or maybe I fell into bad company. I do not remember having any bad company or surroundings. I was a fully mature adult and a student. I performed the act and on the certain animal that I mentioned, and it is no longer around. But living through the incident seemed so devastating that it changed my attitude toward animals with an unusual force and forever. In general this also contributed to my inner upheaval. And if this shameful blemish did not remain on my conscious, I, perhaps, would not now be suffering such a loathing toward every torture or killing of an animal, often even to losing total control of myself.

Of course, hunting as the fundamental means of the existence of several backward tribes cannot be subjected to any kind of moral condemnation, to reprimands the Hottentots[67] or the Goldies,[68] for whom the prohibition of hunting would be the equivalent of death. The same would apply to each of use, should we fall into situation of similar circumstances where we need to support our life and the lives of others by hunting. The life of a human is more valuable than the life of any animal.

Based on this premise, a person has the right for self-defense from predators and parasites.[69] It is also well known that many Indian Jains and some adherents of the extreme currents of Buddhist ethics will not drink water unless it is sieved first, and when the walk on the streets they will sweep the dust from in front of them. There are also some ascetics in India who will

---

[67] Now known as the Khoekhoe.
[68] A Tungusic tribe of eastern Siberia who live along the Amur River.
[69] I suppose he is referring to mosquitoes and gnats and lice and the like.

even allow themselves to be eaten by parasites, rather than killing them. This is a clear example of how some religious concept can lead to an absurd conclusion. The error in such thinking in feeling that the preservation of the life of some insect, and even the simplest form, is more important or valuable than the life of a human, causes any advancement or progress of humanity – social or technical – to become impossible.

So what are parasites and insects? And not from a materialistic point of view, but from a trans-physical. They are creatures with collective souls and hardly remaining on any route. At the present, they are creatures of the least value and survive at the expense and life of creatures of a higher value: animals and humans. We have the complete right to destroy them, otherwise they will have no other existence from this stratum to *Nigoida*.

Predators exist at the expense of the death of those creatures of a value as the same as theirs – animals, and at the expense of humans who have a higher value. Those species of predators, whose predatory nature we are unable to subdue and domesticate, must gradually be destroyed from *Enrof*. I say gradually because this cannot be accomplished immediately, and perhaps over the course of time some means to the domestication of their nature may materialize. The nature of some predatory species, unconditionally, can be changes, especially among the higher mammals. It is sufficient to remember the dog, which evolved from the wolf, and some canine species at present are able to have a meatless diet. As a result, the dog has become domesticated and to the benefit of the human. This hunt for predators, with the present stage of humanity's development, also cannot be condemned.

We have no right, let me repeat, we have absolutely no right to purchase our excitement at the expense of the suffering and death of living creatures. If you have other means of identifying with parts of nature, then do that instead of this. But it is better to remain outside of nature, than to be a monster within it. If you go into nature with a gun and scatter death around yourself for the sake of your personal recreation, you become a pathetic toy of the entity who implemented death, who implemented the law of survival of the fittest, and who gets fat and whose stomach swells from over-eating due to the suffering of living creatures. What is the response I hear from these hunters, "What is an animal? With all the millions of humans in our age that have perished in war and famine and political repressions, you have found a reason to wail on account of a few squirrels and grouse."

Yes, I have found a reason, and even though world wars, repressions, and other of humanity's monstrous atrocities have occurred, what does this have to do with the question of killing animals for pleasure? Since when should animals perish for the sake of the amusement of those who cannot use their time for more constructive and edifying purposes, like stopping the atrocities mentioned above?

Fishing is in the same class, as we gain some thrill from tying a worm to a hook, and watching it suffer as we toss the line into the water, and then watch the fish we catch suffocate as we lure it out of the water. How would we like it if someone would tie our feet together and pierce a hook through our stomach and throw us into the ocean upside-down to use as bait for some shark? We are then experiencing that same pain that worm is.

The following is my program in codified form, a chronological series of measures that need to be implements after ROSE OF THE WORLD attains authority. These need to be put in effect without delay. This is the first list of measures, with the 2nd to follow further in the chapter.

1. The prohibition of killing animals by some torturous means, and especially in the food industry.

2. The prohibition of using live animals in experiments in schools, except in specialized scientific institutions.

3. A complete prohibition of experimentation on live animals unless they are anesthetized or sedated.

4. The creation and finance of strong scientific collectives for research and development of new experimental methods in the natural sciences.

5. The restriction of hunting and fishing as a sport.

6. A rearrangement of the educational system that will promote the development of love toward animals in pre-school and school-age children.

7. An expansive instruction dealing with this new attitude toward animals.

These are mostly prohibitions of its negative facets, and there is really nothing new here. But animals will still be killed to be used as food. The positive side is something actually new, and consists in showing active assistance to the animal kingdom for its self-perfection, to shorten the route and time for this ascent toward perfection. But what does this mean?

This means: the installation of peace between humans and all animals, with the exception of predators; the search for a means for the rehabilitation of certain species of predators; termination of the use of any kind of animals for defense; and a manufactured manner of increasing the mental and religious development of certain species of the animal kingdom. For this zoological development considerable sums will need to be expended. But this is nothing! No matter how much the expenses, or a thousand times more, will ever redeem the damage done by wild animals over the course of millennia. A new discipline of knowledge will arise: zoo-logics, which is the pedagogy of animals. The first species to be included in this course will be dogs and cats, since they are easily domesticated.

Some dogs have already been trained to understand nearly 200 spoken works, and they are not memorized to be repeated mechanically, like a parrot, but they have the mental capacity to actually think of the meaning of the words. This creature truly has colossal possibilities. The ability for dogs to speak is hindered not by its intellectual level, but due to the mechanical obstacles in the structure of its vocal organs, and which are so necessary for proper pronunciation. Following the dog will be the cat, elephant and bear, and perhaps some species of rodents. The horse is still far in the distance for any speech development, but it does seem to have a better ethical base than either the cat or dog. The same would apply to the dear and buffalo

So with the progression of some interval of the reign of ROSE OF THE WORLD, we will now be able to implement the 2nd group of measures:

1. The prohibition of killing of animals for any food industry or scientific and research goals.

2. The strict restriction of killing animals for food or purpose of nourishment.

3. The assignments of large nature preserves or wilderness areas in all the countries for the life of those animals that are not yet domesticated.

4. The free existence among nature and in populated areas of those animals considered to be domestic.

5. A planned work of zoological institutions on a worldwide scale, to transfer such work to higher stages in the research of the problem tied with the development of speech in animals.

6. Especial attention toward research of the problems dealing with reducing, even if artificially, the predatory nature of animals.

So will this creative effort grow for the perfection of animals, an effort that is sacrificial, not inspired by our narrow material interests, but by a feeling of responsibility and feeling of love. This is a growing love, a very wide one, that can be fit within the framework of humanity. A love that is able to resolve problems that seem to be otherwise presently irresolvable. For example, where will all these animals be placed, if we were to curb their massive killing? Otherwise it will be like some areas where the crocodiles increased in the rivers and pose a threat to local residents and farms. It is not for us at present to guess at the measures that our posterity will find and materialize to resolve these issues.

Simultaneously the sum of benefit acquired from these measures will immensely increase and become an ocean of love. For the lion to lie with the lamb and be led by a child is not a utopian fantasy.[70] This will occur. This was the prophetic vision of the great prophets who knew the heart of humanity. Not in zoos, not in preserves, but plainly in our cities, parks, forests and meadows, will the descendents of the contemporary rabbits and tapirs, leopards and squirrels, bears and ravens, giraffes and pangolins, reside, not fearing the human, but rather acting gentle toward him and playing with him, and working with him for the development of themselves as higher intelligent creatures.

---

[70] Isaiah 11:6-7

BOOK VI

THE HIGHER WORLDS OF *SHADANAKAR*

CHAPTER 1

RISE TO THE GLOBAL *SALVATERRA*

It is not a surprise to anyone in particular, that information about these spheres is not only more meager than any of some others, but in essence, is almost non-existent. The reasons are 2. The inadequacy of the concrete reality of these regions by some type or other concept and understanding of ours, and even more the attempt to express them in words, is the first reason. The 2nd is the exclusive height of the spirit of perception that is needed to approach and enter these worlds through personal experience. Almost all that is communicated here regarding them is sourced not from individual direct experience. No, this is only a transmission using words of our language, of what I received from invisible friends. I hope they will forgive me if I somewhere made any mistake, if my comprehension produced something lower, or purely human, or diluted these views with subjective impurities.

All the strata, of which this dissertation will deal from this point, are 5 dimensional. The number of temporary coordinates, that is, the currents parallel to the course of time, exceed the number of 200 in these strata. But this one number is sufficient in order to understand how worthless it is to attempt to express in human terms the content and meaning of all these regions. We will end up having to abandon entirely the customary means of conceptualizing such forms, and the attempt to compensate for this loss by using terms pertaining to energies, zones of activity, and etc, are also doomed to failure.

Above the *sakualas* of the trans-myths of the 5 supreme religions – of which I already spoke comparing them to 5 gigantic pyramids as though fabricated from shining crystal of various colors – the entire *Shadanakar* surges, encompassing the indescribable *sakuala* of the *Sinklit* of humanity, consisting of 7 regions. The sea of shining ethereals – I select this word not having one that is more compatible – of brilliant colors, inconceivable even for the *sinklits* of the meta-cultures, wash the structures in these worlds that are so distant that they can only be compared to the reflections of the crests of mountain ranges, as structures of unimaginable architecture. The primordial dissimilarity between the great monuments of humanity's geniuses and the great creations of nature have no place here, because from the beginning both merged into one, finally into a synthesis that is unfathomable to us. How can we imagine those joyful epopees overwhelmed with dispersed light, with which the surpassingly beautiful spirits, that that now are *stikhials*, are clothed? Or the radiant waves of sounds rocketing to places that are the most blessed bosoms of the heavenly mountains? I will attain my goal, even if only a few of those reading my book will feel the personal presence of such a reality, whether through the unusual composition of words, or through these figures that are almost deprived of any configuration, and to which our spirit can aspire, but to approach to touch is inaccessible to almost every living person upon our dearth and sinister world.

The selected of the select that composed today the *Sinklit* of humanity, will be a number that will not increase beyond, it seems, 7,000. Since not having a specific human figure – in our sense of the word – they voluntarily accept a higher, enlightened similarity when they descend to the lower lying strata. They are capable of traversing the expanse between the *bramfaturas* of the solar system at the speed of light, whose rays will carry them.

Regarding the separate regions of the *Sinklit* of humanity, I do not know anything, except for their appellations, and just to the extent that as I was allowed to render them into the sounds of a human language.

From *Monsalvat* and Eden and the *Sinklit* of the world many already entered into our era, surpassing 100 humans. The ancient and immense meta-culture of India has provided even more. It seems that the last who entered into the *Sinklit* of the world before 1955, was Ramakrishna. In this manner, from the moment of his death in the *Enrof* to the entrance into the highest of these regions, almost 70 years transpired. But more than often, entire centuries pass before an ascent to such an elevation. For example, the prophet Mohammed only attained the *Sinklit* of the world just relatively recently, although any kind of possible movement into a descending level did not interfere with his port-mortem situation. But very soon the ancient prophets Ezekiel and Daniel, and likewise Basil the Great, will rise from the *Sinklit* of humanity, where they presently reside, to a spot far higher than these regions.

This will exhaust all that I have in my possession to say about the regions of this *sakuala*. However, I will have the opportunity to speak regarding the 11 regions of the subsequent *sakuala*, the *sakualas* of the great hierarchs, even less, more brief, just as protocol.

Yes, these worlds are particularly reserved for such supreme entities that we cannot possibly call them anything else other than great hierarchs. Many of them were objects of veneration in the ancient religions of various countries during their era. These exalted entities, as least to a popular degree, were reflected in Egyptian, Babylonian, Greek, ancient German and Aztec forms, and in certain aspects of the supreme deities of the Indian pantheon. But not as they are today, but such as they genuinely were, as they were perceived by the cognizance of the nations during these ancient time that dealt with them. Over the centuries that have transpired from the days of their appearance and the flourish of their religion in the *Enrof*, these hierarchs rose to a supreme elevation.

I can say that the regions of this *sakuala* are arranged in levels, but not based on the principle of the tie of one or another hierarch with his relative meta-culture: these lower strata of *Shadanakar* that are vertically divided into sections, exemplify segments of humanity's meta-culture, and remain far behind, or actually far below. The intervals between the regions of the *sakuala* of the hierarchy is dependent on the principle of the strength and height that is attained by each of these entities.

Once again, just the appellations of these strata was made known to me. But any adequacy of their phonetic physiognomy, the pronunciation of the letters, did not engender in me any kind of assurance of the authentic sound of these names. There is no doubt that the most coarse association pertains to their appellations: *Aolinor, Ramnagor, Pleyragor, Foraygor, Stranganor, Tzeliror, Likhanga, Devenga, Siringa, Khranga, Ganga.*

If we were to allow full freedom of intellect toward this station of meta-historical contemplation, on its own nature it will strive to include in a relative amount the attitudes and specifics of meta-history of the categories of the physical and historical strata to which it is accustomed, and logical norms similar to those of science. In part, its inclination to uniformity and regimentation, naively understood as a symmetry, appears at this occasion such that it seems natural to it, so that – from a meta-historical plane – identical groups of hierarchs, those who participate in its life, would take charge over all these supra-nations. But it reality it is not this way.

True, there is not a supra-nation – and namely supra-nation and not just nation – where its demiurge does not take charge, otherwise it would not be a supra-nation, but an accidental disconnected group of several disassociated nationalities not having anything linking them together. And there is no nation that would have possessed the ideal of the conciliar Soul. But first of all, the ideal of the conciliar Soul from this point forward is not a collection of some kinds of psychological or otherwise qualities of the subject nation, those obvious to us, that have defined its historical physiognomy that made it distinct from others. The ideal of the conciliar Soul is an entity possessing one great monad that retains within itself the precursory of the supreme possibilities of a nation and is clothed in a material woven suit of multi-dimensional spatial expanses. Relative to the measure of the historical position of the nation and its personal maturity of humanity's individualism, the subtle-material portion of each of them, all the more and even more, draws close to it and encompasses it, communicating its character of collectivity to it.

Almost in each meta-culture there exists several national conciliar Souls, but as a rule, one of them will belong to another hierarchy and more than the balance. It is the only one that is divinely born, just as the demiurge of the supra-nation, and only it is connected with them by special secret, spiritual and material chains of love. Such conciliar Souls compose the hierarchy of the Great Sisters; there are about 40 of them in the earthly *bramfatura*. Each defined nation possesses a conciliar Soul, but the balance of them belong to the monads that are divinely created.

These younger Sisters are identified with the national spirit-guides, the inspirations of those nations that lead the supra-nation into its structure, but they do not play a role in its history. Nonetheless, some of the younger Sisters traverse their meta-historical route without companions, without their national guides. There sometimes occurs an intermediate stage, often lasting a century and longer, when the nations together with their conciliar Soul and their national spirit-guides remain outside the meta-culture or as though in between them.

The great divinely-born monad materializes also as the demiurge of the supra-nations, more potent, more active, but alien to the conciliar group. It is its own. One of the Great Sisters, the conciliar soul leading the nation, corresponds to it [the demiurge] in that meta-culture. On occasion however, more complex collusions occur.

The birth of the monad of both hierarchies – the demiurges of the supra-nations and Great Sisters – through the Sun of the World from before the beginning of time, cannot be understandable to us or imaginable, and any other logic on this topic is doomed to remain empty speculation. From my point of view, speculations will remain as just attempts to fill the void in our understandings of those stages of the cosmic installation of these monads that preceded their appearance in *Shadanakar*. In what *bramfaturas*, in what forms, according to what stages, did they journey or materialize before they entered the boundaries of our planet? Perhaps I am astray on this matter, but it seems to me that similar alien-*bramfatura* secrets are transcendental for us. In the circuit of the possibilities of our attainments (and these attainments are not in the viewpoint of meta-historical enlightenment, but just in the form of passive acceptance of research regarding this from the mouths of our invisible friends) both of these hierarchies enter and proceed at the moment of meta-ethereal birth. Such a term conditionally denotes the event that consists in their monads entering the five-dimensional material nature of *Shadanakar*. They receive a certain impulse from the planetary Logos, which we can understand as being an entity that is placed as the highest demiurge of our *bramfatura*. This impulse is the creative willingness toward the materialization and expression of itself in the three-dimensional and four-dimensional substance of the soon arriving supra-nation that so far has not existed and which without them could not exist. It is particularly this impulse that draws after itself their release, their attire in clothing that is more solidly material, still four-dimensional, and in this manner is the beginning of their planetary cycle. This is their 2nd birth in *Shadanakar*, or their astral birth. Physically, of course they never undergo anything. I know that it is not very easy to understand this concept, but it is hardly possible to express it any better.

The worlds where these hierarchies reside between these 2 births of theirs, and where their monads reside during the duration of their cycle in *Shadanakar*, comprise the *sakuala* of the demiurges. They are comprised of 3 regions. The birth land of the demiurges and the Great Sisters are the ideal soul of the supra-nations and are called *Rangaraydr*. The appellations of the others are *Astr* and *Oamma*. *Astr* is the birthplace and residence of the monads of the younger Sisters and the spirits of the nation-guides. I am not in a position to communicate anything about the content of *Oamma*.

Yarosvet and *Navna* are names that I have selected conditionally and arbitrarily to denote the hierarchies of the Russian meta-culture. The actual names of the demiurges and Great Sisters are unknown to me. Nevertheless, they cannot be in general pronounced using a human language.

The meta-historical mission of the marriage union, and all of life in general in the *Shadanakar* of *Yarosvet* and *Navna* – the missions of planetary significance – can be more precisely sketched as being born of them, or should it be better described as the ethereal incarnation through them, a certain great Womanhood monad. It is foolish of course, to think of this as some corporeal personal incarnation. It is prepared to spill at the proper time into some ethereal container, one that is enlightened, individual, living and immaculate. It thoughtfully surfaces simultaneously with its materialization in *Enrof*: the worldwide Fraternity. The Russian nation seems to think that its demiurge is still unenlightened in *Enrof*, but what is already enlightened in the heavenly Russia is the ethereal-physical substance out of which the mutual – the physical and ethereal – containers of light will be created, and at the same time being an arena where this theurgic act will be consummated.

Here is where the strata of the residency of the sole church of our *bramfatura* begins. They pervade this *sakuala*, of which I spoke earlier, in the same manner as the 3 regions of those *sakualas* that are higher: the Elite of *Shadanakar*. The oceans of diverse illuminated and spirit-created matter vibrates about it. Their shining crests do not encounter the ridges of its transparent boundaries, but enter inside in waves, and developing the Perfected residing in this habitation they

communicate to it all the fullness of life. And the humanity of
Enrof, and the humanity of the demons, and the humanity of the
moon and angels and *stikhials* and even the animal kingdom,
whose meta-physical meaning has appeared as such a profound
riddle – all find their supreme vindication, their concluding
transformation of existence in the bosom of this pinnacle of
paradise, combining rest and potency, bliss and creativity,
perfection and an immeasurable progress further and further
along a blinding route. This pertains to all of those who see from
a distance the global *Salvaterra,* the highest of all steps on the
staircase of *Shadanakar* for any of its monads, those born of God
and likewise those created of God, except for the planetary
Logos, the Virgin-Mother Mary, and the great Womanhood
Spirit.

All that I can say about the Elite of *Shadanakar* is that it
repeats some of the list of those great person-spirits who have
attained the Elite world, and some of them being: Akhenaten,
Zoroaster, Moses, Hosea, Lao-tze, Gautama Buddha, Mahavira,
Ashoka, Chandragupta Maurya, Patanjali, Kanishka the Great,
Nagarjuna, Kanishka, Aristotel, Plato, all the apostles except
Paul, Tertullian, Mary Magdalene, John Chrysostom, Dante,
Augustine, Joan d'Arc, Leonardo de Vinci, and Francis of Assisi.

So have we led the review of the structure of *Shadanakar* to its
conclusion, to the supreme pinnacle of the *sakualas,* through the
3 regions encompassing our entire *bramfatura:* the region of the
planetary Logos, the region of the Ever-Virgin Mary, and the
region of the great Womanhood monad.

Among the number of the objective reasons that I adopted
the name of this concentration and summit of *Shadanakar* as the
Global *Salvaterra* is that this is a name, of course, that is fully
conditional, even accidental, and do note that there is no
identification of the least sort with Salvatore of the Crusaders of
the Middle Ages or Palestine.[71] I do not insist on this appellation

---

[71] This is a reference to Salvatore Varagine of the 4th Crusade.

in the least degree, but am forced to use it due to not having anything better.

The global *Salvaterra* penetrates the entire *Shadanakar*, except for the 4 worlds of the demonic *Osnova* and *Sufetkh*, but in different stages. The majority of its fullness is tied with the highest levels of the atmosphere. The religious meaning of the word – heaven, is not some produced aberration of dark comprehensions of antiquity, but an expression of reality that high souls have presaged and foresensed thousands of years ago.

All that is providential in the history of *Shadanakar*, in the history of humanity and individual souls, evolves from *Salvaterra*. Here the underlying matter of the highest cosmic substances is concentrated, and which expresses itself in the installation of the galactic universes as much as in our installation. The creed applied to the global *Salvaterra* – The Heavenly Will of Brilliantly Shining Crystal – is not just poetic. Uninterruptible waves of grace and powers pour from these heights, from these depths. How can such words, as shining gospel or resurging brilliance, help us to draw near to a comprehension of them? That, upon which we can allude similar illusions, remains deeply below, in the worlds of angels, in the *sakualas* of the Supreme Obligation, in the *Sinklit* of the world. Even that passage that attempted to express the Biblical legend of Jacob's ladder, ends here, traversing the entire *Shadanakar*. Great entities and great essences ascend and descend by the steps of material existence from *Salvaterra* to the ground and from the ground to *Salvaterra*. It is the heart of the planet and its internal sun. Through it and only through it are the heights, widths and depths of the spiritual universe unveiled, which encompass the star-filled archipelagoes and the oceans of the meta-galaxies, which seem to us to be so desolate.

The spirit universe is inexpressible in any language and can be experienced, of course, just in the most extreme state of awareness. The very highest spirit-rapture among the mystics of Christianity, the highest stage of ecstasy among the Hindus, the Buddhist abhijna – all of these are the states particularly of these extreme awarenesses. The regimented mentality attempts to pour them into a solid model of teaching in order to attribute much to them and in the process creates nebulous reflections, similar to the teachings of Tao, the Pleroma,[72] the Empyrean,[73] and the respiration of the Para Brahma.

When those who wander about the other worlds speak of Eden, such as the teachers of Semitic religions, or of the chambers of Brahma and Vishnu, or the heavenly Iranian Ashur, or the Hindu Devas, or the land of bliss Sukhavati, or even about Nirvana – they accept as the ultimate goal just the separate stages within *Shadanakar*, the separate summits of the meta‑culture and supreme trans‑myth of religion, otherwise, in conclusion, the reality of the global *Salvaterra.*

When humanity – the tangible as well as the intangible – concludes its colossal cycle, when it and all the realms of the planetary nature conclude, they will consummately and simultaneously merge with this planetary paradise. Then the global *Salvaterra* will begin its revelation, like a flower opening to accept its expanse of the spirit universe. The sun of the world will shine over this flower, accepting its fragrant rays into its heavens.

But the final goal will still be immeasurably distant. At the present it lies beyond the limits of any type at all of even the most blinding state of awareness.

CHAPTER 2

THE LOGOS OF *SHADANAKAR*

To the extent that I now know, all the innumerable myriads of monads dissolve into 2 ontologically diverse categories. One are the monads born of God; there are few of them. They are measurably more solid, they directly evolved from the unfathomable depths of the Creator, they are predestined toward

---

[72] The totally of divine powers
[73] The place of the highest heaven

guidance of the worlds and from the very beginning enter the task, not knowing what is it to fail or collapse, and in the future they grow from having glory to more glory, from having strength to more strength. The secret of their divine birth does not affect and never affects anybody, except for themselves. In *Shadanakar* the planetary Logos, *Zventa-Sventana*, the demiurges of the supra-nations, the Great Sisters, and some of the Supreme Hierarchs, all belong to the quantity of the monads born of God. Not one demonic monad of *Shadanakar* enters into their quantity, although they desperately know that Lucifer appears as a monad that is born of God, but he is the only one of all the monads born of God that incurred apostasy from God.

The other category are all the remaining monads of the world, the monads created of God. The secret of their creation by God can be fathomed by each of them, although, of course, only when they ascend to the extremely high stage of ascension.

The planetary Logos is the great monad born of God, the divine intellect of our *bramfatura*, the most ancient and the very first of all His monads. Its distinction from all the remaining consists in that it expresses itself in the same manner the Word expresses the Person speaking, one of the hypostasis of the Trinity: God the Son. The Logos of *Shadanakar* accomplishes a route of ascension and creativity along the cosmic ladder that is absolutely ineffable.

Not even one *bramfatura*, except for the demonic, exists or can exist without some monad. Because one such monad appears in each of the *bramfatura* at its dawn and remains the concentration of Providential powers and divine Spirit for the entire duration during the installation of all its *sakualas*.

The planetary Logos descended into *Shadanakar* as soon as the materiality of the *bramfatura*, as created by the hierarchs, was able to occupy It. The stratum into which It entered first became later know as the *Iroln*. By way of the creativity of the Logos this stratum was prepared in order to accept a large number of young divinely-created monads. However this creativity could not safeguard *Shadanakar* from an invasion by

Gagtungr. The planetary Logos and multitudes of bright monads were forced to enter into a struggle against him.

The beginning of first humanity – the angelic – was instituted by the planetary Logos Himself, and so was *Leeleet*, the substance that was still at the time free from the demonic *Eytzekhore.* Simultaneously with the incessant struggle against the demonic camp, *Olirna* was created; the *sakualas* of the supreme Obligation, the great Hierarchs, the highest *Stikhials*, were all created, and these strata were prepared and then became the *sakualas* of the Invocations of other planets of the Sun and *Astrafayr.*[74] Some of the strata created at the time no longer exist, for example, those where the person-angels – having attaining enlightenment – ascended during those eras. But because the materiality of these entities was not poisoned by any *eytzekhore*, the ascension of angelic-humanity was not defiled by any failure.

The scenario of the entrance of primordial sin needs to be understood in the following manner, what occurred between *Leeleet* and *Gagtungr* who was thrown into her world. The result of this is that all created entities carry the satanic seed – *eytzekhore*, and due to this generation of a solidly-material succession of posterity, *Leeleet's* participation is included. *Eytzekhore* even reigns over the monads in demonic entities, among the balance it is a worse situation: it is over the *shelts*.

As far as the legend of Adam and Eve is concerned, it seems that all the strata, eras and hierarchs are mixed up in it, and it is better not to touch this tradition. In any case, the general redemption, which is the restoration of all the *eytzekhores*, would have been accomplished in the long run by Christ, if His mission in *Enrof* was not interrupted.

Using a mirror to reflect on the descent of the angelic monads into *Shadanakar*, *Gagtungr* created a solid-material stratum where the more frail demonic entities acquired their incarnation, those that eventually in time were turned into the monsters of our days: the *yuitzraor*, *voglea*, *rifr*, *igva*, angels of

---

[74] The center of the universe

darkness. And parallel to the ascension of angelic-humanity was the appearance of organic life in *Enrof,* as foretold to the animal kingdom. This kingdom was conceived as a grandiose association of new and young monads, created or born of God, who are invited to enter the greater stable strata of materiality in order to enlighten them. When *Gagtungr* succeeded in distorting laws of life in *Enrof,* insert his hand into the animal kingdom and so overthrow Providential objectives, then the planetary Logos with his power created a 2nd humanity – the titans, whose assignment consisted of the same as all the other associations of Light: the enlightenment of material. In time they are supposed to cross into *Enrof* and there guide the animal kingdom and some of the *stikhials* – whether demonic or the apostatized – using processes of enlightenment.

The revolt and fall of the titans surfaced as a new catastrophe. The subsequent suppression of this 2nd humanity served *Gagtungr* as a source for the restoration of his potent power, one that he had never yet experienced. And if he would have at that time put the brakes on the development of the animal kingdom, and have the titans thrown into the worlds of Retribution – although they later escaped the place – then the lunar-humanity created by the planetary Logos and his powers, would have, after the titans, endured another and greater destructive blow and, after passing through a phase of the demonization of almost all of its *shelts*, would have vanished from the face of *Enrof* completely. This occurred about 800,000 years ago, when in the earthly *Enrof* the human began to evolve from the animal kingdom, while in other three-dimensional strata the humanity of the *daimons* was created by the planetary Logos and his camp. His creation was summoned as a result of urgent necessity and due to the increase in size of the camp of light, and what occurred next was the emanation of new and newer myriads of monads from the Father's womb, and they sought routes to descend to these solid-material strata for their enlightenment. The task of the enlightenment of the animal kingdom was not assigned to the *daimons*, because their stratum was in no way connected with animals, but one of their tasks still remains and this is the enlightenment of the apostatized *stikhials*.

The planetary Logos incarnated in *Zheram*, the world of the *daimons* corresponding to our *Enrof*, about 10,000 years ago, when Atlantis experienced its bloom among us. *Gagtungr* was unsuccessful in interrupting or distorting Its mission in the world of *daimons*, to earlier put Its incarnation to a physical death, before it could reach the complete fullness of the powers of the Logos. The route of the Logos in the world of *daimons* was transformed into Its apotheosis, and this entire *sakuala* entered the route of successive enlightenments. The mission of the Logos in regards to the world of the *daimons* was similar to Its latest missions in regard to our humanity, but here it was led to a victorious end and this initiated a subsequent and speedy development of this *sakuala*.

Before attaining incarnation as a human, which would fully reflect Its essence, the great Spirit completed a preparatory descent, having incarnated as a human about 7,000 years earlier in Gondwana. There He was the great teacher. However, humanity was not yet prepared to accept the concept of spirituality poured upon them through the incarnated Logos. At least a profound and immaculate esoteric teaching was founded there, the first seeds were scattered and carried by the winds of history on the fertile fields of other countries and cultures: India, Egypt, China, Iran, and Babylonia. The incarnation of the Logos in Gondwana still did not carry the character of such a fullness as It was essentially preparatory. Later it displayed in Jesus Christ.

What pertains to what we call the dawn of humanity, that is, the era of the evolution of the human form apart from the animal kingdom, this was an unusual and remorseful dawn. The caveman era of humanity can and must be regretted and there is no need to idealize it. It was cruel, base and crudely utilitarian. It knew of absolutely nothing that was spiritual, except magic, while the magic was utilitarian and self-centered on its own merit. A microscopic minority did retain a minute amount of feeling of an existence of great *Stikhials*, and the first shoots of a feeling of beauty, although not understood by any of them. The first massive acknowledgement of the trans-physical side of things occurred at the experience of the flow of *arungvilta-prana* everywhere.

The gradual process of the spiritual into the sphere of their cognizance trickled along millennium after millennium, drop after drop. Occasionally it would seep into the subconscious, but over the course of centuries, as though a recognizable charge of energy, a kind of spiritual faucet, it would burst into the soul and intellect of the individual. These were the first people of bright missions, its generation of announcers. Small fraternities were created around them and they opened reachable branches of routes of self-perfection. It is difficult to assign a timeline when this occurred in history, but in any case, the bursts of light were noticeable even at the end of the Cro-Magnon era. Then a long regress started, followed by new flares on the American continent and, finally, on the eve of the formation of the Altantis culture, they flowed forward in uninterruptible streams of light.

The nation, culture and country that was supposed to become the arena of the life of Christ was not immediately defined. As an unconditional prerequisite, it had to be specifically monotheistic, and not just confessed by a few, but accepted by the entire population of the nation. The psychological field, indispensable for the revelation of God the Son, would be absent without this. But the geographic and historical conditions, defining the cultural and religious character of the nations of India and China, did not provide a sufficient grounds for the appearance of the monotheistic idea in the cognizance of the national population. The monotheistic teaching of Lao-Tze, and similar tendencies in Brahmanism, remained a field for esoteric doctrines.

The 2nd emanation of the powers of Global Womanhood in *Shadanakar* summoned in *Enrof*, like an echo, something like an amelioration of the psychological hardness found in the essence of many people: without this the formation of the Church on earth by Jesus Christ would have been impossible. The Christian churches in their disconnected and incomplete form, as we know them according to history, are pale, rudimentary, limited, and just a distorted reflection of the Church of *Shadanakar* that resides in the highest strata.

* * *

From the age of 14 years and up to the age of 30 years, Jesus was in Iran or India, where he passed through a course of profound wisdom, the highest that is possible attainable at the time for humanity, and he left it far behind him.

Do why did Jesus not codify the exposition of his teaching in written form? Did he prefer to entrust this task to his disciples? Of course, even if they were divinely inspired, the evangelists were still human, and the great enemy did not hesitate to intervene, and even in the books of the New Testament are clearly found places that he has distorted. But Christ was not able to expound his teaching in a book because the teaching was not just his words, but his entire life. His teaching began with his immaculate conception and birth on a quiet Bethlehem night illuminated by the songs of Angels; his conversations with the *Gagtungr* in the desert and his wandering about the roads of Galilee; his poverty and his love, healing of the sick and resurrection of the dead; walking on water and the transformation on mount Tabor; his torture and resurrection. Such a teaching could be expounded, although with some omissions and mistakes, only by living witnesses of this divine path of him. But the primordial enemy intervened into the omissions. Penetrating into the human intellect of the authors of the Gospels, he was able to corrupt many testimonies, distort and discolor the concepts, debase and limit the ideals, and even attribute to Christ – words that the Savior of the world could not have spoken. We still do not have the abilities to segregate the original from the erroneous. There are no precise criteria, no testimonies from personal eyewitnesses. Each person reading the New Testament tries to remember at least that Christ's teaching is his entire life, and not just his words. The words that are attributed to him are all truth providing they are in accord with the spirit of love. What is erroneous is obvious when a spirit of malice or harm is present.

It is difficult to say at what moment an alarm rang in Jesus' soul during his earthly life, or doubt in the ability to complete his mission in its fullness. But during the final phase of his evangelical activity, what becomes more apparent in his words, to the extent that we know them according to the Gospel, is his preparation for the forthcoming event that the sovereign of sinister powers many just gain a temporary and partial victory. Actually, the visible forms of such a partial victory is manifested as the treachery of Judas and then Golgotha.

The subjective motive in the treachery of Judas consists in that Christ with his very human attributes destroyed within Judas' soul the Hebrew fantasy of a messiah who would be a national king or world sovereign. This fantasy burned hot in Judas's heart his entire life to the day of his meeting with Jesus, and this crush of his fantasy was for him a great tragedy. Judas did not sense the least doubt in Jesus' divinity, and the treachery appeared as an act of mortal hate, a discriminate conscious act of deicide. By paying someone 30 silver coins was just a masquerade. He could not publicly display the true motives of his crime. It is particularly the character of these true motives that summoned such an unprecedented form of cosmic vengeance, which culminated in his discard downward into *Zhurch*.[75]

Based on the above it is clear what limitless significance the events that unfolded in Jerusalem after the triumphant entrance of Jesus Christ into this city had. At this moment, the planetary Logos still could not prepare his state of incarnation for a transformation: Golgotha doomed him to a torturous human death. He did not want to escape the execution, although he could have, because this would be apostasy, and even then the *Gagtungr* would have somehow killed him at a later date. But after his death there appeared a possibility for him of a

---

[75] An analogy to the 9th and lowest circle of Dante's hell.

transformation of another type: a resurrection. And between these 2 acts there occurred something that shook *Shadanakar*, his descent into the worlds of compensation and the opening of the eternally locked doors of these worlds, and all of which truly allowed Jesus to obtain the appellation of Savior. He passed through all the strata of the magmas and the cores, all of which were earlier inaccessible, except for the threshold of *Sufetkh*. All the remaining thresholds were moved aside, the obstacles were removed, the martyrs were raised – some to the worlds of Enlightenment, others to the *shrastras*, a 3rd group to the higher strata of Retribution who are beginning their transformation from residence in eternal purgatories to temporary purgatories. So was the beginning of the great amelioration of the law of karma installed and increasing as time went along.

The physical body of the Savior, resting in the coffin, was enlightened and, being returned to life, entered another, much higher stratum of the 3-dimensional corporal nature – into *Olirna*. These qualities of his flesh that were noticed by the apostles between his resurrection and ascension: the ability to pass through objects of our stratum and, along with this, the ability to eat food, the ability to traverse distances at extraordinary speed, can be explained particularly as a result [of this enlightenment]. The quite new, 2nd transformation that is described in the Gospels as the ascension was nothing else other than the transfer of the Savior from *Olirna* even higher, into the subsequent stratum, the next one of those existing at the time. After some interval of time, through another transformation he surpassed the Virgin-Mother Mary, and then after several decades later he surpassed apostle John.

Consequently the transformations of certain other great human souls were also completed.

Gradually progressing from power to more power, the Resurrected One has headed the struggle of the radiant principals of *Shadanakar* now for 19 centuries against the demonic principals. During the initial centuries of Christianity, new illuminated strata were created: *Fayir*, *Nertis*, *Gotimna*, then *Yusnorm*, and the movement of many millions of such enlightened ones through this *sakuala* was accelerated. A potent stream of spirituality surged through the Christian churches, refining and enlightening human souls all the more. Spectacular *zatomises* of the Christian meta-culture with its large populations appeared and flourished, all causing the *sinklits* to become brighter. The most grandiose process of the conversion of places of torture into places of purgatory reached about half-way to its goal by the time it got to our era. The transformation of the *sakuala* of the magmas is expected, while the purgatories themselves must gradually change even more. Those elements of retribution that are among them will be estranged entirely. Such will apply to the souls that possess a burdened ethereal body: this will be replaced by spiritual help from the side of the *sinklits*, now to be compared to solely a healing, and no longer felt as a punishment.

During these centuries the Virgin-Mother Mary consummated her ascension from world to world. The Helper of all the sufferers, and especially all those tormented in the nether regions, she is the general Intervener and Great Female Sympathizer of all and for all. She, along with her son, resides in the global *Salvaterra*, receiving a brilliantly radiant ethereal wrap in order to descend into the strata. The Savior, residing as the planetary Logos, in the inner chamber of *Salvaterra*, has already many centuries possessed authority to clothe others in a light-possessing ethereal body, one that he has created. In this state he descends into the *zatomises*, communicating there with the *sinklits* of meta-cultures. His potency has grown immeasurably. However we are not in any state to accept the meaning of the processes that have been consummated during these 2 millennia in the very highest of the worlds of *Shadanakar*, even though from the point of view of meta-history they contain what is the most important, and this is obvious.

But even if the struggle of Jesus Christ on this side against the demonic powers was marked by a series of global victories, the incompletion of his mission in *Enrof* still affects several unended tragic situations. The very teaching seems to be distorted, confused with elements of the Old Testament, just as with those elements that were overcome by Christ's life, and even if this life of his on earth was not disrupted, it would still have finally concluded.

The affect of the incompletion of Christ's mission is that the material principle in nature and the corporeal in a human were too late to attain their predestined enlightenment in the general extents, including not attaining the substance of Christ himself. And so remaining unenlightened they were discarded by the Christian church beyond the borders of where they were enclosed, and where they were accepted and blessed. The sacraments of baptism and communion severed the neophyte from the gentile justification of the self-oppressing corporeal principle; no other type of proposition, or a higher one, was provided. This ascetic tendency of Christianity, hardly ameliorated by the compromised institution of the sacrament of marriage, this polarization of the understanding of spirit and flesh that drew after itself Christianity in all of the cultures that it absorbed and that brought to the final end a civilization that was without religion – all of this was not a plain accident or just a manifestation of only one historical plan. On the contrary, here was reflected something special, a quality unique to Christianity and its meta-historical fate, a feature that was predestined particularly due to the disruption of the mission of Christ in *Enrof*.

What is primary is that in *Enrof*, there was no essential change: the laws that were there remained the same laws; the instincts remained the same instincts; the passions remained the same passions; the illnesses remained the same illnesses; death remained the same death; the state remained as the same state; wars continued as wars as before; and tyranny continued its tyranny. The formation of the church in humanity, overwhelmed by its earlier conceit and not barricaded from sinister influences, could not summon that driving progress that was spiritual and moral, and which would have accomplished what was needed, but the *Gagtungr* disrupted Christ's life. This is why 19 centuries of humanity has stumbled along its ill-fated, broken, zigzag, unlevel and imbalanced route. It has been effected equally between the effort of Providential powers and the ruthless affect of *Gagtungr*.

Even though the character of the victory of the great demon was only half accomplished, it still thrust him into prolonged activity that is impossible to compare with anything in humanity, except ultimate rage. This bestial fury also overflowed into *Enrof*, birthing unprecedented turbulence on the surface of worldwide history. A series of tyrant-monsters on the throne of the Roman Empire, by which the First Century AD was defined, their malice being incomparable with any other that proceeded after them, their insatiable thirst for blood that could never be rationalize, their arrogance, insanity, their inhuman search for new methods of torture – whatever they could think of doing, the ugly distortion of their creative impulse that motivated them to erect edifices that were beyond just massive and unheard of in history, like the Coliseum, or else the completely absurd performance of the rotten Caligula. All of this were echoes of his monstrous rage when he[76] saw his immemorial enemy[77] at that time. Although [Christ] was somewhat restrained, but he became more powerful and now increases with more credit attributed to him.

Even several centuries before Christ, the *Gagtungr* found influential instruments: he succeeded in incarnating certain large-scale demonic entities in their relative and compatible strata and began the first generation of *yuitzraor* in Babylon-Assyria and Carthage. One of these shoots, the Hebrew *yuitzraor*, voluntarily assisted their master in his struggle against Christ during the life of the Savior in *Enrof*. It would hardly been possible without this *yuitzraor* to overwhelm the will of Judas Iscariot and many religious leaders of Judaism in their entirety, all of whom imagined that by the persecution and execution of Christ they were defending the interests of their people. And in addition to this, the *Intelligent Spirit* knew well

---

[76] *Gagtungr*
[77] Jesus Christ the planetary Logos

that the creation of 2 or 3 or several predatory entities of the same plane, of the same stratum, and in accord with the law of the fight for survival of the fittest will lead to the victory of the strongest among them, until the strongest of the strongest expands his authority in the future into all the *shrastras*, and his authority over his person-weapons through the entire earthly *Enrof.* So will all be prepared ahead of time for his absolute tyranny. Particularly as the materialization of this intent, dynasties of the *yuitzraors* in Iran and Rome will likewise be created, and the Roman will become the most powerful of them all.

It seems that during the first century after Christ's resurrection, the *Gagtungr's* chief hope was placed particularly on *Forsuf* – the *yuitzraor* of the global Roman empire. In addition to this, it seems that even the powers of the *Sinklits* did not at the time possess assurance that the insanity of *Gagtungr*, even with doubling its strengths, would not bring the appearance of the antichrist to the near future, and not shorten the period of the first Eon, increasing the very number of spiritual sacrifices to such an unprecedented quantity by doing this, while relocating the task of the 2nd Eon to some back burner. This alarm is explained as that apocalyptical or, more correctly said, eschatological, mood, the expectation of the end of the world in the near future days, that enveloped Christian communities and Judaism during the initial decades after Christ's resurrection. Fortunately, these dangers will not justified. The power of *Gagtungr* at the time was sufficient enough for the absurd fantasies of the bloodthirsty insanity of the Caesars and their attempts to physically destroy the Christian religion. However other trends are noticeable in the activities of *Gagtungr* during the middle of the first century. Taking advantage of the situation that Christ's mission in *Enrof* remained incomplete and – instead of installing a worldwide apotheosis – the church that he founded barely smolders, considering the handful of small communities crushed under the heavy bulk of state institutions created by the *yuitzraors*, and under the rigid and massive weight of involuntary psychological pressure, the *Gagtungr* powers begin to intervene into the personal life of the church.

The person [Paul] was a bearer of a special mission, unconditionally bright, but his personal and inherited traits that are all so apparent distorted his own understanding of this mission. In place of continuing Christ's task, in place of strengthening and enlightening the church through the spirit of love and only through this spirit, the 13th apostle unfolds a grandiose, extensively wide, organizational effort cementing the disconnected communities using austere regulations, his infallible sole authority, and even intimidation, to the extent that they feared excommunication in the event of some disobedience. And so a spiritual terror was born from the bosom of the church. The circumstance that apostle Paul never met Jesus Christ personally during his life and so he was subsequently deprived of all that grace that directly emanated from Jesus. This circumstance is no less significant than another, that Paul did not experience the descend upon himself of the Holy Spirit as did the remaining apostles. As a result the remaining apostles as though ascend to a 2nd plane, and each of them narrows their activities to local tasks, to the development of Christian communities in one or another country, while Paul, who was deprived of this grace, gradually increases as the central figure and exalts himself over all of the communities, connecting them all together and dictating to all of them what it is that he feels is the continuation of Christ's work.

This, perhaps, is the first clear display of the decisiveness of *Gagtungr* at the root to change the demonic plan. At the end of the first century, the situation and entire atmosphere at the highest levels of the Roman government suddenly changed. The final beast on the throne, Domitian, falls as a sacrifice of the conspirators. The era of Caesarian insanities is sharply and abruptly interrupted. Continuing further for an entire century, fully worthy monarchs take turns on the throne. They of course execute what the logic of authority obligates them, which is the will of the *yuitzraor Forsuf,* so they strive to strengthen that government system that will secure such an inexhaustible stream of red nutritive dew – and it is called *shavva* – for the *yuitzraor*, but they no longer have in their sight the previous fiery fantasies of worldwide autocracy, or delirious intentions of construction projects, or live torches, which were Christians smeared with tar and then set on fire, and which Nero used as lights for his orgies.

Subsequently state life entered into a more or less normal course. In other words, the *Forsuf* worried over the prolongation of its existence, and the drive for worldwide authority no longer swayed it. The axis of the higher demonic plan has changed. The ideas that led the Roman Empire to the stage of planetary sovereignty were discarded. At the head of the corner a new goal is installed: to seize the Christian religion from the inside.

During all the distortions introduced into Christianity by the religious short-sightedness of thousands of persons, the Christian religion, and later denominations, appeared as the source of a potent spiritual flowing stream that originated from the planetary heights. In the eyes of the Intelligent Spirit, the church became a factor of first-stage importance, and so all means had to be used to seize it from within. The Semitic religious exclusiveness, the Greek ecclesiastical separatism, the Roman ruthlessness, and the thirst for political hegemony, in every facet that any of it existed – it was all utilized for help during the 2nd, 3rd, 4th and 5th centuries AD. To attain this essential goal it needed to detach the church from its direct tasks, to confuse it with a spirit of hate, to draw it into an ocean of political storms, to exchange its immutable spiritual goals with those that are inconsequential and mundane, to subject its Eastern half to the authority of the emperors, while the Western half to the principals of a pseudo-theocracy – and this was fully attained. The church became a world-dominating power, which only made matters worse for it! Humanity is still far from that high level of moral integrity upon which it is possible to combine world-dominating leadership with ethical immaculacy.

My lack of thorough information bothers me. I do not speak to draw a panorama of the 19 centuries of struggle between the *Gagtungr* and the power of the Resurrected One, or even to sketch its chief stages. What is more or less clear to me are only a very few individual links in the history.

So for example, the meta-historical significance of the person and activity of Mohammed can be little by little explained. Standing on the point of view of some type of orthodoxy, whether Islam or Christian, it is equally easy to provide one or another, positive or negative, evaluation of this activity. But attempting to preserve objectivity, you unavoidably run into the wall of such conclusions and reflections whose contradictory nature does not permit you to ascertain a final conclusive evaluation. It would seem that the religious ingenuity of Mohammed, or his sincerity, or the obviously spirit-filled inspiration of his high ideals, or the distinctive fiery persuasiveness of his preaching, which forces the issue of recognizing him as the genuine prophet, that is, the messenger of the celestial world, is not subject to any doubt. From another side, it is not understandable as to actually why it is possible to ascertain the progressiveness of his teaching as comparative to Christianity, or why was it even needed for humanity. The attitude toward Mohammed of being a pseudo-prophet also does not help in explaining the situation, because then it remains completely incomprehensible in what manner this religious pseudo-teaching was able to nonetheless become a certain channel by which spirituality was poured into the masses of large populated nations as a fiery worship of the Sole God while raising the ethical level of millions and millions of souls.

Meta-historical comprehension provides these questions an unexpected answer, regretfully however, unacceptable in the same manner for both Christian and Islamic conservatives. The matter is that we can find the correct answer if we will just assure ourselves that Mohammed appeared at that historical moment when the *Gagtungr* was already prepared ahead of time to appear on the historical arena as a genuine pseudo-prophet. He was a figure of such immense scale, and just as immense should his religious danger be, relative to the manner he towered so high above humanity. The pseudo-prophet must be able to tear from Christianity a series of outlying groups of people who will superficially adapt this religion, then draw after himself a series of other nations, those that have not yet adopted Christianity, and then within Christianity itself motivate the most powerful movement in a straight demonic direction. The immature Christian religion was a vacant field upon which this poisonous seed was able to provide a wealthy abundance of harvest, complemented by a group of both known and secret adherents of *Gagtungr* at the helm of religious and state authority.

Prophet Mohammed was a vehicle of a supreme mission. Its meaning can be summarized in his effort in creating a movement for the young and uncultured Arabic nation that had hardly at all been affected by Christianity, and so summon it to a direction of religious reformation that would have an impact on the Christian religion. This had the intent, first, to cleanse Christianity from its extreme asceticism; second, to remove the church from under its subjection to state authority; third, to sever the church from the theocratic autocracy that the papacy was able to acquire. But Mohammed was not only a religious evangelist, he was a poetic genius, and even more a poet, as he was a messenger of the celestial world. He was one of the greatest poets of all times. This poetic ingenuity, combined with certain other qualities of his nature, tended to draw him astray from a strict and undeviating religious path.

The current of a mightily poetic imagination was projected into the channel of his religious responsibility, so distorting and confusing that revelation that was assigned him. In place of the reformation of Christianity, Mohammed permitted himself to be drawn away by the concept of the creation of a new religion, one in its most immaculate form. So he founded a religion. The revelation was sufficient enough to preach a new gospel following Christ that was likewise truthful, however the new religion did not develop into one that was progressive, comparative with Christ's teaching, but regressive, although not fallacious and not demonic. This religion definitely drew into its current those nations that, without Mohammed, would have become the spoils of some other installed by *Gagtungr*. As a result the conclusive evaluation of the role of Mohammed cannot be either totally negative or totally positive. Yes, this was a prophet, and the religion he founded is one of the great religions of the right hand. Yes, the appearance of this religion provided security for humanity from great spiritual catastrophes. But rejecting many of the fundamental concepts of Christianity, this religion regressed toward a simple monotheism. It, in essence, does not provide anything new, and now it is understandable why, among the number of the Great Trans-myths, among the number of the 5 crystal pyramids that shine brilliantly at the summits of *Shadanakar*, there is no Islamic trans-myth.

Here I will indicate just one more trend of the demonic plan, without which knowledge it is impossible to understand the future, and which must be transformed at the proper time– in history as well as in meta-history – into a main highway, if I can say it in these terms.

What I am saying is that no demon of any type, no matter how grandiose his scale, is in any condition to birth even one monad. I hope that necessary attention will be paid to this circumstance. After the human-incarnation of the Planetary Logos, humanity became the decisive arena of struggle, and in the demonic mind the dream was crystallized: to create, and allowing this to be gradual, such a person-weapon who would have the power to materialize absolute tyranny in the historical plane, and to convert the earth's population into a diabolic humanity. Again the creative meagerness of demonic principals appeared and nothing of what he conceptualized was unable to endure and so failed. The contradistinctions we notice can be assigned to laws of contemplation and we can draw a graph of the mirror-images of these powers and routes of Providence: Cosmos versus Anti-cosmos; Logos versus the Principal of forms; Divine humanity versus diabolic humanity; Christ versus antichrist.

Antichrist! With the introduction of its understanding in the range of present concepts, I will repel more readers now than perhaps the series of preceding chapters have repelled. Its understanding has been discredited in many diverse ways:

whether pointless, trivial, or using vulgar terms, or putting words into his mouth. Others maliciously accuse political enemies of being servants of antichrist. But if with the introduction of this resurrected understanding I repel 10 times more people than I would repel otherwise, it is all the same, the understanding of the antichrist is here introduced and tying all the concepts together with strong threads, and none of this will ever go away since it will definitely materialize.

In other places I have focused on certain very important meta-historical collisions that had a place in the course of recent centuries. Just as Jesus Christ also foresaw, this progress of development led to the decisive battle being closer and unavoidable in the light of the immemorial aggressiveness of the demonic principle and its drive toward universal tyranny.

The worldwide potency of he who was Jesus Christ grew immeasurably over these centuries. If he should again appear new in *Enrof*, performing all the miracles that he could, it would eclipse all the miracles of the Gospels, all the miracles of the Hindus and the Arabian legends. But this is not needed for the meanwhile. There still remains 2 or 3 centuries before his 2nd arrival, and after this duration he can still attain such potency in order to accomplish the magnificent act of history and meta-history – the change of Eons.

The change of Eons will execute the change of the quality of the substance of human creation, the birth of all the *sinklits* of the meta-cultures in the illuminated corporeal bodies here in *Enrof*, the entrance of those who will comprise diabolic humanity for their redemptive route into other strata, and the installation in *Enrof* of that which in the holy traditions is called the millennial reign of God's holy people. This act of the 2nd arrival must consummate simultaneously in a large number of regions of the earthly *Enrof*, so that not one entity would be deprived of seeing and hearing him. In other words, the Planetary Logos must attain such unimaginable powers in order to appear simultaneously in so many figures, as many as necessary, so all in *Enrof* can comprehend what is occurring. These ethereal-corporeal figures, however, will remain just for a short duration as an expression of his sole Image, and they will merge with him for their continuous residency in the enlightened *Enrof.* The prophecy of Christ and his 2nd arrival particularly speaks of this, that it will occur like lightning shining from east to west, so all nations and countries of the world will see He who is traveling on the clouds of heaven.

CHAPTER 3

WOMANHOOD

I now approach a decisive thesis. And even then no matter how important it may be, I am only able to just say a few words about it.

The dogma of Christian teaching has existed almost 2,000 years, with which we will presently deal. The most diverse of creeds have been subject to doubt, and raskols,[78] sectarian groups and heresies have evolved from their different interpretations. Even the most meaningless ceremonial variations grew in time into immense crevasses, dividing schismatics from the state-supported church. But during the entire duration of 19 centuries, it seems that there has never appeared any disagreement on what is considered the foundational base: the 3 hypostases of the Triune Deity – God the Father, God the Son, and God the Holy Spirit.

I do not see the need to subject the fact of the emergence in the Christian church of this particular understanding of the Triune Deity to any historical or psychological evaluation. I do not have sufficient resources and neither do I have the erudition needed for this, and even if I did possess one and the other, it would be terrifying for me to subject this mystery having such spiritual depth – a concept that surfaced and was defined in the

---

[78] Schisms within the Russian Orthodox Church during the 18th and 19th centuries.

initial centuries after Christ – to a biopsy, my equivalent of an intelligent analysis.

I will permit myself only to recollect one page of the Gospel narrative that indicates, as it seems to me, an item that is not on the same side of this understanding of the secret of the Triune Deity, but on another. The canonical gospels of Matthew and Luke confirm clearly and distinctly that the conception of the child Jesus was from the Holy Spirit within the virgin girl Mary. If this is so, it is possible to conclude that it is not God the Father who is the father of Christ the person, but the Holy Spirit. So how can this be? Could the primordial birth of God the Son from God the Father be otherwise expressed as a mystery in the historical, human world, as only the birth of the person Jesus from the power of that Specific hypostasis? Of course not. The Gospel narrative is entirely distinct. What is indistinct is the other: the understanding of the 3rd hypostasis by the Christian church. The dogma of the 3rd hypostasis has not been fully developed throughout the entire history of the church. What is also striking is the contrast between the detailed exposition of the teaching of God the Son and that almost empty region where the dogmatic exposition of the Holy Spirit is supposed to be located. But essentially, there is nothing strange here. This is the reason this dogma of God the Holy Spirit is too much of a nebulous generalization, unclear, with an absence of completion, and often also a contradiction in dogmas that pertain to the other hypostases.

It was not accidental that the Christian religion named particularly itself – Christian. Other than specifying its origination from Christ, this appellation includes the reflection of that fact that this religion is the revelation of God the Son for the most part, that it is not so much a religion of the Triune Deity, as much it is particularly of the Son.

So whom can God the Father Himself be except for the Spirit? Only the Spirit. And so particularly Holy, in distinction from all other spirits that He created, because each of the divinely-created and even divinely-born monads can assume, and many have assumed, a negative choice evolving in apostasy. It is totally apparent that the Father cannot apostatize from Himself. He is primordial, immutable, unambiguous, and untarnished, and He is called Holy particularly in this sense. So what positive effect can be apply to this emanation from God the Father of the 2 primordial essential qualities attributed to Him – His spirit-ness and His holy-ness? But where is the bases that we need to abstractly apply a completely autonomous meaning to this quality of the 3rd person of the Trinity? In general, based on what words of Christ, on what witness of the 4 Gospels can we base the teaching that God the Father is one of the hypostases of the Trinity, while the Holy Spirit is another? There is no indication of this in the Gospels. The words of Jesus that enter as the capacity of the argument is His popular prophecy, "I will send to you the Spirit Comforter and he will guide to unto all truth." Due to a diverse interpretation of particularly these words there even surfaced a great schism that severed the one body of the Christian church into eastern and western halves, even though both of their interpretation evolved from a common postulate, from what somebody felt was an indisputable statement: that as though Jesus here implied that the Spirit Comforter in particular was the 3rd hypostasis. But know that in these words there is not a shade of indication that the Comforter, which the resurrected Savior was to send, is the 3rd hypostasis or even is a hypostasis. Here there is no indication that the use of the expressions – Spirit-Comforter, and – God the Holy Spirit, are to be understood as meaning both are one and the same. It would be more instinctive and more conclusive and more understandable from all points of view to completely have another resolution, particularly a resolution in this sense, that God the Holy Spirit in particular is God the Father, because God the Father cannot be anything else than Holy and Spirit.

Once again, I am here dealing with the roots of this great teaching, and placing just one opinion opposite such a mighty choir of individuals, more than the eye can see, and who have been echoing for so many centuries that there can be no doubt in the character of its proponents, even if something else might be noticed by someone else. I even understand that in the eyes of some I will appear guilty of a great spiritual offense and I will be ascribed to committing the sole unforgivable sin according to the Gospel: blasphemy of the Holy Spirit. I will triumphantly announce that I worship the Holy Spirit, honor It and pray to It with the same veneration as do other Christians, and I cannot see this as being anything blasphemous toward It, and there is not the least amount of reduction of Its image in this concept, that It is God the Father and that God the Father is God the Holy Spirit, that these 2 identities pertain to one and same – the First – Person of the Holy Triune Deity.

I also need to underscore that my statements here are my personal opinion, with no pretensions on any other. True that this opinion is my derived conclusion and one more among the many and many more that I will derive over time. However this item was affirmed by a divine incident that remains for me as the sole decisive authority. But I count no one to possess such supreme authorization or empowerment to insist on one sole and absolute validity of this concept, on its dogmatic orthopraxy. The Eighth Ecumenical Council could become the legitimate, generally accepted institution that is empowered to resolve such a question, where representatives of all the other existing Christian denominations, and ROSE OF THE WORLD, would subject this thesis to deliberation, just as with the thesis regarding the absoluteness of the veracity and infallibility of the statutes of the ecumenical councils in general and, perhaps, the review of other points of orthodox dogma. But until this should be accomplished, no one in ROSE OF THE WORLD can affirm the full inerrancy of the old dogma. It seems that a person can only believe as his conscience and his individual spiritual experience dictates, and so work toward a unification of the denominations in order to eventually resolve all dilemmas.

However the concept expounded here now opens the road to the resolution of another that is no less a cardinal problem.

It is popularly known that during the duration from the Gnostics to the Christian thinkers of the beginning of the 20th century there lived a vague, although fervent, and persisting sentiment of the Global Womanhood Principle, a sentiment that this principle is not an illusion, not some corporeal category transferred into the cosmic plan, but a higher spiritual reality. The church intended, obviously, to provide an entrance for this sentiment, sanctifying with its authority the cult of the Theotokos in the east and the cult of Madonna in the west. In reality, ahead of the reverential veneration of the Motherhood Principle – a veneration irrationally inherent in the national masses – there appeared a concrete image to which this [principle] endeavored. But that mystic sentiment of which I speak – the sentiment of the eternal Womanhood as a cosmic and divine principle – remained unsatisfactory. The early and irrefutable dogmatization of the teaching of the hypostases placed the bearers of this sentiment in a precarious dilemma: in order not to be identified as heresy, they were forced to circumvent the root question, not deliberating it to its conclusion, often identifying the Global Womanhood with the Ecumenical Church or, finally, perform a diversion from one the attributes of the Deity – Its Wisdom – and then personify this abstractly, calling it the Holy Sophia. The higher ecclesiastical institutions avoided a statement that would somewhat define this question, and maybe now they are to blame for not doing this. The concept of Global Womanhood cannot but grow into the concept of a female aspect of the Deity and this, naturally, threatens the dogmatization of the definitions of the persons of the All-Holy Trinity with a fracture.

I met several persons who were very scholarly and possessed undoubtable spiritual experience in a cultural and mental environment and who, however, were surprised and even insulted by such a principle: as it seemed to them, it was exchanging genders, and in general this transfer was forcing a corporeal category into worlds of supreme reality and even into the mystery of Deity Itself. They had the impression that this was the result of an ancient inclination to the anthropomorphism of the spiritual spheres by way of our limited human comprehension. From very similar psychological states there evolves, for example, the protest of the austere Islamic monotheism against the concept of the Triune Deity and against the cult of the Theotokos. And so having such intolerance, deism and contemporary abstract cosmopolitan monism are driven from the conceptualization of the Trinity, from faith in the ecclesiastical hierarchy and finally from the concept of Eternal Womanhood. This accusation of polytheism directed by Mohammed toward Christianity from 1300 years back is repeated, as funny as it may be.

There lies at the base of similar accusations either an overly simplified understanding of Christian concepts, or else a plain lack of desire to investigate the depth of such questions. Not in historical Christianity, and no less in the subject topic, is there any transfer of a corporeal category into the Deity, but what we have is something principally opposite. The singularity of God is not being subjected to any kind of doubt. It would be naïve to here search for a return to the times of Cartharge, Ur or Heliopolis. The hypostases are diverse manifestations of the Sole Entity from the outside. This is the manner It reveals Itself to the world, but not the manner that It resides within Itself. But this manifestation from the outside is just as absolutely real as Its residence within Itself. As a result the hypostases cannot be accepted in any case as an illusion or as an aberration of our cognizance.

This is why we name the Divine Womanhood – Mother of the Logos, and through It [she is the mother of] the entire universe. But the immemorial union between Father and Mother does not change her primordial essence. Particularly this is why we name the Mother of worlds – Ever-Virgin.

So in the teaching of the Trinity and of the Female aspect of Deity, what is distinct is not the transfer of something corporeal into the celestial sphere, but on the contrary, the understanding of the objective polarity of our strata – the male and female principles – as the opposite poles in the essence of God that are incomprehensible to us. Apostle John said, "God is love." The centuries will succeed each other, then eons, finally the *bramfaturas* and galaxies, and each of us, sooner or later, will attain the Pleroma, the divine fullness and enter the birth womb, but no longer as a child, but as God's brother. Our present conceptualizations of Deity will vanish from our memory, as pale, colorless, unneeded, and no more than a shadow gone. But then the truth that God is love will not lose its veracity. God does not love Himself – such a proposition would be scandalous, but each of the inscrutable facets that comprise Him and hiding within Him are turned in love toward others, and a 3rd is born out of this love: the basis of the universe. Father – Ever-Virgin Mother – Son.

The pinnacle of secrets, the inner secret of Deity, the secret of the love of Father and Mother, from this point is not reflected in human love, whatever type it is. Nothing in this temporal world can be comparatively measured or identified with the essence of that secret. But nothing in the world, with the exception of what exits from principles of apostasy, can be but on the same side of this secret. Human love, that is, the love toward all that lives, expresses – but not reflects – the essence of the Triune Deity: that essence is love. In love, men and women express – and not reflect – the inner secret of the union of Mother and Father to the same extent that it pertains to us, being refracted by a large series of cosmic layers. This is how we can conclude the fundamental, ontological distinction between the 2 spheres of our spiritual life: not having between themselves almost anything common, but the same thing being expressed in our language by using the same term.

Love toward all that exists has long been the fundamental basis of all religion, at least in concept if not in practice, and not just only in Christianity. We need to expect in the future an even greater expansion of all that love will grasp. True, in the religionless teachings of our contemporary era a reversion backwards is clearly expressed, and at least pertaining to love in its fated sense. This is evident in the attitude toward our state collectives, our allies, other governments, our families and our friends. But this attitude is especially temporal, and due to the conditions of the character of this religionless epoch and its limited and reduced morality, but its duration will be no different than any other religionless stage of evolution. As a result the subsequent religious epoch will be a new one, and will announce and strive to materialize a love encompassing all humanity, all the kingdoms of nature and all the ascending hierarchies. In the distant future even greater spiritual possibilities will be unveiled. Even love toward demons will become accessible and necessary. Just in the recent past some of the saints have towered to this specific level of love. But to outpace ourselves, to nurture this in our soul, is still not free from temptations, still far from encompassing humanity and the animal kingdom.

To love the immemorial enemies of God and all that lives signifies to subject our individual soul to the risk of an ascending route. The demons are just waiting for someone to have pity on them. But they wait, of course, not because they need this empathy, since they are controlled by pride and they disdain any human pity. But because as soon as a person feels sorry for them, this is one step toward that person doubting in their wrongness, and once this doubt is instilled in a person, stretching your hand is helping them in their struggle against God and tempting them to rebel. Then this rebellion turns against the person who helped them and will cause his soul to fall to a cruel compensation and will birth suffering in the soul, the *gavvakh*, and it will increase. This is what demons dreams to do to support their inherent strengths. This is why love to demons in a high degree is dangerous for every person, except for those few enlightened souls.

The enlightened soul will understand on its own how love should be displayed, but not interfered by any sympathy or humanitarianism. Such love can be expressed only in a sense of great sorrow, having faith in [the demons'] eventual enlightenment and in the preparation to give all for the sake of their enlightenment, except for your own fidelity to the Deity.

The other facet of love comprises both the inner and external areas of our life, and namely the love between a man and woman.

That burning hot coal within each entity, the unquenchable instinct for the propagation of the species, the source of self-sacrifice, the unrestrained passion, fantasy inspirations, crimes, accomplishments, vices and suicides: is it strange that particularly this love was the greatest rock of stumbling for ascetics and saints? They attempted to differentiate the duality of the type within themselves: the corporeal love in contradistinction to the platonic; the fleeting passion and immutable love; love with no strings and the child-rearing obligation; perversion and romantic infatuation. Often they differentiated the dual nature of the trans-physical sources of love: the celestial Aphrodite or the terrestrial Aphrodite. But in concrete terms, in real feelings, in daily attitudes, all was interwoven, intermixed, merged one into the other, and consolidated into a bundle that could not be unraveled. It began to seem that it would be better to uproot this love, rather than have it burn like brush and interfere with your route to heaven.

So did now begin the great ascetic era in religion. I think there is no good reason to repeat the truths as to why Christianity and Buddhism had to follow such routes and be reborn as ascetic sects, hating life and likewise themselves hated by it. Marriage was sanctified by a sacrament; childbirth by a blessing; but the higher state continued to be counted as celibacy, and this was emphasized.

A casualty of love evolves from it being one-sided and so ends in human tragedy. This particular specialty of love will not last long, only until the 2nd Eon. There are 2 types of love-initiated tragedy. First is when humanity tries to normalize a complex life and it creates preferences, such as customs and norms. So when the love of 2 people conflicts with established customs, social views or state laws, and there is nothing they can do, then this is the tragedy of the first type. When they love each other and possess a harmonic union, but it cannot materialize as a result of some family or social status or condition, this is a tragedy of the 2nd type. This is why customs and laws must be reconsidered in time in order to reduce such tragedies to a minimum or to none at all.

It seems to me that the correct religious response to the question of love between a man and woman can be only one: this love is blessed, beautiful and holy to the extent that this love is creative. What do I mean by this?

The conclusion I have is that the greatest prevalence of the display of creative love in our eon appears in the birth and nurture of children, but this is far from the only display of creative love and loving creativity. Collaborative effort in love evolves from the spheres of culture, educating one another in the better facets of personality, mutual self-perfection, inspiration of one another in the artistic, religious and any other area of creative effort, finally, even the simple happiness of young, fresh, passionate love that enriches, strengthens and escalates both of them. All of this is divine creativity that leads to their growth and enlightenment, to increasing the size of the global ocean of love and joy. Radiances of beautiful love between a man and woman are exalted as high as the pinnacles of the world, strengthening them, and it is these worlds that were characterized in one of the preceding chapters as Waves of Global Womanhood. Even if both lovers direct their simultaneous creative effort toward an erroneous side, if both of them, for example, labor in some direction that only possesses a harmful intent for society, even in this situation it is only the direction of this effort that deserves condemnation.

Until humanity is corporeally transformed, love to that point between a man and woman will remain as though firmly attached to the instinct of propagation of the species. In time matters will not be this way. The intention of love will alter its instinctive goal. The topic of the propagation of the species will no longer seem commonly applicable to transformed humanity. At that time a place will be reserved for the incarnation of monads in enlightened bodies, materializing completely differently. But of course, due to the conditions of our eon, the fundamental display of love's creativity will remain nonetheless as the birth and nurture of children.

Chapters at the end of this book are dedicated to the problems of nurturing. Here it seems opportune to me to just note some particulars of those historical tasks that are placed in front of a woman presently beginning this repetitive cycle, pertaining to nurturing and other general aspects of life's various cycles.

On occasion we will have the opportunity to hear a positive confirmation from men and from some women, both providing essentially the same conclusion, that as though the cultural and creative tasks do pertain to both genders,. But if up to this time we should notice that women yield to men in societal, political, scientific, technical, philosophic and even artistic matters, in volume of knowledge and significance, this can be explained with the situation that women over the course of history were always in a state of subjection and oppression. This opinion is actually far more extensive than we would like to think. It is sufficient to just call it temporal.

However, were women always and everywhere committed to an oppressed position? It has already been 200 years that doors to creative effort in the spheres of literature and art in Europe and Russia were opened to women just as they have been to men, but of course, just to those of the privileged classes. Do we really need to recollect that not even one woman over these past 2 centuries – those having displayed a irrefutable talent and ascending to become famous artists and musicians – has enriched the pantheon of musical genius? It is also cruel to mention that among the coryphaeuses of global literature, for the 200 or 300 male names, there are only 6 or 7 women. It has been almost a century now that women have the right access to higher education in many countries. But she has successfully replaced men in a wide region of professional activity: in hospitals, laboratories, at the head of schools, and even in conducting scientific experiments. But where are the hundreds of names of outstanding female scholars who would balance the hundreds of male names who have become famous worldwide in this same period of time?

DANIEL ANDREEV

Are women gifted any less than men? It is completely inarguable that in some matters – Yes. But it is also just as inarguable that in other matters they possess gifts that a male does not possess and will never possess. It seems to me that it would be absurd to deny that a woman could not be a good geologist, a conscientious engineer, a talented artist, a qualified chemist or biologist, or be able to decipher her own abilities in these or other vocational spheres.

So what areas is a woman especially and unlimitedly gifted? In motherhood; nurture of children; domestic responsibility; care of the sick and elderly and their healing; the moral restoration of criminals; nature or gardening; care of animals; family love. It seems that wherever qualities of compassion, kindness, empathy, self-sacrifice, patience and tolerance, attention and consideration are particularly required, these are inherently part of the congenital female character.

For thousands of years in humanity the male or manly principle abounded and triumphed: strength, boldness, pride, valor, drive, cruelty, militarism. Millennium after millennium waves of wars have washed and continue to wash over the face of our world, and revolts, revolutions, terrors, insane and ruthless violence, and these waves have been comprised of men's wills and men's intentions. Often though we hear of women's cruelty. But, my God, has the bloodthirsty nature of Genghis Khan, Tamerlane, Napoleon, horror of torture chambers, rage of the Jacobite terror, damage to countries due to colonialism, the oppression caused by the fascists and other dictations – has any of this been started and headed by women? History is aware of repulsive females, those who murdered their brothers, children, who were sophisticated sadists, but there is not one female of historical significance who can be placed alongside the impact of Tiberius and Nero, Assargadon, Alā al-Dīn Muhammad II, Tomás de Torquemada, Pissarro, [Fernando de Toledo] Duke of Alba, Robespierre, Ivan the Terrible and Maluyta Skuratov, Himmler and Beria.

Forced into the hidden recesses of domestic responsibility, the womanhood principle was preserved from annihilation because without it, the male is impotent, and so the physical continuation of the human race is impossible without her.

* * *

In the meta-history of the most recent era, a most secretive event is occurring: a deluge of new divinely-creative strengths into our *bramfatura*. The hearts of the most exalted, the minds of the most refined, dreamed of this event from ancient times. And here and now it is occurring. The first link in the series of events is an event of such significance that it can only be compared with the incarnation as a human of the planetary Logos, and which had its place at the end of the 19th century. This was a waterfall of the strengths of the Ever-Virgin Mother, but not impersonal, as this had its place already twice in the history of humanity, and with its incomparably intensive and personal character.

From the summits of the universe a great divinely-born monad descended into *Shadanakar*. This epiphany in *Raoris*, one of the supreme strata of our *bramfatura*, where It entered at the time, was foretold almost a hundred years ago by Vladimir Solovyov, when in an Egyptian desert on a star-filled night he experienced a tremendous upheaval of comprehension and before his very eyes he saw the Great Womanhood Entity. She was beyond radiance and goodness, an expression of the Female hypostasis of the Trinity that we call *Zventa-Sventana*. Now her residence is in *Bayushmi*, in one of the spheres that enters into the *sakuala* of the waves of Global Womanhood. The day is getting near for her long-awaited descent into one of the highest cities of the meta-culture. There she must be born in a body of enlightened ether, as a child of the demiurge and one of the Great Sisters. A large crowd of the most towering of souls will descend with Her from the elite stratum of *Shadanakar* into this *zatomis*. Here She is! Our hope and reliance, light and divine beauty. This birth will be so reflected in our history such that our grandchildren and great-grandchildren will even see it: the installation of ROSE OF THE WORLD and its expansion through the circles of all countries. And if a horrible upheaval of humanity does not discard it and downward into depths of darkness, then the arrival of ROSE OF THE WORLD will ascend as the supreme authority over all the world.

But this will not yet signify the concluding victory of the powers of Light: let us remember the horsemen of the Apocalypse! But the order of the horsemen in history does not coincide with what was foretold by the visionary on Patmos Island: the first to hurl by was the Black, the era of the sovereignty of the hierocracy with the feudal system. Now the route for the 2nd horseman is prepared, the Red: every person understands what hides behind this symbol. We wait and hope on the White horseman – ROSE OF THE WORLD, the golden age of humanity! The appearance of the final horseman, the Pale, will not repulse anything: the *Gagtungr* will procure its birth in the human figure of the one it has nurtured already several ages. But the epoch of the reign of ROSE OF THE WORLD will summon likewise the termination of spiritual sacrifices, the amount of which have been innumerable. It will succeed in educating a series of generations in a noble fashion. It will strengthen the power of the spirit of millions, even billions of the unstable population. Warning of the approaching antichrist, and directing attention to him when he appears, and disarming him, fostering irrevocable belief in the heart of humanity, while an understanding from the meta-historical perspective in the intellect, along with a global religious panorama, it will make the arriving offspring of darkness inaccessible to temptation in the future generations and generations.

And now only will ROSE OF THE WORLD reflect the mystery of the birth of *Zventa-Sventana* in *Enrof,* the growth of the powers of Womanhood and their significance will occur in one of the *zatomis,* and their contemporaries will announce this wherever they can. By means of this and first of all will a general drive toward peace be stipulated, a repulsion to all blood. Disappointment and coercive methods of change will vanish. The growth of the societal significance of women, increasing their kindness and worry over children, a thirst for beauty and love, will materialize. We are entering into the cycle of epochs when the female soul will cause all to become fresher and cleaner. This will be the cycle of epochs when Womanhood in humanity will reveal itself with unprecedented strength, balancing a perfected harmony with the male authoritative principles. Who has eyes will see.

Book VII

The Meta-History of Ancient Russ

Chapter 1

Kievan Russ as a Meta-Historical Appearance

The drama of historical Christianity consists in that not one of its denominations transformed into a form that is entirely beneficial to the welfare of that nation, that is capable of expressing and materializing the Christian covenant in its mystical and ethical meaning. The reason for this is rooted anyway in the disruption of the mission of Jesus Christ, accomplished by the *Gagtungr*. So the blame lies on the churches because they are just people's fraternities and are absent of serious, sincere and true currents in the direction of [Jesus'] mission. For if Catholicism, striving to replace the Kingdom of God on earth with its hierocracy, succumbed to one of the oldest infra-physical vampires of worldwide history – and even fortunately just for a short interval – then Orthodoxy, still involved with Byzantium – the cornerstone of the state as Dostoyevski expressed it – has completely rejected this task. This task, one of the key ones, if not the very key of all the tasks, that appeared in the presence of humanity, has now traversed with all unreasonable difficulty and danger the route demanded of it toward the hierarchies of Russian meta-culture.

The Christian myth is potently poured into the cognizance of the [Russian] nation, mesmerizing and drawing the hearts using images of the Almighty, the immaculate Virgin and the saints, at one time ascending to the heights of integrity from the dark nether-regions of Judaism and Byzantium. From the sanctuaries of Jerusalem and Athens, from the merchants of Constantinople, white rays shined warming the soul and allowing it to commune with the joy of Orthodox creativity: the artistry of monks, imitation of the lives of saints, ecstasy in the sphere of the spirit, humility, construction of temples, fasts. And from there incessant warnings were reported, the alarm of horror in the face of the worlds of Compensation, so terrifying, that the burden of recompense beyond the grave in the Byzantine meta-culture would not be mitigated by purgatories of any type.

In the furthest corners of the culture, in the lower national levels, the ancient Slavic ideology yielded to decay. But the great forests trustfully preserved within their depths the bound of human substance with the *stikhials*; and the sorcery of the wizards, dances to the credit of creation powers, the chants of witches, rites tying together a person with the unseen residents of masters of nature, prolonged their existence. Never in worldwide history could the required asceticism become the guiding principle for the masses, and which did not occur here either. Life displayed all of its own needs: propagation of the race, welfare of the family, defense of the country from attacks by the nomads of the steppes. No matter how much the monks prayed in their monasteries, all remained the same: these prayers did not liberate the masses of population from military obligation, from all-day regular work, from the destructive attacks of the Polotzi,[79] and from the joyful passions, life in its fullness rewarding all of us.

So did the concepts of dual-belief[80] evolve, and which did not disappear from Russian in its entirety until the 20th century.

---

[79] Pagan Slave tribes of the Ukraine in ancient Russia.
[80] An amalgamation of Christian beliefs with the existing Slavic superstitions and mythology.

[Orthodoxy] began to gradually decorate its edifices using native colors those artistries that seemed to be more connected with the myth of Christianity. This can be ascertained in icons and frescoes of the Kievan, Suzdal and especially Novgorod styles.

At the time when the national religious intuition of many other meta-cultures expressed its knowledge of the existence of *zatomises* and the majority of it based on transmitted legends, Russia begins to express its religious knowledge pertaining to its heavenly expression and counterpart – the heavenly Russia – using the language of another artistry: architecture. From the 11th to the 18th centuries, all the centers of Russian religious activity and especially the religious life of the tribes that earlier were attacking us, aspired to development, perfecting and repeating one and the same figure. This architectural ensemble, whose axis appears as white limestone – a white cathedral with gold cupolas and bell towers in the shape of pillars, while surrounding it are several chapels and smaller churches, often of diverse colors, but almost all of them having gold cupolas. Further away dormitories, kitchens and dining halls would be located, and the entire corporate assembly would be surrounded by massive walls of defense with towers at each corner. The entire facility would be located near a river for water supply.

This design appeared along the Dnepr River at the beginning of the 11th century, and now is repeated along the Volkhov River, and variations of it start to multiply: in Pskov, Smolensk, Vladimir, Pereyaslav, Chernigov, Rostov, Kolomna, Nizhni-Novgorod, Yustug, Troitzi-Sergeev,[81] in large and small cities, and often in some rural area distant from any city, in groups of monasteries and kremlins.[82] In succeeding epochs, it will attain its apotheosis in the Moscow Kremlin.

This is worth thinking about. Hardly would the attempt be crowned with success to exhaustively explain this appearance as solely military-political, technical or even popularly-cultural innovations. Other countries, arranged in similar geographic

---

[81] Today known as Sergeev Posad
[82] Kremlin is the Russian equivalent of citadel.

conditions, during the feudal epochs, and in similar religious climates, however created completely other types of artistic-mystical symbols, other aesthetical figures and, in part, architectural canons. Such an architectural ensemble in general, far from everywhere grew into a primary symbol, into a composite reflection of the trans-myth, into a concrete likeness of the City that was sought.[83]

*   *   *

Now to discuss the matter that consists of nation-building being of several types, and to understand that the diversity of these types is important in the highest degree. I am convinced that the proposed table provides several of the primary types, at the same time I do not attempt to exhaust all possible forms, and have also deleted most of the temporal forms or those with insufficient information.

1. The State with a Fluid Composition:
    Rudimentary centralization of state authority.
    Constant altercations of weakly organized composite units.
    The might of tribal egregores and vampiric organizations.
    The effect of dyads of the supra-nations.
    Still young, with the majority in an ethical and religious level of cognizance.
    Examples are: Egypt during the epoch of the nomes; Vedantic India, Greece during the epoch of the polises; Europe during the early Middle Ages.

2. The State with a Firm-Viscous Composition:
    Sufficiently soft for transforming internal effort.
    Limited tyrannical tendency due to a balance of societal-political strengths.

---

[83] Heb 11:10

The demiurge materializes in state leadership via the egregores.

Its marriage with the ideal conciliar soul.

Examples are: Egypt to Tutankhamen; Buddhist states of India and south-east Asia; the Chinese empires of Tan and Chin; Athens during the era of Pericles.

3. The State with an Extremely Firm Composition:
Colossal despotic sovereignty.

Tyranny of the demon of autocratic domination.

Preservation of the ethereal incarnation of the conciliar soul, but extremely critical of its freedom of activity.

At the end of this stage, and perhaps earlier, the demiurge removes its sanctions from the state demon.

Examples are: the great tyrannical empires of Assyria, Carthage, Rome, Baghdad; the empires of Genghis Khan, Tamerlane, Spain of the 16th century, Britain of the 18th–19th centuries, empire of Napoleon, Hitler's government.

4. Hierocracy:
Where the egregores seize autocratic authority of the church. Either its growth is similar to the vampiric monsters announcing their worldwide pretensions and transferring its residence from the *sakuala* of the egregores to the *Gashsharva* (the papacy of the end of the middle ages); or else the closure of ethical borders and utilization of strictly internal sources (Tibet).

In the first instance, its struggle against the diads of the supra-nation and *sinklit*, while rising against the distorted myth of international religion. In the second instance, from one side, the limitation of the freedom of activity of the bright diad of the infra-physical meta-culture; from another side, the powers of the supreme trans-myth of the international religion.

5. The fracture of the sole structure of the supra-nation into many solid state entities.

    The development of local strengths, removed from under the control of the hierarchy.

    Weakening of the latter's active creative strengths.

    The composition of the conciliar soul is similar with the composition of a deep malady.

    Examples are: the Mediterranean region of the 4th–5th centuries AD; the Islamic regions after the early Caliphates; Germany after the 30-Year War.

6. Alien Enslavement:

    Situation of a nation that is become an instrument of other hierocracies that have their own intentions, one not having any connection to the subject supra-nation.

    The condition of the conciliar soul in the various meanings of the condition of slavery.

7. The State Structure of an Ameliorated Type, created under the conditions of a societal-ethical maturity of a supra-nation and the absence of external dangers.

    The subjection of government principal directly to the powers of the demiurge.

    The beginning of the defeat of the principle of violence.

    The possibility of preparation of an ideal national structure, unveiled to the hierarchies.

    The position of the conciliar soul as the spouse of the demiurge.

    Examples are: Scandinavia, Switzerland for the most part, and a few small countries in isolated areas.

8. Inter-supra-national Unification

    So far this is just a contemplated theoretical government structure, and a means of entrance to planetary unification.

    A creation of the demiurges.

9. Ideal national structure.

Abolition of the state.

Conversion of the state structure of humanity into a fraternity.

The completion of the community and societal structure. Only then can the ethereal expression of Eternal Womanhood, born of the hierarchies, be accepted.

* * *

When the geographic concentration of Russian meta-culture was defined, naturally and unavoidably, this national spiritual center and citadel of government was supposed to be crowned with the corporeal likeness of the summit of the supra-national trans-myth: the earthly Kremlin. The demons and other powers of the demiurge that it sent into the soul, mind and will of the Moscow princes and metropolitans, monks and aristocrats, architects and iconographers, the credited and the unknown, unveiled to them these images of the heavenly Russia and *Fongaranda*, which awaited their reflection in rocks and bricks. And this reflection began to appear: slowly, difficultly, from year to year and from century to century, heavy, disorderly, eternally being rebuilt, distorted due to accidents, crippled due to fires, invasions by aliens and the capriciousness of authorities, with the gold crown of the kingdom upon the forehead, and with the glue of slavery and wounds of torture upon the body; and what is the most beautiful of all is that this was possible in the religious and material level of Russia of the middle ages.

CHAPTER 2

THE CHRISTIAN MYTH AND PRE-RUSSIANISM

The detailed analysis to a somewhat certain extent of the general, and to a high extent the wide and complex question, of the meta-historical significance of the Orthodox Church, and even more the entirety of the Christian myth – is a topic for a multi-volume work or even for an complete series of works. But it is clear and natural that the inner mystical life of the Russian church was defined by the connection particularly with the general Christian trans-myth and with those hierarchies and essentials – both cosmic and planetary – that are venerated by the Russian church: the Logos, the Virgin-Mother Mary, angelic ranks, and the great religious activists of the general Christian or Byzantine past. The high level of their ascension opened before them the possibility of active assistance from top to bottom, from the *zatomis*, from the Heavenly Jerusalem and *Sinklit* of Humanity to the strata of concrete historical effectiveness, and to the *Enrof.*

Over the course of many centuries the Christian myth penetrated and shrouded the religious life of Russian society, imbedding itself decisively in every area of culture, even to the point of decorating tableware and cloths with religious themes.

This ideological attitude, and as long as we speak about the Russian national past, surfaces to draw out from under the layers of the Christian myth, either with the help of a painstaking scientific analysis, or else by the route of meta-historical contemplation and meditation, this ideological approach I have name pre-Russianism.

Pre-Russianism is, in essence, nothing else other than the first stage of the development of the myth of the Russian supra-nation.

On its own merit the general trans-myth of Christianity does not contradict and cannot contradict the trans-myths of the supra-nations; it does not collide and cannot collide with them. On the contrary, the global *Salvaterra*, completely penetrated by the Logos and Ever-Virgin Mother, that is, the supreme reality of the trans-myth of Christianity, remains at the same time the pinnacle of pinnacles, indistinctly traversing through the trans-myths of the supra-nations. Historical perspectives of the future would be morose and joyless if our belief did not illuminate them in the light of such an arriving ideological attitude, when the Christian myth will be mutually supplemented with the myths of the supra-nations, merging with them into one harmonic whole. But in the historical past, the mature Christian myth as if cloaked the barely sprouting myth of the Russian supra-nation. It cloaked all the historical churches with the strength of its essence and with its damaging parochialism, the demands to confirm its religious aspect of the world as the one sole universal truth, and excluding even the possibility of the existence of others.

No matter how respectful was the subjective attitude of the meta-historian to the Christian myth, or how highly he valued the role of this myth in the cultural history of Russian, but this can hardly separate it entirely from feelings of bitterness and compassion, even from some unaccountable offense, while studying something from Russia's arts of the Middle Ages. He will feel that it was cold and torturously oppressed for these shoots of the immemorial national ideology, which so many attempted to display and even in art.

I would have said laughing, that love for it, an infantile joy of life, sunshine happiness and spontaneity, is hardly bold enough to disclose its existence in brightly colored paints of nature, in fairy tales, in the style of mosaics or carvings, in the icons, where flowers, stars of the skies and magic animals create a marvelous collection, radiating a touching, pure, pantheistic love toward the world.

Then monastic asceticism entered, and the creative activity of the *Dingras* debased the corporeal body of human life. The contiguity of spirituality with the corporeal side of love seemed scandalous: love became a sin and marriage had to be sanctified by a rite.

Then the Christian pantheon was introduced, and the soul, trapped by the respiration of the hierarchies of the supra-nations and *stikhials*, was not bold enough to provide to itself an account of the existence of these hierarchies that could not find a place in the Christian pantheon since they were not sanctioned by ecclesiastical authority. The truths of divine knowledge and secular knowledge seemed exhausted by the contents of the 2 Testaments and teaching of the ecclesiastical fathers, and every independent work of thought would seem to be suspicious, if not heretical.

This led to the attitude of art introduced as a second-level view of expression of all those truths of the Christian myth. Secular artistry was suppressed, sculpture was accused of being pagan, poetry stagnated with the boundaries of folklore, dancing was barely tolerated and only in the form of orderly circle dances, while productions of theater performances were cruelly uprooted.

Looks like we have only defined the actions of the Christian myth that applied brakes to the myths of the supra-nations. But there is also another side to this process. Behind the Christian myth there also flickers a light, not a transparent oscillation of incidental shades, but a higher reality, the Christian trans-myth: the heavenly Jerusalem and the spheres of the global *Salvaterra*. The approach of the higher order to these treasures secluded within itself an inexhaustible source of spiritual powers, providing a potent push to the impulse of inner self-realization. Of course, this self-realization moved forward, but essentially only along an ascetic, monastic route. Although [Orthodoxy] respected secular rectitude, however it viewed it as inferior and just a preparatory step toward monasticism. But if the Orthodoxy was able to construct and materialize ideals of rectitude as good as those of the civil, domestic, societal and state areas, then this would signify that it had reached such a stage of humanity's self-perfection incomparable to anything else attained in the world. In other words, this would be possible, but only in 2 circumstances: either that the mission of Christ was accomplished, instead of being interrupted, or else that a new stream of cosmic spiritual strengths would rush from the macro-*bramfaturas* into *Shadanakar*, thereby weakening *Gagtungr*, and acquiring the potential to transform humanity.

* * *

The gift of holiness is the same type of gift as ingenuity or just as the infallible axis of the heroic psychological structure that makes a person capable not for some specific heroic act, but to the conversion of their life into a heroic tale. All 3 of these gifts (which includes the gift of being a national hero, but this is discussed in another trend) can be summarized in the fact that one of the *daimons* is sent to the concrete human individual as a child (or greater if mature), assigned according to their inherent capability to accept the bright inspiration of the hierarchy. Messengers, such *daimons* from the world of winged humanity,[84] where Christ's mission was victoriously consummated and where humanity itself immeasurably assigned us for our spiritual development, see one of their principle tasks as the assistance of those located lower and who have fallen behind in general from ascending the strata of existence ahead of them. Keeping watch over people who possess this bright gift, which is the special mission, *daimons* are installed as guides through whom the effectiveness of Providential principles are poured into the mind and will of a person. Particularly this sensation of their presence summons such persistent objects into life, such as the assurance of many poetic geniuses that they are in the presence of inspirational muses, or religious activists who are assured they are being guided by their guardian angels, while certain thinkers are assured of the positive effect that such *daimons* have upon them.

Resuming the topic, we can say that the absolute significance of the Christian myth is comprised within itself. While its private and positive significance for the Russian meta-culture consists in that it has released to the supra-nation the subjective comprehension of that depth and height of the supreme spheres of *Shadanakar*, to which the demiurge itself strives while drawing after itself the supra-nation as its creation. The Christian myth includes that general planetary obligation that lies farther or higher than any of the *zatomises*, any *stikhials*,

---

[84] Meaning the angelic, with the display of angels always having wings.

any hierarchs, even though it is barely released into the Christian myth.

Of all the cultures of humanity existing to this era and fully defining themselves, only 2 have appeared as able to exit their local regions and promulgate their principles to the extent of almost the entire world: the Roman Catholic culture and the European culture. No matter how many reasons of their influence the historian may disclose – societal-economic, geographic, cultural – and no matter how many attempts were made to suppress the dissatisfaction or insufficiency of their explanation, for the meta-historian, none of any of these rejected comparative means, and the mechanisms of these reasons will be considered the primary, but will remain in its own category. He will search for the superlative reason in the fact that the Christian myth from times immemorial is tied not only with Eden and *Monsalvat*, but with the reality of the heavenly Jerusalem and the global *Salvaterra*, and communicated its true immense scale to the European spirit and so made it capable of effectively having a worldwide mission.

Two other Christian meta-cultures, the Byzantine and Abyssinian, were so oppressed, so squeezed by demonic powers, that the existence of one of them in *Enrof* terminated entirely, while the other on its route was hopelessly restrained.

The 5th meta-culture penetrated by rays of the Christian trans-myth was the meta-culture of Russia. In light of the series of external and internal reasons, it developed slower than its western sisters, but nonetheless it overcame the series of fatal dangers, resisted the tremendous invasions and attacks, and entered the global arena just at the dawn of the 2nd millennium of its historical existence,[85] and so has become formidable for its friends and its enemies with its obvious potential that applies to all humanity.

It is true that other international religions were tied, even in part, with strata of *Shadanakar*, much higher than any *zatomises* of the meta-culture. It seems that they could

---

[85] This would be year 1900, with the initiation of Russian history being about 900 AD.

distribute proportions of the spirit indispensable for the tasks of such a worldwide scale by using their supra-nation. But in the Islamic myth 3 layers are noticed in the meta-historical impression. One is the reflection of the trans-myth particularly of the Islamic supra-nation and it is only applicable to this trans-myth, that is, to the *zatomis Dzhannet*. The other provides its own humiliated and distorted variation of the Christian myth, but nonetheless, one that is reliant on spiritual reality. And the 3rd is as though attempting to break into the meta-*bramfatura*, but it does not acknowledge the existence of the global *Salvaterra*, the existence of the planetary Logos, and as a result created a boundary for itself, dooming itself by not disclosing Islam as a religion having a potential especially applicable for all of humanity.

This is particularly why Islam, as an expanding religion, quickly dissipated, and now has no more drive to expand any further than it has succeeded in recent centuries.

The Buddhist contemplation, with the exception of, it seems, the Abhijna[86] of Gautama Buddha, stops at Nirvana, or more correct, at the world of the supreme aspect of the Buddhist trans-myth, and not striving to grasp even the higher spheres of *Shadanakar*. The feeling of profound hopelessness, unbelief in the possibility of the transformation of worlds and enlightenment though law, penetrates this religion from every direction. This is natural for all religions that appeared before the incarnation of the planetary Logos as a human in *Enrof*. It is natural likewise that this hopelessness paralyzes every aspiration toward worldwide expansion. If we can be amazed at something here, it is quickly that Buddhism nonetheless has found within itself strengths to overflow sideways, although, of course, any proselytism on its part is now in the past.

As far as Hinduism is concerned, because Hinduism remains almost completely alien to proselytism of any type, this is the same reason for its destiny in history.

---

[86] The concept of higher knowledge in Buddhism.

Book VIII

Regarding the Meta-History of the Muscovite Realm

Chapter 2

The Egregore of Orthodoxy and Infra-Physical Fear

Russia is destined for a unique, sole and unrepeatable role, a mission of global perspective was being prepared within it and for it. And the materialization of this mission could have been earlier doomed if its unstable culture, the spiritually untempered nation, unprepared country, was thrown into the orbit of the more mature meta-cultures of the West, that is, was transformed into one of the many nations of Catholic or European culture.

The demiurges of the supra-nations are not the highest of meta-historical institutions. There are others. There is the *Gridruttva*, the white chamber, where the enlightened, raised from the *zatomises* into the *Sinklit* of the world, simultaneously create the spirit plan of humanity's common ascent. There is the *Sinklit* of humanity, there is the Elite of *Shadanakar*, there is the Global *Salvaterra*. The fathomless depths of thought of these institutions are disclosed just in small portions over the course of centuries. Then will begin the illumination of the 2nd and exceptionally profound level of teleology, but only in loose, individually scattered reflections that will arise as teleological plans of all the demiurges of humanity – the creation of great spirits, but nonetheless, limited. Such plans are still incomplete or excessively narrow even with all of their majesty, and not anticipative of all items, not contemplative of all items, and not encompassing of all items.

So the Great Turmoil[87] brought the nation out of an infantile state. It provided it meta-historical experience that enriched it. But the incorporation of this experience required a prolonged period of time, and it has not been fully incorporated, as is apparent, even to this time. The 17th century in its entirety stands under the sign of this incorporation, this transfer from adolescence to youth.

The events of worldwide meta-history are well-known, when the warring egregores surfaced and invaded religious communities. The turbulently surfacing tendency became militarist, and even more vampirical, as they densely merged with the religious-societal global ideology that seemed to be better witnesses of a strong religious egregore, actively demonized by the *Gagtungr* and transformed from a simple unavoidable obstacle of the Providential process of meta-history into its active and conscious enemy. It is sufficient to summon our recollection of the history of Judaism and the blood-filled expansion of early Islam.

We already spoke of the immense and – as a result – most fortunate significance of Russia that consists in the personal decision of Prince Vladimir the Great pertaining to the state religion.[88] Now it is indispensable to remember that it was Vladimir who introduced into Russ particularly that religion, which according to its almost 1,000 year tradition, due to the circumstances of its formulation in the cultural centers of Byzantium at the very foot of the emperor's throne, that

---

[87] Referring to the Time of Troubles, 1598-1613, in Russian history.
[88] The introduction of Christianity into Russian in 988 AD.

remained alien to any extreme theocratic tendency. In comparison with the egregores of Islam or Calvinism, and even more, with the monsters that surfaced from behind the back of Judaism and the Papacy, the egregore of Russian Orthodoxy was inert, amorphic, non-aggressive and weak. From a long while back, the Church's position was that of a religious ally of the state, and later from being its ally it was transformed into its spouse and then into a servant and, with the 3rd *Zhrugr*,[89] into a slave, and only once did it attempt to reveal its pretensions for the supreme autocratic role.[90] No matter how sorrowful from a religious-cultural, and even more from the Orthodox confessional, point of view, this humiliation of the Church to the subjection of the state in stages, all of this was the lesser of 2 evils, if we were to place it side by side with the opposite extreme.

The dark-ethereal egregore gained firm control over the Russian Orthodox Church on the field of that psychological climate that was oriented in the country as the result of the struggle with the Mongols and the establishment of a national militarist autocracy. The egregore was formed from these shoots of the majority population participating in the church, from just any soul that entered, or those who did not attain any rectitude, or those who did not apply themselves to veneration, humility or love, and those just involved in mundane matters. They promoted the growth of the egregore in a fatal manner and especially the growth of the Middle Ages' semi-magical piety that forced adherents to donate immense amounts to monasteries as a requiem for their souls, and the princes contributing large parcels of real estate to monasteries, while the monks themselves accepted all of this as though they deserved it. This imbalanced enrichment of monasteries, secularism of the monastic vocation, and in general the clerical, was an excellent luxurious field for a dark-ethereal wart on the body of the church. This thick and intense club concentrated at the foot of its

---

[89] Probably referring to Tsar Peter I the Great.
[90] Under Patriarch Nikon who wanted to subject Russia to the authority of Russian Orthodox Church while under the weak rule of Tsar Alexei Mikhaelovich.

synodal meta-ethereal summit, this turbulent fog. With its blind equivalent comprehension it identified itself, obviously, with the very church. The threat of its inflation was presented as an appearance of an invisible barrier between the believer's soul and the trans-physical essence of the church, to which this soul aspired. As a result, no matter how obscurely the believer felt the nature of this danger to be, it was intended to be inscribed upon him as something even more terrible than the vampirical tendency of the *Zhrugrs*.

CHAPTER 4

THE NATIVE THINKING OF PETER
AND THE DEMONIC DISTORTION OF HIS MISSION

Of what did the historical task of Peter I consist? To what extent was this task directed by the demiurge? The layers of this task can be separated in the personality and actions of Peter from the effect of the *yuitzraor* and it is expressed in general in humanity's understanding to this extent. This task is pictured in the following view:

Russia is destined to a worldwide mission, the meaning of which was not provided to the emperor to know. It had to be verified just in one manner – in its global character. His personal task can be summarized in turning the supra-nation upon the path leading from a state of vegetation and national inclusiveness to the expanse of humanity's general purpose. In this light, the Russian nation has the responsibility to place itself within the circle of foremost nations, not in the capacity of some or another satellite or lesser historical partner, but in the capacity of a great dominion that other nations will be compelled to accept seriously right from the beginning. Such a turnaround is possible only under the condition if Russia will accept objectively the foremost principles of its neighbors, the older culture, because this culture is just one of the 2 that is able to discard the aristocratic hereditary limitation within itself and the local isolation in regard to the balance of the world.

In order for such a turnaround to materialize and for its results to be stable, a complete inner transformation is required, this will abolish the boyar class as the governing group, which just showed its inability to be on the same level as historical demands, and will transfer the leading role of the royalty to the middle class.

BOOK IX

PERTAINING TO THE META-HISTORY OF THE PETERSBURG EMPIRE

CHAPTER 1

THE SECOND *YUITZRAOR* AND ITS EXTERNAL EXPANSION

The preliminary consideration is that certain occurrences of history, those that on their own remain evil, and because they have caused suffering and death for masses of people, can be at the present time, and this is completely obvious, the lesser of evils and can ameliorate the dilemma. War is the source of suffering of nations and the decrease of their moral level, subsequently – evil. But meditating on this, evil can be even worse, for example, evil that is prolonged, encompassing, depleting, and enslaving of the nation. And if we had to make some historical selection between these 2 manifestations of evil, then choosing the lesser of them would be justifiable. The struggle against the Mongols, the Polish invasion of 1612, against Napoleon – all of these wars cost colossal sums of suffering and sacrifice, however no one doubts that these sacrifices were justified.

From the point of view of meta-history, the irreparable failure of the fulfillment of its meta-historical and historical purpose actually surfaces as the most terrible catastrophe. Any other meandering historical route, that would at its conclusion continue such a danger, must be circumvented at any cost. And when a similar danger presses on one of the dishes of the scales, no magnitude of the sum of personal suffering can rebalance it.

Of course, such a law is cruel. But it is not the demiurge, and not God the Creator, who is at fault. It is impossible to find another moral deliberation, by way of the biological and historical law that reigns presently in *Shadanakar*, except to recognize them as a duality. To understand the burden, the distortion of the initial original principles of the general ascent as created by Providence, we accept the reason as the interference of demonic powers. But the illumination of the law is the task of the grandiose periods. It will not be consummated in a blink of an eye or just by some gesture. We live within the law, are subject to it and are forced to deal with it as a fact. More than this, the law is no worse than what is possible. To be worse than what is possible – its further distortion and burden – is a dream against God. This is why in many situations it is proper to approach the law itself as to the lesser of evils.

I do not want to abandon this thesis without concrete historical examples. How should we approach, for example, the fact of the colonial expansion of the European nations during the 16th to the 19th centuries? From the point of view of absolute humanism, this was an unbreakable chain of the violence of the strong against the weak, and in part it was badness defeating goodness. The results of this violence enriched the higher classes of the western European society, and emaciated the others. Not only from the point of view of some types of theories, but plainly from the point of view of our immediate living conscience, this is monstrous.

So it is. Now, what is the meta-historical point of view?

As far as meta-history is concerned, it is meta-history because it is not possible to investigate even one distinct human life, or the existence of an entire nation or humanity, separately from its religious pre-existence and post-mortem state. The trail of cosmic installation of any entity or their groups is blazed though the layers of other types of matter, a series of worlds, ascending the staircase of various forms of existence and, having surpassed the forms in which we presently reside, to strive, perhaps, to immeasurable reaches of time, into a new order of the transcending and illuminating worlds. This segment that we live through in comparison to the whole can be compared to a 10 second wait at a railway crossing at some nighttime steppe where a gigantic continental passenger is crossing. And as long as we do not accustom ourselves to contemplating historical and cosmic panoramas in all of their majesty, as long as we do not adapt to such proportions, large scales, and consistent patterns, our conclusions will differ little from the conclusion of some insect or animal having the ability to approach the materialization of life only from the angle of vision of its personal interests or the interests of a crumb-size group.

Our unobstructed conscious is agitated by the sight of suffering, and is therein right to be so. But it does not have the ability to ascribe to either the possibilities of yet a more bitter suffering that somehow circumvents the subject sufferings, or any of the unseen futures and indescribable complexities of spiritual verdicts as monads or as their unification. This is its limitation. No matter how correct or how limited all the humanitarian norms are, they are all born from the impulse of this conscience.

The meta-historical ethic is built upon absolute trust and surrender. In other situations the meta-historian can disclose the reasons – and which may seem to be insane – such historical sacrifices were brought and how they are to be redeemed. Yet in other situations this exceeds the capacity available for its cognizance. A 3rd group will explain that the subject sacrifices, and even the historical circumstances that summoned them, are a demonstration of the powers against God summoned crossways and sideways with the intents of Providential principles and so are not justified in any case. But in all of these situations, the meta-historian is faithful to his sole dogma, "You are goodness, and Your goodness is providence. What is sinister and cruel does not evolve from You."

And so it is proper to respond to the proposed question candidly, to the extent that such an exposition will not collide with individual moral concepts. Yes, the worldwide tasks of the 2 western supra-nations appears as the creation of such a level of civilization upon which the unification of the earthly sphere becomes a possible reality, and the materialization in the majority of countries of certain amounts of morally-correct norms, although not very high ones, but providing the possibility for them to sprout and engender ideas, but not those that proceed from the western demiurges and not guided by them. The ideas of the transformation of the state into a fraternity is parallel with the process of their unification, first, into a worldwide federation and, finally, into a monolithic humanity, where diverse nationalities and cultural associations will not be therein mechanically unified through the operation of state violence, but woven together through its spirituality and high ethic. This process will be headed by all the emerging cohorts educated in the new generations of humanity's ideals, persons of the noble form. However this stage is yet to be found beyond the present limits of the obligations of western cultures, such as those we have discussed.

What is primary is that sooner or later the Russian supra-nation has the obligation to stand at the forefront of the creation of an inter-religion and inter-culture. It is possible that in the future the leading roles in this process will transfer to other nations, but the task of installing the foundation obviously lies, and particularly, on its – the Russian nation's – shoulders. It is indispensable for such a nation to have, and more than any other, not only knowledge, but an intrinsic understanding of foreign psychologies, the ability to compositely transform and love other mental scopes, cultural atmospheres, conventional ideals, other races and national expressions of attitude. What is there that will more strongly promote this, if not a mutual interpenetration that is fraternal and, of course, not just through one layer, but particularly, several wide layers, with the historical realities of other cultures? This should have occurred in our history, but to our great sorrow and that of the entire world no cultural pilgrimage to the east and south was ever accomplished.

Until we are liberated from our national-cultural arrogance, until we stop feeling as though Russia was indeed the best country in the world, nothing will be gained even due to our immense land mass, except a despotic threat for humanity.

And further, that we, first, are resolving the question of the 2nd *yuitzraor* of Russia, of its attitude to the world's land mass, and as to what it did right and as to what not right. And second, and this is already well known to all, we learn particularly from the mistakes and omissions of the past. Recognizing, finally, what we particularly have missed, how we have disfigured and restricted our historical road by doing this, and how we have made the materialization of the mission of the supra-nation difficult, then in another epoch we can strive to catch up to what we have missed and while in new conditions.

With this in mind, I understand, of course, that no attempts of any type should be made to return Russian America to us,[91] or to invade and occupy Iran. At present Russia and the entire world is approaching a completely different stage, and it is clear to all that under contemporary conditions similar intentions would only be a humorous and harmful anachronism, remembering the story of the man who danced at his funeral because he missed the opportunity to do so at his wedding. I conclude something entirely different. This education of particularly such an attitude toward other cultures, other psychologies, social structure, political ideologies, such an attitude that is friendly and sensitive, filled with empathy, interest, toleration and love; such an attitude which essence appears as the aspiration for a spiritual wealth to enrich ourselves and to spiritually enrich all – this needs to be applied to us, our nation and in its widest limits.

---

[91] Referring to Alaska

Now the 2nd *yuitzraor*, over time almost strangling itself due to its fantasies of its physical, that is, military might, was not only not able to raise the needed level of the worldwide tasks of itself as a supra-nation, not only did it not saturate this idea of external might with some type of content, but it did not even display itself on the level of these epochal tasks that were placed before the earlier imperial empire. It remained deeply provincial. Since every nationalism – if we can understand this word as meaning the preference of your own nation over others and the progression of its interests at the expense of the remaining nations – is nothing else but provincialism raised in principle and professed as a world ideology.

So did the 2nd *yuitzraor* prove its instability in regard to the external expanse, and it is so lacking in dealing with its own task in regard to its inner expanse.

CHAPTER 2

THE SECOND *YUITZRAOR* AND THE INNER EXPANSE

If we were to correctly understand the comments about the inter-religion, inter-culture, the transformation of the state into a fraternity, which I have already brought to your attention in the preceding chapters, then we cannot but make a bitter conclusion: the scene of the [Russian] supra-nation, summoned from non-existence for the sake of similar ideas and after a thousand years still having 80% of its population in the state of slavery – such a scene summons alarm and profound sorrow.

What is sorrow about this issue is not so much the fact of feudalism: the most popular attitude was that this was an evil hardly considered unacceptable, and dependant on a series of objective reasons known to all, which do not need to be repeated here. Sorrowful and irreparable was the late date in its emancipation.[92]

---

[92] The feudal system was abolished by law in tear of 1862 and all serfs were emancipated.

The gaping abyss between the obligation of the supra-nation and the ethical quality of the national structure, which it has permitted within itself for so many centuries, terrifies us. The fissure between the reality of the ethical level of the supra-nation and that level that is required for the materialization of its missions scares us. Likewise the postponement of the emancipation had a series of very close and direct consequences that resulted in what followed: the post-revolutionary epoch with which we need to deal.

So which of these results are the most important from the point of view of meta-history?

The first result is economic and cultural. This is the troglodytic level of material prosperity and the demands of livelihood satisfied by this level. I am not mentioning this as though it is a complete, irrelative evil, since it is not exalting a person, but demeaning him. We need to understand that without this factor the formation of the 3rd *yuitzraor* – this monster of the 20th century – would not have acquired the possibility to unfold its method, conceivable in the society already accustomed to every possible deprivation, squalor and destitution.

The 2nd result is moral-psychological. These are the persistent habits of servile ideology long deeply ingrained into the psychology of the national masses: the absence of the complex of civic feelings and ideas, humiliating subjection, disrespect for the individual and, finally, the inclination to convert to despotism, if the game of change raises the serf above the level to which he is accustomed.

The germination and pompous bloom of the 3rd *yuitzraor* would be likewise impossible without difficulty, and over a long while, depleting its psychologically characteristics.

The 3rd result is the religious in its wide sense. From a servile psychology, from the squalor of needs and aspirations, from a narrow periphery, from destitution, there evolved a paralyzed religiously-creative impulse. No one should sit in front of a smoldering log with a stomach swollen due to malnourishment, with a destitute mind from not ever reading a book, with a brood of starving and naked children as religious rites are performed. The nation, as represented by its best citizens, displaying its spiritual talents, depth and span of religious possibilities, for many centuries did not produce any religious movement among its large populace, although much that is theological, except for the Old Believer dissention.[93]

A review of Russian sectarian groups leaves an indelibly heavy impression, and especially upon the person who even has a superficial familiarity with the history of religious thought in antiquity, such as Byzantium, India and Germany. Russian sectarianism is either a resurrection of ancient mystic elements mixed with undecipherable and mixed strains of Christianity and transformed into a weak blend of religious self-realizations; or else they are rationalist sects of the western European evolution, freed from mystic inclinations and extreme asceticism. In either direction, they have little to contribute relative to our Orthodox Christianity.

There were 3 results of centuries-long slavery[94] of the population and the ecclesiastical politics of the empire. There is hardly any need to prove that it would have been impossible for the huge 3rd *yuitzraor* to emerge in its murderous and ruthless form, as it did materialize in history, without these results.[95] The later overflow of primitive materialism did not occur in the entire expanse of the innumerable working class and the partial-intellectual level. The unthinkable religious ignorance of the new soviet generations did materialize.

---

[93] Or, Staro-Veri.
[94] Meaning the feudal system of Imperial Russia
[95] this is communism in Soviet Russia under Joseph Stalin.

Book X

Toward a Meta-History of Russian Culture

Chapter 1

The Gift of Annunciation

In 18th century [Russia] there occurred a clear and obvious dearth of spiritual rivers that nourished the roots of Orthodox rectitude. Now we have a meager number of influential religious activists. Less and less figures of immaculate and high ranking shepherds of souls in the presence of society are appearing. In the 19th century there were just a few of such individuals: the venerated Seraphim of Sarov, Theofan the Recluse, Ambrosi and Makari Optinski, who had the likeness of those saints that enriched our land in previous centuries. Finally, during the pre-revolutionary epoch, there was a completely empty desert on the horizon of the church.

If this is not enough, this fracture of the scales of personality seems to be only one of the manifestations of a general destitution of [Russian] Orthodoxy. Year after year the Church even more falls behind the needs and questions of the quickly changing epochs, as a result this tardiness even enters the effectiveness of certain principles: the ecclesiastical hierarchy looks at itself as the treasury of irrefutable and absolute truths, independent of change of eras and humanity's psychology. But just as this view is not confirmed either by the immaculacy of the life of these shepherds, or by the intensiveness of the religious efforts, or by the wisdom of their responses to the socialist, political and philosophic questions birthed by the new epochs, then the authority and significance of the Church is speedily collapsing.

The recent religious efforts from the side of the Church were summoned by the storms of the Revolution. An entire series of unremembered heroes and martyrs surfaced. With the end of their life-long paths, the creative spirit even further leaves the Orthodox Church and, becoming a plaything in the hands of diplomatic politicians, the guidance of the Eastern Christian religious community turns into a panderer and an instrument of the state's anti-religious propaganda.

But to the extent that the church squandered the significance of religious leadership of the community, a new institution arose, upon which this obligation now fell and which, in the person of its high ranking representatives, sharply assimilated this obligation.

The announcer is the one who, being inspired by a *daimon*, provides people the means of feeling a higher truth and light, one that flows from other worlds, through images of art in the wide sense of this word. Prophecy and annunciation have a close definition, but are not identical. The announcer acts only through art; the prophet can materialize his mission using also other means: through verbal preaching, through religious philosophy, even through the example of his own life. From another side, the definition of annunciation is close to the definition of artistic ingenuity, but it is likewise not identical with it. Ingenuity is a higher level of artistic talent. And the majority of geniuses were during their era – announcers, to a greater or lesser extent, but however, this is far from all of it. Other than this, many announcers possessed not an artistic ingenuity, but only talent.

The century that passed from the Fatherland War[96] to the Great Revolution was in the full sense of the word an age of artistic genius. Every one of them, and especially the geniuses of literature, were masters of the thinking of entire generations, society looked upon each of them as upon preceptors of conduct and purpose of life. The colossal growth of the educational and scholastic role of literature was likewise expressed in the activities of the majority of talents. The influence of several of the talented became more intensive and wider than that of the geniuses. Beginning with the 1860s, this diversified fact was clearly defined, although it was completely unrecognized by society: the influence of ingenuity and the influence of talent became, in a certain very profound sense, contradictory one to another. The artistic genius of this era – Tutchev, Lev Tolstoy, Dostoyevski, Chekov, Musorski, Tchaikovsky, Surikov, and later Vrubel and Blok – did not institute any kind of societal and political programs capable of satisfying the questions of the epoch's populace, but they penetrated the intellect, the heart, the volition of the smart people, not in a horizontal direction of societal transformations, but with vertical depth and height of spirituality. They disclosed the expanse of the inner world and pointed the direction of the immoveable vertical axis toward them.

Those of talent, at least those who were the more influential of them, were assigned the comprehension of that generation's problems and the needed societal and political effort. Such were Herzen, Nekrasov, Cherneshevski, Posarov, all who were of the 1860s, and those later, Gleb Yuspenski, Korolenko, Mikhailovski, Gorki, and then the talented trail blazers: Leskov and Aleksandr Konstantinovich Tolstoi, who were essentially isolated. Such were rowing against the current, so to speak, not encountering among their contemporaries their due attention or proper evaluation.

---

[96] War against Napoleon and the French Invasion, 1812-1814.

CHAPTER 2

MISSION AND DESTINY

All that the demiurge *Yarosvet* creates, all that appears on the
historical scene on which it has some influence, has either a
direct or indirect relationship to its supreme task, the
materialization of which must justify the thousand-year route of
the blood-filled and horror of the institution of the [Russian]
supra-nation through its torturous methods. Regarding this
task, I have already spoken to the extent it is practical and
expressible in the language of our understanding, but I will
repeat it once more. Meta-historically this task-goal consists in
the birth of the *Zventa-Sventana* through the demiurge and the
ideal conciliar Soul of the Russian supra-nation. Historically it
consists in the materialization of ROSE OF THE WORLD, that is,
the religious-moral institution that – presenting itself as being
irreproachable and pure, aesthetically wealthy and having a
wide cultural omniscience – would acquire a supreme authority
in the eyes of the world's nations; through a worldwide
referendum would accept ethical control over the activities of all
governments – the members of the worldwide federation; and
gradually institute a diverse system of cultural means for the
noble education of generations of people. In this manner it would
create an environment, not just for an amelioration, but for a
complete transformation of the very essence of the state into an
all-inclusive fraternal humanity.

Orthodoxy, as a teaching and a practice, advanced from its
basic form while yet in Byzantium, on long-passed stages of
general cultural cognizance. It is natural that it could not at a
later date be freed from certain archaic primitivisms, from its
obvious myopia and oppression of cultural cognizance and social
thinking. This type of cognizance and thought was supposed to
yield to the primary role of a new type of cognizance and
thought, to one that was announced by artistic geniuses and

especially by the profound talents of Russia, who would turn it into a new historical factor of high level importance.

So without particularly what preconditions would this task of the *Zventa-Sventana* be irresolvable, which I for brevity and only for the sake of brevity have denoted as a transformation of the governments into a Fraternity? We will number just a few of these prerequisites, those that are the more important, obvious and simple.

First, this transformation is impossible until the obstacles between global religions are removed or, at least, reduced; until such a religious angle of view is acquired, by which Christian dogma and the dogmas of other religious of the right hand will no longer exclude one another, but mutually complement one another instead. Then ROSE OF THE WORLD will be able to unify all Christian denominations based on new rules, while other religions will draw tightly to each other based on the principle of a free eclecticism.

Second, the transformation of the essence of the state is impossible within any local boundaries. If such a process is accomplished in one country, while the balance will just continue their previous mode of polity, then they will utilize force and violence to occupy and swallow this transformed fraternity into their own state. Subsequently the task is irresolvable as long as countries are disconnected and as until such time that a global government is instituted. This is impossible to implement until a new attitude toward the state, to the general structure, appears and is inculcated in the cognizance of Russia and the entirety of humanity, applying equally to borders, wars and dictators. Such conditions also need to be created, by which the possibility of an aspiring development, the requirement of a unification of the entirety of humanity, a repulsion toward force, and revulsion in the face of tyranny, is made available.

Is this not strange, that in the development of such feelings in a person, to a known extent, it is actually the *yuitzraor* that are responsible. A revulsion of tyranny can be just an indication that someone has been personally tyrannized or someone close to him has. More than anything a repulsion of violence develops as a result of a person himself becoming a sacrifice of violence. The need for the unity of all humanity is for those for whom fragmentation has made life intolerable. In this manner the activity of the *yuitzraors* themselves and anti-humanity summoned dialectically that class of people that appeared as the prerequisite for the paralysis and defeat of the *yuitzraors*. However, for the implementation of the character of this state to attain such a trait for it to become one of the psychological reasons for the general unification and the end of global disassociation, the world would be compelled to traverse a stage of redevelopment of governments into a type of tyranny and affliction, into a system of suffering, into an unprecedented mass oppression, and war becoming a tragic annihilation of entire countries and nations. But even during this the danger would remain that the apparatus of tyranny would materialize stronger than the sum of active protests that would arise as a result. So the powers of demiurge, or more properly stated, all the demiurges of humanity, must indispensably direct their strengths into people having this complex of sensations and ideas, who are actively directed particularly toward this struggle against tyranny, to defeat global disassociation and to unify all.

Third, the transformation of the essence of government is impossible any earlier than when a certain level of general material welfare will be attained, and when such a prosperity being the right of every person will become a inalienable axiom. For this to occur, from the one side, the persistent class-related, national and societal antagonisms and prejudices need to be entirely obsoleted; a feeling of social compassion needs to be motivated and inculcated; and successive generations must be taught the knowledge of rights that transcend any birthright, class or nation. From another side, the progress of science and technology must be categorically compelled, while Providential help must be provided for the development of compatible intellectual and volitional qualities in a person. Every decade's interference of *Gagtungr* in this process will widen the gap between the levels of humanity's technology and humanity's ethic.

Fourth, the transformation of the essence of government is impossible without the society being solidly informed of the flaws of the old form. Subsequently, a considerable amount of effort needs to be allotted to the means of disclosing its flaws.

Fifth, the transformation of the government into a fraternity is impossible as long as the contradictions between the 2 immemorial cultural tendencies are finally removed: the tendency of denying the world through ascetic religiosity and the tendency of confirming the world through the corporeal or what is called pagan; as long as Nature is not perceived as something dual, both as a source of joy, happiness and light from the one side, and as an arena of warfare of the demonic powers from the other; as long as we do not see an object of high morality and creative obligation in the face of Nature; as long as we do not grasp activities of love; and until an attitude of spiritual and corporeal friendship is incorporated in the worlds of the bright *stikhials*.

And finally the triumph of Rose of the World is impossible as long as the new profound meaning is hidden, and this is the aspiration of religious humanity toward the eternal principle of Womanhood. It will not materialize until the excessively fiery-consuming severity of the Male principle is ameliorated, and the respiration of *Zventa-Sventana* is allowed to flourish. Until this time the fullness of ethic, religion and community will not reign.

There have been of course a series of other prerequisites of a historical nature, not to mention the meta-historical, without which the basis task could not be resolved. But it seems to me that the few that I have numbered and mentioned above should be sufficient.

So the following are the closest, concrete goals of the efforts of the demiurge: the reduction of the barrier between the diverse historical types of religiosity that were installed; the increase of ideas and feelings in the soul of people, those directed to a struggle against tyranny in order to defeat global disassociation and in order to unify them all; the increase of the depth of feelings of social compassion, the thirst of socialist justice and the comprehension of general socialist rights; the disclosure of those potentials of intellect and contemplation in a person that will provide him the ability to aspire to the progress of science and technology; to expose the aggressive and vampiric essence of governments; to remove the antagonism between the religiously-ascetic and the pagan tendencies from the cognizance of crowds of people; to develop a composite attitude toward Nature; to activate in historical operation the materialization of the eternal principle of Womanhood, whose expression in Russia – *Navna* – has been powerless and tormented and held captive for many centuries.

The enumeration of these objectives of demiurgic cooperatives are sufficient in order to explain how unequipped the Russian Orthodox Church is in order to attain this goal. But it was the complicity by the demiurge and *Navna* of the great artistic geniuses and the especially profound talents of Russia, those whom we call announcers, that particularly initiated the start of all these ideas. It seems that the psychological picture was assembled with the large number of purely human factors: cultural, societal, individual-biographical, and often by the affect of the potent emanation from the great spiritual receptacle of preceding ages: Orthodoxy. Likewise, inspiration was also often instilled from the demonic worlds, and especially from 2: *Druekkarg* and *Duegguer.*

So what are these ideas and what particularly are their forms?

The first cycle are the ideas tied with the task of exposing the demonic nature of the government and strengthening the complex by liberating the moral aspirations of individual souls and entire nations. Here pertains the idea of the unforgiveness of a crime committed by the highest of authorities, which is the cognizance of the insolvency of that authority which is based on the violation of ethical norms. Here pertains the idea of the irresolvability of the contradiction between individual and state, between the individual and the demonization of the world's laws, both on the intellectual-logical plane, and the humanitarian-conscience plane. Along with this the idea of the revolt between the lower, conceited or selfish freedom of the individual and societal harmony is connected. These ideas affecting the comprehensions of masses of people are often communicated through literature to the conclusive idea of the primacy of ethics over government principals, culminating in the establishment of a highly ethical controlling and directing principal over an amoral government.

The 2nd cycle of ideas is tied with the task of the change in attitude of Christian humanity toward Nature. This is interwoven with new adaptation or perception of the very process of life and its daily mundane form. All of this, just as with the preceding, has progressed crosswise from the ascetic period and blazed a trail toward understanding the distant approaching tasks of Rose of the World, the task of penetrating spirituality and the religious-poetic elements of all facets of life.

The 3rd cycle of ideas is tied with the task of unveiling a new profound meaning of the human religious aspiration toward the eternal Womanhood principle, and so, it seems to me, is stated not only by the respiration of *Navna*, but *Zventa-Sventana* itself. The idea of eternal Womanhood as a transcendental cosmic principle pertains to this cycle.

Before the descent of the *Zventa-Sventana* from the cosmic heights to *Shadanakar*, which was before the 19th century, the residence in *Shadanakar* particularly of the ideal Conciliar souls of the supra-nations was made possible by the penetration of the powers of Womanhood into the corporeal human *I*.

Up to this time I know of 3 great contemplators in our culture who evolved from both abysses – the abyss of the celestial world and the abyss of the demonic strata: Ivan the Terrible, Lermontov and Dostoyevski. The 4th I would suggest selecting Aleksandr Blok, but he is considerably lesser in comparison to the large scale of these 3 individuals.

There is nothing comparable, and not only just in Russian literature, in the gallery of humanity's figures as those created by Dostoyevski. Next to Leo Tolstoy, there is not one Russian writer that has achieved such a magnitude of worldwide credit.

Every person is aware that the philosophic, cultural, religious, moral, psychological, societal-historical ideas promoted by Dostoyevski are truly innumerable. The mission of Leo Tolstoy was tied to the promotion of the unity of a love of peace and love of life that is indispensable. This is why I limited myself to mentioning these 2, because from a meta-historical point of view, their significance is completely special.

CHAPTER 3

MISSION AND DESTINY

(CONTINUATION)

Speaking of prerequisites, without which the birth of ROSE OF THE WORLD is unthinkable historically and psychologically, I noticed that one of the most important of them is the removal of the immemorial contradiction of 2 principles: the ascetic-religious and what is called the pagan. The ascetic principle, as self-inflicting, was justified by meta-historical dialectic during early stages of many meta-cultures. In the Christian meta-cultures, as already stated more than once above, it was tied with the interrupted, uncompleted mission of Christ. And we need to particularly stick to this stage in order to continue to think seriously, as if the goal of this global institution is to apply salvation to several hundred thousand righteous. A similar thought is possible with a periphery of the first centuries of Christianity. Historical Christianity was formulated depending on facts supplied particularly from this periphery. Also other religions that were formulated 1-1/2 or 2 or 2-1/2 thousand years ago were not much wider. The sole attempt to make a success in changing some to the dilapidated dogma was the Reformation. But the Renaissance and Reformation present themselves as extremely complex meta-historical knots.

The trans-physical monster presented as the Inquisition began its activity considerably earlier than when it actually appeared on the historical arena and caused a fracture of the bright powers due to its actions. One of them strove to the purging of Christianity, but there was also no unity among them: 2 directions were defined within this camp. The first was to clear what was extremely cloudy in the Reformation; the second was internal, and although a weak aspiration of Catholicism to purge its church of the vile sins of the preceding stage. The other portion of the bright powers counted it indispensable to temporarily distance itself entirely from the historically arranged forms of Christianity, hoping that Europe, while on the route of secular and civic development of humanism, will gradually arrive at a new comprehension of Christ's ideals. In this manner, the Renaissance and Reformation surfaced under a sign of 2 opposing powers: the above noted powers of bright principles deprived of unity and a common direction, and the demonic powers. So now, how was external religious compulsion to weaken, with streams from various dark worlds – *Mudgabr*, *Yunukamn*, *Duegguer* – gushing into the unprepared soul? The influence of the *karossa* increased. *Yurparp* also had much affect. Apparently, they inspired a widening of the crevasse between science and ethic in order to bring science to a complete isolation from morality, religion and spirituality in general. Specialized entities strove in this direction, playing the role as if being dark *daimons*. They interfered and directed their activity even toward people of a completely bright will. Even Copernicus, Galileo and Descartes were not free from their influence. So did a *daimon* stand directly behind Leonardo [da Vinci] his entire life, although toward the end of his life the complicity was suppressed by the influence of Light.

The leaders of Protestantism did not unfold an enrichment of the world through religious ideas, visions and inclinations on this path, but they vomited upon it due to its destitution on account of the elements of mysteries and magic, and likewise on account of the role of the religious-ethical element weakening. Meanwhile during the heat of the struggle with Rome, reliance of any type upon religious leadership was rejected by the state from the side of the religious-ethical institutions, although to them it was just a fantasy of the distant future. This damage caused by Protestantism could not be redeemed by just a partial justification of secular authority.

Luther distorted his obligation and arbitrarily assumed this mission. He could have become pope, since he could have acquired authority over those purging the church through its reformation. In place of this he did what he did: he was responsible for fragmenting the western church[97] and broke it in half through his religious desolation.[98] It is not surprising that he ended up having to experience a descent after his death, but it was only recently that he was raised to the *sinklit* of Germany.

The application of the meta-historical dialectic to this process consists in the following: it is necessary to understand the duality of the Russian movement in culture. We have the brightness of the *stikhials*, which is the justification of some of its facets, and then the dark demonic on other facets. It is a progressive movement on the one stage, and a regressive movement on the other. I understand regressive, of course, as those manifestations that express a struggle against Providential principle in humanity and in the cosmos.

Love of the world is not only justified, but immutable. Without it, nothing is possible, except love of yourself that aspires to individual rescue. So there is love and there is love.

Love of the world, that is, the sphere of nature and the sphere of culture, as with sources that are useful only to us and to be enjoyed only by us, and so such sources that must be turned fully toward our service and servitude – this is what we can do without.

Love of the world as something beautiful, or something that is even ruined, dirty, suffering and which must become beautiful, clean and prosperous over the ages and eons of our efforts on its behalf – this is the love without which we cannot live. This does not mean, of course, that the powers of Nature cannot be utilized

---

[97] Referring to Catholicism
[98] Referring to the separation between the Lutheran church and the Calvinist.

by a person, this only means that after its use, something must be returned, the use of a person's strengths for the benefit of nature.

Love of life needs to be the sum of happiness. Love of life is like the global stream created by God, hierarchies and people, a blessing unto all, from the constellations and suns to the electrons and protons in everything, except for the demonic, and all is waiting for our participation in them on behalf of love. Without this attitude, humanity will revert to absolute tyranny and to religious self-effacement.

Anyway, this does not mean that sensual joy on its own merit is something prohibitive for people. On the contrary, this only means that such joy is justified, as long as it does not increase the amount of suffering of other entities, and balances our life, and prepares us to receive from life not just joy, but also sorrow and work and responsibility.

Book XI

The Meta-History of the Previous Century

Chapter 2

The Struggle against Spirituality

There exists a constant supposition that as if the material destitution of the society is a reflection, and directly, of its religious destitution. And on the contrary: material wealth likewise summons – or is certain to summon –religious wealth.

Objective historical observations do not confirm this thesis. Up to the latest phases of capitalism, one or another of the privileged classes or groups utilize their own wealth, but it did not contributed to society as a whole. And it was not the middle classes of these societies that were characterized as important, but the material levels of these wealthy groups. To attach the understanding of material abundance to society as a whole can only occur at the final stages of historical development. We can speak of abundance and wealth – at least at certain defined periods – of such societies, as contemporary Sweden, as Netherlands of the previous century, as Switzerland. We can also speak of the wealth of the United States, although with some essential corrections, because the difference of the materialistic level of the various groups of the population in this country is very great and their entire society has been far from prosperous even in the best of their times. I will not bring to mind what pertains to the countries of the Socialist camps because these specifics deal with a much later historical period.

I would be very interested if someone was able to convincingly show me that the above mentioned societies that have attained a high level of general material welfare, as for example: Sweden, Netherlands, Switzerland, displayed likewise at the same time a genuine spiritual wealth. True that they contributed and do contribute some things for the benefit of global science and technology, but science, as with technology, pertains basically to categories that are not spiritually, but intellectually, valued.

From its very beginning it is proper to learn to make the distinction between these 2 categories of display. The mood that is much presently promulgated does not distinguish the spiritual from the intellectual. The humanitarian sciences, art, sociology, ethic, religion, the sciences of physics and biology, and mathematics, even some aspects of technology, are all dumped into the same pile. The compositions of Kalidasa and Darwin, Hegel and Edison, Ramakrishna and [Alexandr] Alekhin, Stalin and Gandhi, Dante and Pavlov, are viewed as displays of one and the same sphere – spiritual culture. This aberration could be called barbarian, if some of them were not civilized people of a highly intellectual character. But meanwhile it is clear as day that here before us are 2 complete different categories of displays: spiritual and intellectual. Almost the entire sphere of science and even more technology belongs to the 2nd [intellectual] category. Included are likewise philosophic, ethical and moral scopes to the extent that they are liberated from other-worldly associations. Entering into the same category are all social movements, political agendas, economic and socialist activities, even their art and fictional literature.

The spiritual category consists of humanity's displays that are located tied particularly with the understanding of the multi-stratified existence and with the perception of the diverse strings that tie the physical plane of life with the planes that are spiritual or of a different type of matter. The spheres of religion, spiritualist philosophy, meta-history, ethics and personal integrity, and the greater profound compositions of literature, music and spatial arts, in their fullness belong to this category.

If we can understand and grasp this distinction of the 2 categories of display – spiritual and intellectual – then it becomes clear that spiritual wealth is by no means going to be in direct proportion to material wealth. It is foolish to expect that spiritual effectiveness is dependant only on 2 extreme levels of material sufficiency: destitution and luxury. The first compels the individual to exert all efforts just for the struggle for existence, while the 2nd leads to the race for the increase of wealth to the point of either saturation or desolation, a tug of war of psychological fat.

It is not Sweden, not Netherlands, not United States, but poor Thailand, the half-civilized – it seems from the point of view of the Europeans – Ceylon, Burma and Cambodia, the half-barbaric Tibet and Nepal, the half-destitute India, that present themselves as examples of societies whose life is penetrated with artistry, daily participation of the masses in the creation of highly esthetically valuable productions, intensive ideological searches and that psychological warmth that a person will only find in the countries where the moral climate has reigned for centuries, one created by immense pools of spirituality, and all much more than the societies of the west.

However we have become accustomed to concentrate our attention on the economic deprivation of these countries: on Indian destitution, on Tibetan lack of education, on the primitive life of Ceylon, on the perennial class system of India, while in Tibet it is theocratic feudalism, an imperfect family arrangement. And we consciously close our eyes to the other side of the life of these countries: that side whose strengths are created and supported by the cities half-filled with temples of bewildering beauty and enlightenment, whose towering heights beautify the landscape and testify to the ingenuity of their marvelous architects. As a result, sacred rivers flow through these countries between banks crowned with innumerable memorials of humanity's aspirations to spirit, light and beauty.

The exchange of spiritual understanding with intellectual understanding, while at the same time isolating particularly the term – spiritual, is so prevalent in Russia and even in the west, that its meaning and goal has become completely obvious in a new form. Its meaning and goal is the aspiration to bring humanity's psyche from the sphere of the higher treasured items into the sphere of what is valued as utilitarian. This aspiration and its effective materialization comprises one of the principle sides of the stage of cultural-historical process that we are encountering. Of course, this is tied also with the emasculation of the distant socialist ideal, of which I already spoke, and with the efforts to implement this gradually and clandestinely, society little by little is emasculating itself and degenerating and not noticing the appearing vacuum, and not noticing how the most valuable of its treasures are being replaced by others of lesser value.

Material sufficiency on its own is an unconditional treasure. This is the sole level of a person that indicates the worth of his external existence. It presents on its own his material dignity because this is the very armor of external prosperity that provides the possibility to calmly mature and for his soul to be productive. But to proclaim that material sufficiency and external subjection of the strengths of nature for the sake of some or other material abundance of humanity is the basis of value and the supreme measure of accomplishment, the goal of organized struggle of the masses in all the world, the ideal of social development, in whose name entire generations are subsequently brought as a sacrifice, including all that pertains to the spiritual category of treasures – this is either a tragic mistake or a halfway-decipherable deceit.

However there is particularly this false concept that often is declared with a loud voice, that often is not explained fully to the end, but always is residing in the complex of revolutionary ideas of our century, defining the character of ideals that crown this complex and the methods that it adapts to use. This much-encompassing socialist-political and philosophic doctrine that was produced in the middle of the previous century in the West and gradually gained the hegemony in the sphere of progressive revolutionary thought, we will plainly here identify for simplicity sake as – the Doctrine.[99]

It is not difficult to ascertain that this Doctrine is tightly woven genetically with the preceding clamor of western philosophy and scientific thought, and even with Christianity, but one that is revised however with the active help of those strengths that worry about the teaching that *might is right* that must become the guiding force in humanity. This has definitely followed the staircase of the socialist ideology becoming the replacement of the social, cultural, psychological and technical state, and now there just remains one short jump to an absolute autocratic tyranny. If we were to permit such a premise, then the beam of the projector – through which we are accustomed to glaze at the displays of culture and history – will suddenly and sharply shift its direction and they will be immersed in the shadow of the movie, which up to that time seemed to us to be so distinct and precise and, to make things worse, phenomena will ascend from the darkness, that which we earlier did not suspect, or else to which we did not bother to turn our attention.

The Doctrine is stiff as iron and is not willing to yield even one footstep, literally with foam on its mouth insisting on the concept of dialectical materialism. It is fiery consuming to the point of rage; inciting hate toward everything that can even be suspected as religious, mystic or idealistic; fully excluding all spiritual treasures, equating them with obsolete antiquity, while affirming just material and intellectual categories of values; placing at the head of the corner ideas of the material prosperity of the majority; blessing any means of implementing this goal; announcing the dictatorship of the proletariat; and subsequently replacing the proletariat with one sole political party; and then later replacing the party with one figure of autocratic despotic leadership; the proclamation of an extreme absolute necessity of the subjection of all remaining classes of society. Then subsequent is the physical annihilation of interfering classes;

---

[99] Marxism as implemented in the communist Soviet Union

strict control of the state, which is through the dictatorial political party; censorship over all ideological and cultural productions of society; a colossal role determining technology, automation, industry, equipment of all processes of manufacturing, and its social implications; and even the psyche of the population. All of this and acquiring much more under this new point of view, a new and sufficiently malicious intent.

It was the propaganda machine of the Doctrine that blazed its trail by using slogans of freedom. Then at the beginning of the era of its reign, it banished the national gathering of representatives, and selected only those to participate who would provide it a majority. The result was the gradual prohibition of the activities of all the other political parties and political organizations, and the abolition of free press, except their own.

* * *

In the meta-cultures of antiquity, including Byzantium, society still did not make a final selection between this first [religious-spiritual] route of development and the other, the 2nd one, which in brevity we can label as scientific-technological. True, in the panorama of ancient Roman Empire, in the plane of ancient social cognizance, there can be seen traces of what almost no longer remains from the concept of the first type of development. They became the legacy of esoteric and partial-esoteric societies, mystical cults, and some circles of sacerdotalism. But the socialist-economic conditions of ancient Rome, Byzantium, and even the western Middle Ages could not promote a speedy movement forward of society along the 2nd route. Their limitation can be considered ending about the 15th century, with the epoch of the creation of gunpowder and printing, with the discovery of America and India, and the colossal economic and psychological accomplishments that all of this summoned.

From the beginning of the 17th century the tendency toward development of the 2nd route, and the forceful quench of the potential of the first route, became ultimately clear.

The 2nd route of development is characterized by several specialty items. First, the connection between science, that is, the cognizance of the surrounding world, and some type of spirituality, is sharply and completely severed. Spirituality is finally thrust into the sphere of theology, religion, mystical philosophy and art, that is, into that sphere where science does not bother to take the least interest. Second, the method of cognizance is constricted by rigorous empiricism and purely intellectual generalizations of an empirically acquired knowledge. Third, scientific activity in its fullness is emancipated from every possible type of connection with practical ethics. Of course, karmic consequences of a foolishly directed scientific or technological activity, for example, the spoils of war will consume and torment every person involved, and will continue after his death since during his life the person is often alienated from the consequences of his actions or is distant from consciously acknowledging them. Fourth, the intents of science in principle become obvious for every person who is stubborn or inquisitive. This final severance between the spiritual and the intellectual categories becomes an infallible reality.

From a meta-historical point of view, how can we evaluate this choice of a route that was selected by western humanity, and later in other meta-cultures with the maturity of their mental directions? If Christ's mission was not disrupted, humanity would have received a potent impulse toward a forward movement particularly along the spiritual route. Then at that time those methods would have been opened and incorporated to allow the national multitudes to proceed on this route, and including those who already are on this route in India and the Buddhist countries.

The person who interrupted Christ's life at its very beginning just continued his own profound purpose, a satanic intellectual activity that continued into the distant future. And of course he added considerable strength to it in order to silence all shoots of spirituality, and instead promoted in its place the turbulent growth of scientific and technological concepts. There is no need for an explanation as to why particularly he needed to do the first. He needed the second additional route because it would have been unthinkable to unify all of humanity into one monolith without the highest available technologies, and without this unification it would be impossible to install a worldwide tyranny, a sole despotic tyranny, one that was labeled absolute.

The unification of humanity is the goal, truly, the indispensable station on the route to its terminal goal, and not only for demonic principles. The unification of humanity is the station for the attainment of the terminal goal likewise for Providential principles. Because as long as unification is not reached, humanity will be tormented by wars and revolutions, and wars that will be more and more destructive. The days will arrive when their destructiveness will turn into a threat for all organic life on the surface of Earth. Outside of a general unification, both political and societal, there are no other means of avoiding this threat. And to the extent humanity has chosen to take the route of scientific-technological development, to the extent it has likewise made it impossible to change in a short while its corresponding path in the spiritual direction, to the same extent Providential strengths are forced to move humanity along a scientific-technological route. The powers of Light are worried only about directing the scientific mind, to the extent that it depends on them, along such a route that will pose as little as possible a threat of destruction.

Although the intellectually minded Einstein, Plank, and Curie, accomplished endeavors in their fields, all of it was utilized by other minds for the development of nuclear bombs, all to be used by the eternal enemy of humanity.

If we were to disregard the vast amount and increase of the destructive forces of war, the development of technology still provided a paramount and contradictory significance for humanity.

Of all the other manifestations of spiritual and intellectual categories, even from pure science, technology differs in one area in a significant degree, moved by the sense of a thirst for knowledge: it cannot be anything else other than utilitarian.

People's psyche, those who continually daily work in technology, regarding technology, with technology, are accustomed to approach everything in the world from a critical pragmatic point of usefulness. If a person cannot on his own discover this danger, if he will not install an invisible wall as a barricade in front of that sphere of his life and activity where technology reigns, and apart from the remaining spheres of his life and soul, then he transforms into a religious cripple, spiritually impotent, spiritually blind. There is no better means to extinguish within yourself the spark of anything that might be spiritual; there is no more reliable a route to diluting the psyche regarding understanding art, love toward nature, attraction toward religion, worry for global harmony, desire for love. In our eon, the development of technology is inescapable and unavoidable and justified because without it, it is impossible to unite humanity, to install a general material equity relative to a person's merit. But woe and disaster upon the person who permits technology to rule over their soul.

That circumstance that the Doctrine applied first of all to the proletariat, and particularly that the proletariat was initially summoned by the Doctrine as the future class-hegemony, is validly legitimate based on iron-clad historical logic. Now it was also possible to lead minds into a delusion, playing on people's feelings of justice and pity, and wailing that the proletariat is so far only creating materially-valued commodities just because it has no rights, or is oppressed, suppressed, destitute, uncultured, naked. Naive enthusiasts believed that once being free from exploitation and assuming authority, this class would create such highly-valued commodities, that masterpieces of the past would fade behind their shadow. So what happened?

The feudal aristocracy exploited the population, but the volume of cultural treasures created by this class was not subject to either cataloging or to inspection. The priests and prelates exploited the ignorance of the mass, as this has become so well-known to us today as well as even to infants, but they created not only religious concepts and cults, but also created eternal memorials of architecture, paintings, poetry, music, philosophy.

They created highly theological concepts. The bourgeoisie is guilty of all its mortal sins, but the cultural creativity of this class comprises at least the majority of all that is considered a cultural legacy. The peasantry remained at the bottom of the social scale, but nonetheless it still composed songs and tales, ornaments and legends, artistic creations and folklore.

And the working class? I live in a country where the working class remains the hegemony for already a 5th decade. So what has it created other than treasures of a material category that were possible from a technological or manufacturing standpoint? They will perhaps say, "But how did all the working intelligentsia, that is, those who evolved from the working class, become engineers, economists, jurists, scholars, authors?" Sorry, but this is not the working class. These are those who outgrew it, who had nothing more to do in this class and who forever separated from this class and its character of activity and circle of interests and material conditions of life.

The monk, decorating the church with frescoes, remained a monk. The artisan, who wrote novels and poetry and painted while in his garden or his city flat, was still an artisan. But the worker who ascends to being part of the intelligentsia, stops being a worker on his own. A spiritual – in the exact meaning of the word – production of the working class does not generally exist. Any production from the intellectual class is worthless.

It is valid and logical that in particular this human formation of the Doctrine is raised and set on a pedestal. In particular, cadres of the autocratic political party are created from it. In particular, it is raised over humanity as though it is the most valuable of all of humanity's strata, as an example that all the others must follow to the extent of their strengths.

The impact of industrialization – one of the most important measures that the state undertook in the 20s and 30s of this century – was not underestimated, because this measure increased the defensive potential of the country, and simultaneously raising the country's material level, although at a snail's pace. The impact of industrialization also applied to implementing the compulsive rupture of the psychology of peasant and intellectual, having forced Russia to think mechanically.

The strategic course that the state took at the beginning of the revolution in its attitude toward religion was of course profoundly logical. But the tactic was forced to vary dependent on the situation and on the vigilance of those who guided the course at that specific period of time. The Doctrine was hardly able to grasp authority when the great person-weapon of the Third *Zhrugr* already declared that religion is the opiate of the people.[100] Due to the weakening of the Russian Orthodox Church, which for a long while was dominating over the minds of the vast majority of the national population of Russia, and especially over the peasantry, they took the initial opportunity to attempt to undermine the monolith of Orthodoxy, by giving the impression of permitting every sectarian group freedoms. But they soon discovered that it was impossible to undermine the [Orthodox] Church by implementing such ameliorations, and what now occurred was on the contrary: the spirit of religious aspiration began overflow in every direction. Suddenly the sects now became subject to persecution, just as was the [Orthodox] Church. Their fate was then shared by other religious, philosophic and mystic organizations and associations, even those that existed among the intelligentsia: anthroposophy and theosophist lodges, the occult circles, and religious-philosophic societies and religious orders of any shade.

The activities of anti-religion organizations, and the first of them was the society called *Atheist*,[101] converted all their edifices into clubs, lecture halls, exhibition halls, grandstands, stadiums, print shops, movie theaters and stages, and even into city and villages squares. On ecclesiastical holidays, the churches would be surrounded by crowds of young people, adorned in clown outfits and other sacrilegious decorations, in parades to ridicule the ecclesiastical processions occurring at the

---

[100] Vladimir Lenin
[101] Bez-bozhnik

same time. Members of the Young Communist League dressed as priests with inflated stomachs, high mitres sloping over, holding wine bottles. These clowns would parade the streets parallel with the ecclesiastical procession. But this gave them little success due to their lack of foresight and plain rudeness and inconsideration.

It soon became obvious that these techniques were powerless to lure any significant number of people away from religion, the lovers of spiritual opium. And the result was the opposite of what they expected: the churches now were so full, more than ever occurred since before the revolution. And when in 1925, Patriarch Tikhon died, who had been under house arrest for several years, his funeral turned into an attendance of millions, and far greater amount than what occurred the year before with the mummification of their first leader that was arranged by the Soviet government.[102]

After the failure of this tactic, a new approach was to ruin the church from the inside with the patriarch's successor, who issued a widely distributed declaration: from that time forward the joys of the atheist government would be our joys, and its sorrows would be our sorrows.[103] Increasing the authority of his ordination, the supreme prelate of the Russian Orthodox Church included in the text of the great *eksteni* a petition regarding the governing authorities, that they would reside in all benevolence and purity. It is very believable that the subject motives that guided the supreme prelate to make this compromise was that it was better to take this route to preserve the church from complete physical destruction, and at least secure the means for the church to be able to provide the parishioners the performance of its basic rites: the sacraments of baptism, confession and holy communion.

But one way or another, this was a means of initiating that political course from the side of the church that would soon transform it into a clueless slave of the anti-religious

---

[102] The death of Vladimir Lenin, January 21, 1924.
[103] In 1927, Patriarch Sergius issued a directive where he professed loyalty to the Soviet government.

government. It was only natural that such a change in direction summoned a sharp division among both clergy and laity. The majority of priests either rejected the validity of the successor, or else declined from including the reference to Soviet authority in the liturgy. The result was massive persecution. Over the thousand years of its existence the Russian Church hardly enumerated among its saints a dozen or so martyrs. Now this deficiency was completed by an abundance. Thousands of priests and faithful laity perished in prisons and labor camps. Churches were subject to closure and demolition and in their place secular or business establishments were erected. This destructive storm turned churches and monasteries into piles of rubble, those that were once advertised with global popularity as unique monuments of art and architecture. Bells that for centuries swung over cities and fields of Russia summoning its adherents now rang for the last time and were thrown from crumbling bell towers and carted to be melted for secular utilitarian purposes. By the middle of the decade of the 1930s, out of 600 functioning churches in Moscow, hardly 40 remained. While in Kiev, for example, one sole cathedral remained open for services. All the other denominations and religious groups suffered the same fate as the Orthodox Church.

But no matter how solid their positions, the employment of the Doctrine in the struggle for human souls, within each of these souls there continued to flow an almost invisible constant eye, often not even noticed by the intellect of these very people, watching over the opposing struggle. Continually, in their daily life, in their family, friends, love, in secret movements of the human heart, in turbulent sorrow, in doubts, in strings of love poured into the soul from great creations of earlier ages, the resistance of an undefeatable spirit is proclaimed. Such were the stages that culminated in the struggle against the clergy in the decade of the 1930s, when a gigantic terrifying human institution was drawn over the map of 1/6th of the surface area of the world, and with unbelievable speed, one that that already was foreseen and foretold by the great prophets of Russia.

CHAPTER 3

THE DARK SHEPHERD[104]

During the initial days of March 1953 there occurred a decisive duel between *Yarosvet* and *Zhrugr*. The channel of invocation uniting the entity of the *yuitzraor* with its human weapon was severed at the blink of an eye. If it was possible to have done this earlier, so then much earlier would the life of the human weapon been severed. When this did occur, there were no human strengths available that were sufficient to restrain the burden lying upon this psyche and on this physical organism. This occurred about 2 o'clock in the night. After half-an-hour his cognizance vanished, but the agony persisted, as we know, for several days. The *Yurparp* grasped the ruptured end of the channel of invocation and attempted to pour into the perishing person some strength and consciousness. This did not succeed, and in part because several men, standing alongside his death bed, made sure that he would not return to life.

The motives that guided these people were diverse. Some feared that if he were to remain as head of the state, he would release a war, a war that they pictured as a great calamity for every one and a fatal danger for their Doctrine. But among those that were close to him stood one who for many years guided the rudder of the mechanism of state security.[105] He knew that the leader already marked him as the next serial sacrifice, next in line to be silently purged, knowing that the nation was complaining about him. It would have been proper to place before his eyes the full responsibility for the masses of millions of innocent persons he destroyed. The end of Stalin would provide for him another chance to replace him, take his position. The course of his activity during the life of the leader delineated 3

---

[104] This selection deals with the death of Joseph Stalin on March 5, 1953.
[105] This was Lavrenti Beria who was head of the NKVD, National Committee for Internal Affairs, which he later merged with the MGB, Ministry of Government Security or Safety.

motives: to confuse Stalin, inflating and innovating physical dangers, as though they were threatening him on every side; to retain the country in the reins of fear and mutism and so be able to quench his personal thirst for blood. Such a person was the agent of a dark mission, including the increase of national sufferings, but his comprehension was planar, flat and non-mystical, like a tabletop, while the size of his individuality and talent was worthless. He was the Maluita Skuratov of the 20th century.[106]

Finally the great minute arrived: Stalin released his spirit.

Gashsharva quaked at this strike against him. *Druekkarg* echoed with wails of terror and anger. *Zhrugr* howled from rage and pain. Hordes of demons exited from their lower depths to the higher strata of the infra-cosmos, striving to slow the fall of the dead one into the depths of the magma below.

A sorrowful demonization was transmitted to *Enrof.* The funeral of the leader, or better said, the transfer of his body to a mausoleum, was transformed into an idiotic erection of a monument. The manipulation of his name and actions was so great that hundreds of thousands of people regarded his death as a tragedy. Even in prison cells some wept over the fact of his demise. The crowds, who were never considered sufficiently worthy to see the leader while he was alive, now hungered to see his face at least in his coffin. Moscow displayed itself as a picture of an insane asylum, one as large as the capital city itself. Crowds flowed into the center of the city attempting to get close to the Palace of Unions, where the corpse of the tyrant was set for public viewing, and where anyone could join the mourning procession. The adjoining streets turned into Khodynka Field. People died in the process, crushed against the walls of houses and street lights, or were trampled underfoot, or falling from the roofs of many-storied houses, hoping to somehow bypass the medley of crowds below. It seems, that as though he, having nourished himself all his life with the odor of suffering and

---

[106] Skuratov was the henchman of Tsar Ivan IV the Terrible.

blood, even now in his coffin, was still drawing people into his infra-cosmic sorrow of sacrifice.

CHAPTER 4

TOWARD A META-HISTORY OF OUR DAYS

We have arrived at the meta-history of the contemporary. But our present is distinct from the past in this manner, that we never arrange in our knowledge that sum of facts regarding the present in the manner we absorb what pertains to the darkest of epochs of the past. This even more pertains to the countries having the type of regime that suppresses freedom of speech and does not publish almost any statistics of data, keeping almost everything confidential, beginning with expenses of military armaments ending with the number incarcerated for crimes, or suicides, or sacrifices for somebody's personal advancement. No less a silent cover of secrecy are the government pools where some people vanish and others appear in their place. Citizens become spectators of some type of strange pantomime: some secretive figures that are credited and magnified in every manner of promotion and propaganda (these figures exalted to some unattainable height, as if in the stratosphere of society, and seen by everyone on the earth's sphere, whose volition materializes with just some wave of the hand or nod of the head or some motion), all of a sudden disappear to some unknown somewhere, and they take their family circumstances, habits, tastes and character to the grave with them, now preserved in total silence. Such are replaced by some subsequent individual — now it is his turn — whom humanity will gaze upon and be tormented by some indefinable anxiety and wondering what the purpose of this enigmatic ballet is.

It would have been better for me to write this book not when at the brink of war, not just when only threatening news is daily beaten on the drums of people's brains, one after the other! It is good to be assured at least in this, that tomorrow will not turn into an annihilation, and so that city in which we live[107] and the hundreds of other cities in all the countries! It is good to be assured that this book, which interweaves all of life, will be at some time read by some type of attentive eyes and that some type of soul would be enriched by the spiritual experience that is here expounded. Be assured, finally, that this book will enter into the foundation of the arriving humanity as one of its bricks.[108]

If the world should permit the avoidance of a massive war, ROSE OF THE WORLD will appear, inevitably and indispensably, first in one democratic country, then in others, and will overshadow gradually all the lands of the world. If war should unravel the base principals of darkness, opposing the powers of all the supreme hierarchies of light, then ROSE OF THE WORLD will resurrect from its ashes. Perhaps at that time it may not extend the shade of its flowering branches over all countries and not transform the earth's landscape into a meadow of a golden age, but it will unite thousands of people of an honorable and noble spirit into a union, to all the ends of the world, and will become still another obstacle placed on the road to impede the entity who already arose from the abyss and is nursing the great demon in *Gashsharva*, the one who will materialize the infinite tyranny over all the world, posing as a prince of peace.

July 5, 1958

---

[107] That is, Moscow.

[108] *Rose of the World* was first published underground in the Soviet Union in 1989; and not publicly released until 1991, about 30 years after its completion.

Book XII

Possibilities

Chapter 1

The Noble Education of a Person

The birth of *Zventa-Sventana* in one of the *zatomis* is fully pre-ordained. Consequently, so is the birth of ROSE OF THE WORLD in humanity also pre-ordained. But it is beyond our efforts to foresee in detail as to when in particular, how in particular, and with what stage of fullness, that this historical event will occur in history. The great dilemma that is much closer to us in time, that hangs over us as a Sword of Damocles, appears to be the choice between a 3rd World War and the coexistence of worldwide peace. If war will be unleashed, humanity will be discarded so far into the rear, while demonic hoards will be so increased as a result of the abundance of *gavvakh*, that in time it will even be possible for a 4th World War and total physical suicide of humanity to occur, or at least an unending series of more local wars and upheavals, or at least finally the unification of the world under the aegis of either the American *yuitzraor* or some other. Even if ROSE OF THE WORLD should sprout among humanity during an interval, but it will likely be nothing but an undercurrent, as a hardly tolerable organization (and later it will be completely intolerable), like a weak lamp in a catacomb crypt.

I think it will likely not be implemented through a worldwide referendum for its ethical control over the universal sovereignty, because they will prefer to enter a route toward universal tyranny. The interval between our days and the arrival of antichrist will decrease many times and its physical, and primarily its spiritual sacrifices will increase just as many times.

Even if a choice for the side of peace will be presently made available (even though the chance for this selection occurring will be pathetically small) ROSE OF THE WORLD will acquire the possibility to sprout in all of its fullness, but this is just a possibility. It's very appearance will be totally surrounded by another atmosphere: it will appear under the conditions of a democratic association of many countries, gradually expanding everywhere and drawing the best representatives of humanity into its ranks. Then the following dilemma will occur: this will be the rise of the unavoidable choice for people between the unification of the earth under the ethical guidance of ROSE OF THE WORLD, or the unification upon some other basis, perhaps the cosmopolitan concept of America, in any case, upon the basis of something less spiritual, something religionless and damaging to morality. If the former will be selected, ROSE OF THE WORLD will ascend to authority and a route will be opened before it to the materialization of all its tasks. In the opposite situation, ROSE OF THE WORLD will descend to a position that is barely tolerable, having almost no influence to organize, the same situation it will have after the 3rd World War, with this one, however, difference, that in the period between the first and the 2nd dilemma, it will succeed in attaining a wide diversification, it will create a large number of cadres, motivate considerable excellent activists, impose its influence on the course of the general cultural development, and spread its seeds over the entire earth.

Turning attention to the diverse possibilities of the future, I concentrate only on a few of them in order not to get lost in infinite verbosity. I will speak of what the operation of ROSE OF THE WORLD seems to me in that situation if a benevolent resolution of the chain of the nearest dilemmas will provide it the possibility to present before humanity the question of its implementation as the universal authority. In order to narrow the problem, and even then it is immense, and not to distract off to the side, from this minute I will not any more mention the negative possibilities, that is, those that may in the future pose unsurpassable obstacles for ROSE OF THE WORLD on its route toward materializing its tasks on a universal scale. We will instead speak of the bright future! The heart is already tortured sufficiently by horrors of the past and present. We need to illuminate the circle around our soul with contemplations of the most beautiful of all the possibilities of what is to arrive!

Its basic task is to decrease the sacrifices of the dark camp. This task is the creation of such a religious climate, such an enlightenment in humanity, that the life of not just hundreds and thousands as at present – but millions will be prolonged. This task is to repel the dangers from millions, and even perhaps the billions, of human souls from their enslavement to the coming antichrist, that is, from the ruinous damage to their present persons and from the long road of redemptive tortures that they will enter upon death.

If we were to place this goal in front of us, a certain program of activity will inevitably evolve from it. This program consists of a series of tasks that need to be resolved in series or in parallel. So I will recollect the basis tasks of ROSE OF THE WORLD once more: the noble education of a person; the implementation of general material sufficiency; the assistance of development in humanity of higher capabilities and enlightening creative principles; the consolidation of efforts from all teachings directed toward education; the transformation of our planet into a garden, and the worldwide federation of states into a fraternity.

If there is only one means for all these tasks, then ROSE OF THE WORLD needs to be able to approach their resolution a lot sooner than its entrance to universal authority: this is the noble education of an individual. Because in order to install the foundation of this new and even more inspired pedagogy, there will be no more need for worldwide control over all the schools on our planet. The new pedagogy can be developed on its own in certain and separate educational institutions found in the arrangements of ROSE OF THE WORLD. It is able to implement freedoms that are normal for every democratic country by using such educational institutions, even if they are on the level of some religious-charitable organization. The experience accumulated in the course of such a preparatory period can subsequently be transferred to a general educational and training system.

The ability of education will insert a creative principle into every effort and will remain one of the cornerstones of pedagogy. If the necessity of creative labor will not arise as an indivisible quality of the individual, then under the conditions of general sufficiency and progressive decrease of the working day the person will be threatened with lethargy, uselessness and paralysis of the spirit.

The person of the succeeding century will be benefited with material sufficiency and later with abundance. An aggressive attitude of the person toward nature will also evolve, but this will be counterbalanced with the idea of a harmonization of the mutual tie between nature and humanity. After a precise investigation of the character of nature, its providential principles, humanity will intervene into the life of nature in this manner, with implementing an intense commitment. Humanity will be concerned not only about deriving new and better energy resources from it, but also to promote the increase of the population of the animal kingdom, to promote the growth of plant life and to beautify the landscape and scenery with the use of plants, and to utilize nature to the maximum extent possible as a means of peace and friendship between cultures and regions.

The real and defined passions of these epochs will be:

First: growth of spirit of love;

Second: creativity, a precise divine constructive motivation in many forms;

Third: utilization the benefits of nature;

Fourth: the removal of the obstacles between the physical world and other worlds;

Fifth: life's happiness, ebullient in the *Enrof* and in many other worlds;

Sixth: higher forms of divine cognizance and experience.

The drive to this particular and specific future will distinguish the person of a noble character from the person of all preceding cultural stages.

So how can we characterize the mental form of such a person? Uninterruptible growth of a thirst of knowledge; a habit of independent contemplation and intellectual autonomy; a liberated and happy feeling in submission to the display of the Great and Profound Entity.

What characterizes his aesthetic views? The development of an inalienable need of artistic expression; highly developed cultural taste; knowledge and understanding of the art of the past and its monuments; some need of artistic creation, but these have a limited range; a liberated and happy feeling and exuberance when viewing something beautiful.

What characterizes his ethical views? An active effort on behalf of those who surround him; the ability to have a fervent compassion and empathy with others; the feeling of a common union with all of humanity; the feeling of unity with the cosmos; the liberated and happy feeling of reverence in the display of the Supreme Entity.

What characterizes his religious attitude? A passionate residency in our material stratum as one of the strata of *Shadanakar*; inner effort toward the disclosure of religious acceptance of various concepts; the daily sense of life as a mystery; the knowledge of religious forms of the past and present; the ability to identify with all religions, that is, to understand the experience and teaching of each of them as a reflection of any of the series of spiritual reality; an imperative need of personal participation in a religious life and in its advancement in humanity; the ability to possess a feeling of joy from involvement and participation in such a life.

So finally how can the external, physical figure of such a person be characterized?[109] It seems to me that his body's form would be on the slim side, with a flexible movement, taking light steps, firm and somewhat muscular, and the face would indicate transparency, highly intellectual, filled with friendliness, and as though bright from the inside. From childhood he should be involved in sports, dance, recreation. Understanding that he has a dual nature, he will not allow the intervention of any dark powers, but conduct himself as a sun-filled child. Clothing to match the seasons and always colorful. He will be the elder brother of birds and animals and converse with Angels, a transformer of the land, a builder of beautiful cities, a climber to the top of mountains, a hiker through forests and deserts, a master over the planet-garden. He will be everybody's son and friend. This is how the future person of a noble education, possessing such an inner vision, will conduct himself.

Apart from nature, the development of these qualities would be extremely difficult. As a result, it seems to me that the fundamental type of general obligatory middle school should be the college-boarding school, located either outside the city or at the edge of the city. These colleges would provide this service to young people living in a house in the city and must at least secure for them a vacation for the entire summer and away from the city. And there should be nothing frightening about classroom sessions having to continue 8 or 9 months of the year, but only 7 months, and the course of study at elementary and middle schools combined would not be 10 years in length, but even 12 or 13 years attendance. Young people would also not need to incur any military obligation after their graduation. Any type of weapons accumulation or competition between 2 political-economic systems will not exist to increase life's tempo, and if a person will complete his higher education even at the age of 30 years, this will indicate only that he is entering life not with

---

[109] Daniel Andreev seems to based this paragraph on himself as the example.

some narrow specialty, but as an experienced and educated person.

Of course, such schools will require special attention from its instructors for their preparation, subtle pedagogical tactics and a profound understanding of their task. The boarding house needs to be something halfway between a fraternity and a family. All that pertains to state aridity, regimentation, government coldness, and especially disciplinary drills, will not be allowed in the curriculum or at the boarding house. The individual personality that will be developed here must be capable of living in a society based on voluntary integrity, and not on compulsion. Of course, a system of prohibitions, discipline and encouragement to some extent will remain, and especially at the beginning, but this will only play a supplementary role and be implemented at a minimum. A goal is to develop qualities that will motivate an accomplishment of activities that might seem unnecessary. Neither fear nor ambition will be the source of motivation for the student not to lie, insult the weak, disdain instruction, conduct himself in a antisocial or anti-fraternal manner, or be cruel to animals. All such conduct will gradually become impossible for the student, because he will be nurtured to love friendship, virtue, integrity and compassion.

The schools will accustom the young people to work, to have a taste for creativity, a taste for inner and external culture. Only by doing this will a repulsion of idleness, a repulsion of ignorance, a repulsion of cruelty, conceit and irresponsibility, occur organically and naturally. I am not an instructor, and this is not the place and nor am I in a position to suggest further methodology of educational projects. Here I can just speak of the tasks of the pedagogic system of Rose of the World and its fundamental principles.

The lamentable consequences of such archaic disciples, such as, for example, the coercive memory of Orthodox creeds, must be considered in the student's religious-ethical and religious artistic education. It cannot be enclosed in some immoveable dogmatics, or crowded into one narrow discipline that might be irreconcilably contradictory to other things, but it must be a genuine education, penetrating and refreshing. Sports, swimming, strolls, planting gardens, planting flowers, tending domestic animals, recreation – all of this is linked to a happy, poetic, joyful effect that leads to the cult of higher consciousness.

Instruction occupied with arts, reading, singing, visit of museums and churches, conversations on the themes of culture, history and metahistory, with profound and festive ceremonies, will lead them into the cult of the *Sinklits*. The fully-occupied active day, having provided a wealth of experience for the mind and heart, would only be consummated with reading Sacred Books aloud in the presence of others, but no more than one chapter each evening, and that everyone gathered – boys and girls in order – would have an opportunity to read this aloud. If the teachers are unprepared to do, and as a series of necessary and obligatory duties, then only great misfortune will arise. The task is to open the inner verse and rhyme, beauty, and depth that is dormant within every child, and to raise their spiritual consciousness. If all of this is felt and understood, then a natural desire to do this will surface, and there will be no need of any compulsion.

Alongside the development of feelings of individual religious peace within a person's soul, the student also needs the availability to systematically acquire religious knowledge. It seems to me that the student can source such knowledge from special disciplines: general history of religion that expounds everything in an objective manner, as well as a person's spiritual evolution, as much as possible. This needs to be tightly knit with a course in political history that, in its own order, must be intensely expanded and made interesting by the inclusion of material dealing with the history of art, science, philosophy and culture. These disciplines will on their own, of course, become more valuable, to the extent that time and means will be provided: demonstrations of films, staging exhibits, televised affairs, working in groups, visit of sacred sites of various religions and the centers of national religious life.

In general the creative principle will considerably impress and encourage in every manner possible the growth of even the smallest shoots of creativity, in the areas of music, oratory, theater, architectural, scenery, portrait painting, philosophy, and religion. The creative attitude toward every subject will cultivate, as I already mentioned above, a repulsion toward violence and destruction and the suppression of making demands.

There is no need to further talk about the certain recreations, such as fishing, hunting, or creating entomological collections. We have no need of hunting. It would be best for our teaching to concentrate on addresses pertaining to development of goodness and love and at the same time tranquil contemplation, rather than have their underlings be entertained with the torture of animals. Truly the time will come to begin to categorically prohibit similar amusements, and then a repulsion to the torture of living animals will organically arise from a love toward them, a love that will progress as they care for tame animals. Gradually the feeling of closeness to the elements will begin to penetrate their daily life; it will carefully support the state of preparation for this vocation of care for animals.

Physical exercise in time will firm the body's organism, less clothing will be required as the body is exposed to the effects of the elements, as much as the climate will permit. Shoes will no longer be worn, except for the few hours if exposed to freezing weather when outdoors.

I also feel the need to touch on one group of customs that are tied with the above, but more private, ancillary, but in my view are practically important.

It is natural that the profile of the future college will change considerably with the contemporary middle schools: they will increase the depth and expand the humanitarian curriculum. An increase in courses in history and the introduction of courses in the history of religion in a wide aspect of understanding will demand a large number of additional hours, and these hours will be provided by an increase in the length of the school year. It is possible that in the upper classes we will need to adapt to a system of 3 disciplines: humanitarianism, natural science and technical. And independent from this, to prepare the student to enter a higher educational institution or prepare for practical work, he must be permitted a year's stipend for travel, whether in a group or as an individual, to some country that he finds interesting, or a series of countries, in order to widen his periphery, to familiarize himself with nature and culture, to develop ties. The network of special tourist centers, operated by highly qualified instructors, for young people in all countries and work in these centers will prevent the majority of students from squandering this golden time on trivia or non-essentials, and will help them escape incidental and fruitless amusements.

The question easily arises: how can such an expansion of humanitarian curriculum be justified? Because in the initial epoch of ROSE OF THE WORLD colossal numbers of cadres of other workers will be needed, workers of technical sciences and engineers in all areas of expertise. Will not the assurance of general material sufficiency first of all presuppose the utilization of energy resources of nature.

But alongside these cadres there is required a considerably large number of cadres of workers who will be dedicated to social reforms. Other than this, the natural-science and engineering-technology workers of the new vocations will be distinct from their predecessors, that instead of having a concentration in some narrow specialty they will appear as persons with a noble education. And 3rd, after the course of a few years, with the completion of material sufficiency, the need for engineering-technological intelligence will begin to decrease, while the need for humanitarian cadres will grow.

*   *   *

I have already spoken several times about the future transformation of the surface of our planet into a garden, to occur in soon time under the guidance of ROSE OF THE WORLD and the efforts of several generations. This should not agitate the adherents of the present virgin nature. Over the course of thousands and millions of years the surface of the ground has remained virgin. However, by the time the 21st century arrives, only about half the surface will actually be virgin. Presently this is a sorrowful condition but there is no other route of development or exploitation and seems there cannot be. Population growth, technical progress and the discovery of gigantic resources of energy have doomed the future undeveloped nature right under our eyes. The dilemma consists not in the choice between the wild nature and nature as a garden, but in the choice between nature as a garden and anti-nature.

I understand anti-nature as the transformation of large regions, the entire surface of the ground into a urbanized complex with the inclusion of modified remnants of nature just for pleasure, to use for leisure and physical contentment.

I understand nature as the transformation of large regions into a garden, and then the entire surface of the ground into a series of mountain parks, meadows and forest parks, and fields, constructed with the assistance of higher-level technical people, with conservation areas of virgin nature reserved for animals, city parks and village parks, with the purpose that not only humanity's life, but also the life of the animal kingdom, the plant kingdom and elements, would rise to the highest possible harmony, while the world landscape would ascend to a supreme artistic level.

In this effort, the strengths of many sciences and many skills will crisscross with religious-ethical effectiveness and with the elements. New dimensions, new needs, new technical and scenic innovations will transform the old-fashioned garden into something categorically new, and not just superficially, but qualitatively. They will be placed side by side with monumental architecture and sculpture. It will also subject to itself forestry, horticulture, agronomy, selection of plants, decorative painting, zoology, irrigation, vegetation of the deserts, and much more. This skill will unite the efforts of the most diverse of professions and qualifications, and it may possibly cause the most popular, massive, and beloved of all skills of all the known historical periods to even arise.

It is also understandable that the work of compatible scientific institutions – educational and scientific research – will be rearranged for the purpose of this application to these tasks. But all this will still not exhaust what is available in higher education institutions and the entire scientific-research complex. This will be supplemented with a series of effective religious-cultural educational institutions of a new type – from high school to university.

It seems to me that a humanitarian college dormitory for young adults from 12 to 20 years of age is the best possible first stage in this series. The initial task is selection of students for such a college that have an inclination toward skills or humanitarian sciences combined with moral integrity. The 2nd stage consists of a religious-philosophic university. Clergy will deal with the 5 cults of ROSE OF THE WORLD. The members of its faculty will consist of new social activists, religious and philanthropic instructors, organizers, philosophers, psychologists, publicists, literary editors and commentators, artistic directors, and many others.

We should not forget that ahead of us stands the goal and titanic effort of having to destroy this armor of pseudo-scientific ignorance and anti-religious prejudices which have shackled hundreds of millions of persons, our innumerable nation, during the first half of this century! It is sufficient to remember that during the course of 2 or 3 generations, immense countries were deprived entirely of even the most fundamental, elementary and necessary religious literature, just the Bible and Koran, not to mention the other serious works or the popular religious treasures of the past. Ahead of us stands the work of distributing millions of copies of the canonic texts of Christianity and other religions, fortified with scientific explanations that will answer every question of a contemporary reader. Likewise the publication of many series of editions of books on art and school textbooks, that will reproduce the monuments of worldwide religious culture; editions of scientific research that are capable of satisfying profound interest in the religious history of humanity; special and popular series to inform the society that has devolved into atheism or indifference toward all this; and with the great compositions on spirit, from the Vedanta to Schopenhauer, from Gnosticism to anthroposophy and existentialism. Such workers will prepare the curriculum of the religious-philosophic university. Finally, this series of educational and training institutions will be consummated with a worldwide religious-philosophic academy, with its ideological work coordinated and directed from within Rose of the World. I have the impression that similar academies of national scale will be formed in every country.

But there will be also other spheres of activity that will demand such a large quantity of workers in the humanitarian curriculum, and which are impossible to characterize with any other epithet except that they are grandiose. The transformation of the worldwide sovereignty into a fraternity is impossible with solely external means. We will discuss in the subsequent chapter some external means, some initial prerequisites for this transformation. This is an opportune time to point out the manner of education needed for the generations for a noble person, in order to permit him to progress to the process of this transformation.

Similar to that generation of Israelites who, after leaving with Moses from Egypt, had to yield their place to other generations after the tribes were to enter the promised land, so will it be for the generation of the middle 20th century, poisoned by the atmosphere of the epoch of worldwide wars, who are destined to descend from the arena in order for the long awaited system to reign, while illuminating the way for us through the enfilade of the 3 succeeding enlightened periods. This system is not to be installed from external forces. Only when the moral façade of the new generations become unable to further utilize freedoms for malicious and malevolent purposes and drive itself toward anarchy will this be organized and become naturally indispensable. No measures of any type of reeducation will be sufficient to transform the psyche in the root of 2 billion persons who have long been inculcated by this other, by blood and an atmosphere saturated with monstrous cruelties. Of course, the millions of them who presently live that have done better will respond with a higher need of that distant epoch. These would also be part of their education along with future entire generations in the way of ROSE OF THE WORLD to be people of a noble and refined character.

The transformation of the essence of the state – of what does this consist? Demilitarization of them all? A genuine democracy? Reduction of laws? Amelioration of punishment? It seems, but all of this is just a small part. The essence of the present state is soulless or impersonal automation. It is guided by the material interests of the majority or minority of humanity's masses, understood as a corporate entity. It does not consider the interests of the individual at all. It is likewise uninformed, unaware and inconsiderate of its religious inclinations or religious welfare, whether this be the individual or the nation.

The meaning of the first stage of ROSE OF THE WORLD government is confined in the attainment of general material sufficiency and in the creation of the prerequisites for the transformation of the Federation of state-members into a corporate monolith. Immense unions of legislators, instructors, psychologists, attorneys and clergy will review all legal codices, reforming the system of legal rights, procedural standards, amelioration of the scale of punishments and even the principle of punishment will begin to yield its place to the principle of rehabilitation of the criminal. Cadres of workers of a new type will be prepared for this period, who will be indispensable for the introduction of universal reforms that will be significant in the subsequent 2nd stage. This stage will be the transformation of the corporate monolith – now having become a subdued state – into a fraternity or sorority.

We need to suppose that the general judicial reforms will occur at an interval during the beginning of this 2nd stage.

Well of course, prisons as a form of punishment will depart forever into the history of the past. The words *concentration camp* now likewise will very much be compromised: it will just summon people's memory of the picture of every Potzma,[110] Buchenwald, and Norilsk.[111] Now they will try to reeducate them somewhere with the assistance of labor. It should not be a surprise if the results are initially meager. The majority of criminals are found on a very low social-cultural level. These are people who have gone astray from the path since adolescence and have become accustomed to a repulsion toward labor. What is primary is to raise their social-cultural level, then will they sense the attraction of labor and will fully voluntarily dedicate themselves to handicrafts or manufacturing, while others to mental labor. And I understand the idea of their ascension to this social-cultural level not as some type of training in a technical specialty, but particularly something more general, that is, a mental, ethical, aesthetic, social and religious culture. Some items are being done presently in this vein, it seems, some religious-philanthropic organizations abroad, and especially the Catholics and Methodists. We should take all measures to attract them to our work, learn their experience and incorporate some of their features. In any event, the desire is not to increase our mental baggage with anybody's incarceration, but the intent is the restoration of the criminal. The more successful he passes a course of general humanitarian education plus a special course of some type of socially useful profession, the sooner will the group of his re-educators acknowledge his preparation for release and liberation, and the sooner he will leave the walls of the prison.

The state is comprised of people. Some of the people who materialize state authority in every level of its government are for the most part callous, perfunctory, dry or cold officials, as we have at present, or bureaucratic. The Rose of the World system will prepare cadres of the worldwide government in a manner that these negative qualities presently possessed by government officials will be replaced by the opposite, so that

---

[110] Concentration camp in Kosiu, Komi, Russia. Daniel's wife Alla was confined at labor camps in this region.

[111] Center of the Norillag GULAG concentration camps in central Siberia.

every person who turns to a representative of state authority or enters some government office will not incur monotone bureaucrats with an unprofessional atrophied attitude, or with those fanatics who solely have the state's interests in mind, but to meet with brethren who have empathy.

It is these features that will cause the worldwide fraternity to be distinct from the present forms of government ministry, and a person of noble education to be distinct from the preceding bureaucrats. But in time many other characteristics will appear, and those that will inspire future generations.

CHAPTER 2

EXTERNAL MEASURES

Having spoken of the problem of a person's education in a noble fashion and of the problems that are tied with this in the transformation of the state into a fraternity and the planet into a garden, for the time I excluded from the field of vision another immense problem. This is the problem of those external social-political, economic and cultural measures that will promote the implementation of general material prosperity and harmony of humanity's society.

My thought is that the entire period between the appearance of ROSE OF THE WORLD and its entrance into ethical control over state authority needs to be viewed as preparatory. During this period its structure will be arranged and installed and its religious, political and cultural organizations will increase. Its teaching and its concrete historical program will be cultivated on every facet. The widest means of instruction will unfold – literary and verbal – in all the democratic countries and in all languages. And its cadres, those who at the beginning were limited to perhaps a few dozen or hundred persons, will advance to a multi-million worldwide fraternity.

During this interval, in every country where the existence of ROSE OF THE WORLD will be permitted by the constitution, its participation should also be permitted by the political organizations in the general national elections alongside other political parties. It is obvious on its own merit that not one word of falsity, slander, arbitrary promise, self-recognition, discredit of opposition, even plain unjustifiable claims, should exit the mouth of even one of its proponents or candidates during the pre-election debates or at any other time. They need to conduct themselves such that in the eyes of the nation ROSE OF THE WORLD will not contain even one blemish. It needs to sustain a political victory in complete concord with its own ethical objectives and orders.

Most likely, ROSE OF THE WORLD will gain control over state authority at different times over different countries. And it is possible that some of these countries will be able to unite in this federation considerably sooner than it would be possible for a general unification to become a reality. But the social and political obstacles that will prolong this preparatory period can be so diverse and so indefinable or irresolvable, and at the present we cannot even determine the route that ROSE OF THE WORLD needs to take to become a worldwide ramified organization, to arrive at having control over authority on a worldwide scale. We can only state that just as it can have this right with the adherence of normal democratic processes and at least implementing a majority of voices in all the countries, then we can suppose that the decisive act will have a form that is compatible with some type of referendum or plebiscite. It is easy to imagine that such a referendum will provide it a victory in a majority of countries, but not in all. Time however will work in its favor, while its ideals and methods will be so attractive for such innumerable masses of humanity, that after the passing of a few years, a 2nd referendum will attract the last of the opposing governments into the worldwide federation. When the first stage of its ethical control over worldwide state authority begins, national councils of ROSE OF THE WORLD will accept control over national governments.

If a general and complete demilitarization is not attained any earlier than this moment, then an order for an immediate, general and absolute demilitarization will be put into effect. We need to suppose that this is the manner ROSE OF THE WORLD will signify its entrance for ethical control. What would be created, for example, is a Ministry of Disarmament in the government of the Federation and in cooperative ministries in the governments of all the member-states. What also needs to be taken into account is the immense economic problem that is tied with the general demilitarization and with the conversion of military industries into peace-oriented products, and likewise to secure a new vocation with the release of several million persons who are involved in the military. It is apparent that this process of general demilitarization will occupy no less than 5 or 7 years.

The cost savings from general demilitarization was already long ago calculated. We do not know when or how this will occur and the actual amount of savings is just a conjecture. However, it is likely that the general savings will not be far from a trillion dollars. One way or the other, the savings will be immense. Particularly this sum will permit the possibility of introducing great reforms.

During the first period of the government of ROSE OF THE WORLD, national and local special political administrations, and the traditional social institutions of the various countries, will remain in place and only gradually change, and not from the outside, but from the inside, as long as the universal state does not lose its peculiar bureaucratic character. In general, the entrance of ROSE OF THE WORLD will not expect a fast review of the constitutions of the member-states, with the exception of that sole point, which should change or be supplemented in this sense, in order to stipulate the recognition of ROSE OF THE WORLD as the institution that will limit state sovereignty. In the distant future changes in many statutes are possible and perhaps even inevitable, but it seems to me that from the beginning they will be distinguished more due to their technical character than principle character. In any case the population of each country on its own will define the extent of its freedoms, whether to subject its political administration to a slow and categorical transformation or should it be preserved in its basic state. It is possible to find, for example, even such countries where the adherence to their traditional monarchial system will appear sufficient and solid. Is it so hard to imagine that the conservatism of this type will surface in England or Japan? Of course, in similar situations the monarchial principle must be preserved. When the contemporary understanding of government begins to die on its own, being transformed into the understanding of a business-oriented mechanism for the most part, the person wearing the crown will now remain as the honorary head or the living personification of the glorious past of their nation and its tradition.

The very same pertains also to the social-economic structure of out-lying countries. Subsequently, when the general socialization gradually draws all the nations into its process and the material level of the different countries balance, then also will their social-economic structure level. By this time the majority of vocations – manufacturing, agriculture and commerce – will already be transferred into the hands of general associations. As a result, each of them will become an autonomous collective, a corporation, utilizing all income from its companies, with the exception of the sum that is assigned to the government. The government will finance the creation of new unions, evolving from the needs of the material requirements of the society and secure them on the basis of long-term financing. The reorganization of private endeavors in such unions will be stimulated. Probably the acquisition of finances from the population will then take the form that is similar to the contemporary method of tax collection, but in a more sophisticated manner.

As far as political parties are concerned, they will function as in the past. There might be one sole obstacle for them: their aggressive-nationalist, aggressive-class, or aggressive-religious character. It is only the right of the institution of Rose of the World to qualify one or another party as aggressive. Nevertheless, the complete prohibition of such parties will not be imposed during the first, relatively austere stage, although they will be deprived of any right to verbal and printed propaganda of their views. Eventually, as maximum freedom materializes, they will likewise be freed from such prohibition and control. But it seems to me that this will not be permitted any earlier than the 2nd stage when the stratum of the general cultural development will itself serve as a guarantee against any reoccurrence of aggressive or separatist ideas.

General material welfare should be attained during the course of the first stage. Nothing similar or compliant with communist fantasies will exist in the activities of ROSE OF THE WORLD. Any citizen, independent of nationality, residency or ethnicity, will be provided assurance that all of his basic needs will be satisfied in full: food, clothes, home, a vocation that is compatible with his character and aspirations, recreation, leisure, medical care, elementary comforts for his family, higher education, participation in arts and science, and religious associations. These gigantic sums that to the present in capitalist societies go to unlimited expenditures to expand production, as well as repair, unemployment, crises, will be assigned for new enterprises. I have in view the construction of cultural innovations of a worldwide scope. Cadres of the world's working strengths will have the responsibility to – from the one side – to terminate unemployment, and – from the other side – initiate a gradual diminishing of the working day. Further growth of technology and manufacturing strengths will lead to the reduction of the working day to just a few hours. The departments dedicated to preservation of health and social security will expand the web of its medical clinics and hospitals to the most isolated corners of the world, encompassing all levels of society, including in this number – the peasantry, which to this time has not factually been able to utilize any of these rights.

Is it worth mentioning here about the more private accomplishments in this sphere, for example, about the worldwide scope of the sanitary-hygienic vocation which will permit the eradication of parasites and viruses? Or about the accomplishments of medicine that will bring to non-existence many of the illnesses that presently infect and pain humanity?

It is not my affair to predetermine the purely economic aspect of these reforms. I would even say that this is not a matter of my generation, the type of economic perspicuity that some of its representatives should possess in the future. The time will arrive and the authoritative institution will then construct and, with general approval, introduce a practical worldwide economic reconstruction.

There does exist a known logic of technological development, a logic of civilization. Whatever may be the convictions and ideals of some person, but if he is capable of a perspective thought process, that is, to meditate on the future, he has to be able to deal with the problem of the reclamation of the Sahara or the Arctic, or the worldwide construction of residences, or the direction of great future highways or arteries to connect every area of the globe.

So in order to escape economic crises should they occur during all of this restoration, colossal sums must be stored also for the creation of charitable, welfare, and non-profit institutions. They will be dedicated to the task of religious-cultural development, and the demand over the next 100 years will be inexhaustible.

Such construction of course will take many forms, which at present are hardly imaginable, and they will begin development by diverse but parallel routes. I would like to mention here one of them: the creation of great centers of new religious culture, because I have visualized almost the entirety of my conscious life the architectural ensembles that will accommodate and express these centers, having seen it with a clear precision and a persistence that I could not escape. I was hardly 15 years of age, when these images began to form first in front of me, and a year later I attempted to record them permanently with the help of a pencil. I was not an architect or an artist. But the images of these ensembles, their exterior and interior, are so majestic that I wanted to compare them with celestial mountain chains of white and pink marble, crowned with gold medallions and their slopes covered in flowering gardens and forests. All of this was so defined from one decade of my life to the next. Whether ROSE OF THE WORLD will materialize similar ensembles, or not materialize them, but this book, I think, will not suffer any if this mirage of distant and approaching epochs appears on its pages. Know that the components of the mirage definitely exist, although in a great distance, while the mirage itself will only draw them near to the traveler who is wandering the desert sands.

These great centers of religious culture together with the web of their numerous divisions will gradually induct greater and greater circles of humanity into a wide channel of the creation of a prosperous and sun-filled religion, into a channel of personal and social perfection, into a channel of consummate divine knowledge and a close attraction to other worlds as a result of love, nature, creativity and sacerdotalism.

Religious-cultural implementation will not be completed until humanity is guided by ROSE OF THE WORLD and until the spiritual thirst is alive in the human soul. In the end new and newer forms will be united to those forms that will be implemented initially. There is no reason to surmise or guess at the character of many of these structures – incredible due to their grandiosity – that will signify the 3rd stage of the government of ROSE OF THE WORLD, or even their assignments. I would like to at least mention some of the basic types of these structures that, as it seems to me, will be erected every place during the 1st and 2nd stages. It is beyond our faculties to grasp their diversity, even where they pertain to those eras that are in the near future, those still accessible to our foresight.

What I visualize is that centers and sources of a new religious culture will be installed in the greater cities of the world, and then in general in all cities. From my youth I am accustomed to apply to them the appellation of belief-city. This appellation is not entirely successful, but is conditional, but I do not know what its name will then be in reality. These are architectural ensembles. The axis of each of them will be the temple of the Sun of the World, surrounded by a crown of lesser sanctuaries. All of this will comprise a complete facility with a system of parks, ponds, streets, forests and squares, indivisibly composing portions of each belief-city, especially in the established cities. Health centers and medical clinics, theaters, museums, religious-philosophic academies and universities, galleries, libraries, temples of *Sinklit*, temples of higher mysticism, and stadiums. The belief-city will also include several groups of residential areas. Located within them will be complexes concentrating the religious and cultural life of the city and region, the center of national holiday celebrations, award ceremonies, religious rites, parades, sports events. All of them are freed of their earlier impersonal and secular character and now joined with an attitude of radiant endeavors. Such will be the centers of religious-educational, religious-artistic, religious-scientific work, the sources of solidarity, joy and self-confidence.

In order not to subject the center part of the city to complete demolition and reconstruction, the belief-city will be subdivided with large regions of the outskirts to be used as residential areas. Several wide and green spokes or rays will extend from the center of the belief-city. I will sketch a few names for them that are entirely conditional, and which I have thought of. The names of the green parks that connect the belief-city with the outlying city, and assigned for holiday celebrations, for leisure and strolls, for parades: Golden Route, Triumphant Gardens, and Park, with a special name of some artistic or historical significance.

This is an ensemble raised to the highest level of artistic quality and combining the rich numbers of planted trees with the strength of the sculptural-architectural surroundings: arches and monuments, bridges and fountains, and primary is the inclusion of monumental groups of yet-unknown categories. An ocean of flower gardens with lawns and ponds will be scattered between them. These parks will be created for the purpose of developing a sense of style and artistic taste through a high aesthetic pleasure, a historical and meta-historical awareness, a sensation of cultural universalism and community.

I imagine one of such parks to be the Triumphant Gardens, connecting belief-city with the historical complex of the city center. They will be dedicated to the historical memories of the subject nation. It will be very difficult for us and our posterity to imagine our capital deprived of the Kremlin. If you can imagine the future Moscow, for example, a wide green expanse with areas dedicated to trees, lawns and flower-beds, stretching from the future temple of the Sun of the World to the Kremlin. Cultural institutions, hotels and residences will line this route, buildings several stories high, with sidewalks for pedestrian traffic.

But to contemplate great cities of the future whose purpose is isolated in honoring only their own national culture means to construct the future based on the model of the past. In the cognizance of people of the 21st century, every decade will erase some memory of the boundary between culture and nationality. Moscow, for example. Such epochs cannot be imagined without memorials dedicated to Plato, Copernicus, Shakespeare, Raphael, Wagner and Gandhi, and monuments to Moscow specifically, such as [Patr Nikon] Minin and [Dmitri] Pozharski. It is possible that the memory of the geniuses of other cultures will be connected with the 3rd green park extension of belief-city.

The Golden Route will be a highway-park of entirely special significance. It will begin several kilometers from belief-city and have its terminal point at the temple of the *Sinklit* of the World. It will be distinguished by special architectural surroundings. Each of them will express one of the great meta-cultures of humanity with its *sinklit*. Parades consisting of immense crowds will be held along the Golden Route during the time of corresponding holidays. In front of architecture that will symbolize *Eyanna*, *Sukkhavati*, *Olymp*, *Meru*, *Monsalvat*, the heavenly Kremlin and the *Arimoiya* the priesthood and the people will here perform a profound sacred rite that will bind the hearts of those presently living with all of enlightened humanity.

This is how I imagine the accesses to the belief-city. The belief-city itself is arranged with 3 architectural complexes: temple, cultural and residential.

Relative to the growth of the religious-cultural construction, many cities will be converted into belief-cities, while more will be built within cities having a large population, until a satisfactory number are built in all the cities of world to attend to the entire world population. The individual components of belief-city, especially the temple of the Sun of the World, the temples of higher spirits and higher philosophy, can be erected independently from the balance of the ensemble.

So will the belief-cities be connected with many cities and enter into the interests of the population, into the daily activities of the national masses. Alongside them or even within them, temples of other religions can also be erected. The heart of the belief-city is the temple of the Sun of the World, *Sinklits* and *Stikhials*. Concluding this sketch of the impending universal transformation, I consider it absolute to at least quickly clarify their assignment, their construction, and indivisible from them, the diversity of religion as their respiration.

CHAPTER 3

RELIGION

Providential forces are always on guard. They are always ready to come to help each of us. They constantly labor over every one of us, over our soul and its destiny. Every soul is their course of struggle against demonic principals, and the entire life of the soul is an indivisible chain of choices that arise in front of the *I*, the choices that will either empower or paralyze the strength available for it from the side of the radiant principals.

The soul is similar to a traveler attempting to cross a shaky bridge. A hand of assistance is stretched to it from the one side, but in order to accept this assistance the traveler must stretch his own hand. Every good choice, every correct action and every bright movement of the soul, and every prayer, is such a hand that is stretched to encounter the powers of light. Here the kernel of the answer is contained: Why a prayer? And why divine ceremony?

The word – prayer, I utilize here in a very wide sense. This is an isolated conversation of the soul with God or with the powers of light that He created; this is a state of humiliation, reverence and spiritual ecstasy that grasps the heart during contemplation of the Beautiful, Supreme or Great; this is that catharsis through which revelatory compositions raise a person's soul; this is its participation in activities of the temple that cleanse and exalt it.

Prayer can be performed privately in a monk's cell, or together in a congregation, when its non-verbal song is poured as a triumphant stream of divine ceremony. Both these manners are equally indispensable. The isolated prayer is the type of tension on the soul that it – distant from the spiritual Concentration of the world, but tied with it as a single and unrepeatable musical string – forces this string to vibrate with a high note that has the ability to dissipate the shadow of night. Congregational prayer is the cohesive tension of thousands of such strings. This is a choir of song filling each distinct soul with a premonition of general harmony. A divine rite is not an arbitrary activity devised by people, but a mysterious activity, that is, one that displays the harmonic reality of the highest spheres and relegates its strengths into our heart. It is from here that the most profound justification of what we call religion evolves. And it is from here that the cohesive prayer-filled life evolves into the creative and mystic life of the soon-arriving temples of ROSE OF THE WORLD.

What is ceremony? This is sacerdotalism that is implemented on the foundation of the inner experience of a person, for the sake of his search for help from supersensitive powers of radiance, or to repel repulsing malicious influences from the side of supersensitive powers of darkness.

What is sacrament? This is a specific sacerdotalism during which performance the supra-cognizant roots of human volition accept divine grace, and then overwhelming strengths materialize for the movement toward harmony between the individual and the universe, spirit and flesh, the corporeal and the divine.

The effectiveness of the sacrament is not reduced due to the lack of participation of the devotee's cognizance or insufficiency of belief. The conclusion is the possibility to perform the sacrament on non-believers, critically ill, and children. But the participation of the intellect and individual belief eases and quickens the speed of the stream of grace from the supra-cognizant roots of the will to the sphere of daily comprehension.

The trans-rational and supra-personal nature of the sacraments determine their effectiveness under the conditions of a lack or even absence of belief and the mystical concentration. The result is the independence of the effectiveness of the sacrament from personal qualities and from the psychological state of the priest. But his concentration, belief and attention to the meaning of what he is performing, what is being attributed to the person for whom the sacrament is being performed, eases the recipient's acceptance of this stream of grace.

A sacrament can be performed by any person, but for greater effectiveness it is preferable that it be performed by people who have passed a relative probation, a religious and cultural training, culminating in an ordination, which is also on its own one of the sacraments. An austere probation of several years, through which a priest is required to complete, secures the knowledge he needs to approach the performance of this activity, the concentration of his volition and belief during the course of the sacrament and in this manner his greater effectiveness. Nonetheless, the performance of sacraments by layman should not be prohibited. In situations where the sacrament cannot be postponed and must be immediately performed or in the absence of a priest, such an action by a layman should be welcomed. However, if the petitioner has insincere motives the sacrament should not be performed.

Recognizing the mystical effectiveness of sacraments implemented by ancient Christians and performed by priests of Christian churches, we cannot but notice that as a result of shifts that occurred in worldwide religious comprehension over the past few centuries, our understanding has also changed and strives to introduce an essentially new meaning into certain sacraments, for example, into the Eucharist. What is primary is that the new religious awareness increases the psychological necessity of such sacraments, [questioning it] and to the point that the patriarchs of the great Christian churches and the founders and establishers of non-Christian religions cannot but worry over it. And not only the sacraments, but this demand expands to the entire sphere of sacerdotalism. It worries over congregational prayer that is directed toward certain institutions of the unseen world which the creators of the ancient religious rites could not comprehend. It thirsts for ceremony that would sanctify and bless all life: not only the movement of the human soul upwards in a vertical direction – which is psychological ascension, but also the movement of a person in the horizontal – which is using it for the expansion of the size of their soul. This worry, which has appeared long ago and has never fully been extinguished, reached its apogee in the epoch of worldwide wars. It has attained this level of power, that a wail ascending to the spiritual heaven cannot but summon a response.

Humanity has waited too long for a new voice to sound from ecclesiastical pulpits and ambos. All the existing denominations seem to only be capable of preserving the ancient contents and ancients rites. A voice echoes from an unexpected place, from the depths of daily mundane routine, from unknown quarters into the denseness of large cities, from prison cells, from identical midnight rooms, from silent forests. Its heralds are not the ordained priests of the Orient or Occident. And not any Orthodox patriarch, or Catholic bishop, or Protestant theologian, has acquired a comprehension of what they speak. But the day will come that what they proclaim will be the focal point that theologians and patriarchs and bishops of all religions will approach and, forgetting about ancient disagreements, they will say, "Yes."

Whether I will live to that age when these sacraments will be presented visibly and clearly, not in a artistic exaltation, but in temples raised on the belief-city squares and filled with singers and crowds of devotees, I do not know. I beseech God to prolong the term of my life at least to those days when, having succeeded to conclude all that remains that I must accomplish, I will be able to listen to and experience a divine rite based on Rose of the World, the last of my books. What can I do – here and now? At least provide some fleeting indications in an emaciated and impersonal language regarding the inner environment of these sanctuaries and the significance of some of them.

The center of belief-city, its heart and at the same time, its pinnacle, is the temple of the Sun of the World. Without many other paraphernalia it is possible to install belief-cities in medium-size cities, but not without a temple of the Sun of the World.

Almost from childhood years I have had a mental vision of this temple standing in front of me. I see it very generalized in order to provide it in sketches and in artist's outlines. But the sensation of an incomparable majesty envelopes me every time that it appears in front of me. It's front is made of something that is similar to white marble. It rises upon the crests of hills over a serpentine river, and several wide bridges are located to lead to it. A colonnade encircles the temple. A staircase is located on each of its 4 sides, starting from the ground and to the temple. The top of each staircase ends at a high white wall with 3 doors in the form of a half-circle. At the top of each door is a gold emblem: A winged heart inside a winged sun. Over the colonnades and over the central wall is a roof, consisting of a complex system of gold steps that serve as though pedestals for 5 white ascending towers, slightly narrowing upwards. The center tower was larger than the others, but all 5 were decorated with narrow vertical grooves and crowned with gold cupolas. It seemed that clouds would clasp the crosses on the top.

Essentially, each tower crowns a special area that is confined below it. Under the central tower are slanting roofs to shelter the inner vast space of the sanctuary located beneath it. The cupola on the central tower is at a head-spinning height, and light shines though slowly changing blue emblems of the fiery sun, inscribed upon a cross with 4 penetrating rays.

It seems to me that the nave of the central sanctuary is bordered by rows of supporting columns and turned toward a wide ambo, which is separated from the main altar by an arcade. Holy day services will be performed when the stained-glass window behind the altar is moved, opening a high access into the outside expanse. The north-east section of the horizon is visible now and the morning disc of the summer sun, rising fiery from behind the city rooftops to begin its journey over the heavenly arch of the longest day of the year.[112] Through the access formed behind the altar, the parishioners exit to an opened terrace overlooking the city, turned toward the north-east. Here, visible to all those gathered on the square and to those praying in the temple, the supreme preceptor performs a divine celebratory service to the sun in its 3 significances: as the materialization of the great life-creating Spirit; and the bosom of the Father, out of whom the corporeal substance of all the world and all that is material evolved; and as the image and likeness of the Supreme Entity.

Designed very technically, the temple is arranged in a manner to isolate it from any outside interferences or noises for the parishioners, and also to secure the outside area for large crowds during complex and celebration events. One area will be dedicated to an organ, and for an orchestra and choir.

It seems to me that the area on the right and left sides of the altar, where the primary liturgy will be performed and which is pointed at the First Iconostas, will be dedicated to the Ever-Virgin Mother and God the Son. They are connected with the central hall via 2 high arches. Thick curtains enclose the slots within these arches on regular days. To the side of the main entrance, another 2 arches, similar in design, can be seen as parishioners enter and these lead to the areas dedicated to the *Sinklit* of Russia and *Sinklit* of the World.

---

[112] That is, at the summer solstice, and when the sun in Russia rises from the north-east.

In the belief-cities of the medium-size cities there will not be any absolute necessity of having individual temples dedicated to one of the hypostasis of the Triune Deity or individual temples of the *Sinklits*. The need for this portion of the religion can be satisfied by liturgy in respective areas of the temple of the Sun of the World. But in the larger cities it is indispensable to erect special temples with these dedicated areas particularly for this assignment.

The religion of the Sole Supreme, the religion of the Sun of the World, will never exhaust what Rose of the World will provide to the events of history, the events of culture, the events of a person's individual life. The sacrament at birth; the rites accompanying the various growths of children and their maturity; the sacrament at marriage and the sacrament of dissolution; the sacrament or rite of sworn fraternity, blessing the union of 2 souls in a supreme friendship; the blessing of creative artistic, educational, medical, social; the creation of love; creation of family – all of such rites will enter the liturgy of Rose of the World, directing some of the situations to apply to the Christian trans-myth, while others apply to the *Sinklit* of [their specific] meta-culture and the *Sinklit* of humanity, to the Great *Stikhials* and to the Mother-Earth, and finally, to the One upon whom we rely and we approach.

There exists a vastly immense sphere of human life to which one sacrament of the Christian religion up to this time is directly connected: this sphere is the attitude between male and female and the sacrament of marriage connected to them. In my chapter on Womanhood, I already indicated that the great ascetic era that was so rigidly and sternly impressed on historical Christianity, concluding with marriage and childbirth needing to be sanctified by a sacrament, but the superior state continued to be acknowledged as monastic celibacy. To more correctly state this, marriage and childbirth are arbitrarily tolerated. However when God's will was declared in the union of 2 people in love, it was announced not in thunder and lightning, not in a marvelous burst of the hierarchy in our corporeal world, but plainly in the voice of love spoken in 2 hearts and in their individual and mutual will of this union. This voice of love was truly the divine voice. The sacrament of marriage is a most mysterious activity having the goal of bringing the higher spiritual strengths into the will of both, and these will help them materialize this love in a compatible married life, not one that is confused, not distorting and not exhausting the love.

Suppose the want for dissolution speaks in their hearts? Christ's statement, "What God has united a person should not disconnect," is not a legal contract, but a moral covenant, a spiritual warning. It means that if God, which is the voice of mutual love heard by 2 hearts, unites both their lives, let each of them be cautious on dissolving this union, capitulating to a temptation that is just a human or carnal impulse. This base compulsion, a self-centered and egoistic freedom, is just a fleeing amusement and passion, and is due to lust and impatience.

As a result we sanctify the union of the loving couple through the sacrament and do not want to sanctify the pain of their dissolution through some other sacrament. So there must be available a certain mysterious efficacy that would have the goal of penetrating the will of both should they decide to dissolve their marriage by providing new spiritual strength, helping them to cleanse their hearts from mutual animosity, trivial disappointments, envy, jealousy, conceit, insults, to leave them mutually respectful, mutually condescending, mutually grateful and friendly, to raise any inner intent of dissolution to a higher plateau and so leave them as a quality couple.

Yes, the wedding itself can have different forms and maneuvers. It seems to me that when the young man and woman stand before the altar, it would be proper for them to ask help not from some institution of Christian trans-myth, but from the Mother-Earth and even from the international Aphrodite of humanity. Only after the course of several years, if the union seems to be solid and love between them has not dried, other sacraments directed only toward the Mother-Earth and to the Sun can be performed to provide gracious assistance for a prolonged period of their marriage. If the marriage still continues and is strong without any notice of possible dissolution and they wish a blessing from on-high for their love as love forever, then the priest of the Ever-Virgin Mother will consolidate their spiritual destiny with the sacrament of eternal marriage, an eternal companionship one with another in all worlds.

As far as the architectural figure and artistic style of the temples dedicated to the Ever-Virgin Mother, I have a mental sketch that it will be a variation of the temple of the Sun of the World. It is easy to guess that the prominent inside colors will be shades of blue, while the outside façade of the building will be either silver-blue or a combination of gold, lilac and white.

And it is natural to suppose that alongside the temples of the Ever-Virgin Mother, the temples of God the Son will have a spot dedicated to the person of Jesus Christ. I do not think that this religion will be sharply different than the religion of ancient Christianity. The significant differences are however unavoidable. The obsolete liturgical texts are over-loaded with their legacy of the Old Testament, and specific elements in Christianity that await a review.

From another side, not even one indication can be found in the Christian religion of what Jesus Christ's ascending path, activity and creativity consists after his transformation, which is mentioned in the Gospels as his ascension. And meanwhile, over 19 centuries have passed since that day. The Savior and his great friends, in an indefatigable struggle against the powers opposing God, have transformed entire systems of the world in all the meta-cultures, modifying circles of eternal suffering into purgatories. The greatest of the enlightened are those who enter the elite of *Shadanakar*, who created and create astonishing worlds. I remind you that the bases of *Yusnorm*, the level of eternal ceremony of all the humanities of *Shadanakar*, were created by that great spirit, and the final time it traversed the world was in the person of Apostle John the Divine.

We must not at all likewise forget that plans for such worlds, like the heavenly Russia, the Roman Catholic Eden, the

Byzantine Paradise, *Monsalvat*, are created by great spirits known to us by the names of the apostles Andrew and Peter, and John the Baptizer, and the legendary Tertullian who is permanently impressed only in esoteric narratives. So is it proper at such times to preserve a total silence on behalf of the large number of those who accepted and are accepting this uninterruptible struggle of Christ's powers against the thousands of progeny that oppose God and negatively affect the minds of the world's population? To what extent and on whose behalf should we create a façade that as if we do not know anything about any global perspectives that are awaiting us, about the impending antichrist, his realm and destruction, about what was encrypted two thousand years ago in prophecy regarding the 2nd arrival and awesome judgment? Who gave us the right to restrain this head-spinning joy beneath the 7 seals, to hide the knowledge of the inescapable impending millennial kingdom when millions of enlightened – those who have entered or are entering or soon must enter the *zatomis* of the meta-cultures – will be born on the renovated world, and when these millennia will begin, whose meaning is the salvation of all those fallen into the lower levels of *Shadanakar*, our assembly with them, the struggle for the restoration of all demonic powers and their return to the ascending path, the illumination of all the levels of *bramfatura,* and the redemption of even the supreme entity opposing God? All of this and much more cannot any longer remain undisclosed in the religion of the Savior Christ. We are unable to remain silent any further about this in the liturgies of the Logos.

The 3rd of the hierarchies of the ROSE OF THE WORLD clergy will be connected with this religion. If the first of them, the hierarchy of the Triune Deity – honored under the banner of the Sun of the World and its first hypostasis God the Father – can be assigned the gold color, then the 2nd hierarch will be blue or light-blue, which is consistent with the mystical tradition of the clergy of God the Son, the planetary Logos, Jesus Christ, who is validly represented by being clothed in clothes of a white color.

All 3 of these hierarchies, all 3 religions possess a universal, cosmic meaning. Due to their own essence they can and must be united on behalf of all humanity.

As long as meta-cultures exist, with all of their specific historical expressions, a sole teaching will refract through various cultural prisms, and various historical conclusions, categories of knowledge, accumulations of wisdom and historical requirements, will be indicated in these reflections. Alone in its supreme displays, ROSE OF THE WORLD will, in each culture, create for itself as though a foundation in view of a certain ethical and meta-historical teaching that is accompanied by the religion and turned toward the subject supra-nation or populace. Such a teaching will speak of the levels of the subject meta-culture, of its *sinklit* and its *zatomis*, its *shrastra* and its anti-humanity, its destinies and the figures of its great heroes, geniuses and statesmen – about all of this, what directly and fervently touches only those who belong to this culture. It will teach its intelligence of the past and present, it will explain the tasks that stand ahead of his supra-nation, the tasks that are individual and historically distinct from, and do not pertain to, the tasks that stand ahead of nations of other meta-cultures. Educating the posterity, it will concentrate attention on the molding of primarily those facets of the personality that lead to more activity, development of the student to excel in creativity for the materialization of historical tasks of his specific culture.

Such an aspect of the sole teaching directed, for example, to the Japanese nation could apply to the reformation of Shintoism. Such an aspect applied to the Hebrew nation could apply to the reformation of Judaism. Such an aspect directed to the German nation could be first founded on the basis of a meta-historical revelation pertaining to the culture of Germany. Such an aspect directed to the Indian nation, although it would be more correct, if I do not error, to call it Bharatavarsa, would likewise apply to the Hindu experience of that nation.

This aspect of the religion pertaining to all humanity which will apply to the Russian nation, and only to it, is Russianism. It teaches about our meta-culture, our *sinklit*, the historical and national activities of Russian heroes, geniuses and saints. It teaches about our good and bad clerics, who displayed their will in our culture and history, about the religious, cultural and social needs of our supra-nation, about both Russian social and personal morality. It prepares Russia for a service unto all humanity. It builds the Russianist corporate complex.

From here forward we have the inevitability of a 4th religion and 4th hierarchy of ROSE OF THE WORLD. The color that pertains to it will be, if possible, purple. For the peoples of Russia this religion will be for Russians, this clergy will be a Russian clergy. But as in Russia, and so in every country, there appears what I am accustomed to call their respective religion, and in lieu of not having anything else to call it, a more correct word or pantheon: Temples of the *Sinklit* (of the subject nation).

*   *   *

Now I approach the end of the exposition of my concepts. I fully take personal account of its extreme complexity and likewise the certain few people who will be found whose spiritual need will be sufficiently strong enough to compel them to overcome the difficulties of this book. In time the number of such people will grow, and then interpreters will come along and popularize it. But from another side, the educated will be supplemented by the spiritual experience of many and many others, and during the epoch of the reign of ROSE OF THE WORLD, the complexity of the teaching will become so great that just a handful will be able to grasp it and assemble all of its parts. So let it be this way! This is good, for esoteric depth to remain in the teaching. This should not be all or always displayed in the public square, even if this is the public square of belief-city.

And those hours when I will have the privilege (and often this will occur entirely on its own) to catch some of the echoes of that great celebratory liturgy it will be for me so especially joyful. It will be performed in the presence of many tens of thousands of persons, and all 5 priests of ROSE OF THE WORLD will participate in it, each one once a year. The sounds of the gold trumpets will reach my heart, higher and higher, under the very cupolas of the highest tower of the great temple. The city is sheathed in darkness, while the cupola and these trumpets will already be reflecting the morning sun's rays: the day of the summer solstice begins. I will hear a melody, I will see how the passage in the temple behind the altar will swing open, how the crimson disc will appear in the presence of the people, still jagged due to its rise over the city's horizon. I see the representatives of all priesthoods around the sacred table in the altar, and among them the female deacon of the ministry of the Ever-Virgin Mother and the female deacon of the ministry of the Great *Stikhials*. I can tell the difference as to how the 7 of them[113] that are present stretch their right hand over the altar table. I cannot distinguish what particular sacrament they are performing, but I see a harmony in their slow movements and hear how the eldest of them, the supreme pontificate of humanity, approaches the sun, "Glory to you, ascending sun!"

The thunderous choirs will repeat these words and the gold trumpets will again trumpet from outside the temple under the cupola.

"Glory to you, exalted heart!" is the distinct 2nd statement of the supreme pontificate, and I will see how he is accompanied by prelates of all the priesthoods, and how he is walking through the open passage to the eastern terrace. And when the voices of the loud choir subsides, the trumpets a 3rd time will repeat their chorus. I will see how the supreme preceptor approaches the parapet over the square, standing over the radiant crimson disc of the winged heart and sun, and he declares, "Blessed is this desirable encounter with the dawn!"

---

[113] The 5 priests and 2 female deacons.

Chapter 4

The Prince of Darkness

We need to clearly envision that atmosphere of harmonic tranquility that will reign in the world toward the epoch of the 7th or 8th pontificate of ROSE OF THE WORLD. These generations will only learn of the despotism of states, wars, revolutions, famines, calamities and epidemics, from books and memorials. Not inclined toward socialist struggles, their strengths will be dedicated to spiritual and physical self-perfection, to quenching their thirst of knowledge and thirst of creativity, to incomparably enrichment, orientation and expansion of their personal life.

To the extent that I can identify this, although this does amaze me, a permanent capital of the world, that is, a city that will permanently remain as a residence of the supreme preceptors and the Supreme Council of ROSE OF THE WORLD, will not appear. It seems that with every new pontificate the world's capital will be transferred to the chief city of that country, the residence of the supreme preceptor at that time. In any case, Delhi and Moscow will be installed as capitals twice each. The final revealed residence of the supreme preceptor, when the factual despot of the world will be the antichrist, and the sole Church of humanity will begin to descend into the catacombs, to the extent that I can remember, the city will be Tokyo.

If ROSE OF THE WORLD ascends to ethical control over world-wide state authority, then between this moment and the change in Eons, there must elapse, if I am not mistaken, about 26 supreme pontificates. But of this number there will elapse, it seems, 7 or 8, but not more than 9, during the epoch of the sovereignty of ROSE OF THE WORLD. The balance will elapse during the period of the reign of the antichrist and in the subsequent period of the final historical cataclysms. Some of the very final pontificates will be very short, and the end of these supreme preceptors will be a martyr's death, because the despots of the world will seek a means for the premature termination of their earthly course of life. Among the number of the supreme preceptors who will predominantly follow in authority one after another, will be Russians and Indians, Chinese and those natives of the various countries of the Americas, then Germans and Abyssinians, Spaniards and Jews, Japanese and Malayans, English and Arabs. But not any of them will have the responsibility of transferring the divine work. The last of the supreme preceptors, the one who will be in office when the change in Eons occurs, will arise from a small, destitute, northern Asiatic people, one that in our present age is hardly associated with other civilizations.

In this gallery of the world's leaders, I differentiate more or less distinctly 2. One of them is destined to become supreme preceptor, it seems, immediately after the referendum who will predetermine the method of turning the Worldwide Federation into a monolith. The character of such a giant of spiritual maturity is depicted directly before me. The wisdom and other- worldly tranquility that will respire from this person will make this impression on our mind that, if we were to imagine Gautama Buddha crowned and uniting the dignity of Nirvana with the supreme authority over humanity, then we can approach a representation of the brilliance and majesty of this destiny and this soul. His figure compels me to suppose that this person will arise from the womb of China.

Several times I already indicated how the uncompleted mission of Christ was reflected in the damage of Christianity of the Middle Ages, and how from the psychological climate created in the West as a result of this damage to the Christian Church there appeared reactionary movements: the Renaissance, Reformation, Revolution, religionless science, and the demonization of technology, all of this a speeding flight of the red horseman of Revelation. With the white horseman, all that is possible will be made available in order to liberate science and technology out from under the authority of demonizing rulers.

The thirst for authority and the thirst for blood will secretly draw many souls to their bottom. Not finding satisfaction in the conditions of social harmony, they will push some people to acquire doctrines that will battle on behalf of certain social and cultural changes, and who will promise them future contentment in these unmerited passions. While boredom will weary others.

From the time of our genetic formation to a self-sufficient extent the instinct of moral-social self-preservation restrains the sexual elements in a tight rein. The healthy instinct of self-preservation states that the removal of prohibitions from all displays of the sexual elements, complete liberation of mores, leads inherently to the destruction of the family, the development of sexual perversion, the weakening of the will, moral dissipation, and in the final end, the general degeneration of both the physical and spiritual state. The instinct of moral-social self-preservation is strong, but not enough in order to prevent society from this danger without the help of state regulations, juridical norms and generally accepted decency and modesty. This health-related instinct is strong, but when the external restraint is severed from the instinct of sexual liberation, the drive often seems stronger.

A person's sexual sphere hides explosive material of unimaginable power deep in itself! The centrifugal instinct of moral-social self-preservation binds us one to another, it solders together the elements of the personal life of each of us. But if we were to find a convincing and glamorous teaching that would pacify humanity's fear of what would occur should the restraints be removed from absolute sexual activity, a moral catastrophe would occur, one that has never yet occurred. The liberation of this centrifugal energy that is contained in this instinct could cause such a destructive social-psychological upheaval, should a chain reactive occur, and the same type as the liberation of atomic energy in the sphere of technology. And yes, there are many millions of the masses that thirst for sexual freedom.

Liberation from the bonds of goodness will cause the following condition of many and many more at the end of the Golden Age: first it will be subtle or underlying and then become more open and subsequently demanding its advertisement. Humanity will decline from spiritual light. It will weaken from lack of moral uplift. It will grow hateful toward virtue. It will be saturated with secular and social freedom – freedom toward everything. But it will never seem to exhaust itself in 2 spheres: the sexual sphere and the sphere of violence of one toward anther. The setting sun will cause the red brilliance of the mysteries and temples of the Sun of the World, on the cupolas of the pantheons, one the sanctuaries of the stikhials with the assessable pools and terraces, to slowly decline. The blue-gray dust of perversion, the gray fogs of boredom will already begin to expand to base levels. Monotony and thirst of sinister passions will grab at half of humanity in this indifferent moral anarchy.

Then humanity will yearn for a great person who knows and is able to accomplish more than all the balance, one who will demand restrictions and their obedience in opposing all these changes of unlimited freedom, to enforce various laws curbing all such types of sensual gratification.

Know that ROSE OF THE WORLD will consist of not just virtuous people, but of people who stand on the most diverse of levels of moral development. The tasks of the worldwide church from its very beginning will be so immense, they will be so wide and large in quantity, that to limit the number of active members of ROSE OF THE WORLD solely to people of high integrity and unimpeachable character will not at all be pragmatically possible. Even in the sphere of the Supreme Council there will be found individuals who will not be able to withstand the temptations of the prince of darkness, while people on the lower strata who will attain moral perfection will appear in time in significant numbers.

All the pontificates of ROSE OF THE WORLD, from the epoch of the unification of religions to the appearance of this monstrous entity in the historical arena, will concentrate their efforts on this impending and cautionary work. But no weapon will remain in their hands except the press during this immense ideological and cultural freedom. However due to pressure from extreme sinisterly circles of society, the removal of the last statutes that still allow freedom of the press will unnoticeably and eventually occur. This will no longer deal with the prohibition of social shameful conduct and the prohibition of sacrilege. Particularly this will unveil a wide access for the predecessors of the great progeny of darkness into the hearts of humanity.

CHAPTER 5

CHANGE OF EONS

Not during the reign of the antichrist, but particularly 2 or 3 decades after him, the revelry of evil on the world's surface will reach it apogee. As it writes,

> Then war broke out in heaven. Michael and his angels fought against the dragon, and the dragon and his angels fought back. But he was not strong enough, and they lost their place in heaven. The great dragon was hurled down—that ancient serpent called the devil, or Satan, who leads the whole world astray. He was hurled to the earth, and his angels with him. Then I heard a loud voice in heaven say, "Now have come the salvation and the power and the kingdom of our God, and the authority of his Messiah. For the accuser of our brothers and sisters, who accuses them before our God day and night, has been hurled down." They triumphed over him by the blood of the Lamb and by the word of their testimony; they did not love their lives even to death. Therefore rejoice, you heavens and you who dwell in them! But woe to the earth and the sea, because the devil has gone down to you! He is filled with fury, because he knows that his time is short.[114]

Unexplainable phenomena will start in nature introducing terror as a premonition of some type of cosmic catastrophe that has not

---

[114] Rev 12:7-12

yet occurred. Only a miniscule handful who will withstand, scattered throughout all the ends of the world, will understand these phenomena. They will understand that now over two thousand years after Golgotha, the planetary Logos has entered, finally, into the fullness of his power, sufficient in order to execute the transformation of the world.

> A great sign appeared in heaven: a woman clothed with the sun, with the moon under her feet and a crown of twelve stars on her head. She was pregnant and cried out in pain as she was about to give birth. Its tail swept a third of the stars out of the sky and flung them to the earth. The dragon stood in front of the woman who was about to give birth, so that it might devour her child the moment he was born. She gave birth to a son, a male child, who will rule all the nations with an iron scepter. And her child was snatched up to God and to his throne.
>
> The woman was given the two wings of a great eagle, so that she might fly to the place prepared for her in the wilderness, where she would be taken care of for a time, times and half a time, out of the serpent's reach. Then from his mouth the serpent spewed water like a river, to overtake the woman and sweep her away with the torrent. But the earth helped the woman by opening its mouth and swallowing the river that the dragon had spewed out of his mouth. Then the dragon was enraged at the woman and went off to wage war against the rest of her offspring—those who keep God's commands and hold fast their testimony about Jesus.[115]

What does the Woman clothed in the sun signify? This is the *Zventa-Sventana*, enveloping the planetary Logos and giving birth to the Great Spirit of the second Eon. In world history this reflects ROSE OF THE WORLD, in its extreme pains it is preparing

---

[115] Rev 12:1-2, 4-5, 14-17.

humanity in the era prior to, during, and after the antichrist, for the arrival of the vessel to contain this birthed Spirit.

Finally, one of the portents is read as a sign that in the higher worlds of meta-history all is prepared and that the old Eon is entering its final days.

Several dozen persons, all who remain from ROSE OF THE WORLD, will install a tie with those few from among people and the semi-*igvies* who, independently of the Sole Church and even not knowing about it, have performed an inner selection of the bright course. A sign will be provided that the time is arriving for the unification of all, those remaining alive from the brethren of light, at one point on the surface of the world. Overcoming all obstacles, 100 or 200 of the faithful will gather as a corporate body and the last of the supreme preceptors will head them. In the Revelation of John this place is called in Hebrew – Armageddon. I do not know what this word signifies. It seems to be that this great event will occur in Siberia, but it was not revealed to me why this region was selected as the final encounter.

And at this hour the entire *Shadanakar* will shake from top to bottom.

In the worlds of angels, demons, *stikhials*, in all the worlds of the ascending series, the one who traversed the roads of the earthly Galilee several ages ago will appear. These worlds will be enveloped with an unimaginable celebration, and their residents will traverse through one more and the brightest transformation. He will appear among all the *zatomises* of humanity and all the *sinklits* will drive toward him as he is descending into *Enrof.*

The prince of darkness who terrorized people, will appear in 3 or 4 physical figures at the same time.

Christ will meanwhile appear to so many figures, as many that there will be in *Enrof* who have the cognizance to recognize him. He will display himself to each of them and speak to each of them. These figures will at this time be molded into one supreme entity arriving on clouds in indescribable glory, unfathomable in comparison to anything else. And not one person will remain in

Enrof who will not see God the Son and not hear his words. And all that is allegorically stated in Scripture as prophecy regarding the awesome judgment will be consummated.

The expanse of the *Enrof* will not yet be changed, but the material composition of the human will change. Those at that time who will attain being among the living in *Enrof* will not endure any death, but will undergo one of 2 contradistinctive transformations. Some of the people, those who remain faithful, will physically transform. Their material substance will be immediately illuminated. They will remain in *Enrof*. The majority, all of those who comprise diabolic humanity, will undergo an opposite transformation. Not dying, they will corporeally change such that they will be moved to the worlds of compensation. First to the higher purgatories, then to the lower and lower, each one relative to his personal karma.

Some of the *igvies*, some insignificant number, will remain in *Enrof*, where they will become as if a special race, guided by enlightened divine humanity. The balance of the *igvies* will fall to the bottom of *Shadanakar*, but later will rise to a level of gathered *shrastras*.

The higher animals, those who survived the antichrist's destructions, whose change of Eons will occur in *Enrof*, will be rewarded for all their sufferings. They will undergo the same transformation as the minority of humanity and will complement their population in the world during the 2nd Eon.

The Savior, who attained the divine potency, will descend to these other levels. The *igvies* of all the *shrastras*, in confusion and agitation, will see his face with their eyes, the one exuding waves of love and light. The appearance of the planetary Logos, which their earlier perverted mind perceived as an insurgent and terrible tyrant, will summon the alteration of the direction of their minds and, leaving them in their *karrokhs*, they will mentally change in a gradual illuminating process, opposed to what they were before: anti-humanity and fugitives of the world. Something similar will apply also to the *raruggas*. There will not be any demons in the sovereign state near the days of the change of Eons. All of them, except for one, will considerably earlier fall into the *Yuppum*, and their salvation will be included in the number of the task of the 2nd Eon.

The shackles of the sufferers languishing in purgatories and magmas will be overcome, their imposition will be ameliorated, the ability of religious affiliation will be opened to them, and the captives will begin their ascent by steps in an ascending series.

The formidable demonic entities will be thrust down, since the *Digm* will be destroyed much earlier, at that meta-historical moment of which the Apocalypse speaks about their defeat in the heavenly war and about their discard down to the world. They will be preserved in the *Gashsharva*, *Tsebruemr* and in the lunar hell.

And the Savior will descend even lower, to that level where no one to this time was able to penetrate, except for the superintendent of the *Gagtungr*. In the *Sufetkh*, the cemetery of *Shadanakar*, the gates will collapse, freeing those residing there from the beginning of time, and streams of divine light will pour from one edge to the other edge of the desolation, until the entire region is radiant with lilac light of the anti-cosmos. The discarded corpses will rise to greet the life-providing rays. The breath of the resurrecting Logos will breathe new life into these half-living remnants of souls destined to a second death, those not having lived through the minutes of the final collapse of their *shelts*. The cemetery of *Shadanakar* will terminate its existence for ever.

The *sinklits*, all 34 *sinklits* of humanity, all the myriads of illuminated souls, and those having placed the beginning of their ascending route to the ancient civilizations of Atlantis, Gondwana or Egypt, and those who have entered the route during latter ages, and those attaining the brilliant *Arimoiya* through martyrdom during the final ages of history – all will descend into *Enrof* following the Savior Christ. They will not be born but will appear and populate the world.

> Then I heard something like the voice of a great multitude and like the sound of many waters and like the sound of mighty peals of thunder, saying,

"Hallelujah! For the Lord our God, the Almighty, reigns. Let us rejoice and be glad and give the glory to Him, for the marriage of the Lamb has come and His bride has made herself ready." It was given to her to clothe herself in fine linen, bright and clean; for the fine linen is the righteous acts of the saints. Then he said to me, "Write, 'Blessed are those who are invited to the marriage supper of the Lamb.'" And he said to me, "These are true words of God."[116]

So shall the mystery of the first Eon be consummated – the struggle of darkness against light for the possession of the world and the defeat of darkness.

Then the wedding feast will begin. The planetary Logos and its Church will marry in an inexpressible love in the inner chamber of the Worldwide *Salvaterra*, located at inaccessible heights.

The 2nd Eon, to which the prophesies testify as the millennial kingdom of the righteous, will begin when it deems proper. Its goal is the salvation of all without exception: who was torn away, who went astray, who fell into the depths of the worlds of compensation, and the transformation of all *Shadanakar*.

Because the powers of *Gagtungr*, the fugitives of *Enrof,* will still retain authority in some other worlds, so there will remain multitudes of those who committed fatal mistakes during the final historical epochs, still in purgatories and dungeons. And the task begun by Christ, the completion of the transformation of sinisterly worlds during these 3 great days between Golgotha and his resurrection, will begin. This includes the transformation of the inescapable dungeons located in temporal purgatories, and purgatories located in worlds of spiritual healing and the deliverance of all the prisoners through these levels into the world of illumination.

Divine humanity in the world, not further comprehending any disunity with Christ or with *Zventa-Sventana*, but having

---

[116] Rev 19:6-9

437

him at the head and being guided by him, will begin the work of the transformation and spirit-enlivenment of all that remains of its predecessors in *Enrof:* maimed nature, cities and civilizations.

The 2nd Eon will not perceive the existence of human birth, illness and death, suffering of the soul, enmity and struggle. It will just recognize love and creativity for the sake of the deliverance of those who have perished and the illumination of all levels of material creation. Because this is the reason for the existence of the entirely of humanity and all fraternity: and ours, and the angelic, and demonic, and the animal kingdom, and the elements and all the hierarchies of light. For this purpose we were here incarnated, in a corporeal body, but not yet with illuminated matter.

These distant eras will arrive when their task will be the illumination of the levels of the most corporeal, most difficult, lowest. And who will resolve this task, if not the virtuous and willing martyrs? Because they, leaving the enlightened *Enrof,* will be allowed to descend into such darkness, and not even one minute's residence there will cause any immense torment.

Crime will no longer reside in humanity, but the sinisterly powers will yet cause opposition in the demonic worlds. No one knows, except for the All-Omniscient, how many millennia the kingdom of the righteous will prolong in the world. Time will become different than it is at present. It will be transformed into a gold symphony of parallel strings of time, and what we call history will emaciate and vanish. It will no longer be history, but a growth of worldwide harmony that will define time.

All levels of compensation will become desolate in the middle of the 2nd Eon. Not one emanation of suffering, not one evolution of malice, not any divulgence of lust, will sustain the camp of demons. And the entities involved in opposition to God will fall one after another from their demonic nature. At the exit of the 2nd Eon, the very *Gashsharva* will be transformed, the Bottom will vanish, and now the *Gagtungr* in the inaccessible *Shog* will admit its defeat and will no longer draw strength from the anticosmos of the galaxy.

If the planetary demon, *Gagtungr*, defeated by his confederates, continues to be obstinate in evil, remaining on a one to one fight against the principal of light among the transformed *bramfaturas*, no powers of Lucifer of any type will be of any help to him to prolong the struggle against the powers of Providence. Then he, defeated, will withdraw from the *bramfatura* entirely, seeking a new harbor and new routes to its tyrannical dream in other edges of the universe.

Eventually *Gagtungr,* still isolated from the transformation, will finally say to Christ and God, "Yes!" Then *Shadanakar* will enter the 3rd Eon. Evil will disappear from the cosmic *Enrof* (just as did the planet *Daiya* disappear at some time), and this will complete the task of the 3rd Eon: the redemption of *Gagtungr.*

The great angel of Revelation swears to the impending arrival of the 3rd Eon, saying, "Time will be no more."[117]

So, traversing from light to light and from glory to glory,
All of us populating the world at present,
And those who lived and those who will appear to life in
the future,
Will arise to the indescribable Sun of the World,
In order to sooner or later assimilate into It,
And to merge into It,
To celebrate together, and to create with It
Creations of universes and universes.

December 24, 1950 – October 12, 1958

---

[117] Rev 10:6

APPENDIX

(BY THE TRANSLATOR)

Because Daniel Andreev's eschatology is very complex and lengthy, and scattered through Books 11 and 12, I have provided a short summary of it, instead of translating the entire verbose text dealing with this topic.

Brief Eschatology of

Rose of the World

The hallmarks of Rose of the World are the transformation of government into a religious fraternity and the creation of an intra-culture and inter-religion, one enveloping all governments, cultures and religions. This is also the specific purpose for the Russian supra-nation, that is, the union of the nations of Russia, Belarus, Ukraine, Georgia and Armenia. This corporate group was summoned into existence from non-existence to accomplish this mission.

   Even in the most optimistic of scenarios, the anti-christ will institute a universal tyranny, but after an interval of some time, and as a result of the assigned activity of the planetary Logos, he will be deposed. After this the world will devolve into a chaos of anarchy and a final global war of all against all. This will be terminated by the second arrival of Jesus Christ. At the time of writing ROSE OF THE WORLD, Andreev felt this would occur in about 250 or 300 years. As Andreev wrote:

> To what extent and on whose behalf should we create a façade that as if we do not know anything about any global perspectives that are awaiting us, about the impending antichrist, his realm and destruction, about what was encrypted two thousand years ago in prophecy regarding the 2nd arrival and awesome judgment?

During the course of the 20th century, an event occurred of such significance that it can only be compared to the incarnation as a human of Jesus Christ, the planetary Logos: a female divinely-born monad having the name of *Zventa-Sventana* descended to *Shadanakar*. As Andreev describes it, while he was writing *Rose of the World*, she resided in the highest strata of *bramfatura*, and later she is to descend into the *zatomis* of one of the meta-cultures. Later Andreev received a revelation that it was the Russian meta-culture. This meta-historical event is reflected in the earthly *Enrof* as the materialization of ROSE OF THE WORLD.

Andreev envisioned the reign of ROSE OF THE WORLD on earth in the 23rd century. During the era of ROSE OF THE WORLD, pontiffs will govern the land. They will be selected at Supreme Councils of ROSE OF THE WORLD. With the election of each new pontiff, the capital of the world will be moved to the primary city of that country where the Supreme Preceptor has his origin. Delhi and Moscow will arise as the capitals at least twice each, and Tokyo will become the world capital during the reign of the Eighth Pontificate.

But even this harmonically developing civilization of the future will still not be able to remove all the undesirable remnants of the evolution of humanity. The general abundance will sever the roots of material envy, but the roots of spiritual envy will remain untouched. The more gifted persons will serve as guides for the less gifted. Other than this, technical intellectualism will play a subjective role in the humanitarian direction of society and will be alien from governing the people. What is most important is that ROSE OF THE WORLD will not uproot the impulses of the thirst for authority and unrestrained sexual freedom that smolders deep inside the human subconscious. The thirst for authority will encompass thousands while the thirst for complete sexual freedom will envelop millions. Even the members of the Supreme Council of ROSE OF THE WORLD will still retain deep in their souls latent fantasies of complete authority over people and luxurious comfort.

Under such conditions, a demonic religion will evolve and be animated from the darkness of the underground, having been cultivated by its agents from the infernal regions. Those people who depart from the era of goodness will resurrect the Prince of Darkness – *Gagtungr*. Initially timidly and then more boldly, the social consciousness will be inculcated with the inclination to worship him as the eternal revolutionary, the one who is struggling for full human equality, for the complete freedom of human nature, and nothing to be limited by God or by moral rules. A quasi-religion will arise, announcing the soon arrival of the anti-logos.

Under the pressure of radically developed layers of society, those teaching that violating morality is wrong will be prohibited, while religious sacrilege will be promoted. People will arise who will proclaim the coming posterity of darkness. The best of them will evolve from France and become a talented and perspicacious creator of a grandiose cultural-historical and social-moral doctrine. In his fundamental work, *The Revealed Route*, he will show that once the people receive such a large amount of freedoms, they will realize that humanity was deprived of sexual freedom and moral dissipation as a result of the puritan morals of ROSE OF THE WORLD, that they have stupidly fallen into a captivity of a false sense of shame and old-fashioned ethics. This teaching will captivate the ears and hearts of millions of people, and who impatiently will now await the arrival of the Dark Messiah on earth.

The thoughts and expectations of humanity will be hungrily devoured by the residents of the infra-physical civilizations of Atlantis and Lemuria, where an evolutionary error occurred in deep antiquity, and so they devolved into ethereal bodies of the suffocating worlds of our planetary cosmos. These worlds are characterized by the smallest number of space and time dimensions., Due to the increased dissolute aspirations of peoples from the expanses of these worlds, they will descend into *Digm*, the residence of *Gagtungr* himself. The Prince of Darkness will emigrate from there to the earth, now captive to him. This will occur in the 23rd century.

On the eve of the birth of the anti-logos in Latin America, his mother will as if appear out of nowhere, a young woman of demonic nature. Her life will be surrounded by dark legends of ties with horrible entities of other worlds. Having conceived the physical body of the coming anti-logos from an ethereal body of a dark monad – a former female servant of *Gagtungr* – she will disappear from this world just as enigmatically as she appeared here earlier.

For 33 years the incarnated anti-logos will be the greatest of all geniuses of humanity, generally accepted as a leader of global science. He will not only have a gigantic intellect, but also be the greatest of poets. He will complete a series of fundamental revelations, incorporating principles of magic and rational knowledge. He will be handsome, and his appearance and speech will draw mesmerism and favor toward him, and all the women of the world will go out of their mind over him.

For 30 years he will be a member of the Supreme Council of ROSE OF THE WORLD and begin to weave plans of a physical estrangement of the pontificate. For 33 years he will accomplish the greatest miracle – turn his physical body into a body of strong *agga*, a substance of alien-materiality consisting of elementary particles, deprived of freedom of volition. This body will become invulnerable to any physical impact, no matter how strong it might be and he will not be affected by death.

He will acquire new abilities. Any person touching his *agga* will be overwhelmed by a powerful discharge. Every person whose eyes meet his will experience a living terror. Women in ecstasy will tear their hair from their heads, and want to fall into his clutches. But when he unveils his plan of accomplishments for his pontificate, he will meet with a roar of laughter and people's contempt. Then he will secretly murder the Supreme Preceptor and through a route of fraudulent elections he will place the tiara upon himself and declare himself the final Messiah of humanity. A woman-demon, the physical incarnation of alien-materiality of the elementary powers of female fertility and sexuality, will become his faithful companion. Together they will perform black magic miracles.

The Asian nations will not subject themselves to the usurper and will select for themselves a new Supreme Preceptor. But the majority of populations of the planet will follow after the anti-logos as the personification of their latent aspirations long hidden from the Supreme Council. Then the adherents of Rose of the World will be subject to the worst of persecutions and repressions. Not possessing weapons, they will be forced to endure martyrdom.

The anti-logos will triumph. He will raise his hand against the great mission of Jesus Christ and vehemently prosecute the teaching that 2,400 years earlier in Palestine a divinely-born monad was incarnated in a human body as the virtuous Jesus, becoming God the Son and residing on Earth. Assured of his infallibility, the anti-logos will announce himself as the first and last incarnation of god the son on our planet. He will declare his dissolute female companion to be the incarnation of the great Female Principal. This diabolic couple will create a cult best described as a global theatrical sex-show, the same as was practiced at some time in the past in Atlantis. The world will grasp the sexual orgiastic element and the blood-thirsty violence, and overwhelm those who exhibit the smallest protest against such bestial behavior. All of this will be exaggerated by an intellectual and refined technology serving to demonize humanity.

The entire world will serve as an arena of unfolding monstrous sexual entertainment. All religious temples surviving from white period, will be either removed from the land, or be converted into pagan temples of Satan and the great Prostitute. There they will curse the name of the Supreme as though He is a vile usurper of the universe. New temples will be built in the form of short cones or square pyramids with smooth sides and top, and they will serve as memorials of this phantasmagoric majesty of the mysteries of the long-gone Lemurians and Atlantisians who were completely morally corrupt and deprived of any rationalism.

Over the course of 50 years, all material means of retaining information will be methodically annihilated, including all that testified to humanity at some time possessing great religions, highly developed philosophies, geniuses of literature and art, and virtuous sages. The Prince of Darkness will be intoxicated by his authority over humanity. He will perfect his corporeal body, converted to a material that is foreign to our world, and will have the ability to appear at different parts of our planet simultaneously, demonstrating the increase of his global presence to the shocked populations. He will be convinced that he is not subject to corporeal death, and subsequently immune to any post-mortem retribution. He will foster the notion that all the planets of the solar system will sooner or later become his patrimony. These fantasies will just remain fantasies, but he will genuinely be able to migrate in a transformed body to distant infra-physical worlds and communicate there with the ethereal bodies of the priests of Atlantis and Lemuria.

At the beginning of his reign this Dark Despot will move the new capital of his world to the summits of the Alpine Mountains, and will reside there for the most part of his era. The city will be credited for its baroque architecture. Its population will attain a population of several tens of millions of persons.

It is only obvious that during the era of the despotic and autocratic authority of the tyrant, a large population will protest his demonic bacchanalia manner of rule. But clever and intelligent equipment will allow the Prince of Darkness and his associates to completely retain control of the thinking of any person and in time he will take reprisals against those he feels useless. Some virtuous people will prefer a quiet suicide instead of serving the incarnated devil. Such suicides will not cause post-mortem retribution, since this voluntary departure from life will be perceived as a lesser evil than being of service to the demonized world and the loss of human decency.

After death of the corporeal body the majority of human souls will descend into the infra-physical worlds of retribution, where they are nourished by the energy of redemptive suffering. This energy will provide so much nourishment to demonic entities of other dimensions, an amount incomparable to that provided by all the world wars, revolutions and repressions that humanity has experienced, all summed together. In addition to this, the anti-logos will initiate a chain reaction of uncontrollable release and transportation of the sexual energy of male and female animals in human form to the lower worlds of the nether-regions.

Taking advantage of the vices and weaknesses of human nature, the Price of Darkness will begin to contemplate on his cosmic mission. It will not be easy for him to perfect the art of communication with alien worlds. From there he will summon a massive exodus to the land of demonic entities, the *Igvies*, the residents of the infra-physical civilization of Atlantis and Lemuria. Surfacing from the cellars of our planetary cosmos, these residents of other planets will infiltrate our lands along with civilizations from other galaxies. Mixing with humanity, they will breed a race of semi-human and semi-*Igva* entities. They will intensely multiply and within 2 or 3 generations will attain a population of millions, and together with the anti-logos they will acquire the leadership of humanity. They will prepare sanctuaries on Earth and on the surface of nearby planets to accept and welcome the new race. All animals will be destroyed.

The catastrophe for the Prince of Darkness will occur unexpectedly. The groans of the humiliated and degenerated humanity will reach the higher strata of the space-time dimensions of our *bramfatura*. The active laws pertaining to freedom of choice and freedom of personal development in the evolutionary process of humanity will be temporarily suspended.

The planetary Logos – Jesus Christ – will descend onto the infra-physical world and remove the demonic anti-logos from there. The soul of the Prince of Darkness will begin to collapse into the empty bottom of the galaxy, long expecting him.

The beginning of this process on our planet will occur very graphically. Right in front of the eyes of many people and semi-*igvies*, those rejoicing at the moment over the triumphs of the anti-logos, the body of the Prince of Darkness will suddenly begin to lose its durability and will be transfigured into a fog. The Dark Despot will clearly understand what is occurring and he will become something that they never saw before. He will begin to violently wail, and in the course of a hour he will dissipate into the atmosphere and disappear from sight. After this defeat of the anti-logos, his female companion will disappear somehow to some unknown place. Her physical body will dissolve into infinitesimal particles and vanish without a trace.

Not during the reign of the Prince of Darkness, but 2 or 3 decades after him, the evil on the surface of the Earth will attain its apogee. Everyone will begin gnawing at each other and create discord among the closest confederates of the anti-logos, and the dark masses will be drawn into this issue. All those tied with the name of the ruined Prince, will sufficiently and speedily resign to a cynical ridicule and self-destruction. The morally corrupt masses will finally and to the maximum extent possible receive their long awaited sexual freedom. Sadism and sexual cannibalism, earlier accessible only to the elite, will now be available to everybody.

Mutual hostility between full-people and semi-*igvies* will acquire an especially cruel form. The semi-*igvies* will disdain full-people as though they are a lower race of degraded cretins. Full-people on the other hand will hate these rationalist masters of refined technology, as though they are insolent usurpers, animated mechanical robots in the role of implementing a vile plan for the enslavement of humanity. This mutual hate between full-people and semi-*igvies* will quickly grow into a final global war. But because no attention was turned toward the development of military technology during the reign of the Dark Despot, the means of an armed struggle will be poor for the enemies on both sides of the field, and this will prolong the war. The semi-*igvies* will conquer the world capital, but this victory will have more of a symbolic significance. By using their large population full-people will suppress the semi-*igvies*. During the course of the war, the capital, a super-megatropolis, will eventually be taken by the full-people and be subject to cruel annihilation.

During the course of the blood-filled bacchanalia, which will overwhelm the entire world, religious movements of the bright direction will begin to surface. Secret underground organizations will begin to unearth documents and testimonies of the era of Rose of the World. Several dozen persons, adherents of the rebirth of Rose of the World, will implement a connection with those few from among both the full-people and semi-*igvies* who have internally selected the choice of the bright direction.

Unexplainable apparitions will occur in nature that will inspire people with a mystical fear and reverence. Some of them will understand the true meaning of these signs. All those of the Brethren of Light remaining alive will gather at one sacred point on the surface of the planet, which is in Siberia. Here the portal for a transfer to other dimensions will open. A select number of representatives of humanity, about 100 or 200 persons, will experience a transformation of their bodies due to their integration with the higher energies of the cosmos, and will observe the process of the 2nd arrival of the planetary Logos – Jesus Christ.

Jesus Christ will appear to every person residing on Earth. Diabolic humanity will bodily change and descend into the worlds of retribution for cleansing through the energies of the infra-physical subterranean expanse. The currents of energy of suffering and sexual dissolution from the three-dimensional physical world of the Earth will terminate. Infra-Lemuria and infra-Atlantis will begin to separate into distinct regions.

From this moment, only virtuous people will be born on Earth, since there will no more be any powers from other worlds that would attempt to paralyze humanity and take advantage of the weakness of human nature.

The posterity of the Brethren of Light will acquire new ethereal bodies and settled all over the world. The new humanity will initiate the transformation and spirit-enlivenment of all that remains from its predecessor on the planet: the crippled nature, cities and civilizations. This period of intelligent life on Earth will recognize only love, creativity and labor for the ascent of those fallen human souls in the worlds of retribution to the bright strata of the planetary cosmos. In the final end, these worlds will be emptied. No emanation of suffering, no emanation of malice, no emanation of lust will any more nourish the lowest levels of the worlds of demonic bases. Such worlds will speedily crumble and as long as it takes for their broken pieces to fall to the bottom of the galaxy.

All the people living in the three-dimensional world will labor for the unification of their souls with the spirit body through the knowledge of the laws of nature, cultural creativity and advancement. Souls enlightened due to their spiritual labors will rise only vertically upward during their post-mortem existence, to the highest worlds of *bramfatura*, our multi-dimensional planetary cosmos. As a result of this progress, the supreme stratum of *bramfatura*, the global *Salvaterra*, will increase the quantity of its space-time dimensions and make it the same as the number of the multi-dimensional Absolute. Then the window into the world of God the Father will open, where the high strata of the planetary cosmos will be transferred by a single space-time dimensional whirlwind. It will attain the quality of the eternal mother of the creations of endless quantities of future worlds.

Made in the USA
Middletown, DE
24 July 2022

69951972R00269